Decline, Renewal and the City in Popular Music Culture: Beyond the Beatles

SARA COHEN
University of Liverpool, UK

ASHGATE

© Sara Cohen 2007

Published by
Ashgate Publishing Limited
Gower House
Croft Road
Aldershot
Hampshire GU11 3HR
England

Ashgate Publishing Company
Suite 420
101 Cherry Street
Burlington, VT 05401-4405
USA

Ashgate website: http://www.ashgate.com

British Library Cataloguing in Publication Data
Cohen, Sara
  Decline, renewal and the city in popular music culture : beyond the Beatles. – (Ashgate popular and folk music series)
  1. Popular music – England – Liverpool 2. Music – Social aspects – England – Liverpool 3. Music – Economic aspects – England – Liverpool 4. Liverpool (England) – Social conditions – 20th century 5. Liverpool (England) – Economic conditions – 20th century
  I. Title
  781.6'3'0942753

Library of Congress Cataloging-in-Publication Data
Cohen, Sara, 1961-
  Decline, renewal and the city in popular music culture : beyond the beatles / Sara Cohen.
    p. cm.—(Ashgate popular and folk music series)
  Includes bibliographical references.
  ISBN-13: 978-0-7546-3242-9 (hardback : alk. paper)
  ISBN-10: 0-7546-3242-3 (hardback : alk. paper)
  ISBN-13: 978-0-7546-3243-6 (pbk. : alk. paper)
  ISBN-10: 0-7546-3243-1 (pbk. : alk. paper)
  1. Popular music—History and criticism. 2. City and town life—Social aspects. 3. Popular culture. I. Title. II. Series.

  ML3470.C623 2007
  306.4'84240942753—dc22

2006016412

ISBN 978-0-7546-3242-9 HBK
ISBN 978-0-7546-3243-6 PBK

Printed and bound in Great Britain by MPG Books Limited, Bodmin, Cornwall.

Contents

General Editor's Preface

The upheaval that occurred in musicology during the last two decades of the twentieth century has created a new urgency for the study of popular music alongside the development of new critical and theoretical models. A relativistic outlook has replaced the universal perspective of modernism (the international ambitions of the 12-note style); the grand narrative of the evolution and dissolution of tonality has been challenged, and emphasis has shifted to cultural context, reception and subject position. Together, these have conspired to eat away at the status of canonical composers and categories of high and low in music. A need has arisen, also, to recognize and address the emergence of crossovers, mixed and new genres, to engage in debates concerning the vexed problem of what constitutes authenticity in music and to offer a critique of musical practice as the product of free, individual expression.

Popular musicology is now a vital and exciting area of scholarship, and the *Ashgate Popular and Folk Music Series* aims to present the best research in the field. Authors will be concerned with locating musical practices, values and meanings in cultural context, and may draw upon methodologies and theories developed in cultural studies, semiotics, poststructuralism, psychology and sociology. The series will focus on popular musics of the twentieth and twenty-first centuries. It is designed to embrace the world's popular musics from Acid Jazz to Zydeco, whether high tech or low tech, commercial or non-commercial, contemporary or traditional.

Professor Derek B. Scott
Chair of Music
University of Salford

Acknowledgements

The preparation of this book has been a long and at times rather tortuous process, and throughout it I have depended a great deal upon the support of others. There are therefore many people to thank, so many that it is not possible to name all of them here.

The book draws upon the findings of a series of distinct research projects conducted over a 20-year period. I would like to thank the organizations that funded those projects, particularly the Leverhulme Trust and the Economic and Social Research Council of Great Britain, but also the University of Liverpool, which provided pump-priming funding. I would also like to thank all my co-researchers, particularly Kevin McManus, Adam Brown, Abigail Gilmore, Justin O'Connor, Connie Atkinson, Rob Strachan and Tricia Jenkins. It is important to emphasize that the book's failings have nothing to do with them but are my own responsibility: none of them were involved in the writing of the book or saw any of its draft chapters. In addition, I am extremely grateful to the many people who agreed to participate in our research. They surprised us with their generosity and they were kind enough to allow us access to their lives and their music events, networks and organizations. They taught me much about music and its urban setting and I apologize if I have misinterpreted or misrepresented any of them in any way.

I am grateful for the opportunities that I have been given to publish some of the research findings elsewhere, and to present papers based on the research at various seminars and conferences. This has involved many individuals, groups and events, but I would particularly like to thank Martin Stokes, Peter Manuel and Michael Talbot; Shirley Ardener and the Institute of Social and Cultural Anthropology at Oxford University; the Popular Music Section of the Society for Ethnomusicology; and members of the International Association for the Study of Popular Music who have done so much to make popular music an academically rigorous field of study, but one that is also hugely enjoyable and rewarding. Colleagues, research fellows and research students at the Institute of Popular Music (IPM) and School of Music at Liverpool University have been especially supportive and have contributed to the production of the book in different ways, and I would particularly like to thank Mike Brocken, Mike Jones, Marion Leonard, Debbie Ellery, Holly Tessler, June Maxwell, Lars Kaijser and Frances Hunt. I am especially indebted to three other IPM colleagues, Jan Fairley, David Horn and Jason Toynbee, who commented on various parts of the book in draft form and made critical and typically astute comments whilst also managing to encourage and inspire. Derek Scott and Heidi May at Ashgate Publishing have been extremely helpful and accommodating, and I am grateful to Stuart Wilks-Heeg, John Connell and Chris Gibson for sending me drafts of their articles or books, and to Sandra Mather for providing the illustrative maps.

Finally, I would like to thank my friends and neighbours in Liverpool and, most of all, my family. My sons Ed and Alfie arrived after I had started work on the book and provided a major but very welcome diversion from it. My greatest debt, however, is to my partner Colin and my mum, both of whom provided much encouragement. Colin will be more delighted than anyone to see an end to the book but without his patient support it would never have been finished.

Introduction

You could argue that pop is a metaphor for the city; certainly, that it is a continuation by other means of the urban mind. …The simple fact is that pop is better on cities than on anything else, apart from love. It's taught us to be intrigued by cities, to fear them, to face up to them (Nick Coleman, *The Independent,* 11 April 1995).

During my second year as a postgraduate research student at Oxford University's Institute of Social Anthropology, my fellow students ventured off to conduct research in the Bolivian highlands, Sudan and other distant places, whilst I hopped on a train and travelled just a couple of hundred miles north to engage in fieldwork on rock culture in Liverpool, a provincial, maritime port city on the north-west coast of England (see Figure 1) and within the wider region of Merseyside, whose population stood at 439,400 in 2004. Yet in a letter addressed to my funding body, my supervisor supported my application for travel expenses by emphasizing my bravery in going to Liverpool on my own. At that time, during the mid-1980s, Liverpool's economic problems were more severe than those of any other British city, and the national media was using the city as a symbol of urban decline. Given such negative media representations, I was stunned when I first visited Liverpool by the unexpected beauty of the city centre and waterfront, and the faded grandeur of so many city buildings, as well as by the city's expansive suburban parks. I was also enchanted by the warmth, friendliness and humour of so many of the people I met.

I had only been in the city a few weeks when I met Roger Hill, who broadcast his own regular rock show on BBC Radio Merseyside. I was sitting in Probe Record shop, trying not to look too much like a novice ethnographer, when Roger strode into the shop sporting a luminous pink, green and white Mohican hairstyle, a black leather jacket and tight, pink leopardskin trousers that disappeared into long, black boxer boots. We were introduced to each other by the shop's owner, and Roger immediately took an interest in my research and discussed it with me during this and subsequent meetings. Since moving to Liverpool in 1978 Roger had been an astute commentator on music in Liverpool. He was particularly interested in what he referred to as the 'localness' of local music, and he had a theory about the 'Liverpool sound', which he described as the sound of grief, of the loss of people and industry, and of the city's soul. I dismissed Roger's theory as rather fanciful and over-romanticized but it touched upon themes that had already begun to interest me and it began to haunt me. I started to ponder over certain questions that it seemed to raise: how is popular music connected to cities, for example? How does de-industrialization affect a city's musical life, and why would music be perceived as the expression of a city's soul? This book, as I shall now go on to elaborate, attempts to address such questions.

Popular Music and the City

Popular music and cities have always been closely connected. The emergence of commercial forms of popular music during the nineteenth century was bound up with industrialization and increasing urbanization. Rhythm and blues and rock'n'roll developed in North American cities, such as Memphis and Chicago, in the 1940s and 1950s following mass migration to those cities from rural areas and the subsequent mixing of rural blues and country with urban jazz (Hall, 1998; Shepherd and Manuel, 2003). More recently, the label 'urban music' has been used by major record companies to market contemporary rhythm and blues and other styles of so-called 'black music' or 'music of black origin' (including, for example, reggae, hip-hop and jungle). Cities have also been key sites for the production, promotion and dissemination of popular music and for music-related consumption and entertainment. The city has thus been ingrained in popular music culture; hence twentieth-century styles of rock and pop have been described as 'the sound of the city' (Gillett, 1983) and as 'urban rhythms' (Chambers, 1985). Schafer (1977: 114–17) argues that rock and pop emerged in parallel with the increasing and continuous low-frequency hubbub of cities and factories, a process that was reflected in the incorporation into the music of high-intensity, low-frequency noise.[1]

In addition, popular music has represented the city in various ways. The modern city, as Raban (1974: 17) points out, has been 'a dream pursued, and found vain, wanting, and destructive', and it has been a metaphor for the decline of civilization, a place of decay and disease, sin and moral corruption, crowds, social tension and discontent. Yet it has also been an embodiment of hope and personal freedom (Simmel, 1997 (1903): 180). Thus many rock and pop songs have associated the city with excitement, presenting it as an escape from the restrictions of family and home and rural or suburban living. 1950s and 1960s crooners, for example, celebrated the city as a place of affluence, fun and endless possibility, as illustrated by celebratory songs about New York, Chicago and other cities, and about the joys of 'Downtown' (Petula Clark, 1964). Other rock and pop songs, as Connell and Gibson (2003: 73–9) point out, have presented the city as a place of action or hope, forbidden pleasures (for example, 'Walk on the Wild Side', the Velvet Underground) or uncertainty ('People are Strange', the Doors), whilst country music has presented the city as a place of seduction but also sin. Suburbia, meanwhile, has been a place of 'contempt and comedy' (for instance, 'Well Respected Man', the Kinks), 'dreary' and 'soulless' (as in the music of Blur) or a place of 'alienation, repressive stability' (the music of Suede).

But how are musical representations of the city shaped by specific social and economic circumstances, and how does popular music influence not only how cities

---

1   More specifically, Schafer (1977: 108) argues that increasing urbanization was paralleled by a growth in the size of orchestras so that they could compete with factory noises and reflect 'the thicker densities of city life' (ibid.: 104), but when the electric revolution arrived the amplifier and rock and pop began to replace the orchestra in order to match the increase of urban noise.

are represented and interpreted but also inhabited and experienced? Moreover, what can popular music tell us about cities, and in turn what can a focus on cities tell us about popular music? These are important and topical questions. Within a 'post-industrial' context the role and significance of cities, and the relationship between cities and culture, have become the focus of considerable debate.

Popular Music and the City in a 'Post-industrial' Context

The global economic recession of the 1970s, resulting from a crisis in the global capitalist economy based upon so-called 'Fordist' methods of mass production, provoked dramatic changes in Liverpool and in many other port and industrial cities. It encouraged and intensified a process of de-industrialization and depopulation that gave rise to intense debates about the future of such cities and their role and significance within the global economy. At the same time, however, other cities grew in size and wealth, including 'hub' cities that occupied a central position within global networks of finance and capital, trade and distribution, media, communications and information (Sassen, 1991), and it has been frequently pointed out that more and more people (amounting to over half of the world's population) live in cities than ever before. As a means of compensating for and overcoming their economic problems, many port and industrial cities (commonly referred to as 'post-industrial', but also as 'shrinking' cities)[2] began programmes of economic restructuring. They turned to more specialized, 'post-Fordist' systems of production involving new 'information technologies', and to more flexible and decentralized labour processes targeted at specialized or niche markets (Harvey, 1990). There was a parallel emphasis on the marketing of such cities and on their physical regeneration involving strategic economic development targeted at specific urban areas. Increasingly, attention was also paid to the contribution that 'culture' and the so-called 'cultural' or 'creative industries' could make to that process of local economic restructuring and urban regeneration.

So what happens to the musical life of a city once the economic infrastructure that the city was built upon collapses, and how has popular music been implicated in the regeneration process? How have such developments in global capitalism affected the relationship between popular music and the city? In tackling such questions this book has two interrelated aims. The first main aim is to examine the impact of urban de-industrialization and economic restructuring on popular music culture. In turn,

---

2   The term 'shrinking cities' was used by the US Department of Housing and Urban Development to describe the population decline and rising unemployment experienced by around 24 per cent of America's central cities ('State of the Cities, 1999'. http://clinton3.nara. gov/WH/New/New_Markets_Nov/factsheets/hartford2.html, accessed July 2004). Research by the United Nations and other demographers has shown 'that for every two cities that are growing, three are shrinking. Some cities that were bustling centers of commerce just a generation ago have become modern-day Pompeiis' (Kate Stohr, *New York Times*, 6 February 2004).

the second main aim is to consider how the specificity or distinctiveness of popular music might have an impact on the city.

Method and Approach

Meeting these objectives requires an approach that recognizes music as a social and symbolic practice encompassing a diversity of roles and characteristics: music as a culture or way of life distinguished by social and ideological conventions; music as sound; speech and discourse about music; and music as a commodity and industry. The book considers how particular popular music practices are connected to social, cultural, geographical and economic characteristics of the city, to its 'citiness' (Massey, 1999) and to the way the city is represented, thought about and reflected upon. This involves thinking about the particular role and significance of popular music within urban life and why music matters, how and to whom. Moreover, the book explores the relationship between popular music and the city in some detail by using Liverpool as a case study, and it examines that relationship over a 20-year period (the 1980s and 1990s) in order to consider how it is affected by social and economic change. The book thus focuses on the popular music culture of Liverpool and, despite the reference to 'culture' in the singular, it illustrates how urban popular music culture is in fact broad and diverse, consisting of many different cultures 'scenes' or 'worlds'.

Whilst the book focuses on Liverpool I have nevertheless incorporated some comparative references to other provincial port and industrial cities, particularly other culturally rich cities in Britain and North America such as Manchester, Sheffield, Glasgow, New Orleans and Memphis. In doing so I want to show how the issues and themes that the book addresses have a broader relevance, and to highlight common global trends. My main interest, however, is in studying those general trends within one particular city and thus in studying the global within the local, considering how global trends are mediated by local (and also national) socio-economic circumstances, as well as by the social and ideological conventions that inform popular music production and consumption and genre-based cultures or scenes. I also want to study the general within the particular by using 'small' ethnographic details and encounters to address the big themes, issues and questions highlighted above. Each of the book's chapters begins by focusing on a particular music-related event and moment: a musical sound, a genre-based scene, a music business, a music industry meeting, a music convention and festival and the launch of a musical 'Wall of Fame'. The chapters describe the encounters that those events and moments involved between individuals, groups and institutions that were part of different and overlapping social networks and had particular interests in music and the city. The chapters also highlight the social and ideological conventions that informed those encounters and the particular social practices and understandings of music and the city that emerged. I try to avoid using these specific ethnographic events and encounters as a basis for making generalizations about Liverpool or its popular music culture, or about local experiences of de-industrialization and economic restructuring. Instead, by shifting focus from one event and moment to another the book offers a kaleidoscopic view of the city that reveals just a few different perspectives on the city and its popular music culture, and different patterns of social interaction and understanding.

The book thus adopts an ethnographic approach, drawing upon ethnographic research conducted in Liverpool during the 1980s and 1990s. Some of that research was conducted by me alone, and some in collaboration with other researchers. Much of the research took the form of a series of individual projects involving unstructured, face-to-face interviews, conversations and oral histories that were tape-recorded and transcribed. Each project had its own specific aims and objectives, which were distinct from those of this book, and together they resulted in single- and joint-authored scholarly publications and a range of other outputs. Many people kindly agreed to participate in this research, and they were involved with music in a variety of different ways and were connected to a broad range of social and occupational groups. They included musicians, music critics, music businesspeople, tourist entrepreneurs, music fans and audiences, music consultants and music policy-makers. The research also involved participation in and first-hand observation of a wide variety of music activities and events, including performances and rehearsals, festivals, launch events for specific music initiatives, public and private lectures and meetings about music, music-related guided tours and music seminars, workshops, conferences and conventions. Information and data gathered through these forms of direct contact with people were supplemented by those gathered from a variety of other sources, including popular publications, consultancy reports and policy documents, leaflets and publicity materials, newspaper articles, websites, statistics, minutes from meetings, radio and television documentaries and song texts. (Further information on the various research projects, methods and approach is included as an Appendix.)

Whilst the book is constrained by conventions of academic writing and referencing, I have nevertheless tried to write it in an accessible style and to avoid the excessive use of academic jargon. I have included lengthy descriptive passages that help to provide an account that is detailed enough for particular points to be properly contextualized and for others to use for comparative purposes. I have also included many quotations in order to highlight the terms and perspectives of those who participated in the research. Most of those quotations are referenced as 'Personal Communication' (abbreviated as p.c.), and in order to acknowledge the collaborative, team aspects of the research I have not specified the particular interviewer(s) involved. Likewise, throughout the text I refer to the researchers as 'us', even when comments were directed at myself alone or to individual co-researchers. I have made an exception to this, however, on occasions that involve references to my PhD fieldwork or to my own personal observations and experiences of particular events. In addition, I have adopted the past tense throughout the book in order to make it clear that the events, activities and situations described relate to specific points in time and do not necessarily have a contemporary or continuing relevance. Some of the material presented in the book has been included in a few previously published journal articles and book chapters but all of that material has been extensively reworked for the purposes of the present volume; and considerable new analysis and research material and information have been added. I have therefore taken those earlier publications as a starting point rather than as a foundation.[3]

Structure and Argument

The book has been written up as a series of chapters that are interconnected but can also stand alone and be read independently. It has two general arguments. Firstly, it argues that in Liverpool de-industrialization encouraged efforts to connect popular music to the city to categorize, claim and promote it as local culture, and to harness and mobilize it as a local resource, and that those efforts exposed and generated particular tensions and urban inequalities. Secondly, it argues that popular music's specific role and significance in urban life (and perceptions of it as specific and unique) helps to explain why it was a focus for the production of local difference and for tensions related to that process.

Chapter 1 introduces the key aims and themes of the book in more detail and it also introduces the case of Liverpool and provides some historical background to the chapters that follow by discussing Liverpool's rise to prominence within the global economy and considering how this influenced the city's musical life. The rest of the book can be described in terms of two parts. The first part discusses the musical life of Liverpool during the 1980s and early 1990s, by which time the city had become marginalized within the global economy due to a shift in the geographical focus of world trade, and its economic problems were particularly severe. Chapter 2 examines the appropriation of rock music as a city sound, focusing on Roger Hill's notion of the 'definitive Liverpool Sound', and it considers the influence of rock culture, and socio-economic factors specific to Liverpool, on the representation of the city through rock. Chapter 3 examines efforts to claim country music as Liverpool heritage and considers the influence of country on the production of local identity and difference, and on local narratives of decline and renewal. Chapter 4 then focuses on music as a city business. It examines efforts to incorporate Liverpool into the development of a business brand, and uses this as a starting point for a more wide-ranging exploration of the social, economic and symbolic significance of place and the city in the commercial production of music.

The second part of the book explores music in relation to economic restructuring, urban regeneration and local re-imaging, and it extends the discussion up to 2005. Chapter 5 focuses on the linking of cultural and economic policy and on initiatives aimed at developing a local music industry. Chapter 6 focuses on the development of music as a Liverpool tourist attraction, whilst Chapter 7 discusses the role and significance of music in relation to the physical regeneration and marketing of Liverpool and the creation of urban 'cultural quarters'. The conclusion draws

---

3   Nevertheless, much of the material presented in the first part of Chapter 3 was drawn from an article published in *Ethnomusicology* (2005).

together the findings of the chapters, and relates them to the book's key aims, themes, and arguments.

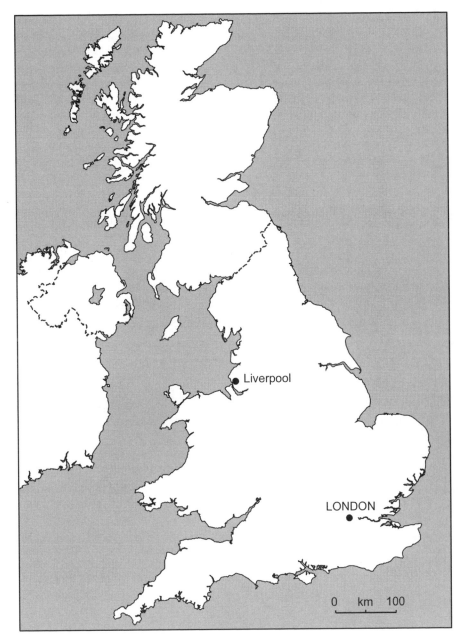

Figure 1   Map of the UK showing Liverpool © Sandra Mather

Chapter 1

Music and the City:
Cultural Diversity in a Global
Cosmopolis

The Liverpool Ladies' Barbershop Chorus are in mid rehearsal in the back room of a pub, which is located on the leafy edge of an expansive park in Liverpool's southern suburbs. We are filming the chorus for an exhibition that will be staged by the National Museums and Galleries on Merseyside. Three tiers of women stretch out in front of us, spanning different generations. Every now and then they sway from side to side or lean inwards. Their hand movements are carefully co-ordinated and their faces animated and expressive, but they relax and break into smiles and laughter whenever the conductor interrupts their singing to offer comment and guidance. They pause for a break and Margaret Blackman rushes across the room to greet us, and calls over her sisters, Bette and Lesley, so that she can introduce them to us. Two other sisters, Geraldine and Terry, also perform with the chorus but are not at today's rehearsal, as does Margaret's daughter, Rachel. Rachel comes over and explains to us that her father, Joe, is rehearsing that night with the men's barbershop chorus in a different Liverpool venue. She is interrupted every now and then by Margaret, who continues to point out to us particular members of the chorus and their family connections. It is a lot to take in so we ask Margaret to tell us more about her immediate family.

Margaret's story begins with her father, Jack Blackman, and the music lessons that his mother sent him to when he was growing up in Liverpool as a young boy. Every Saturday morning she would 'pledge a parcel' in order to raise the money to pay for those lessons. During the mid-1950s Jack sent his own children to music lessons and established a family jazz band, named Jack Blackman and the Black Keys. The band featured his wife Elizabeth on piano, himself on alto sax and clarinet, and his daughters Bette and Margaret on drums and vocals. Another daughter, Lesley, was also part of the band before she joined the local country and western group Lee and the Strollers. We record as much of Margaret's story as we can before leaving the chorus and driving to Chinatown in Liverpool city centre for our next appointment. There, the street names are written in both English and Chinese characters, and tall and shabby Georgian terraced buildings are brightened up with gaudy neon restaurant signs. Concealed behind those terraces are quiet residential backstreets and a square that houses the Chinese Gospel Church, which runs a choir and music workshops. At the corner of the square stands the Pagoda Chinese Community Centre, an oriental-style building where we are due to film next. Inside, members of the Liu family are rehearsing with Liverpool's Chinese classical youth orchestra.

What can the Blackman and Liu families tell us about the relationship between music and the city? How are barbershop and traditional Chinese music connected to the social and economic life of Liverpool and to its history and geography? In order to begin to answer such questions, I must first of all situate Liverpool's popular music culture within a broader and more historical context, considering, Liverpool's emergence as a city, its rise to prominence as a global cosmopolis and the impact of this on the city's musical life. In particular, the discussion will focus on how Liverpool's musical life was affected by the development of the city's port, the city's status as a place of migration and its American connections. It will draw upon a study of music and kinship on Merseyside, introducing case material on families involved with various musical genres and styles.[1] The chapter will end, however, by drawing attention to music's role and significance in producing rather than just reflecting the city, and by relating that process to the book's key aims and themes.

Musical Diversity and the Gateway to Empire

Tony and Beryl Davis live on the Wirral, an area of Merseyside that lies across the River Mersey from Liverpool. When they talked to us about the role and significance of music in their individual and family lives, and about the musical life of the region more generally, they were keen to emphasize the influence of the sea and the port. Liverpool was granted a Borough Charter in 1207, but it remained a small Atlantic-facing coastal settlement with a population of only a few hundred until the construction of the Old Dock of 1715. This was one of the world's first wet docks and it enabled Liverpool to develop and rapidly expand as a trading port strung out along the length of the River Mersey. Through the port Liverpool became a central player within the global economy and a 'Gateway of Empire' (Lane, 1987), and this had a profound impact on the city's economic, social and musical life.[2] Liverpool's folk traditions, for example, are rich and diverse and cannot be reduced to the port and port culture; but they have been described as 'more surf than turf in flavour' (Du

---

1   This pilot study was carried out by Kevin McManus and myself in 1990 and some of the case material was included in the above-mentioned exhibition and accompanying video. The chapter also includes additional information gathered for a longer project on music in twentieth-century Liverpool life (1991–94), which is supplemented here and there by subsequent research (see Appendix). Some of the research materials and publications that we produced on the basis of our pilot study and the larger project have been drawn upon by others who have written on popular music in Liverpool, including Du Noyer (2002); Meegan (1995) and Willis-Pitts (2000).

2   It is significant in this respect that the port runs directly into Liverpool city centre rather than being confined to peripheral areas, as in some other port cities.

Noyer, 2002: 53), and they do illustrate a long-standing interest within the city in songs and instruments connected with the sea and with seafaring culture.

Beryl Davis had published various magazines and articles on folk and sea music but she also played various instruments, including the concertina, an instrument traditionally played by sailors.[3] Her husband Tony was also a musician. During the 1940s and 1950s he performed with various local groups, including the Muskrat Jazz Band and the Gin Mill skiffle group. Yet he was best known as a member of the Spinners, a folk group from Liverpool that formed in 1954 and were particularly popular in Britain during the 1970s when they performed both classic and new folk songs on national television. When we first met Tony he was running the region's annual international sea-shanty festival, and he introduced us to Jack Coutes, who performed with Storm-a-long-John, a local group of around 12 or so shanty singers. Shanties were sung on local clipper ships for around 30 years during the mid-1800s and were passed down by local dockers (Hugill, 1969). Some of the songs of Merseyside rock musicians, such as the rock band The Coral, have been regarded as being influenced by sea shanties,[4] whilst the Beatles performed the sea shanty 'Maggie May' during their earlier incarnation as The Quarrymen.[5] Jack Coutes had been involved with Liverpool folk music since the early 1960s when the city had around 20 folk clubs, partly due to the folk revival of the mid- to late 1950s. By the time we met Jack, however, that number had dwindled and only two clubs remained (Jack Coutes, p.c.).

As a result of its west-facing position and the development of its port, Liverpool began to play a central role within national and international trade and transportation networks. As the city developed trading links with Europe, America, the West Indies, India, China and Africa, it expanded outwards from the central waterfront area and gradually incorporated surrounding villages within its boundaries. That expansion was encouraged by the opening of the Liverpool and Manchester Railway in 1830, which enabled the transfer of people and commodities. By the middle of the eighteenth century, Liverpool had taken over from Bristol as the leader of the 'triangular' slave trade. Manufactured goods from inland cities were transported to Liverpool and loaded onto ships bound for West Africa, where they were exchanged for human slaves who were taken into forced plantation labour in the colonies of the New World. In return, cotton, rum, sugar and tobacco from the New World were shipped back to Liverpool. Liverpool consequently became Britain's 'second city' and a major centre for commerce. 'At its, peak, the port provided direct employment

---

3   Tony Lane, a sociologist who has specialized in research on Liverpool seafaring, told us that during the 1930s a lot of Liverpool ships had their own musical groups 'and there was always somebody with a concertina' (p.c.).

4   The Coral's debut album was described by one reviewer as being 'so nautically inclined you can almost smell the fishing nets'. http://www.nme.com/reviews.10732.htm, accessed April 2005. See also http://www.xs4all.nl/~fsgroen/Albums-C/TheCoralTheCoral. htm, and http://www.earmedicine.com/100207.php, accessed November 2004.

5   http://www.iol.ie/~beatlesireland/zBeatlesfactfiles/factfilesx1/quarrymen/the quarrymen.htm, accessed June 2005.

for perhaps as many as 60,000 people, and almost the same number of people were employed in processing and manufacturing industries that depended upon the port's commodities, such as timbre, cable, latex, tobacco, sugar etc' (Lane, 1987: 35). Liverpool was thus a city that developed and expanded through trade, including not just port-related trade but also smaller trades and businesses – such as the highly specialized watch- and clock-making industry that emerged in the second half of the eighteenth century and was at its height in the middle of the nineteenth (Hall, 1998: 338). Local industries also developed around the building and repair of ships.

Liverpool's wealth, and its status in a national and global context, encouraged the development of rich and diverse local musical cultures. The city became a stopping-off point for sailors, traders, tourists and touring musicians, and it was thus exposed to international musical influences, becoming a place where different social and musical groups met and musical sounds and styles were exchanged. Liverpool has had a strong and long-standing tradition in street music, for example, involving local and visiting musicians. Miriam Collings, who was 74 years old when we met her, had vivid childhood memories of the songs of the street sellers and the music of the foo-foo bands that paraded around playing simple instruments such as biscuit-tin drums and the 'kazoo' made out of comb and tissue paper (Cohen and McManus, 1991: 17). Unwin (1983: 60) notes that 'members of the ships' crews also had their foo-foo bands which provided plenty of entertainment for passengers and the members of the bands alike.' Describing a visit to Liverpool in 1839, the novelist Herman Melville comments on the music emanating from boarding houses, the songs of seamen and strolling musicians playing hand-organs, fiddles and cymbals (quoted in Du Noyer, 2002: 1). Other writers have described the singers, banjoists and concertina players that entertained Liverpool theatre and cinema queues during the 1930s (Shaw, 1971: 34; Unwin, 1983: 97); the sheet-music pedlars selling popular songs for a penny (Unwin, ibid.: 233); the barrel organs that 'drew youngsters like bees round a jam pot'; the buskers who jammed into the pub doorways playing 'battered old banjos or mandolins'; and the local unemployed men who hired instruments for the day from a shop in St Anne Street and dressed up in drag, touring the city and busking in groups of four (ibid.: 94).

A wealth of other entertainment facilities and resources emerged to cater for city visitors as well as locals, including different kinds of venues for live music performance. Local reports and surveys have highlighted a long-standing prevalence within the city of clubs, societies and other organizations devoted to music or involved in the promotion of music performance, and many of those who participated in our study on music and kinship were involved with such organizations. Barrow, writing about the Liverpool of 1756–83, comments on the city's 'highly developed network of clubs' (1925: 136), whilst a prevalence of local music clubs is noted in the *Liverpool Review* of 18 November 1899. The city's wealth of clubs and venues for music, dancing and singing is also highlighted in later reports,[6] thus Jones (1934:

---

6   These include a report by the Liverpool Council of Voluntary Aid on the Uses of Leisure in Liverpool, November 1923, p9, and a later report by Masser (1970: 468).

284) states 'There is in Liverpool no lack of societies and organizations giving musical performances. Some years ago, indeed, there was probably a superfluity of such institutions.'

The grandeur of some of those societies and venues reflected Liverpool's wealth and status. The city boasted, for example, prominent concert halls – such as the Royal Philharmonic Hall, which opened in 1849[7] – as well as numerous orchestras and societies for classical and choral music. The latter included the Royal Liverpool Philharmonic Orchestra that was administered by the Royal Liverpool Philharmonic Society (RLPS) and gave its first public performance on 12 March 1840.[8] During the late nineteenth and early twentieth centuries Liverpool could boast not just an impressive number of concert halls but also many notable music halls; and several of those who participated in our study had relatives who had been involved with music hall as performers, promoters or managers. The halls were targeted at all social classes, including working and upper classes, and they promoted a broad and diverse range of acts. On 20 August 1864, for example, the advertisements on the back page of the *Liverpool Era* included those for the Vine Hotel Concert Hall, featuring 'the celebrated Walton family' and 'the great Irish vocalist' Paddy Doyle; the American Opera House, featuring 'the celebrated comic vocalist W.H. Morgan, the 'great Ethiopian serenaders Hildebrandt and Ormonde, 'sensation vocalist' Mr Robert Frazer and Mr Thomas, 'basso-profunda'; and Scott's Royal Music Hall, featuring the eleventh week of performances by the Alabama Sisters: 'the black sisterhood have already acquired a widespread fame in the delineation of "nigger" character, and the songs and dances of the newest and most attractive styles'.[9] Some of those halls and some local theatres attracted the most successful entertainers of the time, including the well-known female drag artist Vesta Tilley, who married a Liverpool theatrical entrepreneur named Walter de Frece (Maitland, 1986); the US vaudeville entertainer Sophie Tucker, who appeared at the Empire in July 1934 (Unwin, 1983: 73); and the great violinist Paganini, who performed at the Liver Theatre in 1833.[10]

The popularity of music hall in Liverpool encouraged the later development of music theatre in the city. During the 1930s and 1940s local comics such as Arthur Askey and Tommy Trinder became famous for performances that drew upon music hall and helped to promote the city's strong reputation for comedy. However, some local music halls eventually became cinemas, which were a source of employment for many local musicians until the arrival of talking film. The Olympia, for example, was built as a music hall in 1905 but it became Liverpool's first cinema in 1925. On 23 January 1929 it screened 'the Singing Fool' featuring Al Jolson, which was the first talking film to be heard in Liverpool (Unwin, 1983: 183). Eighty-seven-year-old

---

7 During the late 1980s the Royal Liverpool Philharmonic Society took over the hall and thus became the only orchestral society in Britain to own its own performance venue.

8 http://www.orchestranet.co.uk/rlps.html, accessed November 2004.

9 I am grateful to Ellen Loudon, a PhD student in music at Liverpool University, for drawing my attention to these advertisements.

10 http://www.old-liverpool.co.uk/Liver3.jpg, accessed June 2005.

Jack Levy told us what it felt like to see that film shortly after its first screening in the city, and how inspired he had been by the characters and their musical performance, which had reminded him of his own life in Liverpool as the son of Eastern European Jewish immigrants (Cohen, 1998). He, like so many other people we spoke to, also reminisced with great fondness about the dance halls of his youth. Liverpool housed a wealth of such halls in addition to its music halls and cinemas. They included ornate ballrooms such as the Grafton, where numerous dance and swing acts performed during the 1920s, 30s and 40s. Like Glasgow – a city with similar social, economic and cultural characteristics – Liverpool has a strong and long-standing tradition in dance culture, and by the mid-1920s, according to Unwin (1983: 204), the city was 'recognised as one of the leading centres of ballroom dancing outside London'.

Liverpool's role as a port brought the city not just wealth but also severe poverty and striking divisions between rich and poor. Unlike large industrial cities such as nearby Manchester, Liverpool had little manufacturing industry, and the city's port activity was dependent upon an extensive and generally unskilled labour force. Fluctuations in trade and the casualized nature of much dockside labour brought chronic unemployment and deprivation to the city's working classes, most of whom lived in squalid and unhealthy conditions. The city consequently became a national pioneer in social reform and welfare provision, and in the establishment of organizations aiming to entertain the unemployed (Jones, 1934: 314). It was in Liverpool that the free concerts for the poor were first launched during the second half of the nineteenth century (ibid.: 27, 32, 35). A national survey of 'Labour and the Poor' revealed a concert-room industry in Liverpool in 1849:

> The attention of the stranger who walks through the streets of Liverpool can scarcely fail to be directed to the great number of placards which invite the public to cheap or free concert-rooms. Of all shapes, sizes and colours to attract the eye, they cover the walls of the town, and compete with one another in the inducements which they offer to the public to favour with its patronage the houses which they advertise. (Russell, 1987: 74)

In addition to these concerts, a network of welfare and support agencies was established in Liverpool that was unmatched by any other British city, and the city consequently achieved a pre-eminence in philanthropy (Belchem, 2000: 100). Thus in 1923 the Liverpool Council of Voluntary Aid stated, 'Liverpool is probably one of the most advanced towns in the whole country with regard to the supply of public and voluntary institutions for the social and metal welfare of its citizens.'[11]

Migration, Ethnic Diversity and Multiculturalism

It is clear from the discussion so far that Liverpool's role as a port had a huge impact on the social, cultural and musical life of the city. It influenced musical style and

---

11   Liverpool Council of Voluntary Aid. Report on the Uses of Leisure in Liverpool. November 1923, p17.

content and the development of the city's entertainment provision and infrastructure, and it brought large numbers of visiting musicians to the city. It also created local musical cultures that were characterized by class hierarchies and striking divisions between rich and poor. Most of Liverpool's poor were immigrants and immigration had a significant impact on Liverpool's musical life. As early as 1800, large numbers of immigrants crowded into the older parts of Liverpool and its dockland areas (and the city was a place of migration up until the 1950s). According to Belchem (2000: xiii), the city's multiculturalism was 'a pattern not found in other British cities until the later twentieth century'. Our research on music and kinship in the city therefore highlighted family networks that extended way beyond Liverpool's borders in reflection of the journeys and settlements of local emigrants, as well as intermarriage between the city's immigrant groups. The immigrants brought to the city new musical sounds, and through intermarriage and alternative forms of social mixing they and other social groups exchanged musical influences and combined them to form new hybrid local sounds and styles. In addition, both music and kinship played crucial roles in the process through which immigrants adjusted to their new surroundings and created a sense of place, identity and belonging. According to Stokes (1994a: 114), 'Place for many migrant communities, is something which is constructed through music with an intensity not found elsewhere in their social lives.'[12] For many of Liverpool's immigrants music was certainly a focus for the construction of local communities, and it also played a part in the forging of broader, diasporic connections involving relations of alliance and affinity with groups and places elsewhere.[13] Those immigrants had travelled to Liverpool from many different places, particularly Wales, Scotland, Ireland, Africa, China, and Eastern and Western Europe; and I now want to introduce some of the main groups involved and highlight their contribution to the city's musical life.

The Irish

Many of those who participated in our study of music and kinship had Celtic – particularly Irish – connections, including the Coyne family. Eamon Coyne and fellow musician Sean McNamara were founding members of the Liverpool branch of the Comhaltas Ceoltoiri Eireann (Association of Irish Musicians), which was established in 1957 to promote Irish traditional music and song through organized classes, music sessions and competitive events. They also founded the Liverpool Ceili band and, following Eamon's death in 1990, his two sons joined Sean in that band. We watched them perform with the band in Liverpool's Irish Centre, which had first opened in 1964. I had spent a Sunday morning in that centre during my first ever visit to Liverpool in 1985. I was taken there by my Liverpool-based host and I

---

12   On music and migration see also Slobin (1993), Lipsitz (1994), Connell and Gibson (2003: Chapter 6).

13   See, for example, Cohen (1998) on music's role and significance in the construction of Liverpool's Jewish community.

was struck by the strong emphasis on kinship and community within the centre, and by the ease with which people of varying ages – including my host's eight-year-old daughter – sang familiar Irish tunes to each other in such a large and crowded room. According to Du Noyer (2002: 51), 'The Irish shaped many facets of the Scouse character … but their greatest contribution was the view of music as one of life's necessities.'[14]

Welsh and Scottish migration to Liverpool was substantial and long established;[15] hence Liverpool had Welsh newspapers and Welsh chapels that supported local choral groups, such as the Wavertree Male Voice Choir of the early 1930s.[16] The city also hosted the National Eisteddfod music festival on several occasions (Belchem, 2000: 44). From the 1840s, however, the crossing to the New World flourished, with Liverpool serving as the main point of emigration for Britons and Europeans in search of a new life;[17] and the biggest influx of immigrants into the port came from Ireland following the disastrous potato famine of the 1840s. Du Noyer thus suggests, rather too glibly, that, 'If Irish people had green skins, then the typical Liverpool complexion would be a delicate shade of mint' (2002: 50), and he refers to the labelling of Ireland as 'West Liverpool' by the Liverpool comedian Ken Dodd (ibid.: 51). According to Neal (1988: 82), in 1847 alone, during one four-month period 296,231 Irish settlers arrived in Liverpool. Yet they entered a city with a population that was little more than 200,000 – and that included large numbers of residents who were already living in extreme poverty and in shocking contrast to the wealth of the city's elite. Such vast numbers of destitute and often disease-ridden immigrants had huge implications for Liverpool, and although most of them eventually moved on westwards to America and Canada, others stayed. The casualized nature of the dockside labour market meant that many of them were able to gain employment, and a large proportion of unskilled and semi-skilled immigrants settled in cramped, squalid terraced housing close to the waterfront.[18] Between 1821 and 1851 the number of Irish-born people enumerated in Liverpool's records therefore increased dramatically and the city's total population more than doubled.[19]

Irish immigrants have commonly expressed through music a longing for the people and country they have left behind and strong notions of home. These themes and sentiments are evident in some of the Irish-influenced folk songs that have been written about Liverpool, such as 'The Leaving of Liverpool' and 'In My Liverpool

---

14   Scouse is a term that has been used to refer to the distinctive Liverpool dialect and also to native Liverpudlians.

15   Du Noyer states that in 1813 one tenth of Liverpool's population came from Wales (2002: 52).

16   Mentioned in *The Liverpool Review*, April 1934: 21.

17   'Between 1830 and 1930, nine million emigrants set sail from Liverpool' (Du Noyer, 2002: 48).

18   See Shimmin (1856).

19   According to data arising from the national census, the city's population increased from 165,175 in 1821 to 375,955 in 1851, by which time the number of Irish residents amounted to 22 per cent of the total population.

Home'. The former tells the story of a sailor about to embark on a voyage to America, leaving his woman behind, whilst the latter has been used in certain situations as a local anthem.[20] Many Irish songs were passed down through the generations. Tony Davis, for example, lived with his Irish grandmother for a while as a young child, and he told us how she had loved to sing Irish folk songs and how this had influenced his own music-making. Sean MacNamara introduced us to Greg Query, a Liverpool-based Irish traditional musician who ran classes in Irish culture at the Irish Centre. Greg told us about the various 'revivals' of Irish traditional music and dance that Liverpool had experienced over the years. From the 1930s onwards, for example, there were regular ceilidh nights in many Liverpool venues – particularly pubs and parish clubs – involving instruments such as the bodhrán, fiddle and tin whistle. Following a further wave of Irish immigration into Liverpool in the 1940s due to the employment opportunities afforded by post-war reconstruction, several organizations were established in the city to promote Irish traditional music and dance and to ensure their continuity. According to Leonard, those who participated in such events often appeared to be 'more Irish than the Irish'.[21] Although the Irish Centre closed during the 1990s, regular Irish sessions still took place in some of the city's pubs, including the Newstead Abbey pub that we visited to watch Greg perform traditional Irish music with other local and visiting musicians.

The Lane and Collings families also participated in our study, and they drew our attention to the influence of Irish Protestantism on Liverpool's musical life. Philip Lane was Vice President of the Bootle Concertina Band, a marching band that was established in 1904 by a former sailor. For some time members of that band performed in naval uniform, but by the time that we got to see the band rehearse and march the uniform had changed. Philip and his brother David joined the band as young boys, and eventually their wives and children also became members – although women were only allowed to join from 1977 and membership was always restricted to Protestants. George Collings, who ran another local concertina band, told us,

> For a marching street band to be made up of concertinas is something unique that's survived in Liverpool ... These bands that are walking along the streets today are the last of a dying breed ... once they are gone it will be a little part of Liverpool's history that won't be here any more. (Cohen and McManus, 1991: 25)

---

20   It was performed, for example, at a special event held at Liverpool's Anglican cathedral in the summer of 2003 to celebrate Liverpool's success in its bid to become the European Capital of Culture 2008. Jimmy McGovern, the composer of the song, had added some new verses to commemorate the event. During the 1980s the song was compiled onto cassettes sold by Radio Merseyside and featuring local musicians. Those cassettes contributed to a local heritage industry that is described by Belchem (2000: 51) as encompassing the production of books of photographs of pre-1960s Liverpool, collections of children's rhymes and books on 'scouseology' produced by Scouse Press, 'Liverpool's first publisher of local humour and local history'.

21   www.bbb.co.uk/legacies/immig England/Liverpool/article 2.shtml, accessed May 2004.

The music-making of the Lane and Collings families was closely connected with the Irish Protestant Orange Lodge, a religious movement that also provided social clubs offering members practical benefits and local networks. Liverpool became the centre of that movement in England following the dissolution of the Grand Lodge in 1836. By 1900 there were 17,000 lodge members in Liverpool and prominent Orange marches regularly took place through the city, heralded by the marching bands.[22] Those public parades were for some time a focus for local sectarian differences,[23] and although such differences eventually declined, the musical traditions nevertheless continued.

Jewish Settlers

A strong love of and involvement with music has also extended across several generations of the Swerdlow family. Rob Swerdlow was in his early twenties when we first met him, and he had just started to manage a Merseyside rock band called The La's. He later became manager of Cast, another local band that became known nationally and internationally. Rob attended Liverpool's Jewish school, King David, where he befriended the nephew of Brian Epstein, manager of the Beatles. One of Rob's uncles had been in the same year as Brian Epstein at Quarrybank School and also at the local art college. He had designed some of the merchandise for Brian's record shop NEMS, and had also photographed the Beatles on numerous occasions. Another of Rob's uncles had been a member of a Liverpool rock group in the early 1960s, whilst Rob's father, Michael, was an avid record-collector and for a long time ran his own music programme on a voluntary basis for a hospital radio station, in addition to his work for Jewish community organizations and charities. Michael Swerdlow talked to us at length about his family's musical history. He showed us a video recording of a performance by his Aunt Asna, a music hall singer and dancer who married a professional musician from London, and he told us about his uncle who was a theatrical agent and music promoter. From the early twentieth century many Jewish people became involved with Liverpool's emerging modern entertainment industries, either as musicians or as managers, promoters, musical instrument retailers and club owners. During the early 1960s there was thus a strong Jewish involvement in the businesses that helped to support and promote the Beatles.

Michael Swerdlow's brother-in-law was Frankie Vaughan, an internationally renowned 'crooner' of the 1950s who was originally from Liverpool, and whose parents (like Michael's great grandparents) had been Russian immigrants. Ian Broudie, who was known internationally for his rock/pop band The Lightning

---

22   www.movinghere.org.uk/galleries/histories/irish/culture/culture.htm, accessed May 2004.

23   See Meegan (1995: 75–6); McManus (1994b: 5); Lane (1987: 110–11); Nightingale (1980: 75); and O'Mara and Anon (quoted at www.movinghere.org.uk/galleries/histories/irish/culture/culture.htm, accessed May 2004).

Seeds and his work as a record producer,[24] and Darren Michaelson, a rock manager, were also descended from Russian immigrants. Both of them described to us how their ancestors, who did not speak English, had been sold tickets that they were told would take them to New York, when in fact Liverpool was the actual destination; so when they disembarked at Liverpool they just assumed it was New York. During the 1980s a Hollywood film company arrived in Liverpool to shoot a re-enactment of the arrival of Jewish immigrants from Eastern Europe as part of a scene for *Yentl*, starring Barbra Streisand. The film company advertised in Liverpool for extras to play the part of those immigrants, and Betty Cohen, who was born in 1910, became one of those extras. She told us how moved she was to participate in the reconstruction of a real-life event that she had been involved with herself, having travelled to Liverpool from Poland with her family as a small child.

During the latter half of the nineteenth century thousands of Jewish immigrants travelled to Liverpool from Eastern Europe, many of them fleeing the Crimean War; although most moved on from Liverpool to other places. During one of many visits to the Jewish archives at the Liverpool Records Office I came across a late nineteenth-century register from Liverpool's Jewish School. The pupils' names were listed down one side of the page and each day those who attended were marked by a tick. The ticks were outnumbered, however, by crosses to mark the absentees, which were accompanied by brief explanatory notes stating, more often than not, 'left for Canada', 'left for America', 'left for South Africa'. This was truly a population in flux. Nevertheless, around 5000 Jewish immigrants eventually settled in Liverpool. They joined a small, wealthy and anglicized Jewish elite that had already settled in the city, descendants of early eighteenth-century German and Dutch immigrant bankers and merchants. That elite was known for its extensive and impressive charitable work[25] and for its patronage of the city's classical music venues and concerts. By contrast, the new Eastern European immigrants brought with them their own sacred and Yiddish musical cultures. Jack Levy, for example, described to us how his mother and aunts – all first-generation Jewish immigrants in Liverpool – wept as they listened to imported recordings of the great chazans and Yiddish folk songs, which reminded them of their native homelands and evoked strong feelings of loss and nostalgia (Cohen, 1998). Many of those immigrants, like Rob Swerdlow's great-grandfather, established tailoring workshops, and a small Jewish-run tailoring and cabinet-making industry developed in the city centre. By the eve of World War I the city's Jewish population had expanded to 11,000 (ibid.) but over recent years that

---

24   Ian had also been a member of the Liverpool punk band Big in Japan, and he also attended King David School in Liverpool. One of the school's Jewish prayer books was described to me only recently by someone who had come across it by accident. Ian's name had been inscribed on the inside cover, whilst the back cover featured the scribbled lyrics to the Paul McCartney song 'Another Day'.

25   Williams, Bill (1987), 'The History of Liverpool's Jewish Community', http://www.ljgs.org, accessed November 2004.

number has declined quite dramatically.[26] Michael Swerdlow thus described it to us as a 'dying community', and he told us about various projects he had been involved with to document and archive that community, to inform young people about their local roots and to attract Jewish people from elsewhere to migrate to the city.

African Migrants

During our research on music and kinship we were introduced to members of several extended and interconnected families with African connections and a strong tradition of music-making. Liverpool attracted immigrant seafarers from Africa from the mid-eighteenth century, and they were joined by African students, servants and freed slaves (Lane, 1987: 117–18). Some of them were initially catered for by seamen's lodges; but they established the oldest black community in Europe, with its own churches, social clubs and community centres. Robert Amoo was a guitarist and tap dancer who travelled to Britain as a stowaway from Ghana. He earned a living as a performer in London before travelling to Liverpool, where he stayed during the 1930s in a seamen's lodge. There he met his wife Moya, who was of mixed African and Irish parentage, and whose aunt owned the lodge. He also performed high-life and other musical styles in local, black-owned clubs and bars such as the Ibo, the Yoruba and the Sierra Leone. He performed with other local black musicians, including Eddie Jenkins and his brothers, and the brothers Powie and Johnnie Wenton, all of whom came from Sierra Leone. The sons and grandsons of these men also became involved with music-making.

Bernie Wenton was the son of Johnnie Wenton and his wife Eileen Hogan, who was white and Irish. Bernie won a national singing competition on British television impersonating Nat King Cole, and was one of nine children, several of whom were singers or professional boxers, as were two of Bernie's nephews. Charlie Jenkins, Eddie's son, performed cabaret music in clubs across Merseyside during the 1970s and had at one time run his own club. Meanwhile Robert Amoo's sons, Eddie and Chris, were members of a vocal harmony group named The Chants during the early 1960s, as was Joe Ankarah, whose Ghanaian father played the organ at the African Churches Mission. The Chants performed on occasion with the Beatles and were managed at one point by their manager, Brian Epstein. During the 1970s Eddie and Chris Amoo established a soul band called The Real Thing and produced several British hit singles. They were still performing with that band when we first met them in the large house that they and their families shared, which had a recording studio in the basement. At that time Eddie was managing his four daughters – Sara, Michaela, Dionne and Marlene – who sang and danced together as a vocal group.

Sugar Deen was a Music Worker at a local black community and education centre, and he had been involved with music-making for most of his life. During

---

26   This has been largely due to intermarriage and emigration (particularly to Israel and to other British cities). According to the national census of 2001 Liverpool's Jewish population was 2,698.

the 1960s he had performed with various male vocal harmony groups – including the Conquests, the Earls, the Valentinos and the Harlems – and he had passed his love of music on to his five daughters and his son, all of whom performed and recorded together. Sugar's first recollection of music was his father's recordings of African/Nigerian music (p.c.). His father, Saka, was a Nigerian who had performed with a circus group but had travelled to Liverpool as a seaman in 1938. There he met Sugar's mother – who was Scottish and could play the piano and sing. Many African immigrants travelled to Liverpool as single men and later married white, local women. Sugar told us, 'The African seamen settled in Liverpool and married Liverpool white girls. You go to London and 99 per cent of the black people are from the West Indies. You come to Liverpool, 99 per cent are from mixed race.' Small (1991: 512), citing the Commission for Racial Equality, states that this has been a common aspect of Liverpool's black population, which has a 'high proportion of mixed couples and marriages'. Wes Wilkie, an ardent jazz fan, told us that he didn't know of any black Liverpool families that did not include white people. Wes's grandmother, Sarah Samuels, who was of Welsh–Jewish origin, married a West African mandolin player. Her son Derry, Wes's father, fronted the local rock'n'roll or beat group Derry and the Seniors, which in 1960 became the first Merseybeat group to perform in Hamburg.[27]

Liverpool's black population expanded after World War I with the arrival of immigrants from the colonies, and again when hundreds of West Indian volunteers arrived to contribute to the World War II effort. Caribbean musical influences have not been as strong as in other British cities that have more recently established black communities, but some of the Liverpool-born black musicians we spoke to as part of our project nevertheless remembered calypso and mento being performed in Liverpool venues during the 1940s and 1950s and they also introduced us to a couple of reggae-influenced local bands. Also mentioned was Lord Woodbine, a Caribbean calypso singer and business partner of Allan Williams, first manager of the Beatles (Du Noyer, 2002: 31). Lord Woodbine had his own steel band during the late 1950s, which took up a residency in Liverpool's Jacaranda club and also performed in Hamburg. More recently, Liverpool has become home to many North African and Somalian immigrants, although Somalians lived in the city throughout most of the twentieth century.

Chinese Immigrants

In the Pagoda Community Centre, founded in 1982, we met members of the Liu family who had immigrated to Liverpool from China and spoke Chinese. They were

---

27   The group was unusual because it was a white band fronted by a black performer. Some of our interviewees suggested that there was very little collaboration between black and white musicians during that period, and this is also suggested by Jenkins (1994) and Willis-Pitts (2000: 48, 55, 199). Since the arrival of rock and roll in the city, black/white musical collaborations have for various reasons not been as obvious in local rock/pop music as they have in British cities such as Manchester, Bristol and Birmingham.

heavily involved with the Chinese classical youth orchestra (the only one of its kind in Europe) that rehearsed in the centre, and with other efforts to promote Chinese language and culture within the city. Near the Pagoda Centre is the Wah Sing Chinese Community Centre, which is known for traditional Chinese music and dance, and a Chinese gospel church that runs a choir and music workshops.[28] However, many of the city's earlier Chinese immigrants had become highly anglicized. During the 1950s Sugar Deen mixed with Anglo-Chinese youths of his age, and he described to us their interaction with older Chinese people who did not consider them to be Chinese. Chinese seamen had begun to settle in Liverpool from the late 1860s (Lynn, 1982:9; Jones, 1934: 102) where they founded Europe's oldest Chinese community, which established its own newspaper in 1944 (the *Chunguttua Chow Pao*) as well as a Chinese bank.[29] For sometime those seamen, like their African counterparts, were perceived as a threat to the employment of white seamen (Jones, 1934: 102). This encouraged local anti-Chinese sentiment fuelled by the cheap cost of Chinese labour, extensive interracial marriage between Chinese men and white local women, Chinese gambling and racist Chinese stereotypes that were promoted in the local and popular press (Lau, 2003: 18). Liverpool's Chinese community expanded in the early 1900s following the growth of the Chinese laundry business in Britain, and in the mid-twentieth century following the growth of the Chinese catering trade (ibid.: 19, 21; Lane, 1987: 121).[30] Those immigrants brought with them not just traditional and classical Chinese music, but also more popular music such as Cantopop, which combined Chinese music with various international popular music styles.

Other Immigrant Groups

By 1901 Liverpool's population had risen to 704,000 (Misselwitz: 114)[31] and it included many other immigrant groups, amongst them seafarers from Holland, Greece, Poland and Scandinavia. The latter established a network of seamen's lodges, churches and community centres. Italian immigrants settled in Liverpool between 1880 and 1912, whilst Indian immigrants arrived following their country's declaration of independence in 1947.[32] Some of those Indian and Italian immigrants became entertainers, including a successful piano-accordion act featuring the Italian

---

28   http://icliverpool.icnetwork.co.uk/community-id=11-23881, accessed November 2004.

29   Wong, 1989: 3. http://web.ukonline.co.uk/lcba/ba/history.html, accessed November 2004.

30   According to Lane (1987: 120), 'The Chinese population, counted in several hundreds in 1906, had probably doubled by 1939.' In 2001, according to the national census, there were over 5000 Chinese (1.17 per cent) in Liverpool, making it the third largest minority after the Irish and other non-British white.

31   P. Misselwitz, 'Liverpool City Profile'. pp114–17. http://www.shrinkingcities.com/fileadmin/shrink/downloads/pdfs/WP-11_Manchester_Liverpool.pdf, accessed November 2004.

32   http://www.museumofliverpoollife.org.uk/indian, accessed May 2004.

Valerio Brothers.[33] The *Liverpool Citizen* (28 November 1888) mentioned a musical performance by five Italians in native costume at the Trocadero Club, which catered for sailors; whilst Shaw (1971: 132) describes Dom Volante, a boxer from Liverpool's Little Italy whose father 'used to play a barrel organ round Liverpool streets' in the 1920s. In the mid-1980s Liverpool's first annual Asian music festival (MILAP) was launched. More recently, Liverpool has housed more asylum seekers than anywhere else in Britain, and it has received immigrants from Eastern Europe and the Middle East. Within the city performances of music from Iraq, Somalia and many other countries regularly take place in private homes and in local community centres.

Urban Musical Landscapes and Places of Mixing and Exclusion

The Liverpool families and immigrant and ethnic groups that I have introduced clearly contributed to the cosmopolitanism of the city and the diversity of its musical life, I now want to discuss the movement and settlement of those families and groups within the city, and the impact of this on the city's musical landscape and on the creation of place, neighbourhood and local identity (see Figure 2).

Italo Cavina writes that the city, 'does not tell its past, but contains it like the lines of a hand, written in the corners of the streets, the gratings of the windows, the bannisters of the steps, the antennae of the lightning rods, the poles of the flags, every segment marked in turn with scratches, indentations, scrolls' (cited in Short, 1996: 390). As we traced the musical routes of those who participated in our study of music and kinship, and learned about their family histories, consulting related sources of information, I began to perceive the city and its various places and spaces in new and different ways. Familiar streets and landmarks took on a new resonance. Increasingly I came to recognize within the present traces of the musical past and related patterns of internal migration and local settlement. I realized, for example, that my university office was located in an area that had once been a focal point for the city's population of East European Jews. All of a sudden my daily route to work incorporated the site of a 1930s taxi crash that had resulted in the deaths of members of a local Jewish dance band; and I began to notice Hebrew inscriptions on a couple of buildings. Buildings surrounding my office also gained new significance as former synagogues and residences of local Jewish families, and the dance halls that so many Jewish people had frequented. The latter included Daulby Hall and Dayne's, described by Unwin (1983: 224) as 'almost a marriage bureau as so many couples met there for the first time and married'. I began to appreciate how musical venues and events had helped to distinguish the city's social, ethnic and migrant groups and the neighbourhoods they inhabited; but how they had also contributed to social mixing and intermarriage between those groups.

Earlier, I introduced Charlie Jenkins, a guitar-player and singer whose father had been a musician from West Africa. Charlie was one of seven children who grew

---

33   http://www.scottiepress.org/projects/litaly.htm, accessed May 2004.

Figure 2   Map of Merseyside © Sandra Mather

up around Windsor Street. During the early 1990s this was a quiet residential street close to the city centre and flanked by a mix of older, disused residential blocks and newer housing estates. The street lay at the intersection of Liverpool 8 (also known as Toxteth), where the city's black population was concentrated; the Dingle in the southern docklands where many Irish immigrants had settled; Chinatown, which was close to the city centre and waterfront; and the area around the university where the Jewish immigrants had lived. Charlie worked for a local Jewish bakery as a young boy, and he pointed to the close social and economic connections that developed between neighbouring Jewish and black groups (connections that were also mentioned to us by others we interviewed as part of our research).[34] Charlie said that he used to defend the Jews when people made anti-Semitic remarks, adding 'They'd employ "colour", maybe because they were downtrodden as well.' I first met Charlie in 1990 in Windsor Street's Wellington Butts pub. The pub was detached from other buildings and it looked rather out of place in relation to the neighbouring modern housing estates. Charlie wasn't there when I arrived, but the woman behind the bar explained that he had telephoned to say that he would be slightly late, and had instructed her to get me a drink. The pub had a mixed black, white and Chinese clientele, and the walls were adorned with photographs. There were photographs of Liverpool's ocean-going liners; of local black musicians and boxers – including members of the Wenton family mentioned earlier – and of Stanley House, a black community centre that opened in 1946 just around the corner from the pub. Stanley House was where the vocal doo-wop bands of Sugar Deen, Eddie and Chris Amoo, the Wentons, the Ankarah brothers and other black musicians had rehearsed, and it had housed a gospel church.

Charlie soon arrived to meet me and he also greeted, and introduced me to, some of the pub's other customers. They included four white men in their sixties or seventies who were all brothers and were seated around a table. All of them, Charlie explained, had worked on the ships featured in framed photographs mounted on the wall above their heads. Although Charlie had suggested that we meet in that pub, he and the rest of his family had not lived in Windsor Street or its neighbourhood since the 1960s, when many local houses had been demolished as part of an urban renewal programme. Most of the area's residents had subsequently been dispersed to other parts of Liverpool and Merseyside. Charlie told me that he and his family nevertheless still travelled back to the pub every fortnight where they had sing-songs, and they also gathered there for special occasions: 'My roots are here' he explained. I was struck by the way that Charlie talked about his earlier life on Windsor Street and the spatial divisions that emerged so strongly through his narrative. Charlie told me, for

---

34   Ray Costello, who has written on the history of Liverpool's black community, told us that his father used to run a cap factory at the corner of Hanover Street and had business dealings with the Greenburgs over the road; and that strong sympathies remained between Jewish and black communities. Eddie Conway, who had a particular interest in the city's Jewish history, told us about the black women who worked in the Jewish rag trade. Steve Higginson, a local historian and film-maker, told us about his time at King David School, founded in 1840, which took on Jewish and black pupils until the 1960s when it was relocated to the suburbs and further away from the city's predominantly black neighbourhood. Steve had conducted research on the impact of Liverpool seafaring on the city's popular culture, and had discovered photographs of local foo foo bands that indicated, he believed, collaboration between Jewish and black musicians during the late nineteenth century, although the precise nature and extent of that collaboration has yet to be investigated.

example, the story of how he met his wife – a white woman of Irish Catholic descent who had lived across the street – and said that before they met, his wife had never travelled '*this* side of the line'. He was referring to the imaginary line or boundary separating the largely white, working class, Protestant area of the Dingle from the black population of Toxteth, or Liverpool 8; although this was by no means a fixed boundary and other people we spoke to situated the boundary elsewhere. Windsor Street and neighbouring streets were thus symbolic boundaries distinguishing one social and ethnic group from another. As Charlie talked I began to appreciate the significance of the pub in which we sat, and why it continued to act as a magnet for Charlie and his family. Situated at the junction of different ethnic neighbourhoods, it had been a social hub, hosting social and musical events that attracted residents from those neighbourhoods and provided a context for social mixing and cultural exchange.

Certain local ballrooms and dance clubs had also been significant as places of mixing, and Charlie described for me several of those venues during the 1950s. The Rialto Ballroom was situated on the boundary of Liverpool 8, and Charlie described how dancers from the North End of Liverpool would stand at one end of the dance floor, whilst the 'South Enders' stood at the other. 'North Enders' also frequented Liverpool 8 clubs such as the Kit Kat, the Palm Beach and the Ibo, because many were unlicensed and therefore stayed open longer than clubs in the city centre and the city's North End. Odie Taylor and Derry Wilkie, two black musicians from the South End, and Hank Walters, a white country musician and 'North Ender', have also described the social and musical mixing that took place in Liverpool 8 clubs, and how those clubs attracted musicians and music fans from all over the region.[35] They emphasized the variety of musical styles that those clubs promoted, including calypso, African music and country and western. (Derry described how those and other musical styles, particularly Irish styles, had also influenced local sailors, including his own West African father, who met and performed music together on board ship. The ships were thus another place of social and musical mixing.) Joe Flannery was one of many white music fans who travelled to Liverpool 8 to visit its clubs, despite the fact that he had been warned by family and friends not to go there; and he described the area's club scene as a 'magnet for people from all over the city'.[36] Sugar Deen used to perform in and frequent the Rialto and he told us,

> Everybody but everybody was in the Rialto ballroom. It's where we first started meeting people from the North End of the city, girls that is … the white girls would come down there. So we'd come up with the dances first, the movements and stuff like that, then they'd take it back to the North End.

---

35   Interviewed in *Who Put the Beat in Merseybeat?*: documentary by True Corner Productions based on research conducted at the Institute of Popular Music, Liverpool University, and broadcast on Granada television on 5 March 1996.

36   Ibid.

At the same time, however, many music venues and events were a source of social tension and exclusion. Murphy (1995: 125) writes that during the 1940s Liverpool pubs, clubs and dance halls were sites of potential 'race conflict', and a 'colour bar already excluded Black people from the majority of leisure facilities in the city'. Many of the black musicians we interviewed related anecdotes that illustrated how that colour bar had operated within particular venues (sometimes only on certain nights of the week), and pointed to a long-standing and institutionalized racism in Liverpool.[37] The Grafton Ballroom, for example, imposed a ban on black people in 1942 (Murphy, 1995: 108). Charlie Jenkins told us how he was once barred from the Grafton around 20 years later, even though he was with a white girl and both had tickets to see the black musician who had been hired to perform at the ballroom that night. Wes Wilkie told us that during the 1970s he had also been barred from Liverpool clubs that were playing black music, and that his father, Derry Wilkie, had been barred from the Rialto Ballroom despite the fact that he was a well-known local musician, and despite the fact that the Rialto was located in Liverpool 8.

Sugar Deen told us about his experience of living in the North End of the city during the 1950s between the ages of seven and ten:

> No black families lived there and it was a totally racist part of the city. You couldn't walk from one end of the street to the other. Each day, going to school, coming home, bricks through the window, the whole bit ... Liverpool is the most racist city I know ... The North End of the city is still very racist ... most days I'd come home with cuts and bruises from the gang. It was never just one boy, it was always a gang.

Racism, including racist policies and policing, thus served to restrict the movement and settlement of black people within the city, and also the operation of music venues run by black people. Black music entrepreneurs pointed us to local licensing and policing policies that discriminated against businesses run by black people. 'They don't let clubs stay open in L8 now', Sugar Deen told us; whilst during the late 1990s those involved with the city's small black hip hop scene (there was also a white, student-oriented hip hop scene) complained that the events they ran were automatically regarded as problematic by the local authorities, who assumed that they would attract drug taking and violence. Racism also contributed to the Toxteth street riots of 1981 that resulted in the burning down of the Rialto Ballroom. Unsurprisingly, therefore, Liverpool's diverse black population was overwhelmingly concentrated within the Liverpool 8 area, where complex interrelations emerged and developed between Africans, Caribbeans and black Liverpudlians.[38]

37　On racism in Liverpool see Jones (1934: 102–3); Small (1991); Meegan (1995: 73); Parkinson (1985: 15); Lane (1987: 12); Kettle (1981: 60); Law (1981, foreword) and Gifford and Bundy (1989: 82), who conclude 'that the situation with regard to racial discrimination in Liverpool is uniquely horrific'.

38　According to the national census of 1991, 'just three of the city's thirty-three census wards contain[ing] over 40% of its black population' (Meegan, 1995: 73). The Granby ward

Like other similar inner-city areas in Britain described by Taylor, Evans and Fraser (1996: 198), Liverpool 8 was demonized and became a symbol of crime, a 'virtual no-go zone' (Du Noyer, 2002: 92), and it was thus disconnected from the rest of the city (Meegan, 1995: 73; Murphy, 1995: 124, 125). Consequently, the area became host to distinct black music and dance cultures. Until the1930s, for example, illicit 'shebeens' or dance parties were held in the cellars of residential houses within the area – events that were remembered or referred to by many of the people we interviewed. Beth Hanning, who was of mixed black African and white Liverpudlian parentage, told us about the parties that took place in her own family home:

> the Africans, once a month, would go to a house and they'd all pay 4 pence each. I've got a photograph of my father in an evening suit. It's the most wonderful suit with a pin tucked shirt and bow tie, because he was the MC ... It was a social togetherness where they could all play their own music. They always played guitars because only the English played pianos. They played a sort of half African, half Negro American thing – the beat to it (quoted in Jenkins, 1994: 38).

It was hardly surprising, therefore, that Wes Wilkie, like so many of the people we met, described Liverpool to us as not so much a 'melting pot', but as a patchwork of geographical areas distinguished by class, ethnicity, religion and a strong degree of territorialism.

Likewise, Belchem (2000: 63) writes, 'Liverpool lacks a political culture and a historiographical tradition to incorporate its non-celtic immigrants, the long-established presence of West Indians, Africans and Chinese notwithstanding.' He thus points out (ibid.: xiii), 'Cosmopolitanism was a point of Merseypride, a factor that raised Liverpool above provincialism, but it was seldom given an inclusive (or "melting-pot") inflexion,' and he states, 'Liverpool was ahead of other cities in its "modern" spatial segregation, a pattern already established on Merseyside by 1871' (ibid: xv). Similarly, Gentleman (1970: 39) writes of Merseyside, 'There was in the past a tendency for particular elements in the population to congregate in separate communities'. During the nineteenth century Liverpool's residential areas were highly stratified, with the poorest housing at the water's edge, the skilled in inner residential suburbs, [39] and the mansions of the merchant traders and ship owners on the rises overlooking the water. Particular stretches of the city docklands were closely associated with Irish immigrants, and Belchem (2000: 45) refers to the city's sectarian geography consisting of a Catholic North and Protestant South. Yet those Irish and sectarian associations have diminished over the years due to intermarriage, post-war slum clearance leading to the relocation of local residents, and other factors.

As illustrated above, such patterns of internal migration have left their mark on the city's built environment, and particular local landmarks (and also neighbourhoods) have become a focus for collective memory. Eighteenth-century black immigrants

---

that overlapped with Liverpool 8 has been described as 'one of the few neighbourhoods in Britain that feels like a ghetto' (P. Barker, *New Statesman*, 7 February 1997).

39   They included many Welsh and Scottish migrants (Belchem, 2000: 42).

settled primarily in the South Docks area of the city centre, but the black population gradually shifted a mile or two inland towards Toxteth Park, occupying areas that had once housed the mansions of the city's white elite, including those of wealthy Jewish families, and the terraces that supported those mansions. That migration vacated space in the South Docks that white working-class people then occupied. During the 1920s and 1930s there were common references to Liverpool's 'Little Italy',[40] whilst the majority of Jewish immigrants were concentrated in an area around Brownlow Hill that has been referred to as a Jewish 'colony' (*Liverpool Review*, 1899). Following city-centre slum clearance of the 1930s and 1940s, those immigrants gradually followed the route established by the Jewish elite and migrated to the relatively affluent suburbs of South Liverpool and to other parts of Merseyside. Today, Liverpool's Jewish 'community' consists largely of middle-class businesspeople and professionals, and its focal point is a South Liverpool campus that houses a synagogue, Jewish junior and senior schools, and a Jewish youth club and community centre. Ann McKeown works as a cleaner and carer in a nearby residential street that she and her associates refer to as 'the Jewish Mile' because, she told us, 'a lot of Jewish people live there'.[41] From the 1960s Liverpool-born black families also began to move out of Liverpool 8 and into the suburbs, making way for new immigrants from the Caribbean, North Africa and, more recently, the Middle East.

American Connections and Local Sounds

I have described the influence on Liverpool's musical life of several immigrant, ethnic and religious groups, as well as local patterns of settlement and local, neighbourhood identities. This will help to inform the discussion in the following chapter on musical sounds identified with different areas of Liverpool. Du Noyer (2002: 47), however, states that 'the Liverpool rhythm is more than anything else the pulse of America', so I will now turn to that American influence.

Carol Sherry was a registered judge but in her spare time she was involved with barbershop, a style of singing that originated in nineteenth-century America. Carol, her daughter Helen and her mother Joan, all sang with the Liverpool Ladies' Barbershop Chorus alongside Margaret Blackman and her daughter and sisters. Carol's husband Paul, who ran a local newsagent's, sang with the men's barbershop chorus, as did her son David and her father Joe McCartney. Joe's brother Jim ran an American-influenced swing band in the 1920s known as Jim Mac's Band, and in later years Jim's sons, Paul and Mike, established their own bands. One of those bands was the Beatles, whose music drew upon American country music, skiffle

---

40   'Disappearing Communities', a video filmed by Community Productions Merseyside, Liverpool, 1989.

41   Michael Swerdlow told us that his schoolfriends enjoyed visiting his home in post-war Liverpool because it was not located in 'the Jewish ghetto areas' of suburban Liverpool, and visiting it thus gave his friends a 'change of atmosphere and decor and architecture'.

and black American soul and rhythm and blues. The other band was a quirky and satirical group of poets and pop musicians known as the Scaffold. The musical activities and tastes of the Sherry and McCartney families – like those of the other families that participated in our project – were thus strongly influenced by American musical styles and traditions, and American influences were prevalent throughout the city's popular music culture. During the early decades of the twentieth century the Anglo-American music and media industries rapidly expanded, exposing audiences in Liverpool and other parts of Britain to American popular music, which dominated media output. Thus before 1956, 'British popular music was dominated by US sounds,' a 'musical cocktail' that included showbusiness, light jazz and music hall (Chambers, 1985: 18). During the 1920s and 1930s, for example, Liverpool's ballrooms and smaller venues hosted numerous dance bands, but during World War II the popularity of those bands began to decline in favour of popular vocalists and Dixieland jazz and swing (Brocken, 1994). The Merseysippi Jazz Band, formed in 1949, performed at the opening night of Liverpool's Cavern Club in 1957, and four of the band's original members were still performing together in 2005. Lita Roza, who was part Malayan by birth, was a vocalist with various local swing bands, and in 1953 she became the first Liverpool musician to top the British charts, with the American novelty song '(How Much is) that Doggy in the Window'.

Liverpool's American connections were highly valued by many of the musicians we spoke to. The city's trading connections with North America continued after the Slavery Abolition Act passed by the British Parliament in 1833; and in 1840 the Cunard Steamship Company sent out the world's first ocean-going passenger liners from Liverpool, establishing a direct shipping link with North America. That shipping route helped bring to Liverpool American popular music sounds and styles that were not readily available in other parts of Britain – such as early country music and early rhythm and blues – and Chapter 2 discusses the role and significance of local sailors within that process. In addition, many notable American performers visited Liverpool at the start of their tours of other British cities. Visiting Afro-American performers included, for example, the Virginia Minstrels – who pioneered the minstrel show, as opposed to the minstrel act – and who opened their 1843 British tour in Liverpool on 21 May; Pell's Ethiopian Serenaders, accompanied by William Henry Lane (nicknamed Master Juba), who pioneered the 'Tennessee Double-shuffle' and performed in Liverpool in 1848;[42] Hague's Georgia Minstrels (1866);[43] the Fisk Jubilee Singers, a group of predominantly ex-slaves, who visited Liverpool several times during the 1870s to perform Negro spirituals (Fryer 1984); the singer Paul Robeson (1922 and later dates) and the jazz musician Duke Ellington (1933). Charlie Jenkins told us that he remembered Paul Robeson and also the guitarist Django Rheinhardt visiting the house of his father, who had extensive contacts with local music and theatrical businesses. Ray Costello told us about a photograph taken in Liverpool of his great aunt as a small girl sitting on Paul Robeson's knee. The

42   http://www.geocities.com/soulpooluk/index.html, accessed October 2004.
43   A portrait of Sam Hague features in the *Liverpool Town Crier Album* of 1875.

visits of these musicians were mentioned by some of the other black Liverpudlians we spoke to, and seemed to have been particularly inspirational and to have remained vivid within collective memory. The fact that Robeson was the son of a slave, whilst Rheinhardt was a Gypsy, seems hardly coincidental.

Also inspirational were the visits of black American servicemen to Liverpool clubs and dance halls during the 1940s, 1950s and 1960s. The servicemen were based at the American Burtonwood military airbase located a few miles east of Liverpool, which opened in 1943 and operated for 50 years. During the 1950s it was the largest base of its kind in Europe, and black and white American servicemen stationed there regularly visited Liverpool, where they mixed with local musicians and exchanged musical recordings and influences. Eddie and Chris Amoo, like other local black musicians of their generation, told us how inspired they had been by the music, dance, fashion and record collections of the black servicemen, and by their confidence and swagger. They also referred to regular exchanges of records between those servicemen and local black musicians. Sugar Deen told us:

> the American GIs always had lots of records. We couldn't buy the records off them, but we used to nick 'em anyway. The GIs used to bring guitars and stuff and start playing at parties. Many times we'd say, 'What's this guy doing in the army?' Excellent voices and singers. It was like a privilege to sit in with them and sing a few harmonies here and there.

In addition, local musicians performed at the Burtonwood base or went there to hear visiting American musicians – including international stars such as Bob Hope, Nat King Cole and Glen Miller – perform jazz, country, rhythm 'n' blues, soul and rock'n'roll. Thus, as Frith (1987:63) points out, 'The United States' influence on international popular music, beginning with the worldwide showing of Hollywood talkies, was accelerated by the US entry into World War II – members of the service became the record industry's most effective exporters.'

Eddie, Chris, Sugar and their friends and associates formed male vocal harmony groups, such as the Earls, the Valentinos, the Casuals, the In Crowd and the Chants. Those groups adapted the a capella, doo-wop singing styles of Black American groups such as the Ink Spots and Frankie Lymon and the Teenagers. Sugar told us how he and his friends had acquired new record releases from Curtis Mayfield, the Marcels, the Contours, the Drifters and the Impressions by ordering them as imports from a catalogue at Liverpool's NEMs record store. One local music promoter claimed rather conjecturally,

> Liverpool is the most American of English cities. It's got the most intensely aware soul music Black community in the country … they're getting American records in so fast they're probably getting them before they're properly released in the States. They've always been that aware … It's like a sinew that goes across the Atlantic (quoted in 'Liverpool's Second Coming', *Melody Maker*, 24 July 1976).

Local female vocal harmony groups and white male 'crooners' also modelled themselves on their American counterparts, copying their sounds and styles; and the Vernons Girls and the Liver Birds achieved some degree of commercial success.[44] Skiffle and American country music were also popular. Skiffle was an improvised and relatively easy to play version of early country, blues and folk that was also influenced by traditional jazz (Chambers, 1985: 47), and it was popularized in Liverpool by Britain's Lonnie Donegan and America's Johnny Duncan. It was based around acoustic guitar and bass but also featured less traditional instruments such as the tea chest and washboard. Tony Davis thus described it to us as 'the punk movement of its day'. Ringo Starr was a member of the Eddie Clayton skiffle group prior to joining the Beatles, whilst the Beatles had originally been a skiffle band called the Silver Beatles.

During the late 1950s, as Chambers puts it (ibid: 38), 'The exposure of rock'n'roll in Britain, on records, in films like Blackboard Jungle, Rock Around the Clock, and later live tours, conjured up for British audiences not the peculiarities of specific cultural realities but quite simply, to employ a Barthian neologism, "Americanicity".' Liverpool's Billy Fury, who had a series of chart hits between 1959 and 1963, is proclaimed by Du Noyer to be Britain's first rock'n'roll star (2002: 10–11); but the early 1960s also saw the emergence of local rock'n'roll or 'beat' groups, including the Beatles who went on to become the most famous band in the world. Hundreds of those groups formed in the city,[45] and they had their own weekly music paper – Mersey Beat – which was at that time unusual. The groups performed across the Merseyside region in local ballrooms, social clubs and town halls,[46] but the venues that came to be most closely associated with the Merseybeat scene, and thus the most symbolically significant, were the city's numerous coffee bars, jazz bars and cellar clubs – particularly The Cavern Club (see Chapter 7).

John Lennon tuned into stations such as Radio Luxembourg to hear early American rock'n'roll as well as American r'n'b and gospel-influenced groups such as the Drifters, the Dominoes and the Coasters. Paul McCartney explains how the Beatles combined those influences with local and family influences, including British vaudeville, music hall and Irish song (McCartney, 2002; Everett, 2001). Similarly, Yoko Ono writes on the sleeve notes of John Lennon's album Menlove Avenue: 'John's American rock roots, Elvis, Fats Domino and Phil Spector are evident in these tracks. But what I hear in John's voice are the other roots, of the boys who grew up in Liverpool, listening to Greensleeves, BBC radio and Tessie O'Shea.' The Liverpool

---

44   http://www.triumphpc.com/mersey-beat/a-z/lesgirls.shtml, accessed October 2004; Du Noyer (2002: 74).

45   Some 500 according to one estimate – www.triumphpc.com/mersey-beat/birth/index.shtml, accessed November 2004. However, Du Noyer (2002: 62) acknowledges, 'Nobody really knows how many beat groups there were in Liverpool', but adds, 'the total would run into several hundred'.

46   Bill Harry, editor of Mersey Beat, cited in Du Noyer (2002: 32), estimates the number of venues for Merseybeat groups at well over 300, although no evidence is provided to support that claim.

groups thus developed new, hybrid and local styles of rock/pop music. At the same time musicians in other small countries, who had also begun by copying American rock'n'roll, likewise began to combine it with local influences to develop their own distinctive sound (Wallis and Malm, 1984). Later still the Beatles incorporated additional influences into their music, particularly psychedelic and Indian influences – hence their interest in the music of Ravi Shankar – and, according to Du Noyer (2002: 33–4), they believed that it was their art school connections that distinguished them from other Merseybeat groups such as Gerry and the Pacemakers, the Fourmost and the Searchers. (Liverpool's art school also influenced the city's popular poets such as Roger McGough and Adrien Henri, and 1970s bands such as Deaf School and the Scaffold.)

The so-called Mersey or 'Liverpool Sound' that came to be associated with the Beatles and other local beat groups was guitar-based and characterized by a strong emphasis on melody and vocal harmonies. That sound, and its connection to Liverpool, has been much celebrated and mythologized. Taylor (1998: viii), for example, describes it as:

> the sights and sounds at the birth of a legend that would sweep first Liverpool, then the United Kingdom, then the world. It is a legend that lives on in the image of four fresh faces singing unforgettable chords and lyrics that are still known today the world over – a sound forever evoking, for all history perhaps, a particular time and a particular place in their lives and ours.

For 51 of the 60 weeks between April 1963 and May 1964 there was a Merseybeat record at Number 1 in the UK charts (Du Noyer, 2002: 61). One of our interviewees, describing the Liverpool of her childhood, told us:

> It was thriving, buzzing and everyone was in a band – there were so many bands across Merseyside. The 60s was a very exciting time here. It just happened that everything came together. And the Prime Minister was from here, and it seemed like the centre of the universe. I was only a child then but you absorbed it and thought it was your inherited right. One of my earliest memories was 'She Loves You' being No. 1. for six weeks and all the kids would talk about it and it was a great source of pride.

Since that time Liverpool and Merseyside have continued to produce commercially successful rock and pop acts, including The Real Thing mentioned above; The Christians, another black vocal soul group who hit the British charts in the 1990s; white electro-pop bands such as China Crisis, Dead or Alive, Frankie Goes to Hollywood and the Lightning Seeds; the female vocal pop act Atomic Kitten; and guitar-based indie rock bands, from Echo and the Bunnymen (1980s), to Cast (1990s) and The Coral and the Zutons (2000s).[47] The 16th edition of *British Hit Singles* (2003, Guinness World Records) awarded Liverpool the title 'World Capital of Pop' because the city had produced more Number 1 singles than any other city in

---

47 See Du Noyer (2002) for a celebration of these and other commercially successful Liverpool acts.

the world. Yet these chart-topping acts are just a few examples of the many diverse musical acts and scenes that the city has produced, over the past few decades. More recent and highly productive popular music scenes include alternative scenes based around techno, electronica and new styles of punk.

As later chapters will illustrate, the unprecedented success of the Beatles has continued to have a profound impact on Liverpool life and on the city's image and reputation. Yet Liverpool's musical past has influenced the present in many other ways. Liverpool continues, for example, to have a diverse culture of street music, which may be partly due to relaxed local licensing policies. During the period of time that I have lived in the city the musicians involved have included various familiar characters, such as the elderly and homeless man sporting a fake, elasticated white beard, who played a cardboard guitar and was nicknamed Mr Plink-Plink; local unemployed youths; students from the Liverpool Institute for Performing Arts and recent asylum seekers from Eastern Europe. The city also hosts Brouhaha – an annual festival of street entertainment – in addition to a variety of other music festivals, from Chinese New Year celebrations to the world music festival known as Africa Oye. Liverpool's strong traditions in dance and club culture have also been longstanding, from the early dance halls to the discotheques and cabaret clubs of the 1970s and rave culture of the 1990s. Likewise, classical and sacred music continue to flourish, and today's local choirs include those supported by the city's impressive Anglican and Catholic cathedrals that stand at either end of Hope Street.[48] Meanwhile, the wealth and grandeur of Liverpool's past are evident in its ornate Victorian and Georgian residences; its grand mid-nineteenth-century galleries, museums and libraries; its late-nineteenth-century banks and shipping and insurance houses that characterize the striking waterfront; its impressive maritime warehouses that dominate the docklands; and in the magnificent suburban parks ringed by the large, sprawling mansions built by the city's elite. At the same time the brutal reality of Liverpool's history and wealth is also evident in the streets named after prominent slave traders, and the heads of African slaves and animals carved onto the Town Hall.

Music and the Production of the City

The families we met during our research introduced me to aspects of Liverpool life that I had previously ignored or been unfamiliar with, and they taught me to look at and listen to the city in new ways. It was through them that I began to appreciate the richness, complexity and diversity of the city's musical history and contemporary music cultures. They therefore informed my interest in the relationship between music and the city, and I will now move on to discuss and illustrate that relationship.

---

48   Building work started on the former at the start of the twentieth century but was not completed until the 1970s, whilst the latter was built in the 1960s.

Music Reflecting and Producing the City

To begin with, our study of music and kinship illustrated how Liverpool's musical sounds, cultures and infrastructures were influenced, though not determined, by the city's historical geography and economy. Liverpool's musical life was certainly influenced by the city's position within and access to global networks and routes. This included networks connected to the city's port and trading activities and transportation infrastructures; the geographical routes and settlements of sailors, servicemen, touring musicians and migrants; and the Anglo-American music and media industries that rapidly expanded throughout the twentieth century and extended their geographical operations. Burnett (1996:1) describes popular music as 'certainly the most global aspect of our "global village"', explaining, 'whereas consumption of other media products is often limited by geographical availability and consumer income, almost anyone anywhere can listen to popular music, often regardless of whether they want to or not. Most of us at one time or another have felt pursued by music itself.' At the same time, however the musical life of Liverpool was also influenced by specific local circumstances and Liverpool's distinctive social, cultural and economic characteristics. Thus, as Lipsitz (1994: 180) points out, 'the global processes that shape us have very different inflections in different places'.

Due to its geographical position and its role as a port Liverpool was able to rise to prominence within the global economy and become a 'Gateway to Empire'. This contributed to the diversity and cosmopolitanism of the city's musical cultures. The port brought the city great wealth but it also depended upon a large and unskilled workforce, and it brought into the city destitute immigrants fleeing from hardship elsewhere. This produced striking divisions of wealth and poverty within the city and its musical life and shaped the relations of class, ethnicity, gender and religion that characterized local music practice. The immigrants brought with them classical, traditional, popular and religious musical sounds and styles, thus contributing to the richness and variety of local music, whilst internal patterns of migration and settlement left their mark on the urban musical landscape. The national context was also important, and subsequent chapters will illustrate how socio-economic, political and geographical characteristics of Britain also had a significant impact on Liverpool and its musical life.

In turn, however, our research on music and kinship illustrated how music has not just reflected Liverpool and its particular characteristics but has also shaped the city, influencing the way that the city is lived, thought about and reflected upon. It thus pointed to a reciprocal relationship between music and city. The city is not simply a place where music happens, or a container or inert setting for music activity. Instead, music can be conceived as contributing to the making or 'social production' of the city.[49] In the following chapters the city thus appears as both figure and ground – as a setting for, but also a product of, music practice; hence each chapter discusses

---

49   See Appadurai (1996) on the 'production of locality'.

popular music in Liverpool, but also Liverpool within popular music culture. I shall now go on to briefly describe two particular aspects of this musical production of Liverpool that will be discussed in these chapters.

Music as Liverpool Culture   Firstly, music contributed to the distinctiveness of Liverpool and Liverpool life. The global networks and local circumstances that influenced the musical life of Liverpool combined to produce musical cultures and sounds that were in some ways often peculiar to Liverpool, thus helping to distinguish Liverpool from other cities. They also influenced the way that Liverpool was represented and imagined through music. Most obviously for example, the Beatles contributed to the mythology of Liverpool as a 'music city' through the musical styles they created and their unprecedented commercial success. They deliberately set out to represent Liverpool through lyrics, sounds, videos and other visual materials, associating the city with particular images and ideas and influencing how people thought about it. Moreover, connections between the Beatles and Liverpool have been a focus for discussion within the extensive and diverse literature on the Beatles, and amongst Beatles fans, and a focus for debates about the distinctiveness of Liverpool culture.

The following chapters explore the making and mythology of music as Liverpool culture, by examining specific ways in which popular music (whether musicians or music businesses, musical scenes or sounds) was connected to Liverpool during the 1980s and 1990s.[50] Some of these connections were strategic and instrumental whilst others were less so or not at all. The chapters consider the individuals and groups that forged and contested such connections between music and the city, the activities, interests and circumstances involved, and the influence of local factors and circumstances on that process. At the same time, however, they situate that musical production of the city within a broader context by examining within it the influence of global musical cultures and economic trends, and by drawing attention to local/global relations. Whilst music has commonly been related to place and local identity, accelerations in the pace of globalization appear to have influenced such relations. Despite fears that globalization and increasing global connections would eradicate geographical places and the differences between them (see, for example, Meyrowitz, 1995), such developments have given people a new impetus to think about places in different ways. Over the last couple of decades many social theorists have noted that globalization appears to have renewed an emphasis on the local, encouraging new quests for local identity, the emergence of new expressions of local attachment, and thus a re-imagining of the local. At the same time several influential theorists have reconceptualized local cultures in terms of travelling as opposed to dwelling; routes, rootlessness and displacement as opposed to roots; and in terms of border dialogues and crossings (Clifford, 1992; Chambers, 1994; Gilroy, 1993; Lipsitz, 1994) and

---

50   I prefer to use the term 'connected' rather than a term like 'fixed', because the former seems less permanent and more fragile and I want to highlight fleeting, transient and plural connections between music and city.

global flows or 'scapes' (Appadurai, 1996). Similarly, Connell and Gibson (2003) describe the relationship between music and place in terms of mobility and 'fluidity' whilst emphasizing ways in which music is nevertheless attached or 'fixed' to place.

Music as Urban Culture   Secondly, the musical life of Liverpool contributed to Liverpool's 'cityness' (Massey, 1999) or 'urbanicity' (Martin, 2004),[51] although distinctions between cities and other places are not always easy to make and have in some ways become increasingly blurred. Finnegan (1989), writing about the English town of Milton Keynes, points out that music allows for the meaningful structuring of social activities and interactions in terms of time and space, and its contribution to urban life is extensive and often hidden. We were likewise struck by the number and diversity of people involved with amateur music-making in Liverpool, whether that involved barbershop choirs, Chinese classical orchestras or a cappella doo-wop groups. We were also taken aback by the extent of people's involvement with music, and by the fact that for so many of our interviewees music was a way of life. Through their involvement with music the people we met established regular routines within the city and well-trodden routes around it, thus contributing to the dynamism and general flux and flow of urban life. As part of our research we participated in and conversed about regular music lessons, rehearsals, performances, examinations and competitions. We also learned about the activities of our informants as music listeners, including their music tastes and everyday listening experiences and their regular attendance of music performances or clubs.

These musical routes or 'pathways' (Finnegan, 1989) influenced the way that people experienced the city and perceived its built and sonic environment.[52] In fact our study highlighted a broad range of different and sometimes conflicting perspectives on the city and its musical history and illustrated ways in which the city is haunted by musical echoes from the past. Eighty-seven-year-old Jack Levy, for example, navigated us through an imaginary tour of Liverpool city centre from his armchair in a sheltered home for elderly Jews, pointing out buildings that had once been the dance halls he frequented and worked in as a young man. His memories of and feelings about Liverpool had clearly been shaped by the dancing circuit of his youth, and by the emotions and sensations that he associated with dance culture and the music involved (Cohen, 1998). Music thus contributed to the intensity of experience within dance halls and other venues, and to the way that they continued to be symbolically significant, even if the venue had since been demolished.

Music also influenced social behaviour and interaction within the city. For some, particular music venues and events were a focus for tension and a symbol of social division, such as the ballrooms that operated a colour bar and were perceived as sites of whiteness and social exclusion, and the orange parades that once stirred up

---

51   http://www.urbanicity.us/, accessed April 2005.

52   Lynch (1960, 1972) and other cultural geographers have studied the influence of city routes on the production of mental images and maps of the city.

sectarian conflict. Yet at the same time music provided an occasion and focus for social gatherings and social interaction, sometimes leading to social mixing and an exchange of musical styles and influences. Music thus played a central role in the production of individual, collective and local identity within the city. It helped, for example, to create a sense of place and belonging for local immigrants and ethnic groups. Nevertheless, whilst music provides a resource for the creation of community and identity, it also organizes and regulates people's behaviour, and shapes their relationships, experiences and identities, often without their being aware of it. Some scholars, for example, have examined music's contribution to the soundscapes of public places within the city, highlighting the way that music controls people's behaviour within the city, including people's daily routines (Crafts, Cavicchi and Keil, 1993), how they shop (DeNora, 2000), what they buy and even how much they are prepared to spend (Hargreaves and North, 1997).

Popular Music and Urban Social and Economic Change

The above discussion on music's role and significance in the production of the city helps me to introduce the two interrelated aims of this book that were outlined in the introduction, and I end this chapter by briefly discussing each of them in turn.

Popular Music Culture and its Specific Contribution to the Production of the City

First, the book aims to consider the specificity (both actual and perceived) of popular music and its impact on city-making. Finnegan's study of grass-roots music-making in Milton Keynes suggests that music is commonly regarded as special and as different from everyday experience. Finnegan mentions the 'unspoken but shared assumption among the participants in local music that there was something which was not to be found in other activities of work or of play ... something about music which for the participants set it apart' (1989: 332). Her study 'reveals that music may play a far larger part in the experience and fulfilment of human beings and the patternings of society that is usually allowed by social scientists, musicologists or the conventional wisdom on the topic' (ibid: 341). These findings were confirmed by our own study of music and kinship in Liverpool. Roger Eagle, a Liverpool-based music promoter, told us, 'In their knowledge about music, and how they relate to music, it is very much a religious thing with people in Liverpool. Music is a life-saving thing, you know. It's absolutely essential.' Whilst statements like this contribute to the mythology of Liverpool as a musical city, it nevertheless became clear to us that those who participated in our study valued music highly and generally perceived it as special.

Some of the people we interviewed spoke of their love of music but described themselves as just ordinary listeners, whilst others were more passionate about music and described to us how it had contributed to or changed their lives. Many spent a significant proportion of their income on music lessons, music recordings, music or dance clubs and live music performance events, and they talked about music in overwhelmingly positive terms. Even when music had clearly been a source of tension and conflict people were anxious to emphasize to us how music had nevertheless helped to bring the family or wider community closer together: 'We weren't a particularly close family before barbershop but the music has pulled us together' (Helen Sherry quoted in Cohen and McManus, 1991: 7); 'it has always been through music that my family has expressed its togetherness' (Carl Brown, ibid: 51). In the stories we were told about the histories of particular families, music was often singled out as the one thing that had helped people get through difficult times, including not just personal or family crises but collective experiences of migration and hardship. The musical events that we participated in along with members of those families illustrated how music provided a context in which new social relationships could be forged and social divisions and symbolic boundaries bridged as well as created or reinforced. Many people explained to us how music had helped them to express or work through particular emotions, and had in various ways changed their feelings about or outlook on the world. For Jack Levy, listening to or even just thinking about music evoked people, events and emotions from the past, and enabled him to locate himself in different imaginary places and times (Cohen, 1998).

It was because they valued music so highly that some of our interviewees had turned to music as a source of additional income or as a career as well as a hobby. I first met Michael Swerdlow in 1993 at the premises of his family's kitchen equipment company located in Liverpool city centre. Much of the stock had been emptied and furniture and fittings were being packaged up. The company had recently gone into voluntary liquidation, resulting in the loss of fifty or so jobs. The business had been established by Michael's father in the mid-1940s after he had worked for some time as a chef on the Cunard Shipping Line, and it originally supplied the ocean-going liners. It was a departure from the family tailoring business that had been established in Liverpool by Michael's grandfather, and it became highly successful. Michael and his brothers became involved in the running of the business, and Michael's son Rob joined the business in the late 1980s. Following the closure of the business Michael began to explore possibilities for music-related work, having always been a big music fan. For his son Rob, leaving the business meant that he was able to get involved with the management of rock bands, a career that he had long aspired to.

Subsequent chapters will consider how perceptions of music as special, and as special to Liverpool in particular, contributed to debates and struggles over music as local culture. They will also consider what those debates and struggles suggested about the distinctiveness of music as urban culture. How, for example, does popular music's role and significance in the city differ from those of other arts and cultural industries? How does the specificity of popular music as a social, aesthetic and symbolic practice, or as a text, commodity and industry, contribute to the production of the city?

Urban De-industrialization and Renewal and their Influence on Popular Music Culture

The second main aim of the book is to examine the impact of urban de-industrialization and economic restructuring on the popular music culture of Liverpool and on the musical production of the city. Our study of music and kinship highlighted ways in which music contributed to Liverpool life, but in turn how music was influenced by its local, urban setting and by social and economic change. Liverpool's role as a port, for example, and its central position within the global economy, affected the musical infrastructure of the city and contributed to local music diversity. But what happened when the city's economic infrastructure collapsed? How was popular music culture in Liverpool affected by urban de-industrialization of the 1970s and 1980s, and by efforts to compensate for and overcome the city's economic problems through local economic restructuring? The following chapter begins this investigation by explaining the 'Liverpool sound' mentioned in the Introduction and described as a sound of grieving, loss and economic decline. This is a very different Liverpool story, therefore, from the one related in this chapter.

Chapter 2

Music as a City Sound:
Rock Culture and the Poetics of Loss

Amongst the crowds in a busy street flanked by shops and cafes I spot Gary Daly, lead singer with the rock/pop band China Crisis. I had recognized him from a distance by his distinctive lanky hair and long overcoat. He catches my eye and we exchange greetings. I ask him how things are going. He is quietly spoken but has a dry, razor-sharp wit, and he relates an amusing and typically self-deprecating anecdote about a recent musical event that he had participated in. I drop into the conversation the fact that the local broadcaster Roger Hill has described one of his band's songs, 'Christian', as 'the definitive Liverpool Sound'. He nods. He's heard about Roger's theory before. He shrugs:

> Over the years they just keep on comparing you to yet another Liverpool group, it was just all the time. I'm really surprised people even think we are a Liverpool group. Kirby's not even in Liverpool and it was like so isolated. Growing up in Kirby was like growing upon on the other side of the moon … You didn't even go into town. I don't think I even knew me way home from town … We never felt part of the Liverpool scene because we never gigged and we didn't know anybody. We've never even written about Liverpool. None of our songs are about Liverpool. We don't even sound anything like a Liverpool band.

Why would the music of a city be described in terms of a 'local sound' and what does that mean? What can the interpretation of one particular song by one particular listener suggest about the relationship between music and the city or, more specifically, the relationship between popular music and urban de-industrialization? This chapter focuses on the appropriation of music as a local sound in order to examine how music is interpreted as local culture and connected to tales and mythologies of the city, and the influence upon that process of music genre and local social and economic factors.[1] The first part of the chapter situates the notion of a local sound within the context of rock culture, describing and explaining some of the characteristics, conventions and myths of rock culture in Liverpool during the 1980s and early 1990s, including the 'rhetoric of the local' in rock. The chapter then goes on to examine the notion of a local sound. It highlights contrasting descriptions of and debates about the Liverpool Sound, but it focuses

---

1   The chapter is largely based on ethnographic research on rock culture in Liverpool conducted between 1985 and 1987 for my PhD thesis, and for subsequent research projects that ran between 1990 and 1998 (see Appendix).

in more detail on Roger Hill's description of the song 'Christian' by China Crisis as the definitive Liverpool Sound. Roger's description of that sound was unusual in the sense that it had been thoroughly considered and it was well informed. I have chosen to focus on it, however, because it nevertheless shared certain similarities with other descriptions of the Liverpool rock sound; because it was provocative but also evocative, raising interesting questions about music and the city; and because as a radio broadcaster Roger promoted his ideas to a wider public and they therefore had some influence on the perspectives and discourses of others. The chapter begins with a brief account of Liverpool's changing economic circumstances that will set the scene for the discussion that follows.

Rock Music in Liverpool

Liverpool in Crisis

The previous chapter described Liverpool's development as a hub city situated at the centre of world trade networks. In 1985 however, when I arrived in Liverpool to conduct research for a PhD thesis on the city's rock culture, I found myself in a city that was in deep and worsening crisis; a city that had become known in Britain as much for urban decline and political dissent as for the Beatles and football; a city that had experienced little inward migration since the 1950s and in that sense appeared on the surface to be more monocultural than multicultural. Throughout the twentieth century Liverpool experienced a series of economic slumps and depressions due to broad shifts in world trade and the changing fortunes of its port. This was largely due to the gradual reorientation of British trade from the Atlantic towards continental Europe following the worldwide depression of the 1930s. Britain's industrial centre thus began to shift to the Midlands, and other ports that were more suitably located and more easily accessible became increasingly significant. This contributed to a reduction in the building and repair of ships within Liverpool and Merseyside, which had provided the basis of export and imperialist expansion. The Lancashire textile manufacture, connected to the cotton industry that Liverpool had depended upon, also contracted. Consequently, unemployment rose in Liverpool to become double the national average (Lane, 1987: 36; Belchem, 2000: 50; Gentleman, 1970: 50–51; Jones, 1934).

Following World War II Liverpool's economy improved slightly due to the re-emergence of world trade and port activity and an increase in reconstruction work aimed at repairing extensive bomb damage and at slum clearance. However, although the city had an entrepreneurial small-business sector, unlike the south-east of England and the nearby city of Manchester it lacked mid-sized companies of 500–1000 employees, and there was little expansion of manufacturing and factory work (Nightingale, 1980: 35).[2] Moreover, the mid-1950s saw the introduction of

---

2   Nevertheless there was some development of car manufacture and engineering within the region.

containerization, which replaced the cargo liners and led to a further reduction in the dockside labour force. During the 1960s large multinational corporations arrived on the scene, attracted by the availability of cheap labour. They took over ownership of merchant, industrial and food-processing business and introduced new technologies and production methods, beginning a process of rationalization and restructuring that further hastened the closure of smaller city-centre firms that were less able to compete (Nightingale, 1980: 38; Meegan, 2003: 57).[3] Liverpool's problems deepened during the 1970s and 1980s due to the crisis in the global capitalist economy provoked by the collapse of the so-called 'Fordist' regime of accumulation, involving large-scale assembly-line production of relatively standardized commodities for mass markets.[4] Consequently, Liverpool entered a phase of economic decline more severe than that experienced by any other British city, losing jobs and people 'on a scale and at rates that are exceptional even among the industrial cities of the north' (Meegan, ibid.: 75).[5] De-industrialization and rising unemployment were accompanied by widespread urban dereliction, and by disinvestment and depopulation. Liverpool thus became disconnected from the networks that had maintained its prominent position within the global economy, and the city found itself at the core of one of the most disadvantaged city-regions in Europe.[6]

Throughout the 1980s and 1990s Liverpool was demonized by the British media, which continually used the city as a symbol not just of 'decay on a frightening scale' (*The Guardian*, 6 September 1994) but as, 'a "showcase" of everything that has gone wrong in Britain's major cities' (*Daily Mirror*, 11 October 1982), representing it through shockingly narrow and ugly stereotypes.[7] Such newspaper reporting has

---

3   Between the mid-1950s and mid-1970s about a quarter of all the jobs in the region's manufacturing sector (amounting to 18,000) disappeared (Nightingale, 1980: 42).

4   See Harvey (1990) on the causes and effects of that crisis.

5   This de-industrialization involved the departure of many famous names from Merseyside, such as Tate and Lyle, Triumph, United Biscuits, British American Tobacco and Meccano.

6   During the 1970s unemployment reached three times the national average (Nightingale, 1980: 42). By 1985 53 per cent of local unemployed people had been out of work for more than a year, compared with 39 per cent nationally (Parkinson, 1985: 13). In 1991, 40 per cent of Liverpool's population lived in poverty and 15 per cent of the population (16 per cent of households) lived in intense poverty. Both figures were approximately twice the equivalent national levels (The Liverpool Quality of Life Survey published by Chief Executive's Department, Liverpool City Council, June 1991).

7   As illustrated by articles such as 'No Money, No Jobs, No Future, No Point' by Anthony Bevins: 'Welcome to Utopia in Liverpool. Once people queued to live here. Now they must exist in a decaying haunt of drug addicts and criminals' (*The Observer*, 3 October 1993). Belchem (2000: 54–5) lists other sensationalized newspaper headlines about Liverpool printed in Britain's national newspapers, including a description of Liverpool as 'Britain's Beirut', and the *Daily Mirror*'s advice to Liverpudlians to 'build a fence around [Liverpool] and charge admission. For, sadly, it has become a showcase of everything that has gone wrong in Britain's big cities.'

been described as racist by one Liverpool-born journalist.[8] British television also promoted unhelpful stereotypes of the city through fictional drama series and soap operas featuring caricatures of working-class Liverpool culture. Such negative media representations of the city were fuelled by a series of dramatic events. The Toxteth riots of 1981 had taken place before I arrived in the city, but during my initial period of fieldwork tensions escalated between Liverpool City Council and the central Conservative government led by Margaret Thatcher. The Militants, a Trotskyist section of the Labour Party, had taken over Liverpool City Council in 1983, and Liverpool became the focus of government efforts to control regional insurgency and dismantle and disempower local and regional authorities. Consequently, the leaders of the city council entered into a direct confrontation with the government and threatened to make the city bankrupt unless they received more funding, which resulted in their expulsion from office in 1986.

Lane (1987: 161) refers to those events as a 'tragedy' and their timing as a 'disaster', whilst Belchem (2000: 57) argues that such 'toy town political extremism' contributed to the association of Liverpool with white, working class belligerency. This association was further encouraged by Liverpool's reliance on the docks and shipbuilding, industries known for their strong union involvement; and media images of a volatile and disruptive local workforce served to further discourage outside investment. The city's media image worsened following the death of 36 Italians during a 1985 football match at Belgium's Heysel Stadium, when a wall collapsed due to disturbances between Italian and Liverpool supporters; and also the death of 95 Liverpool football fans in 1989 as a result of crowd pressure during a match at Sheffield's Hillsborough stadium. Both tragedies were constructed as local to Liverpool rather than to one particular team or to a wider region, and the reporting on Liverpool football fans by one tabloid newspaper led to a boycott of that paper in Liverpool that has continued up to the present day. By the national census of 2001 Liverpool's population had almost halved compared to what it had been at the start of World War II and the numbers continued to fall.[9]

Rock as a 'Way Out'

Against this backdrop of economic and political crisis, negative and vindictive media reporting, I discovered in Liverpool a vibrant culture of rock music-making. From the day I first arrived in the city rock musicians began to emerge, as if from out of the woodwork, and before long I was overwhelmed by the number and variety of local bands and the extent and complexity of my chosen field of study. The musicians

---

8   Linda Grant: 'History Broke Liverpool and it Broke My Heart' (*The Guardian*, 5 June 2003).

9   Whilst the population peaked at 870,000 at the start of World War II, by 2001 it had dropped to 440,000 (Meegan, 2003: 54), although the official boundaries of the city had changed during that time and there had also been a relocation of many city residents to other parts of Merseyside.

involved listened to, and were influenced by, rock music from many different places, and they produced many different musical styles and sounds. There were bands that were described as 'alternative' or 'indie rock', and those described as more 'mainstream' or pop-influenced. There were also folk-influenced singer-songwriters and musicians who fused rock with soul and rhythm and blues, as well as those who produced music that was described as 'heavier' or more 'hard rock'. During the late 1980s and the 1990s they were joined by musicians who combined rock with 'contemporary dance music', an electronically generated style of dance music played by 'artist-DJs' in clubs that was sometimes referred to as 'acid house' or 'rave'.

Despite this variety it was possible to detect certain common trends within local rock music-making. Reggae-influenced rock, trip-hop and heavy metal were relatively absent, for example, and there was a notable taste for psychedelia and a prevalence of bands producing a lush, guitar-based and pop-influenced style of rock characterized by a strong emphasis on melody. Du Noyer (2002: 174) writes:

> The curious quality of other Liverpool pop in the 1980s was its willfully lightweight nature. It used to puzzle some observers, who thought a beaten-up old pug of a town like Liverpool should be inciting music full of rage. Instead it was fey, dreamy and pretty. It's striking that Liverpool has never produced a heavy metal band of any consequence. Nor was there much of a market for the hard-core punk, whether cockney boot boy or anarcho-vegetarian, that flourished elsewhere. The local taste was for a playful escapism.

The vast majority of the city's rock musicians were white, male and between 18 and 35 years of age, and they were drawn from both working and middle classes and from all parts of Merseyside and beyond. Many of the musicians I spoke to believed that there were more rock bands in Liverpool than in other English cities, and they attributed this to the city's economic problems and high unemployment levels. Becoming a rock musician, they suggested, was a conventional escape route for local working-class males. That theme of escape was also evident in the lyrics of some local bands.[10] Other studies, however, suggest that there existed a relatively similar proportion of bands within other British towns and cities around the same time (Finnegan, 1989), and the notion of rock as a 'way out' was a familiar cliché or myth that was by no means peculiar to Liverpool. It is evident, for example, in the emphasis on mobility, and on escape from 'humdrum suburban and industrial worlds into dream worlds', in classic American rock songs (such as 'California Dreamin' and 'We Gotta Get Out of this Place'), and in various road or highway songs (Connell and Gibson, 2003: 83).

Nevertheless, it was commonly suggested to me that the desire to join a band and 'get out' was more intense in Liverpool than elsewhere. Likewise, Lawson (1998) quotes Stratton (1983) commenting on Liverpool's beat scene of the 1960s: 'Liverpool was much worse off than Manchester, and even back then they had a

---

10   See, for example, some of the lyrics of the band Cast that try 'to find a way out, out, out' ('Magic Hour'); and wonder 'Will I ever get out of here?' ('Four Walls'), and sing of 'Breaking out' ('Dance of the Stars') and 'Leaving it all behind' ('She Falls').

large pool of unemployed youngsters. For many of them rock'n'roll was the only way out.' Roger Hill, a Liverpool-based rock critic and radio broadcaster, suggested to me that the number of local rock bands had mushroomed in parallel with the rise in local unemployment, and he referred to music that was born out of 'domestic distemper – the frustration of sitting around all day doing nothing but watch TV' (p.c.).[11] A local rock promoter described rock music as being along with sport the 'fastest way out', whilst a musician commented, 'In such a run down area people look around, see how depressed it is and decide they have to get out … It's the only way for young kids. Everyone you meet is in a rock band these days' (quoted in Chappell, 1983: 6). A record label owner told me, 'pop is a way of "getting out of the jungle"', and he added that in Liverpool rock music had begun to follow a local pattern established by boxing and football: 'it's an economic thing. Boxing and football have always been a way out.' Similarly, a local band manager said: 'I suppose learning to be in a band or Fords is the only way of getting out of poverty.' Referring to the Beatles he added, 'I think that there may be a bit more emphasis on music in Liverpool in making your way, because of the history of it … it is a more acceptable route than in other cities that have not had a history of conquering the planet' (p.c.).

For the musicians that I got to know, however, their involvement with rock music-making was significant primarily as a way of life within the city rather than as a desired or actual route out of the city. I was impressed by their dedication to their music-making – the enthusiasm, humour and creative energy with which they approached it, their tremendous confidence in their music – and by the depth of their musical knowledge and interest. Their music-making structured their daily and weekly routines, and it provided them with a particular means of communicating ideas and feelings and developing and performing a sense of self. It also offered them a context for the development of close friendships and social networks, whilst music performance presented them with a challenge and a sensual and emotional experience that could be pleasurable, exciting and rewarding. Nevertheless, those musicians were keen to get their music heard and to achieve critical acclaim, and I was struck by how many of them were driven by commercial ambitions and by a desire to 'make it'. This usually meant not just earning an income through their music-making, but getting their music across to a mass audience by making records that could be widely distributed and would thus attract widespread recognition. Some musicians released their own records, and some released records through small independent record labels; but most were keen to sign a contract with a major record company that would have the resources to properly promote them and their music. Those companies were based in London, so the musicians involved spent much time and effort trying to contact and visit London-based companies, and entice representatives

---

11   It has likewise been claimed that 'Unemployment brings out the guitar in everyone' (*Europe A Go Go*, Channel 4, 5 January 1985), and that in Liverpool 'large numbers of people seek to escape the boredom of the dole by forming bands and playing music' (*Next* 14: 6 September 1986).

of those companies to attend their performances or listen to recordings that they had produced and financed themselves. I have discussed those efforts in detail elsewhere (Cohen, 1991a), pointing out that whilst the musicians involved were commercially oriented, they nevertheless perceived commercial pressures and preoccupations to be a threat to their original and creative music-making. Frith (1981) refers to this as the familiar 'ideology of folk in rock'.

I have also described elsewhere (Cohen, 1991a) the journeys to London taken by particular Liverpool bands, journeys that have become a conventional part of rock mythology and are symbolized by the train trip to London taken by the Beatles in their film *A Hard Day's Night* (1964). For some (but by no means all) local rock bands moving to London was regarded as a development that would benefit their career, and it was generally considered to be a cliché for bands to do so as soon as they had signed their 'deal' with a London-based record company. Thus Roger Hill once related to me an anecdote about a local rock manager standing on the London-bound platform at Liverpool's Lime Street station in the 1960s and begging the departing musicians not to take their equipment with them. Yet that cliché involved not just musicians but also producers, promoters and others working in the business of music in Liverpool. Rock managers felt particularly pressurized to move to London in order to develop business networks with London-based record and publishing companies, and to keep an eye on the activities of the companies that their musicians were involved with (Cohen, 1991a: 129). In 1995 the director of a Liverpool-based contemporary dance label (3Beat) told me:

> there's still a tendency for people from Liverpool, definitely, if they make anything of themselves, to get out of Liverpool, because, you know, no one would blame them to forward their career if there's more opportunities or whatever, to get off. And there's numerous examples of, you know, people from Liverpool having a hit right back to the 60s and then getting off to where the money is, or to where the centre of everything is, which is obviously the capital.

Yet only a small percentage of local musicians ever managed to get 'signed up', and only a few of those musicians went on to achieve the success that they desired. According to one local manager, 'maybe one in a hundred will have a UK hit and maybe one in fifty of those will have success somewhere else and very few of those will sustain it long enough to make a living out if it … it is a very risky business' (p.c.). Du Noyer (2002: 87–8) writes of the Liverpool bands that did not achieve the success they so desired:

> Here's where so many thwarted pop musicians returned back North, careers gone south, their dreams all cracked and battered ... Those compartment trains have gone now. But how many musicians must have sat in them and fantasized about the kind of Beatlehood awaiting them in the smoke, just the other side of signing some papers in Manchester Square and Denmark Street. How many must have sat in those same compartments, gloomily chugging home, wondering why the plans had gone awry … You would spot them, has-beens at 24, standing at bus-stops or telling their war stories in pubs.

China Crisis

The story of China Crisis, as told by the band members themselves, helps to illustrate these conventional rock journeys and clichés or myths, and connect them to the notion of a local rock sound. The two founding and core members of China Crisis – Gary Daly (lead vocalist) and Eddie Lundon (guitarist) – were from Kirkby, a predominantly working-class and relatively deprived district that lay just north of Liverpool and on the outskirts of Merseyside. It was characterized by municipally owned concrete high-rises built to house residents who had been moved out of the city as part of post-war redevelopment.[12] Gary and Eddie met at school when they were 14 years old and became friends through their shared interest in music. They began to make music together as a duo, acquiring guitars through a mail-order catalogue and practising at home in their bedrooms, bringing in like-minded friends whenever it suited them. They attempted to perform covers of well-known rock/pop songs in public, but eventually began to compose and rehearse their own songs in the privacy of their own homes. Roger Hill thus described them to me as a typical 'bedroom band'. This is a familiar label within rock culture that tends to be interpreted in different ways, but usually refers to bands that produce home-made music themselves using domestic recording equipment, as opposed to bands that place more emphasis on live performance and depend upon others to record and produce their music for them.

In 1978 Gary and Eddie left school with no qualifications and signed up for unemployment benefit, agreeing, as Gary put it, that for them 'music was going to be "*it*"' (p.c.). Gary also said that they were able to concentrate solely on their music largely because they were both still living at home with their families and had elder brothers who were working and could therefore contribute financially to the household. They eventually acquired a synthesizer and portastudio and formed a band with some other musicians. The first recording of the song 'Christian' took place at Eddie's house and featured a sound that was produced using the pipe from his mother's vacuum cleaner. They sent a tape of their music to the owner of a local recording studio, who liked what he heard, invited them to record in his studio and released their first two singles on his own independent record label.[13] Those recordings helped China Crisis to sign a recording contract with Virgin Records in London, and they subsequently released several albums and spin-off singles. In 1983 'Christian' reached Number 12 in the UK pop charts, and in 1984 their single 'Wishful Thinking' entered the charts all over Europe and became their biggest hit, reaching Number 9 in the UK. Soon after they made the charts with the singles 'African and White', 'Black Man Ray' and 'King in a Catholic Style'.

By 1985, when I first met China Crisis, they were managed by a company that also looked after the Scottish band Simple Minds. I travelled with them when they

---

12   See Meegan (1988) on the area's social and economic problems but also the resilience of its residents.

13   'African and White' (1981) and 'Scream Down at Me' (1982).

performed at a couple of venues outside Liverpool and also attended their rare performances in Liverpool (Cohen, 1991a: 130–31). A few years later, after I had returned to Liverpool to take up employment at Liverpool University, I invited Gary Daly and fellow band member Gary Johnson to visit the university to discuss their experiences of the music business with a small group of music students.[14] During the session they emphasized how young they were, and how naive they had been about the business aspects of music, when they signed their first record deal with Virgin in 1981. Most of them were 18 years of age at the time but the drummer was younger, which meant that his father was obliged to sign the contract on his behalf. Gary described the band's first visit to their new record company and how excited they were to think that along Virgin's corridors they might actually bump into some of their favourite bands who were also signed to the label, and how thrilled he and Eddie were when they left with their arms full of gift-box sets of Virgin records. Little did they know, he added, that while they were happily clutching their records in the queue at Euston railway station for the return journey to Liverpool, their manger was standing in the Manchester-bound queue with his leaving present – a cheque for around £20,000. In 1989 the band's record contract with Virgin was terminated, and Gary and Eddie went back to writing and recording as a duo in Liverpool.[15] At the end of the session with the students Gary referred to local bands like his own that 'have made it, come back and lived to tell the tale'. This was thus a classic rock tale portraying young and naive working-class lads from the provinces who dreamed of commercial success, took a train down to the Big City in search of fame and fortune, visited a major and seemingly exploitative record company and achieved short-lived notoriety before returning back home.

Liverpool in Rock Music

Later in this chapter I will relate the classic rock tale outlined above to Roger Hill's description of the China Crisis song 'Christian' as the 'definitive Liverpool Sound'. First, however, I want to relate notions of the local, and of a local rock sound, to rock culture and to the Liverpool of the 1980s and early 1990s. I will discuss how Liverpool was represented through rock music and through speech about that music and I will introduce the Liverpool Sound as a social and commercial construct. The discussion will thus consider the contribution of rock culture to the making or social production of Liverpool.

---

14   The talk took place in a university seminar room in January 1991.

15   They released records on small independent labels but also got involved in other activities (Eddie, for example, became an advisor on the British Government's New Deal for Musicians scheme). In 2002 they performed again as China Crisis for a concert tour based on a 1980s theme.

Musical Sounds Representing the Local and Urban Discontent

Music-making is commonly believed to be influenced by its social, material and aesthetic environment:

> if I was sat on a beach in the Bahamas, I'd be writing things a little bit differently. When you live in the inner city, the general landscape definitely has some sort of subconscious effect on you. I like to push a feel good vibe in my music but I also like to contradict that with harsh reality in order to reflect what's going on around me. 'Revenge' was the first track I wrote while living in Whitworth Street. Every night I'd hear the sound of sirens bouncing between the tall buildings (the Manchester DJ and musician Wiawan, quoted in Haslam, 2000: 259).

> You can't live somewhere without being affected. If you leave your door and see cows, horses and green fields you'll make different music. We do live on council estates, there are flats around us and dogs and decay – that's our reality. When I look out of my window I see bars. Why should I make music that doesn't reflect that experience? (Roni Size on living in Bristol, quoted in Connell and Gibson, 2003: 101).

In the quotation at the start of this chapter, Gary Daly responded to the description of 'Christian' as 'the definitive Liverpool Sound' by pointing out that he and his fellow band members had never consciously tried to represent Liverpool or Merseyside in any of their songs. He nevertheless acknowledged that aspects of the local culture and environment might have influenced the music of China Crisis.[16] Rock music is also commonly interpreted in terms of the local and the urban – either because or in spite of the intentions of the musicians involved – and the urban environment is commonly represented through music. Rock musicians, for example, have often deliberately represented through their music the city and city living in general, but also individual cities and specific urban locations. Meanwhile audiences have commonly associated rock-music sounds and styles with images of and ideas about the city.[17] Furthermore, whilst many musical sounds and styles have been connected with cities – including those bound up with classical and traditional music – it has been conventional for popular music, particularly rock, punk, soul, r'n'b and rap, to promote images of urban discontent.

In the Liverpool of the mid-1980s to early 1990s, for example, the 'escapist', 'lightweight' style of music described above by Du Noyer was certainly in evidence;

---

16   See Cohen (1994) for further discussion on this.

17   Musical sounds and styles have commonly been connected to individual cities, hence the naming of styles such as the Vienna waltz, New Orleans jazz and Chicago or Memphis blues. Kurosawa (quoted in Connell and Gibson, 2003: 280) points to the way that cities have also been associated with specific musical sounds: 'In New Orleans it's the wail of a sly trombone from behind a shuttered window in the French Quarter. In many Asian countries it's the yowl of karaoke from basement dives. In Paris there's always a suggestion of Piaf singing in the shadows. In Vienna, it's Strauss – the whole city moves to the tempo of a waltz – while in Salzburg it's Mozart (unless you're on a Sound of Music bus tour, in which case it's Julie Andrews).'

but there were also songs about that city and its particular social and economic problems. Those songs included the passionate anthems of the rock band Wah!, such as 'Come Back' and 'Story of the Blues'. They also included 'Forgotten Town' by the soul group The Christians, which achieved chart success in Britain and has been described as capturing 'the urgent claustrophobia of urban Liverpool in a bleak time' (Du Noyer, 2002: 174). Earlier on The Real Thing, Britain's biggest selling black rock/soul act of the 1970s, produced an album entitled *Four From Eight*, which was a reference to inner-city postal district Liverpool 8 in which they lived and where most of the city's black population was based. Songs on the album drew upon representations of the urban ghetto promoted by North American soul artists such as Curtis Mayfield and Marvin Gaye, but adapted them to suit circumstances within Liverpool 8 at that time (according to one report unemployment levels were four times higher in inner Liverpool than in the city as a whole, and they were higher in Liverpool 8 than anywhere else).[18] Similarly, the lyrics of Liverpool and Merseyside bands of the 1990s, such as the Las, the Stairs and Shack, represented a lifestyle surrounding unemployment and a related drug culture (Cohen and Strachan, 2005), and local journalists celebrated such bands and their music as the 'drug and dole culture' of Liverpool council estates (Cohen, 1994; and Du Noyer, 2002: 181–6).

Themes of urban discontent are by no means peculiar to rock music in Liverpool. During the early 1980s, for example, the music of Manchester's post-punk scene – which has been closely associated with the Factory record label – was perceived as reflecting that city's bleak and decaying landscapes:

> The music and lyrics of groups such as Joy Division, the 'sparse' production techniques of the scene's most prominent producer Martin Hammett, and the visual style of its resident graphic designer Peter Saville, have all been seen by music-makers and critics to work as metaphors for the 'emptiness' of the post-industrial landscape (Cohen and Strachan, 2005).

Saville has been quoted as describing the music of Joy Division as 'an underpass with iodine streetlights through Manchester at night', continuing that 'Manchester was the first industrial city, and even if you don't know that as a kid, you grow up with a certain sensibility' (O'Hagan, cited in Cohen and Strachan, ibid.). The music of a Certain Ratio, another post-punk band associated with Factory Records, is described on one website as combining 'a sparse Manchester bleakness' with American soul, funk and r'n'b, and as expressing 'the depressed, decaying Sound of an industrial city in decline'.[19]

Other popular music sounds – including the dark, stripped down sound of Detroit techno, and the lyrical and visual references to urban dereliction in the music of 1980s punk bands from the German cities of Halle and Leipzig – have likewise been perceived as reflecting decaying post-industrial landscapes (Cohen

---

18   The report was submitted to the Racial Disadvantage Inquiry by the Merseyside Area Profile Group (Kettle, 1981: 61).

19   http://www.souljazzrecords.co.uk/rhythm.htm, accessed July 2004.

and Strachan, ibid.). During the mid- to late 1970s, London-based punk musicians had responded to the national economic depression by rejecting their white, middle class, suburban origins for the credibility of the inner city, and by raging against the conformity, myopia and boredom of suburbia, promoting nihilistic representations of inner-city hardship and unemployment (Connell and Gibson, 2003: 77–9). Rap music, meanwhile, has become synonymous with images of urban discontent and the black urban ghetto or 'hood. Forman (2000, 2002) and Rose (1994) examine how rap has taken 'post-industrial' cities and their depressed inner-city neighbourhoods as its creative foundation. Forman discusses, for example, how the American West Coast city of Compton has been represented in the names lyrics, sounds and visual imagery of local rap acts, in their song and album titles, and in the discourses surrounding the activities and lifestyles of key performers: 'In the music the city is an audible presence, explicitly cited and digitally sampled in the reproduction of the aural textures of the urban environment' (Forman, 2000: 67). The music journalist and author Dan Sicko describes certain strains of Detroit hip-hop as 'an extreme, almost parodied' version of inner city life, which he links to the extremities of urban decline in that city: 'both the horrorcore of hip-hop outfits such as Insane Clown Posse, Esham and (to a lesser extent) the multi-platinum selling Eminem, utilize shocking (and blatantly over the top) narratives to give an over-exaggerated, almost cartoon-like version of urban deprivation in Detroit' (cited in Cohen and Strachan, 2005).

The Rhetoric of the Local in Rock

It was thus quite common for rock musicians in Liverpool to deliberately try to represent through their music aspects of the city in which they were based, and for the music of local bands to be interpreted by audiences and critics in relation to the city and specific urban locations and experiences. In addition to this, there was a common preoccupation within Liverpool rock culture with the distinctiveness of local rock music, and the relationship between rock sounds and the city was a topic of considerable debate. It was evident in the emphasis on local scenes and sounds, which again was not specific to Liverpool but was a feature of rock culture more generally. Hence Straw (1991: 370) critiques the 'musical localism' of alternative rock culture in North America, involving an emphasis on the authenticity and uniqueness of local music scenes; Street (1995: 255) refers to the 'rhetoric of the local' in rock; and Connell and Gibson refer to rock's 'mythology of the local' (2003: 112).[20]

That mythology was promoted by dominant music and media corporations. It has been common, for example, for Liverpool and other cities to receive visits and enquiries from record company representatives anxious to cash in on the success of

---

20   See also Cohen (2003); Johnson (1996) on the Bristol Sound; Mitchell (1996) on the Dunedin Sound; and Connell and Gibson (2003: 98), who summarize the key characteristics of well-known local sounds, such as the Bristol Sound and the Seattle Sound.

local rock/pop musicians. This can result in the signing of a number of musicians from that city who are similar in style, thus contributing to the creation, promotion and marketing of city scenes and sounds.[21] In Britain this trend began to emerge during the 1960s with the success of the Beatles. As Chambers puts it (1985: 52), 'Record companies were soon busily scouring Liverpool's clubs and dance halls, anxious to tap the seemingly inexhaustible gold mine of the "Mersey sound".' During the early 1990s the music press in Britain paid considerable attention to the so-called 'Madchester' scene and sound,[22] and a number of articles drew contrasts between the rock scenes of Manchester and Liverpool – underplaying their similarities or interconnections and dwelling on a long-standing rivalry between the two cities (Cohen, 1994: 124). Throughout the 1980s and 1990s local scenes and sounds were also promoted through the local media and local music publications. Roger Hill, for example, presented a weekly rock programme on BBC Radio Merseyside, through which he disseminated his views on Liverpool rock music and its distinctiveness to a specialist regional audience.

Rock critics and journalists have commonly connected musicians and the musical sounds they produce to particular geographical places:

Bristol's character, particularly its pace, does seem to have an influence on the music produced there ... 'Unlike many musicians in London we're never been rushed, we have time to make music' ... Bristol is friendly, slow-paced and relaxed (*Sunday Observer*, 24 February 1991).

Their sweet, sticky pop songs are suffused with the tang of something wild and strange ... capturing a sense of the South Island landscape – the slow turn of the seasons, and of what it is like to live in that landscape (David Eggleton on the music of a band associated with Dunedin's Flying Nun record label; quoted in Mitchell, 1996: 227).

Manchester is more spacious than London where you can't see more than 200 yards in front of you ... This freedom of movement is all important to the Manchester groups: you can hear it in the slowed down James Brown backbeat which ... has become the year's dominant rhythm (*Observer Magazine*, 7 July 1990, from an article about the Manchester band New Order).

Such reporting can sometimes involve the promotion of reductive and stereotypical representations of local sounds and the places they are associated with. In terms of England's music press, for example, the female singer Björk has been represented in terms of quirky and stereotypical images of her native Iceland (Leonard, 2001: 126–9). Liverpool rock musicians of the 1980s and 1990s often complained to me that they and their music were victims of negative stereotyping, and that they

---

21   However, as Connell and Gibson (2003: 99) point out, those scenes are not always terribly successful.

22   The term Madchester refers to a Manchester-based music scene of the late 1980s and early 1990s, involving bands that produced a combination of psychedelia, indie and guitar-based rock, and house music.

resented the way they and their music were continually compared with the Beatles and with music of the local past. Similar complaints were made during the early 2000s by members of the Coral, who were from Hoylake on Merseyside, following numerous reviews of the band's music that associated it with images of Liverpool seafaring or criminality (Hargreaves, 2005). Connell and Gibson (2003: 126) refer to the so-called 'Britpop' phenomenon of the 1990s, which was closely associated with different generations of British bands such as Blur and the Kinks, as a 'media-inspired creation that had little if any relationship to the musical diversity of the nation'. Music and media corporations have thus promoted not only the notion of distinctive local rock sounds, but also selective constructions of a local rock lineage. Rock journalists writing on Liverpool, for example, have constructed a local rock history that involves a conventional narrative. That narrative is based around a familiar and select group of commercially successful and internationally known bands; and around specific points in time when Liverpool rock music attracted attention from music and media industries, and a distinctive Liverpool scene and sound was perceived to have emerged. One such journalist related to me a familiar story about 'the two waves' of Liverpool rock music: the first associated with rock'n'roll or beat bands of the 1960s, including the Beatles, and with the Cavern Club; and the second with 'indie' bands of the early 1980s, most notably Echo and the Bunnymen, who met and performed at the alternative rock club known as Erics (Dave Sefton, p.c.). Similarly, Du Noyer's *Liverpool: Wondrous Place* (2002) selectively traces, as its subtitle proclaims, the development of Liverpool rock and pop music 'from Cavern to Cream'.

Locating rock music in this way can serve to associate it with roots as opposed to routes, and thus with local authenticity. Moreover, linking rock musicians and their products to authentic local settings has tended to suit a strategic promotion of local authenticity by music and media corporations that is designed to boost the sale of records whilst at the same time obscuring the commercial transaction involved. In this sense the rhetoric and celebration of the local in rock could be described, drawing upon the work of Spivak (1990), as a 'commercially constructed strategic essentialism of place' (Connell and Gibson, 2003: 112), or as 'a fetish which disguises the globally dispersed forces that actually drive the production process' (Appadurai, 1990: 307).[23] As Street (1995: 259) puts it:

> It is true that different cities, like different countries, make different noises. The question is whether these differences signify musically, whether they do more than reflect the circumstances in which the music was made, the clubs and the surviving traditions which became part of the sound. These supply interesting details, but do they become part of what the music means? After all, to see the music as expressing the experience of a place may be to confuse record business hype and journalistic extravagance with reality.

---

23   See also Stratton (1983) who discusses how that ideology of authenticity is promoted and exploited by the music industry. Likewise Connell and Gibson (2003: 87) refer to Allinson's argument that rap turned the city ghetto into a commodity, 'enabling the "marketing of "ghetto authenticity"'.

Street's comments are particularly pertinent to the notion of a local, city sound. In Liverpool there were common references to a specific 'Liverpool Sound', and to sounds connected to other geographical areas within the Merseyside region, although the notion of a local sound was also fiercely debated and contested (see Cohen, 1994). Those local sounds tended to be described in different ways so there was no general agreement on what their characteristics actually were. Nevertheless they were commonly defined through the drawing of contrasts between different geographical places. The Liverpool Sound, for example, was commonly identified and distinguished from that of other cities, particularly the nearby city of Manchester. Similar contrasts were drawn between the sounds of areas within the Merseyside region, particularly Liverpool and the Wirral, which was located across the river from Liverpool and was thus commonly referred to as 'the other side'. (Nevertheless, any rock band from Merseyside that achieved some degree of commercial success and notoriety tended to be categorized in the media as being 'from Liverpool'.) In addition, housing estates on the outskirts of the city centre were described as having a musical world of their own and a 'confident separatism' evident in their 'quirky, distinctive' sounds (*i-D* magazine, February 1991). Even certain streets were sometimes characterized through sound (Liverpool City Council's Arts Officer, for example, described Liverpool's Scotland Road for us in terms of its association with country and western music). More commonly, however, musical sounds were associated with distinctions between North and South Liverpool. A rock manager, for example, told us, 'a lot of the North End of Liverpool, like Huyton, Aintree, Fazakerley, Walton, Broad Green, all around there, pick up guitars, they're a lot more into smoking pot and being into Led Zeppelin, Jimmy Hendrix and Pink Floyd … and in South Liverpool they're a lot more folk music oriented.'

This preoccupation with a local rock sound fascinated me. Although the notion of a local sound was commonplace within rock and other musical cultures and was by no means peculiar to Liverpool, I began to wonder if there were particular local factors or circumstances that had encouraged this way of talking about music. I also began to notice certain features that were common to these narratives of place, and to wonder what such narratives might suggest about music's role and significance in the production of Liverpool.

The Definitive Liverpool Sound

These questions concerning the relationship between music and the city prompted me to invite the local broadcaster Roger Hill to discuss his views on the Liverpool Sound with a small group of music students at the University of Liverpool.[24] Roger presented a weekly rock show on BBC Radio Merseyside, and for a while he and I lived in the same street and I would frequently catch sight of him as he walked to or from Radio Merseyside, or the local youth and community drama groups that he

---

24   The session took place in October 1990 and lasted around forty minutes.

was closely involved with. We also met at various live music performances. During our meetings Roger would often share with me, as he did with his listeners and with local rock musicians, his thoughts on the distinctiveness of Liverpool music. He now presented those thoughts to the students, looking rather incongruous as he paced up and down in front of the whiteboard of the university seminar room dressed, as usual, in black leather and fake leopardskin, and with his characteristic fluorescent and brightly coloured Mohican. He did not speak from a script and he prefaced many of his comments with phrases such as, 'as I often tell people', 'as I always say'. Every now and then he dived into the large pile of recordings that he had brought with him to fish out a particular album. I will briefly summarize Roger's views on the Liverpool Sound below before examining them in more detail in order to consider music's specific role and significance in the construction of tales and mythologies of the city, and the influence upon that process of genre conventions (in this case those governing rock culture) and local social and economic factors.

The Train and the River

Roger explained to us that he was interested in what he referred to as 'the localness of local music', hence his interest in the Liverpool Sound. He described that sound in terms that were eloquent and lyrical but also rather conjectural and abstract, suggesting that there were two contradictory tendencies within Liverpool rock music: 'trainish music', which was about 'being away from home or wanting to be somewhere else', and 'riverine music', which expressed a reflection upon or yearning for home.[25] 'The train is the train that I often travel on', he said:

> Rarely do I travel from Liverpool to Euston without bumping into a rock band heading down to London to hand their tapes to various record studios, producers and record companies in the hope of actually being big in the world of rock music … that train in a sense represents the tendency to get on something with full speeds and rhythm and head on out to the place where things are happening.

Trainish music, Roger suggested, reflected a desire to make music that would be commercially successful, and he played us a series of musical extracts that he regarded as 'trainish' – selecting songs that were actually about trains, or that referred to trains in their title, in order to emphasize his point. He described the music as 'rockist' and 'beatish' because of its emphasis on 'propulsive drumming'. For Roger, trainish sounds expressed the dilemma of an economically isolated city that could not support its own music or 'propel' it to economic success. 'Trainish music is not', he continued, 'Liverpool's natural music … it's the music you go away to make and it's the music you retreat from making if you return.'

'Riverine' music, on the other hand, was for Roger the 'natural' music of Liverpool. He described the music as 'beat less', and said that its creation was not

---

25   Hill took these metaphors from the title of a song from the late 1950s, 'The Train and the River', by the jazz musician Jimmy Giuffre.

motivated by commercial ambition. Riverine music was about 'being here' and perhaps dreaming of being somewhere else, but also about being away yet wanting to return. The sound represented, he told us, 'Liverpool talking to itself', and he suggested that when the city talked to itself it 'grieves'. He related that grief to Liverpool's geographical proximity to Ireland and to the influence of the plaintive and poetic Irish music. To illustrate the riverine sound he delved once again into his record collection and played musical extracts from three songs by rock bands of the early 1980s: one by Pink Industry, which he described as having 'just enough instrumental accompaniment for the voice to ride over – like water, like waves'; one by the band Oceanic Explorers which had a harmony that 'rotates in a circle and comes back again' to the tonic; and a brief extract from the song 'Christian' by China Crisis which for him, he explained, was the definitive 'riverine' sound and thus the definitive Liverpool sound.

I liked the extract from 'Christian', which came from the very beginning of the song, and had heard it before; although for me personally the music of China Crisis had always sounded rather bland. (Their music has nevertheless been described by critics as 'some of the finest, fragrant pop music of a generation';[26] 'Synth Pop' with songs that are 'awash with gorgeous melodies which course through every groove';[27] 'a particularly light blend of synth, guitars and vocals';[28] 'dreamy, understated pop';[29] 'Uniting elements of synth pop, jazz, progressive rock, and new wave'.[30]) The extract started with a breathy but synthesized solo woodwind sound, which traced a melodic phrase that slowly rose in pitch and then descended. The melody was soon taken over by Gary Daly's solo voice, although the woodwind sound returned later for an instrumental break that took the place of a chorus. The vocal had a drifting, effortless quality, and the singing style was relaxed, monotone, rather emotionless and not terribly stylized. Each lyrical phrase began on a high note, slightly dropped in pitch and then rose again before descending to and finishing at the tonic. The lyrics were rather abstract[31] and were sung in English and with an English accent. There was no obvious drumbeat, just a light snare drum that kicked in halfway through the song with accents on the third and sixth beats. It was accompanied by light cymbals and by a dry, tapping bass drum that didn't sound at all big or beefy. At the same time a deep, fretless bass produced a melodic phrase consisting of deep, sustained and sliding notes, which provided an underbelly to the song that occasionally intersected with the melodic phrasing of the lead vocal. In the background, meanwhile, there was a gentle and continuous finger-picking guitar, and during the second instrumental

---

26   http://www.leonardslair.co.uk/china.htm, accessed October 2004.

27   http://www.frannyman.com/boardwalk/reviews.html, accessed October 2004.

28   http://www.awrc.com/review/c/diary_a_collection.html, accessed October 2004.

29   http://www.musica.co.uk/musica/screen_PRODUCT/shop_DYM/affiliate_DYM/category_PP596117.htm, accessed October 2004.

30   http://www.artistdirect.com/store/artist/album/0,,199256,00.html, accessed October 2004.

31   The lyrics appear on various websites, including http://www.lyricsdownload.com/china-crisis-christian-lyrics.html, accessed October 2004.

break sustained, synthesized and discordant keyboard chords emerged that sounded rather like a church organ.

I started to ponder upon Roger's description of this music. I wondered what it was about China Crisis and this particular song of theirs that made it represent, for Roger, the Liverpoolness of Liverpool music, and that made it appear to him to be so definitively 'riverine'. To begin with, the song's musical sounds and structures did not appear to be culturally coded in a way that would signify Liverpool to audiences familiar with British rock music. The distinctive Liverpool accent and vernacular style were not obvious in the lead vocal, for example, and the song did not include musical references to the well-known 'Liverpool Sound' of the 1960s described in the previous chapter and commonly used by the mass media to signify Liverpool. For Roger, 'Christian' was the definitive riverine sound because it lacked a beat, it was 'harmonically rotational' and had 'perfected drift', and its melodic cadences were like the structure of waves ('Even the word emotion sounds like ocean,' he added). He also likened the song's cadences to 'big sighs' due to their repeated rise and fall, which suited his association of the riverine sound with feelings 'of loss, of retreat and of regret', and with a 'yearning to return'. He suggested that 'the soul of Liverpool seemed to be caught in something of the riverine sound'.

Yet there is nothing inherently Liverpool or riverine about the song 'Christian' because musical sounds cannot inherently mean anything, and music is not some autonomous 'thing' from which listeners simply take meanings. Moreover, musical representation is abstract and thus particularly open to interpretation. The same piece of music can be connected to a series of quite different images and meanings. Musical codes, as Middleton (1990: 32) argues, 'leave open a space within which the operation of other elements in the music, its context and reception, can pull them into a more specific place in the network of social meaning'. Reviews of 'Christian' confirm that it does not appear to signify Liverpool, or indeed any other geographical place, to any of the reviewers concerned. Neither do any of the reviewers associate the song with the riverine themes of water, grief, loss and introspection, and those themes certainly didn't seem obvious to me when I listened to the song. After Roger's talk, however, I dug out the original 7″ version of the song, and when I played it I listened to it with new ears. I noticed how certain musical and lyrical features of the song combined to establish a particular 'perspective' (Maxwell, 2004) that might encourage listeners to interpret the song in broadly similar ways. Several reviews, for example, describe the song as sad, peaceful, ethereal and contemplative, and it is not a song that is likely to be described as aggressive or happy. That 'perspective' suited the particular story of Liverpool that Roger wanted to tell. He selected sounds and structures in the song that allowed if not encouraged him to associate them with specific features of the city, sifting through various layers of meaning in order to select those than cohered and rang true for him at that particular time. While I listened to the song I tried, in an extremely rudimentary way, to pick out those sounds and structures and relate them to Roger's interpretation.

River Whilst there are no specific references to river or drift in the lyrics of 'Christian', the song's rising and falling cadences do allow for an association with the circular movement of waves, and I was surprised to find that the record sleeve for the original 7″ single release of 'Christian' features a blue, abstract, swirly and water-like pattern that frames a photograph of Gary Daly and Eddie Lundon standing in front of an extensive rural landscape. Features of the actual song might also signify the rural or pastoral to listeners open to such suggestions (in one popular music encyclopedia China Crisis are actually described as 'pastoral electro pop')[32]. This would have assisted the opposition that Roger constructed between the natural, riverine sound and the more contrived, commercial sound associated with the mechanical and modernist metaphor of the train – an opposition that suggested the dichotomy and tension between urban and rural that has been familiar to Western ideology and tales of the city (Finnegan, 1998: 171). Those 'pastoral' features include the slow tempo of the song and the relaxed, effortless quality of the lead vocal. It is certainly not the rough, tense, harder and louder vocal style associated with heavier ('rockist' or 'trainish', as Roger put it) styles of rock, which tend to convey effort and urgency (Tagg, 1990: 112). In fact the only sense of urgency in the song is conveyed in the singing of the words 'rush over', when the vocal suddenly becomes more emphatic and for the first and only time in the song a second voice appears to join in harmony with the lead vocal.

In addition to this, the sustained notes of the synthesized organ and fretless bass produce drone-like sounds that also help to convey a mellow, dreamy feel. According to Tagg (1991: 43), sustained chords played in slow tempo are often used in film and television soundtracks to conjure up a general feeling of calm in large open spaces, and 'Handel, Beethoven, Schubert, Bruckner, Mahler and Grieg, not to mention Vaughan Williams … all use drones in music associated with calm and peaceful, large outdoor spaces connected with the bourgeois individual's idealized notions of pastorality' (ibid.: 41). After I had listened to the song a couple of times, however, I noticed that the sliding of the bass notes also helped to produce a drifty, dreamy sensation, and that those notes were so deep in tone they sounded almost whale-like, or perhaps even like a blown conch shell. At the same time the addition of reverb to the snare made it sound rather like a splash of water. There was in fact an abundance of reverb added not just to the snare but also to the vocals and many other instruments, and this, as Tagg (ibid.: 44) and Van Leeuwen (1999: 25) suggest, helped to enhance the sense of open space and distance. (Van Leeuwen (ibid.: 21), citing Tagg, points out that the absence of reverb in hard rock'n'roll 'signifies a closer and more crowded acoustic space and thus a modern urban environment'.) The images of wide open space, nature and a sense of remove seemed to become stronger when the reverb was combined with the long-held notes and ascending pitch of the solo woodwind sound at the start of each cadence. Moreover, the solo woodwind instrument, particularly the flute, has commonly been used within orchestral music,

---

32   Larkin, C. 1999. *Virgin Encyclopedia of Popular Music*, p259.

and film and television soundtracks, to signify pastoral, rural settings (Schafer, 1977: 105).

Grief and Yearning   It is possible, therefore, to explain the 'river' in 'Christian', but what about Roger's association of the song with grief and yearning? Van Leeuwen (1999: 111, 103) states that a melodic structure that rises and falls in pitch can convey a sense of relaxation. In the musical extract of 'Christian', however, the solo woodwind sound ascends in pitch but does not descend straight back down to the tonic. Instead it hovers about for a while, dipping slightly and rising back up again, and then dipping again and again before its eventual descent. As I listened to the song I began to appreciate how that structure kept me waiting for the eventual return to the tonic, generating for a while a sense of something unresolved. Maxwell (2004: 207) suggests that in such cases melodic lines can produce a tension and sense of unfulfilment and yearning. Citing the work of Cook, she also states that rising pitch can suggest anything that comes 'out' or 'away', whilst falling pitch can suggest anything that comes 'in' or 'back' (ibid.: 40). It was presumably these aspects of 'Christian' that allowed Roger to associate the song with sighing, yearning and returning.

At the same time, however, Roger also associated the song with sadness and grief, and a melancholic feel is certainly established right at the beginning of the song because it starts in B minor, reverting temporarily to A major before reverting back again to the minor key – a key that is conventionally used to signify sadness. One reviewer of 'Christian' describes the song as 'subdued' and 'haunting', noting that compared to some of their contemporaries, 'the China Crisis brand of haunting is … a much friendlier, softer, less anguished flavour of haunting. A bit sad, yes, but not suicidally depressed.'[33] Sadness could also be suggested by the song's lyrics, particularly the lines 'I can't sleep', 'I could lose myself', 'I may lose my fear', 'long dead cause' and 'I've seen the hand that rushes in as it rushes over you'. Due to the phrasing of the lead vocal, and the way that it descends in pitch towards the end of each lyrical phrase, the words 'war', 'down' and 'fear' that feature at the end of these and other phrases become emphasized. The absence of a typical chorus, which is somewhat unusual for a rock/pop song, also contributes to the song's rather subdued feel.

Roger Hill is not the only rock critic to have distinguished rock musical sounds and structures in terms of beat and flow, being away from and yearning for home. His distinction between the trainish and riverine tendencies of Liverpool rock music has interesting parallels with the psychoanalytic discussion of Reynolds and Press (1995) who, like Connell and Gibson (2003: 98), categorize the music of certain rock bands (including that of the Liverpool band Echo and the Bunnymen) as 'oceanic'. They describe oceanic music as 'nostalgic' and as produced by 'home boys' who yearn for home and mother, and they contrast it with the sounds and lyrics of typical male rock rebels (including the Rolling Stones and the Stranglers) who seek to escape from

---

33   http://www.awrc.com/review/c/diary_a_collection.html, accessed July 2004.

home and create a hard and typically 'macho' or misogynistic style of rock.[34] Here, therefore, is a distinction between macho and oceanic rock, and between rebellious escape and nostalgia for home, that shares certain similarity with Roger's distinction between train and river.

Isolation and Introspection   If Roger's association of 'Christian' with grief and yearning was provoked by the semiotics of particular sounds and structures within the song, then what about his association of the song with the theme of isolation, and his description of the riverine sound as the sound of Liverpool talking to itself? To begin with, certain aspects of the song could have helped to convey a sense of introspection and isolation. The lyrics, for example, emphasize the first person, and the lead vocal has a quiet, soft, breathy and almost whispering quality that could suggest intimacy and confidentiality. The drones that feature in the background mix of the song provide a gentle and dreamy background that could help to explain why some reviewers have described the song as possessing 'a quiet majesty';[35] 'very peaceful';[36] a 'meditative' song that 'mesmerizes the ears with exquisite strings and pensive keyboards'.[37] It is also common for sounds that connote nature, wide and open space and a sense of longing and yearning to be associated with meditation and contemplation (Maxwell, 2004: 124, 204). Some of the sounds of 'Christian' also have an ethereal quality, and China Crisis have been described as a 'restrained, tuneful affair … who had a run of ethereal, murmuring hits' (Du Noyer, 2002: 174). These sounds contribute to the song's dream-like quality and perhaps also to the sense of remove and isolation. The continuous, discordant and arpeggiated finger-picking guitar, for example, sounds quiet and delicate and has a high-pitched, steely, harp-like quality. The sustained, synthesized, ambient and discordant organ sounds that appear during the second instrumental break are also rather dream-like, and at one point they are so high pitched that they suggest outer rather than open space.

Roger Hill thus connected 'Christian' to images of nature, sadness and reflection. It seems relevant that in his study of listener evaluations of 'mood music', Tagg (1982: 17) notes that, ironically, the musical category of 'nature' was opposed to technology and was positively evaluated, yet at the same time it was associated with sadness, and the only other musical category to lend itself to sadness was 'the tiny "Religious" one'. This suggests a more general connection between nature and sadness within music semiotics. Images of nature also appear in lyrics and song titles within the broader repertoire of China Crisis, a repertoire that Roger Hill would have

---

34   Reynolds and Press thus associate the 'oceanic' with the feminine, and women and femininity have been associated with water or liquid by others scholars (see, for example, Theweleit, 1987; and Cixous, 1976), sometimes in ways that can appear to celebrate and/or essentialize female difference.

35   http://www.leonardslair.co.uk/china.htm, accessed July 2004.

36   http://www.musica.co.uk/musica/screen_PRODUCT/shop_DYM/affiliate_DYM/ category_PP596117.htm, accessed July 2004.

37   http://www.artistdirect.com/store/artist/album/0,,199256,00.html, accessed July 2004.

been familiar with. They feature, for example, in song titles such as 'No More Blue Horizons', 'Red Sails', 'Here Comes a Raincloud', 'Blue Sea', 'Hampton Beach', 'Northern Sky' and 'Jean Walks in Fresh Fields'. Interestingly, the lyrics and song titles also feature religious imagery, as in titles such as 'The Soul Awakening', 'Wall of God', 'Sweet Charity and Adoration', 'All My Prayers', Singing the Praises of Finer Things', 'The Highest High', 'King in a Catholic Style' and 'Christian'. When Gary Daly visited Liverpool University to talk to students about China Crisis and their music he was asked about that religious imagery, and he explained it in terms of feelings of guilt and discomfort, thus suggesting the kind of associations between nature, sadness and religion that are noted by Tagg:

> I was a catholic. I went to church for years and years. I was brought up in St Joseph's school in Kirkby, which was regarded as like a really nice catholic school … If I was to say anything important it was usually religious you know, because they had all the fabulous words … There was a guilt thing in there as well because when you're brought up that way, you know, you're wrong to kick off with. That's how I interpreted it. And I suppose … whenever I was in a position where I was doing fine, there would always be this side of me saying 'why are you feeling like this?' Because a lot of the time I wasn't feeling that great in the group but we were having, you know, this success, so I suppose the words would come to mind then and I would use them (cited in Cohen, 1994: 128).

Music, Lament and the Soul of the City

My discussion of the musical sounds and structures of 'Christian' has been brief and rudimentary, but it suggests that they allow for associations with images of river, sadness or grief, yearning and introspection. They cannot explain such associations, however, because music means different things to different people and musical representation is necessarily abstract. They also cannot explain why such images would be connected to Liverpool, and cities are likewise open to interpretation. Mike Brocken, for example, a Liverpool-based music lecturer and folk musician, has pointed to literature and media reports on the Beatles that commonly associate the band and their music with images of working-class Liverpool and its tough docklands (p.c.).[38] He has contrasted them with his own image of John Lennon walking across the golf course on his way home from school, and gazing at Strawberry Fields from the bedroom window of his comfortable, semi-detached house in the leafy suburbia of South Liverpool. Similarly, for some, the music of the Beatles and the Liverpool Sound of the 1960s may be perceived as an authentic expression of 1960s Liverpool, whilst for others it is a tourist cliché. We must therefore turn to the contextual factors that influenced Roger Hill's interpretation of the song, and thus to the interaction of textual and contextual factors on representations of music as local culture. How, for example, did the conventions of rock culture that were described earlier influence

---

38   See, for example, the 1963 BBC television documentary *Beat City*.

the notion of a Liverpool Sound, and how was that notion connected to local socio-economic factors and to local and collective narratives of the city?

Rock Culture and Representations of the City

Roger's 'Liverpool Sound' was informed by, and drew upon, the social and ideological conventions of rock culture that were discussed earlier, and it was in a sense a product of that culture. The train represented the conventional quest of rock bands for commercial success and the journeys they undertook as part of that quest, as well as the notion of rock music as a 'way out' or an escape from place. Moreover, trainish sounds directed at the commercial marketplace were distinguished from 'riverine' sounds that were unfettered by commercial ambition and were consequently a more honest and truthful expression of place. The opposition of train and river thus suggested rock culture's conventional and ideological emphasis on local authenticity, and on an opposition between commerce and creativity. In addition, by describing 'Christian' as the definitive Liverpool Sound, and thus connecting music to the local, Roger Hill made an 'interpretive move' (Feld, 1984) that was familiar to rock culture, and that illustrated the 'rhetoric of the local' in rock. His association of the Liverpool Sound with images of a deserted and grieving city also suited the conventional emphasis on representations of urban discontent within rock music.

At the time of Roger's university session references to a local rock sound seemed to be particularly commonplace in Liverpool, perhaps encouraged by the media-hyped rivalry between Liverpool rock music and the so-called 'Madchester' scene. Distinctions between Liverpool and Manchester rock music certainly preoccupied one group of rock musicians that I got to know around that time.[39] Those musicians described Manchester as wealthier than Liverpool and suggested that its population tended to be better travelled and more open-minded. Consequently, they suggested, Manchester rock music revealed a variety of influences, whilst the Liverpool sound reflected a paucity of influences and a parochial obsession with the past. They also suggested that Manchester's wealth was reflected in the synthesized and hi-tech sounds that they associated with rock music from that city, in contrast to the Liverpool Sound, which they described as 'acoustic', 'basic' and 'raw'. Thus, much like Roger's opposition of train and river, imaginary distinctions between Manchester and Liverpool music were constructed around a series of dichotomies: insular vs cosmopolitan, technological vs acoustic, rich vs poor, honest vs contrived (Cohen, 1994). Similarly, the musicians from North Liverpool distinguished their musical sound from that of musicians from South Liverpool. They described the sound of Northern rock bands as the 'real' Liverpool Sound, and characterized it as introverted and less cosmopolitan than that of bands from the city's 'South End', but

---

39   The musicians participated in a three-month project that was designed to encourage musicians to reflect upon their songwriting and upon factors that might have influenced it, and was based at Liverpool University's Institute of Popular Music with funding from the Performing Right Society of Great Britain.

also as more 'honest' and 'basic'.[40] For those musicians the Liverpool sound was thus a sound that had turned inwards and had been stripped down to its bare, raw essentials.

Media Stereotypes and Narratives of Place

These descriptions of a local, Liverpool Sound shared certain similarities with Roger Hill's description of that sound. Firstly, they connected musical sounds to local social and economic factors and inequalities; secondly, they involved a conventional emphasis on musical authenticity;[41] thirdly, they related the Liverpool sound to themes of insularity, isolation and introspection. Like Roger's description they were also influenced by certain narratives of place that were familiar within Liverpool, and by familiar and sometimes stereotypical representations of the city that were commonly promoted through the media. These included representations of Liverpool as insular despite the cosmopolitan history of the city described in the previous chapter.

For some, Liverpool's geographical position, and its role as a seaport, has meant that the city 'looked outward, not over its shoulder' (Lane, 1987: 11), and that it is 'an island with arcane customs and rituals, loosely attached to the north-west coast' (Sweeting, cited in Belchem, 2000: 63). The city has thus been described as:

> deeply insular, yet essentially outward-looking. It faces the sea and all the lands beyond, but has its back turned on England. There were local men for whom Sierra Leone was a fact but London only a rumour. They knew every dive in Buenos Aires, but had no idea of the Cotswolds. And Liverpudlians speak with merry contempt for their Lancashire neighbours, displaying all the high indifference of a New Yorker for Kansas (Du Noyer, 2002: 80, citing the work of Lane and Belchem).

Yet, despite this dual emphasis on Liverpool cosmopolitanism and insularity (which is discussed in the following chapter), during the 1980s and 1990s Liverpool was more commonly described in a more reductive and stereotypical manner, and references to the city as 'insular' had become somewhat of a cliché. Time and time again the musicians and music enthusiasts I spoke to referred to the city's insularity, and the city had been commonly described as insular in media reports and in popular literature:

> in those days Liverpool was like a city apart. Nothing like as cosmopolitan as Manchester and a very insular and parochial place ... Mike Maxfield recalls that he thought of Liverpool as a 'walled city, apart and alone'. In 1962 the walls began to be breached but it was by Manchester groups going in rather than Liverpool groups coming out ... Groups

---

40   Gary Daly from China Crisis, during his session with students at Liverpool University, mimicked his relatives deriding South Liverpool and describing it as 'full of friggin' cockneys' (that is, people from London rather than Liverpool).

41   As Stokes points out (1994a: 7), authenticity is 'a way of talking about music, a way of saying to outsiders and insiders alike "this is what is really significant about this music", "this music makes us different from other people".'

from Liverpool were hitting Hamburg in numbers but the first steps into London came from the early Manchester groups (Lawson, 1998: 59, 60).

I have never looked upon myself as being a typical Liverpudlian … I don't think I have a Liverpool outlook. It's possibly because I've done such a lot of travelling in my work. I'm not parochial (music enthusiast and radio broadcaster, p.c.).

My feeling about working in Liverpool compared to Manchester, is that Manchester is much more, it's much more like London actually, it's more outward looking (Music Officer of the North West Arts Board, p.c.).

Liverpool is very insular. It's partly self-deprecation. People from Liverpool think that they're unique, they think that they've had a hard time and therefore deserve something, and almost live up to everyone else's stereotype of ourselves (Liverpool-based arts consultant, p.c.).

By describing the Liverpool Sound as the sound of an economically isolated city talking to itself, Roger Hill thus drew upon a familiar local narrative and stereotype of place, as did his description of Liverpool as a grieving city. A couple of years before Roger's talk, media reporting on Liverpool had focused on the public displays and rituals of grief that followed the Hillsborough football tragedy of 1989, including the construction of a shrine of flowers, handwritten poems and messages at Liverpool's Anfield football ground. (At that time it was more common in Liverpool than in other English cities for bouquets of flowers, poems and photographs to be taped and distributed at the specific location of fatal road accidents, largely due to the strong Catholic influence within the city.) The British press responded to that tragedy and subsequent events in an astonishingly vindictive manner: 'In reporting local reaction to the Heysel and Hillsborough disasters and the Bulger case, the quality press have constructed an image of Liverpudlian self-indulgence, self-pity and mawkishness' (Belchem, 2000: 62).[42] One headline in a national quality newspaper labelled Liverpool 'Self Pity City' (*The Sunday Times*, 28 February 1993), whilst a journalist from a national British newspaper spoke of the 'penumbra of tragedy' that was peculiar to Liverpool, and the notion that there is something 'special' about the place. 'There isn't,' he said, adding 'The tragedies are on your own heads.'[43]

Media attitudes towards Liverpool have changed over recent years, although in the autumn of 2004 British news headlines focused on comments about Liverpool made by the Conservative Shadow Minister Boris Johnson in an editorial for *The Spectator* magazine. Referring to the city's response to the beheading of a Liverpool-born man by a fundamentalist extremist group in Iraq, and to the mourning rituals that

---

42   The toddler Jamie Bulger was murdered in Liverpool by two ten-year-old boys in 1993. The incident attracted extensive national news coverage and provoked considerable debate about youth and criminality. Again, however, that incident (and also local reactions to it) was connected by the press to Liverpool, and it was represented as a tragedy specific to that city.

43   Walter Ellis, speaking during a televised debate on BBC2 entitled 'Self Pity City?', broadcast in March 1993.

subsequently took place within the city, he described Liverpool as a city 'hooked on grief'. He also accused Liverpudlians of a 'mawkish sentimentality' and of wallowing in their victim status. In the face of considerable anger expressed by the city's leaders he was later forced to apologize for what he referred to in a public statement as 'an outdated stereotype', and what one Liverpool councillor described as 'old prejudiced and stereotypical views of Liverpool citizens'.[44]

Music, Economic Change and the Poetics of Place

Roger Hill's description of 'the definitive Liverpool Sound' may thus have unwittingly tapped into, and colluded with, familiar local narratives and stereotypes. It also reduced the diversity of rock sounds within the city to one single sound and promoted a romanticized and essentialist view of the relationship between music and city. I now want to argue, however, that his Liverpool Sound was at the same time a genuine and sympathetic attempt to get at the distinctiveness of local music and to consider what music can tell us about cities.

The previous chapter discussed Liverpool's rise to prominence within the global economy, but this chapter began with the city's deepening marginalization from the late 1960s, and its severe economic crisis of the 1980s and early 1990s. Du Noyer (2002: 90) thus describes Liverpool as a Cinderella City: 'When the clock struck midnight its finery, just like Cinderella's, turned back into rags.'[45] Lane (1987: 160) writes, 'The bottom fell out of the port economy too suddenly and with too little counteracting economic compensation for there to be any easy collective psychological adjustment to the brutal fact that Liverpool no longer mattered in the world, that the city's time had passed.' But what impact did this fall have on the musical life of the city? For Roger, it affected the city's musical sounds and resulted in a local, riverine sound that represented a lament for Liverpool and, like the birdsong of the Kaluli from Papua New Guinea (Feld, 1990), a poetics of loss and abandonment. At the sametime however, Roger's 'Liverpool Sound' was a Levi Straussian myth constructed through the opposition of train and river, each of which had a literal but also metaphorical significance. The train represented the journey from Liverpool taken by musicians in their quest for commercial success, but also the journey taken by other local residents who left the city to seek work elsewhere, and the migration from the city of people and industry. As Roger put it during his university session: 'the beat is also the beat of history and the beat of economics and the beat of all those sorts of things. And there is the sense that that beat has left Liverpool behind.' The river was The River Mersey that had once been the lifeblood of Liverpool's port and the 'Gateway to Empire', but was

---

44   BBC news, http://news.bbc.co.uk/1/hi/uk_politics/3758340.stm, accessed November 2004.

45   Similarly, the Chief Executive of the Littlewoods Organisation and Chairman of the Merseyside Development Corporation declared, 'The biggest single shock I ever experienced was the rapid degeneration of Merseyside. I've never seen anything go to hell so quickly' (*The Independent on Sunday*, 3 May 1992).

now more of an isolated cul-de-sac represented through harmonies that rotate and sigh. The musical sounds and structures of China Crisis and other Liverpool musicians, including musical beats, cadences and flows, thus provided Roger with a resource that he could harness in order to represent the city. He applied them to specific local social and economic factors, using them to construct a particular story about the city.

Roger's 'Liverpool Sound' could also be interpreted as an attempt to use music to get at a local 'structure of feeling' (Williams, 1977) produced by specific economic circumstances, although the relationship between culture and the economy is not a deterministic one. Roger nevertheless drew attention to a tension between leaving and returning (or staying) that was prevalent within Liverpool rock culture during the 1980s and 1990s and will reappear in later chapters, and to the relationship between place, sound and sentiment. The rock musicians I got to know in Liverpool often turned to music for help in dealing with or communicating emotions, and expressing sentiments that they perceived to be meaningful and profound. For Gary Daly, for example, music was a means of saying something important and coping with feelings of guilt and discomfort. For Roger Hill music was likewise able to evoke sentiments relating to one particular city that could not easily be put into words. His 'definitive Liverpool Sound' was a sound that was haunted by the local past, containing its affective traces and memories and expressing a sense of grief and yearning. The Sound was an attempt to say, as he put it, 'something universal about the city'.

Likewise, travel journalists often turn to music when they want to try to convey some sort of inner essence or truth concerning the place they are writing about. Like Roger, some promote the idea that geographical places have souls and that music is best placed to express them.[46] This is partly because music has a specific role to play in the structuring of emotion. As DeNora (2000: 169) writes of music:

> The temporal dimension, the fact that it is a non-verbal, non-depictive medium, and that it is a physical presence whose vibrations can be felt, all enhance its ability to work at non-cognitive or subconscious levels ... as a way of happening that moves through time, it allows us, should we latch on to it, to engage in a kind of visceral communion with its perceived properties. We can imagine and 'feel', for example, the close-knit texture of dissonant polyphony, or the 'wide-open spaces' of fifths and fourths, or the 'depressed' character of the minor triad.

Conclusion

The previous chapter highlighted the diversity and cosmopolitanism of Liverpool's musical life, whilst this chapter pointed to different and contrasting styles within the

---

46   Anthony Sattin, for example, writes, 'Feel the rhythm – know the nation: local music gives the traveller a fast track to a country's soul' ('Rhythm Nations', *The Sunday Times*, 10 February 2002). In Austin, Texas, music was promoted as the city's soul by city marketers and tourist officials (Shank, 1994: 210). Soul and r'n'b music has been similarly promoted as the 'soul of Memphis', whilst the director of the Tourist Board of New Orleans declared that, 'The whole spirit of the city is summed up in its music' (quoted in Atkinson, 1997: 96).

city's rock culture. There thus existed many different Liverpool Sounds. During the 1980s and early 1990s, however, the marginalization of Liverpool within the global economy, and the severity of the city's economic crisis, along with negative media representations of the city, encouraged the rhetoric of the local within the city's rock culture, suggesting a symbiosis of culture and economy. That rhetoric of the local involved a musical poetics of loss and abandonment and the appropriation of rock as a local, city sound. Musical sounds were thus connected to the city despite the emphasis in the previous chapter on global musical routes and hybridity, and on music as a mobile, travelling culture. That musical production of the city pointed to the specificity or perceived specificity of music as sound and text but also as an experience.

I critiqued the notion of a local, city sound for promoting an essentialist view of music, and for suggesting that cities can have a 'natural', 'authentic' sound and can be directly mirrored or expressed in music. The relationship between a city and a musical sound is not deterministic, organic or homological and it is difficult, if not impossible, to identify within rock music sounds that are purely local.[47] In addition, a musical sound and also a city are complex entities that can mean different things to different people. Yet both are often represented in partial and reductive ways that reduce them to particular essences or crude generalizations. The notion of a singular local sound involves a fetishization of locality that will be explored further in later chapters, and it reduces the multifarious aspects of music and of the city to a few rigid and narrowly defined characteristics or tendencies. Roger Hill's 'Liverpool Sound', for example, promoted familiar media stereotypes of Liverpool and it neglected the pluralism and diversity of its music.

On the other hand, however, Roger's Liverpool Sound was an idiosyncratic but informed and sympathetic attempt to get at the localness of local music. I discussed it as a social construction and as an act of definition that needs to be understood in relation to the particular musical sounds and structures involved, but also in relation to the socio-economic, geographical and historical context in which it was produced. It was influenced, for example, by the social and ideological conventions and myths of rock culture. It was also influenced by local circumstances. These included specific, contemporary local events such as the Hillsborough tragedy and media constructions of a rivalry between the music 'scenes' of Liverpool and Manchester. They included recognizable stereotypes and narratives of Liverpool, which acted as a form of discursive currency that Roger could adopt but also adapt to promote a coherent and orderly view of the city and its music. They also included specific local histories such as Liverpool's history of migration and its economic crisis of the 1980s and 1990s involving de-industrialization, disinvestment and depopulation. This

---

47   Irish Traditional Music, for example, is often used by Hollywood and by the Irish tourist industry to signify real Irishness, even though aspects of that music – such as a certain style of fiddle playing and pub 'sessions' – were developed by Irish migrants outside of Ireland and later re-imported back into Ireland and regarded as authentically Irish (Kneafsey, 2003: 23).

combination of genre and locality, text and context thus informed the production of music as local culture and inspired the poetics of place that will resonate throughout the next chapter and the rest of this book.

Chapter 3

Music as City Heritage:
Decline and Renewal in the Nashville of
the North

Liverpool used to be referred to in some circles as the 'Nashville of the North' because it had the largest country music scene in Europe, with around forty country bands performing in the city at the same time as the Beatles.[1] Hank Walters has been a familiar and charismatic figure within that scene, and Kevin McManus and I had heard a lot about him before we were first introduced to him when conducting our study on music and kinship.[2] Beneath a peaked sailor's cap was a face that exuded good humour and a strong personality, which, like his deep, husky voice, demanded attention. We subsequently met with Hank on many occasions to watch him perform and to talk to him and his family about their involvement with country music. Hank is an accomplished player of the accordion, guitar, bagpipes and piano,[3] and a skilled raconteur with a wealth of jokes and anecdotes that he enjoys regaling his audiences with. He likes to describe himself as the father of country music in Liverpool, and on the sleeve of the LP *Liverpool Goes Country*, released by Rex Records in 1965, Hank is referred to as 'The Daddy of them all'.

This chapter focuses on Hank Walters and a small core group of musicians involved with country music in Liverpool during the early to mid-1990s. It examines how a music genre that originated in America's rural south was claimed and promoted as the heritage of Liverpool, a provincial city in north-west England. I distinguish music heritage from notions of music history or tradition, drawing attention to the emphasis that heritage places upon the continuity of the musical past, and upon a

---

1   http://www.triumphpc.com/mersey-beat/birth/birth2.shtml, accessed December 2004.

2   The study is referred to in Chapter 1 and discussed in more detail in the Appendix. It was conducted by Kevin McManus and myself in 1991, and it led to a larger research project on music in twentieth-century Liverpool that ran from 1991 to 1994 and included a case study on country music that this chapter draws upon. That case study benefited from the work of Frances Hunt, a postgraduate research student at Liverpool University's Institute of Popular Music – where Kevin and I were also based – who was working on a thesis about country music on Merseyside. The thesis was never finished but was provisionally titled 'Liverpool Goes Country: A Study of a Popular Music Performance on Merseyside'.

3   Some of these instruments were picked up through the involvement of Hank and his family with the Irish Protestant Orange Lodge movement.

sense of ownership rather than just knowledge of that past. The chapter thus builds on the discussion in Chapters 1 and 2 by considering country music as a cosmopolitan, travelling, global culture, but by focusing on how it was at the same time connected to Liverpool and appropriated as local culture,[4] a production of the city through country music that compares and contrasts with the previous discussion on rock music.

Country Music in Liverpool

Hank Walters and the Dusty Road Ramblers

Hank Walters was born in 1933 into a Protestant, working-class family of seafarers. He grew up listening to American country music because his grandfather had a collection of Jimmie Rodgers records acquired during shipping trips to America; and when Hank was 11 years old he joined a band named Spike and the Hillbillies.[5] The band had been formed to perform at a Christmas concert at Hank's school, but they stuck together and eventually began playing outside local pubs where they earned money from pub customers. Later on they played at local weddings and dances and in local social clubs, including Protestant clubs. Hank loved to remind us, however, about the moment in 1949 when he first heard the Hank Williams song 'Lovesick Blues' played on a jukebox in a local cafe. 'I just went ecstatic,' he told us, and from then on he spent his Saturdays at a local record shop, and his income on Hank Williams. In one version of the story related to us, Hank was so moved by the song that he stole the jukebox; but he told us on another occasion that the cafe owner was so moved by Hank's response to the song that he took the record out of the jukebox and gave it to him. Bernie Green, another Liverpool country musician who was roughly the same age as Hank, told us that he was similarly smitten when he heard his first Hank Williams record, and he clearly remembers being fascinated as a young boy by a poster of Hank Williams displayed in the window of a local record shop.

While stationed in the Middle East during his National Army Service, Hank formed his own band named Hank Walters and the Dusty Road Ramblers. The band continued after Hank left the army in 1953 and started working on Liverpool's docks, eventually taking up employment with the Mersey Docks and Harbour Board Company, where he earned and adopted the nickname Hank. Like the few other country bands in Liverpool at that time (such as Phil Brady's Ranchers, Cyl Con and the Westernaires and The Drifting Cowboys) the band began by performing in their own neighbourhoods before venturing out elsewhere in the city. The band's membership changed and expanded and they started to get regular bookings, and

---

4   Throughout this chapter I use the term 'scene' (in much the same way that it was used by Hank and his associates) to refer to the specific groups, activities and institutions involved with local country music-making, and the behavioural and ideological conventions that distinguished country as a genre.

5   Named after the country performer Spike Jones.

during 1955 they undertook their first radio broadcast in the UK. By 1957 they were performing at Liverpool's Cavern Club. One of Hank's favourite and oft-repeated anecdotes is about the time he first met John Lennon at that club and told him that he didn't much like his music, and that the Beatles wouldn't get anywhere unless they 'got on with it and played country' (in McManus 1994a:12).[6] Also in 1957, Hank established his own weekly country music club in a city-centre venue. The success of that club encouraged the launch of other clubs and the formation of new country bands:

> Within the area abounded more such artists than anywhere outside Nashville. On a given weekend you could guarantee that plenty of the three-hundred-odd venues affiliated to the Liverpool Social Club Association had booked The Dusty Road Ramblers, the Hillsiders, The Ranchers and any others from a legion of outfits playing the kinda music folk liked tappin' a foot to (Alan Clayson, quoted in McManus 1994a:11).

Liverpool's Country Music Scene

So what was Liverpool's country scene like during the early to mid-1990s? As in the 1950s it involved a broad and diverse group of musicians that included many solo performers. When those musicians spoke about the local country music 'scene', however, many of them referred to a core, close-knit group of around 25 or so country bands and their followers, and it was that core group that our research focused on. Members of that group were white and mostly middle-aged and working class. Almost all the musicians were male, but their audiences usually included equal numbers of men and women and were also 'nearly always middle-aged' (Hank Walters, p.c.). Only a couple of the bands were professional. Most musicians had day jobs or were unemployed or, like Walters, retired; and most financed their own recordings made in local recording studios, which they sold through mail order and at live performances. They did not employ agents or managers. There were, however, some notable exceptions, particularly the Hillsiders and Northwind – two bands that had acquired a national reputation and were the only full-time, professional country bands based in the region.[7] During the 1960s a few other local country bands had also become nationally known, including Phil Brady and the Ranchers and Sonny Web and the Cascades.

Until 1994 Liverpool had a specialist country record shop, Pat and Gerry Allen's Record Store. Both Pat and Gerry were country musicians and were well known and well liked within the local country scene – as indicated by Gerry's funeral, which was attended by a large and illustrious gathering of country musicians, some of who performed during the event. In addition, the country programme *Sounds*

---

6   See also http://www.triumphpc.com/mersey-beat/a-z/gretty.shtml, accessed December 2004.

7   The Hillsiders formed in 1964 and were fronted for the first ten of their 25-year career by Kenny Johnson, who ran his own country music programme on local BBC radio and also fronted other country bands, including Northwind.

Country on local BBC radio was for some time the station's most popular and longest-running show. The station thus classified country as 'mainstream' and broadcast it during the day rather than in the evening, which was when its specialist music programmes tended to be broadcast. The programme featured a mix of local, national and international performers and its presenter was the country musician Kenny Johnson. Liverpool's main commercial station, Radio City, also broadcast a country programme, presented by the country musician Joe Butler.

Country music was particularly popular in the dockland areas of North Liverpool, which was where Walters and many other country musicians of his generation had grown up. Towards the end of our research on the local country scene we started to contribute a weekly country music column to Merseyside's free newspaper, but the column was only published in the newspaper's North Liverpool issue where it would appeal to a wider readership. Hank told us that his band had 'a good following around the docklands', and that the scene was strongest in Huyton and Walton, which were both North Liverpool districts. As discussed in Chapter 1, the port of Liverpool had once depended upon a large and generally unskilled dockside labour force consisting largely of immigrants, particularly Irish immigrants. They included relatives of Hank, who was of Welsh/Irish parentage, and the Irish influence on the local country scene of the 1950s and 1960s is mentioned by Willis-Pitts (2000: 44–5). Many Irish immigrants stayed and settled in cramped terraced housing in the residential neighbourhoods of North Liverpool, which were close to the waterfront and dockside labour market. Following World War II those neighbourhoods were dramatically disrupted and transformed as a result of planned programmes of demolition and slum clearance involving the relocation of residents to satellite towns and estates, and also the decline of Liverpool's port.

Country's American Roots and Traditions

Country music became popular in America during the 1920s, although as Peterson (1997: 9) points out, 'the term "country music" was not widely applied to the music until the 1940s, and was not fully embraced by all those interested in the field for another thirty years, when the term "country and western" faded from wide usage'. The kind of music made by most of the country musicians we spoke to was traditional country, which is sometimes also referred to as 'hillbilly' or as 'old-time', 'pure' or 'classical' country. This kind of traditional country music-making was particularly popular in the north of Britain and not only in Liverpool but also in Newcastle and Glasgow, which are also port cities. It was strongly influenced by the American musicians Jimmy Rogers and Hank Williams, but the music of other country performers – such as Ferlin Husky, Webb Pierce, Carl Smith and Jean Shepherd – had also found its way into the local repertoire. In the 1960s, following the emergence of rock'n'roll in Liverpool, a distinction emerged within the city's country scene between the 'purists', who played in the traditional manner, parroting the American records and wearing Stetsons and cowboy clothes, such as Hank Walters and the Dusty Road Ramblers – and the new wave such as the Hillsiders, young bands with a fresh approach to the music, who didn't dress in country style, but provided a new and exciting beat to country sounds.[8]

A few local bands were thus more rock-influenced, but the repertoire of many bands included songs by rock- or pop-influenced country artists such as Hank Snow. There was little, however, in the way of so-called 'new (pop-influenced) country' or 'alternative country'.

Adherence to the traditions of American country music took place in several areas, including instruments, lyrical subject matter, repertoire and sound, although the musicians did adapt those traditions to suit their own particular style.[9] Hank Walters frequently drew attention to his own distinctive Cajun style of country music, and he later publicized it on his website as 'a unique sound of Country mixed with hints of Cajun and Tex Mex.'[10] He attributed the Cajun sound in his music to the fact that his grandfather once jumped ship and lived for a while in Louisiana. Hank's stories about his grandfather's escapades – which were repeated to us and to his audiences on many occasions – were entertaining, but it could be suggested that through those tales Hank was also able to connect himself and his family to the American south and thus to the perceived 'roots' of country. In terms of dress, most musicians and their followers did not wear any special clothes for performance events, and although bands such as Hank Walters and the Dusty Road Ramblers used to wear cowboy hats and clothes (another familiar code of authenticity within Country), during the 1990s they preferred to perform in ordinary clothes, and Hank stuck to his favoured flat peaked cap.[11] Besides rhythm, lead and bass guitars, and drums, local country bands often included pedal steel guitar, banjo, fiddle or mandolin. Those instruments had also become established musical codes of authenticity in country (Peterson 1997: 228), and by using them musicians could signify their commitment to tradition, a commitment that was evident in their repertoire. That repertoire was largely based on well-known American country songs, although some musicians had composed their own original songs. The song lyrics addressed familiar country themes, including heartaches and breaks, infidelity and divorce, death and loss.

An emphasis on family and home is also conventional to traditional country music, which has been closely connected to rural, working-class communities (Connell and Gibson 2003: 29; Peterson 1997: 9). In Liverpool it was common for musicians

---

8   http://www.triumphpc.com/mersey-beat/birth/birth2.shtml, accessed December 2004.

9   Finnegan (1989:96) makes the same observation about country musicians in Milton Keynes in southern England.

10   http://stage.vitaminic.co.uk/main/walters/biography, accessed July 2004.

11   Hats have played a symbolic role in country music generally, hence the term 'hat acts' (Peterson, 1997: 232) and the dismissal of Liverpool's country music scene by one of our interviewees (who was not a country fan) as 'the big hat brigade'.

and their followers to describe the music as the expression of 'ordinary' folk of the American South, and to emphasize how they spoke to and for the 'ordinary' people of Liverpool. Similarly, Finnegan (1989: 97) writes that country musicians in Milton Keynes regarded country as an expression of a common humanity and 'the feelings of "ordinary people," treating everyone on a level with no false snobbery or show.' Connell and Gibson (2003: 81–2) suggest that country music has attracted a massive global following because of its simple virtues and certainties, including its sincerity and anguish and its 'simple musical structures and instruments', which have made replication relatively straightforward.

Country Music and Community

Country musicians in Liverpool were tapped into local, regional, national and international country music networks. During the 1960s, for example, Hank Walters and the Dusty Road Ramblers helped to establish the North West Country Music Association and participated in a national country music tour. During the 1990s their performances were largely confined to Merseyside, but they were still connected to a broader country music scene through specialist country publications (and later on also web pages), and through occasional special events and competitions (see also Finnegan 1989: 92–3). At the same time, however, there was a strong sense of belonging to the local country music scene or community. Many of the musicians had been performing together since the 1950s, and despite certain rivalries there existed long-standing friendships, collaboration and kinship connections between the musicians, and between them and their followers. One of the daughters of Hank Walters, for example, explained to us that she had known a lot of Hank's fellow country musicians since she was a baby, and that she and her sisters called some of them 'Uncle'.

A sense of community was also encouraged and signified through live music performance, which was the activity most central to the scene. Shank (1994) points to the social, sensual and symbolic significance of live music performance within the rock music scene of Austin, Texas. In Liverpool live country music performance forged close social connections between the performers and their audiences that reinforced the connection between music and place. In the Liverpool of the 1990s there were no longer any specialist country venues. Performances by local and visiting country bands were regularly held in the region's theatres, leisure centres and ballrooms, and some of them acted as charity events – benefits or concerts arranged on behalf of ill, recently deceased, former or long-standing local country performers, or on behalf of disadvantaged groups. Those performance events were advertised in local gig guides and on local radio. The venues that played the most central and socially significant role in the scene, however, were the public houses and social clubs. Many pubs designated one or more nights per week for country music performances and admission was usually free. The social clubs, which included working men's clubs and political (Labour or Conservative) clubs, were open to the general public as well as to club members.

Performances in pubs and social clubs were usually publicized by word of mouth. Many of the pubs that had once hosted regular country music nights had closed or been demolished, particularly those located in the city's northern and dockland areas, but a few had survived. Such events attracted country fans who used to live in those neighbourhoods before their post-war redevelopment. Like Charlie Jenkins and his family (Chapter 1), they travelled back to the pubs from outer suburban areas in order to participate in the events and engage in reunions with former friends and neighbours. The pubs had thus become a focus for the construction of community, and for a sense of loss and nostalgia for imagined communities and neighbourhoods of old. The Union public house in Kirkdale, for example, hosted regular country performances and was patronized almost exclusively by locals and former locals until it was demolished in the late 1990s. Country performance events were thus social occasions characterized by spontaneity and a sense of collectivity and intimacy. The emphasis was on audience participation and on good-humoured interaction between audience and performers. Audience members requested particular songs, sang along with and danced to the music and bought drinks for the musicians; and I was particularly impressed by the way that the musicians tailored their set to suit the specific tastes of their audience. In between songs the musicians directly addressed individual members of the audience and their collective concerns through storytelling, which has been conventional to traditional American country music (Jensen 1993: 124–5). During the breaks between performances someone (the MC, if the performances took place in a social club) would often take to the stage to make public announcements of one sort or another, including announcements of forthcoming events and of birthdays and special anniversaries relating to particular audience members.

Local country musicians were quick to acknowledge the influence on their music of many different genres and styles. Hank Walters, for example, described country music to us as 'a diamond with many faces', mentioning the way that it had been influenced by English folk and skiffle, by the music of German, French, Spanish and particularly Celtic immigrants in America,[12] as well as by black American music, rock'n'roll and jazz. Hank, like many of his fellow country musicians, was also a proficient and versatile musician able to skilfully perform a variety of different musical styles, including jazz-influenced country, Irish folk and bluegrass. Yet at the same time, despite some crossover between Liverpool's country scene and local folk, cabaret and bluegrass scenes, the more traditional country musicians were anxious to disassociate themselves and their music from anything that was not considered to be 'real' country. This insularity was not just a characteristic of the 'purists' but typified local country music more generally. As in Milton Keynes (Finnegan 1989: 98), the paths of Liverpool's country musicians and their followers seemed quite distinctive during the 1990s, and thus rarely intersected with those connected to other local

---

12   Liverpool's strong Irish connections may have encouraged Hank to emphasize in particular the 'Celtic roots' of Liverpool country music on one website – http://www.mbus. com/bands/genadm/Hank.Walters.and.the.Arcadian.Ladies.htm, accessed July 2004.

music scenes. The symbolic boundaries of the local country scene had perhaps been reinforced by the way that country music was sometimes ridiculed by 'outsiders' to the scene. Research student Frances Hunt suggested to us that this was partly due to the music's associations with cowboys, which some found amusing; partly because it so overtly embraced its North American influences and was thus regarded by some as 'second hand'; and partly because it was regarded even by some within the scene as old-fashioned.

This insularity seemed to have been encouraged by the fame and notoriety of the Beatles and other local rock'n'roll or 'beat' groups that had contributed to the city's 'Merseybeat' scene. Clearly there had been significant interaction between the Merseybeat bands and local country bands, and the Beatles and other local rock bands were certainly influenced by skiffle and country (see McManus, 1994a; and Du Noyer, 2002: 55–6 on the country influence). John Lennon is quoted as having stated:

> I heard country and western music in Liverpool before I heard rock and roll. The people take their country and western music very seriously. I remember the first guitar I ever saw. It belonged to a guy in a cowboy suit and a cowboy hat and a big dobro. They were real cowboys and they took it seriously (Meegan, 1995: 82, citing Wenner, 1987: 102).

Musicians such as Walters, Bernie Green and Tony Allen were keen to tell us that during the 1960s Liverpool country and Merseybeat musicians often performed together in the same bands and events, and exchanged musical styles and repertoire. At the same time, however, they also described with a little bitterness how the commercial success of Merseybeat meant that they lost their younger audiences to the rock bands (McManus 1994a: 12–14, 16). During the mid-1960s those musicians helped to establish the North West Country Music Association in an effort to promote country music across the region, although the association only lasted for a couple of years. Whilst some country musicians adapted their music to embrace the new rock styles, others began to move away from rock'n'roll and to go 'full country' (Hank Walters, p.c.). Those events reflected similar developments within North America during the 1950s following the commercial success of Elvis Presley. There, country fans likewise deserted for the new rock'n'roll and a Country Music Association was consequently formed in 1959 to help promote the music (Peterson, 1997: 231).

Liverpool in Country Music

Country music thus appealed particularly strongly to groups and neighbourhoods in North Liverpool. Those neighbourhoods had always been in flux. From the mid-nineteenth century their residents had experienced the upheavals of migration, struggled with the oppressive uncertainties of a casualized dock labour market, and had their lives disrupted by post-war planning and industrial decline. This may help to explain the popularity of country music, with its emphasis on tradition and continuity as well as kinship and community. Country music was thus connected to a local geographical community as well as to a rather insular community defined through genre. At the same time, however, country music was also authenticated through the way that it was connected to its American origins, and the musicians involved emphasized the music's American and Celtic roots, along with other international music influences that had helped to shape it. They also participated in, and felt connected to, a broader national and transnational country music scene. Liverpool's country music scene was characterized, therefore, by an emphasis on the scene as connected and open but also as bounded and distinct. This could be described in terms of a dual emphasis on, and easy coexistence between, the cosmopolitan and the local, or even in terms of 'rooted cosmopolitanism' (Appiah, 2005), but it seemed more appropriately described in terms of a tension between two paradoxical perspectives. But how were connections between country and the local forged by the musicians involved? In order to address that question I now want to turn from a discussion about the making of country music *in* Liverpool and consider instead how Liverpool was made or produced through country.

Music, Performance and Local Identity

Country musicians expressed strong feelings of attachment and of belonging to Liverpool in various ways. Hank Walters liked to frame his music within a Liverpool setting by referring to the city in his storytelling in between songs, and through that storytelling he was also able to promote his own version of the notorious Liverpool accent and wit.[13] He often introduced the songs he performed with a joke or anecdote that attached them to Liverpool or to himself or a member of his audience, thus ensuring that each song had local relevance and meant something to the people listening. Tales about the Liverpool docklands were a key theme and Hank obviously had close personal and family connections with the docks. Yet the port has also been a recurring motif in the music of Merseyside rock bands such as the Zutons and Tramp from the early 2000s (Cohen and Strachan, 2005), and references to a local industrial past in music, or in writing and speech about music, are by no means peculiar to Liverpool. Motown musicians of the 1960s, for example, are said to have drawn inspiration from Detroit's industrial focus on car manufacture (Perry and Glinert, cited in Connell and Gibson, 2003: 99), whilst 30 years later the city's techno musicians were regarded as harking back to the city's industrial past from a post-industrial perspective.[14] (One techno musician, Kirk DeGiorgio, thus suggested that Detroit Techno illustrated 'a city sharpening a music' – as cited in Toop, 1995: 215.)

In addition to stories about the Liverpool docks, Hank sometimes slightly adapted the lyrics of well-known American country songs to make them refer to Liverpool,

---

13   Other local country performers, such as Lee Brennan, have likewise added a strong Liverpudlian flavour to their performances.

14   There are numerous websites that describe techno in this way. See, for example, http://the.decline.of.d-troit.de/pages/0,6903,341312,00.htm, accessed July 2004.

as in his customized Dr Hook's 'Liverpool Dock Road Café'.[15] [Jensen (1993: 124) points out that this alteration of lyrics is commonly undertaken by American honky-tonk musicians and is an 'important part of the performer–audience interaction.'] Several musicians had also composed their own original songs, which included songs about Liverpool. The first song that Hank Walters composed was entitled 'Sweet Liverpool', and it was based on a Jimmie Rodgers song called 'Mississippi Delta Blues.' (Hank described Rodgers to us as his main influence.) Hank had since composed other songs about Liverpool, including a song entitled 'Everton', which was named after a particular district of North Liverpool. Similarly, Kenny Johnson, who had performed in the Hillsiders and presented the country music programme on local BBC radio, had written a song about growing up in the North Liverpool neighbourhood of Kirkdale, and about the particular street that he had lived on. He told us that he and his friends from the neighbourhood used to rehearse as a skiffle band in the alleyway between two of the street's houses because 'it was a really fabulous echo chamber'. The sentimental and nostalgic aspects of such songs were typical of country music and, as noted and described to me by Frances Hunt, there was also an element of nostalgia in the attitudes of local country musicians and their followers to some of the old pubs that had once hosted regular country events but that now stood as a reminder of the 'good old days'.

Local country musicians also commonly referred to the existence of a Liverpool country scene and sound, even when they were discussing musicians and performance events based outside Liverpool and dispersed across Merseyside. Descriptions of that country sound tended to vary and a few of our informants questioned its existence, saying that local country music simply aspired to sound like American country music. It is significant, however, that there were others who wanted to identify Liverpool in the music. Joe Butler, for example, said, 'I've travelled all over the UK and Liverpool bands definitely play with more meat behind the music. They attack the music a lot more. Out of town they tend to be very "pretty sounding" with a front line singer and a backing band' (McManus 1994a: 15). He also referred to the 'Merseybeat style' of Liverpool country music (p.c.). Paddy Kelly told us, 'Liverpool country music has got a style of its own because we don't use all the gadgets that other bands use.' Like the descriptions of the Liverpool rock sound discussed in the previous chapter, these descriptions of the local country sound suggest a construction of local authenticity, and perceptions of a local sound that was stripped down but also 'meaty' or gritty.

Country Music, Seafaring and Myths of Liverpool Origins

An emphasis on local identity was also evident in discussions about the origins of the local country scene. Hank Walters and Bernie Green frequently argued about who had been the first to start off country music in Liverpool, and each was convinced

---

15   This particular performance was described to me by Frances Hunt.

that it was himself. Hank, for example, declared to us emphatically, 'I started country music off in Liverpool. I was the first one to take it on the road.' He added:

> Before my band in Liverpool I don't know of any other country bands as such. I get Bernie Green saying 'I've been around as long as you,' but if you go to Venice Street School in Anfield you'd find in the records that I had a band in that school when I was 11. Bernie Green is about five years younger than me so I've got to be ahead of him. If you look at the adverts in the paper you'll find my name well ahead of anyone else in Liverpool – before the Beatles or anyone.

Hank also claimed that in 1948 he was the only person in Liverpool in possession of a Hank Williams record, and that it was he who had established Britain's first ever country music club – the Black Cat Club (p.c.). Bernie Green, however, argued that the first club was actually run by him in a room hired from a local Labour club (p.c.). (Interestingly, a website focusing on British country music mentions the Black Cat Club and its launch in the 1950s, but also the York Club, which was Manchester's first country music club and was established in 1956. If that date is correct then it suggests that the York Club was actually launched the year before the Black Cat Club.)[16]

These debates were particularly significant in view of the fact that many local country musicians believed that Liverpool was the one place in Britain where American country music first became popular. Joe Butler, for example, claimed that Liverpool was the first city in Britain to hear, appreciate and make country music (Cohen, 1991a: 12). He, like many other country musicians we spoke to, suggested that this was largely due to the city's role as a port and to its cosmopolitan outlook, and they emphasized the role played by sailors in the emergence and development of Liverpool's country music scene (p.c.). In 1840, as mentioned in Chapter 1, the Cunard Steamship Company sent out the world's first ocean-going passenger liners from Liverpool, establishing a direct shipping link with North America, and Liverpool sailors returned from their American trips with various commodities that were often difficult or expensive to obtain in England. The influence of these sailors on local popular music has been the subject of much speculation and debate. According to John McNally of the Merseybeat band the Searchers, 'Most people in Liverpool had some relation who went to sea and could bring record imports in' (quoted in Leigh, 1984: 30). However, several music critics have suggested that the influence of such sailors has been exaggerated. It has certainly been dismissed by some as an explanation for the Liverpool origins of British rock 'n' roll, and for the success and distinctiveness of the Beatles (Du Noyer, 2002: 56; Chambers, 1985: 63–4).[17] Nevertheless, during the 1950s many local sailors did develop a strong interest in American popular culture and fashion, and there exists solid evidence that those men brought into Liverpool records by earlier black-American r'n'b and

---

16   http://www.gpservices38.freeserve.co.uk/britishcountry.htm, accessed December 2004.

17   see also http://www.triumphpc.com/mersey-beat/birth/birth3.shtml, accessed July 2004.

jazz artists such as Earl Bostic, the Moonglows, the Orioles and the Flamingos.[18] The men were therefore collectively referred to in Liverpool as the 'Cunard Yanks'. They were generally ship cooks and waiters who were not unionized and had an irreverent attitude to work. Many of them, for example, jumped ship and stayed for a while in various parts of America, as Hank's grandfather had done earlier. They also adopted a manner and style that was non-conformist in relation to mainstream British popular culture, and that helped to distinguish them within the city and give them cultural status.

Sailors were also significant for many of the country musicians we met because those musicians had strong personal seafaring connections, and we took seriously their claims about the influence of those connections on the development of local country music. They referred us to numerous examples of country music recordings that were brought into Liverpool by local seafarers. Paddy Kelly, for instance, was introduced to country music through a sailor friend who brought Hank Williams records home with him (p.c.). Belchem (2000: 61) refers to country music records by Jimmy Rogers and others, which were regularly brought back to Liverpool from Galveston and New Orleans by sailors working on Harrison boats (see also McManus 1994a: 2–4). Tony Allen described for us how he was taught on board ship to play country music and the guitar by a Chinese fellow crewman, but he said that was already familiar with the music:

> Everybody had either brothers, cousins, dads that went away to sea, and the same thing happened in our family. My eldest brother went away to sea ... All my father's friends and mother's friends, their sons went to sea, which first got me into country music in about 1950 when I was twelve or thirteen years old. There were few other outlets for getting music in those days.

Other local musicians also told us how they or their relatives had learned to play on board ship; they including Bunter Perkins, who acquired his first guitar following a trip to New Zealand, and Derry Wilkie, who was quoted in Chapter 1 describing how his Liverpool-based West African father had developed a taste for country and other musical styles on board ship.

Despite this emphasis on the role of local sailors in bringing country music to Liverpool, the musicians we spoke to also highlighted other routes through which country music was disseminated to the city. The Anglo-American music and media industries had rapidly expanded during the early decades of the twentieth century, and they exposed Liverpool musicians to a broad range of music genres and styles – but

---

18   The sailors are the subject of a film by Souled Out Film Productions in Liverpool. During a screening of the draft film at Liverpool University in November 2004, the producers suggested that these sailors were forerunners of the teddy boys and mods. They pointed to British rock'n'roll performers who had been so-called 'Cunard Yanks', including Tommy Steel and Billy Fury, whilst the fathers of John Lennon and George Harrison had also worked on the liners. (See also http://www.geocities.com/soulpooluk/index.html, accessed October 2004.)

particularly to American popular music, which dominated media output, although as illustrated in Chapter 1, American influences on Liverpool music extended back to the nineteenth century. During the late 1940s and early 1950s Liverpool musicians had access to American country music through local record shops, and through cowboy films broadcast in local cinemas, which helped to promote and romanticize the figure of the 'singing cowboy' personified by screen artists such as Gene Autry and Roy Rogers (see Shank, 1994). They were also able to listen to country music on the radio. Kenny Johnson, for example, told us that he used to listen to country music broadcast by the European service of the American Forces Network, and he and other local musicians listened to country music radio programmes such as *Stickbuddy Jamboree* and *Grand Ol' Opry*. They also got to hear country music at the American Burtonwood military airbase, which was located a few miles east of Liverpool. Bernie Green played at the base twice a week for four years: 'At that time they couldn't believe it. They thought we were Yanks because we sang in American style. We got on like a house on fire. They in turn gave us loads of records – so the learning material was endless' (quoted in McManus 1994a: 4).

Nevertheless, Sailors thus appeared to have a particularly important influence on the construction of collective and local identity within Liverpool's core country music scene. With hindsight it may be interesting to consider the symbolic significance of the sailor and whether the image of the sailor might have been particularly attractive to those participating in that scene. Lane (1986) attributes much of Liverpool's distinctiveness to the traditions of its ports, suggesting that they gave rise to the city's reputation for masculine exuberance, assertiveness and flamboyance, and for a fierce sense of individualism as well as deep-rooted traditions of egalitarianism and democracy. The figure of the sailor, he argues (ibid.: 10), symbolized a feisty masculinity:

> In a city saturated with port activity it is not so surprising that the idealized seafarer should come to be regarded as the ultimate expression of what it meant to be a man. Here was the free born, free spoken, foot-loose male who respected those who earned it and was unswervingly loyal to his equals.

Lane also describes various ways in which the Liverpool seaman sought to acquire a reputation as 'a real man' and states (1987: 108–9):

> It is hard to exaggerate the influence of seamen in Liverpool life. All those stories – of gambling and illicit trading, of womanising and drinking in foreign ports, of being on the beach in the SA and Australia, of irreverence to chiefs and skippers – produced an image and an ideal of a highly desireable freewheeling life of adventure and independence. Of course the *practice* contained only the merest fraction of the colourful promise – but then the truth of the matter was utterly irrelevant. What mattered was that the *message* of the stories represented an account of 'the sort of people we are.' The meaning of the stories was not in any actual events described but in the contribution every event made to an overall picture of a 'man's life. This picture became a mirror and the people of dockland could then look at it and see themselves with pride.

The masculine image of the sailor may have suited the patriarchal nature of Liverpool's country music scene and its emphasis on hard living and on male authorship and control (Peterson, 1997: 10, points out that early country music in the US was also patriarchal). One of Hank Walters's daughters described the local country scene to us as 'male-dominated', and Frances Hunt documented in her research notes various examples of the lack of respect for women as singers or musicians shown by male country musicians. She states:

> They felt that women were simply not capable of playing musical instruments – and certainly not to the level of competence required for performance. Many said that they felt that the guitar was not an instrument for women – they didn't like to see a woman holding one, let alone playing it, nor did they like the 'affected' way that some women adopted 'American' accents when performing.

There were a few female country musicians in Liverpool with a significant local following (McManus 1994a: 17–18), but only two local bands had female members and both of them were headed by men. They included Hank Walters and the Arcadian Ladies, a band that Hank established in 1991 with his three daughters – Pauline, Claire and Lorna Gail. Hank could be a strict disciplinarian and onstage he sometimes gave his daughters a public if light-hearted telling-off, and discouraged them from consuming alcohol. Hank's claim to be the 'father' of Liverpool country[19] continued this patriarchal theme. When watching Hank and his daughters perform, however, the affection and mutual respect that existed between them were clearly evident, as was the extent of the women's contribution to the band – from the original songs they had composed themselves to their organization of performance events. When the women performed with the band their husbands and their mother Carla took care of their children. Carla also drove Hank to and from his public performances, thus playing – like several other women we met or were told about – an important supportive role within the scene.

The emphasis on the role played by sailors in the development of Liverpool's country scene suited not just the patriarchal nature of that scene but also the sense of nostalgia within it. Like the lyrics about childhood neighbourhoods, and Hank's references to specific dockland pubs and cafes, sailors were a reminder of the lost world of the dockside labour market and the old neighbourhoods and lifestyles connected to that world. In addition, as indicated earlier, sailors signified cosmopolitanism and local connections to foreign places and influences. The country music singer and songwriter Charlie Landsborough was born in 1941 in a dockland area of Birkenhead, which lies just across the river from Liverpool, and was the youngest of 11 children. He writes on his website:

> My brothers were all sailors ... Apart from the guitars and all the music, they brought home gifts from all around the world. I remember sitting enchanted by the scent of the wood in a guitar brought from Spain, my imagination afire at the sight of a small canoe

---

19   A claim backed up by other local country musicians.

carved by natives of West Africa, pistols with real revolving chambers from the US and getting my first pair of dungarees from Canada. Small wonder I so eagerly awaited the return of each brother from another trip ... My brothers of course were returning from their voyages with the first guitars I'd ever seen and wonderful country music from such artists as Hank Williams, Jimmy Rodgers, Ferlin Husky and Montana Slim. They'd often arrive home with a group of friends and a crate of beer and I'd sit enthralled as they laughed and sang the hours away.[20]

Country as Liverpool Heritage

It is clear from the discussion so far, that the country musicians we got to know in Liverpool described their music and music scene in terms of cosmopolitanism, whilst at the same time emphasizing the Liverpoolness of Liverpool country music, and the Liverpool origins of British country music. In fact, the cosmopolitanism of country music and its connection with America and with the culture of various immigrant groups within American, particularly the Irish, appeared to have encouraged a celebration of local difference within the Liverpool scene. That emphasis on the local, and on local sounds, neighbourhoods and communities, was further encouraged by country music's conventional emphasis on 'home' (although 'home' in country is usually rural and is constructed in opposition to the city[21]). In addition to this, country music was connected to Liverpool through narratives of decline and renewal and concerns about the future of the local scene.

Music scenes are commonly perceived by their participants as mortal, fragile entities that require constant nurturing and protection. Rock musicians in Liverpool, for example, have expressed concern about the attentions of the music media, which can result in misrepresentations of the scene and intrusions that threaten the scene and hinder its 'natural,' organic development (Cohen 1997: 33, and 1999: 241). Similarly, Stahl (2001: 106) highlights discursive references to the weakness of Montreal's alternative rock scene. In Liverpool, country musicians pointed to the way that the local scene had been threatened and marginalized by various cultural trends and technological developments. They included the emergence of 1950s rock'n'roll and 1970s discotheques, which took away some of the audiences for country music; the introduction in the 1980s of karaoke, pub quiz nights and singers accompanied by prerecorded backing tapes, which local venues tended to find easier to accommodate and cheaper to hire than live country bands (singers that Hank Walters described to us as 'cheating' and as 'undercutting' him);[22] and the 1990s craze for country and western music and step or line dancing.

---

20   http://www.charlielandsborough.com/biography.htm, accessed June 2004.

21   Various studies of country music have discussed the way that country songs have represented the city as seductive, corrupt and sinful, and they are referenced by Connell and Gibson (2003: 79–81).

22   Connell and Gibson (2003: 110) argue that the viability of original music has always been undercut by 'the incursion of new forms of leisure into household entertainment

Line dancing had attracted new audiences to country music, but the musicians we spoke to felt that there was little or no interaction between themselves and the people on the dance floor, and that their music meant little to the dancers. They believed that they were being used merely as a vehicle for audience self-expression and display, and that their audiences could accomplish this just as easily by dancing to recorded rather than live music. Walters told us: 'The scene has gone foolish all over. Certain places have country music on but it's these cowboy things. It's fantasy island merchants wearing guns and posing, thinking that they're cowboys. It isn't country music. All they're doing is dancing and posing in the gear.' Similarly, Pat Allen told us:

> People dress up as cowboys, Mexicans, Confederates, Unionists and Indians. All they are interested in doing is parading around, showing off who has the largest Mexican hat, the most flashy gun or gun belt, and performing sequence dancing. Nobody appears to be remotely interested in the music or the artists performing. That's not what country music is about and most of the bands don't like it. It makes country look silly and gives it a bad name.

Bernie Green echoed those sentiments: 'I don't agree with it at all. It's derogatory to the music. The music is not about cowboys. I don't mean to be a killjoy, but I don't like them to be associated with country music.'

Concerns about the mortality of music scenes often provoke an emphasis on their continuity and revival. This seems to be particularly the case with scenes that depend on the performance of a fixed and dated repertoire or on the participation of older musicians and fans – as suggested by fanzines and fan websites related to Britain's Northern Soul scene.[23] In Liverpool, Hank Walters and other country musicians of his generation were certainly anxious about the ageing and shrinking of the local country scene, and they continually expressed to us their fear that the scene would not survive them. 'The scene now in Liverpool has dropped,' said Kenny Johnson, 'There's no new blood.' Walters told us that when he was involved with the North West Country Music Association[24] he had a list of 127 Liverpool country bands, but that now, in the early 1990s, there were 'not more than a couple of dozen if there's that.' Paddy Kelly complained, 'There's not many of us left … As George Jones sang, "Who's going to fill their shoes?" There's no-one to fill our shoes … there's no new bands coming up' (in McManus 1994a: 31–2). Bernie Green painted a similarly gloomy picture: 'The unfortunate thing is that there's not so many young lads coming into it now' (ibid.: 32). Yet despite these rather despondent comments, country music

---

(including videos, computer games and Internet surfing and gambling) and competition from other forms of live music, such as cover and tribute bands.'

23   See, for example, http://www.soulfulkindamusic.net/articlensdead.htm, accessed August 2005.

24   The association is also mentioned at http://www.triumphpc.com/mersey-beat/ archives/cw-breakthrough.shtml, accessed June 2004.

performances were regularly advertised in local gig guides throughout the 1990s, and weekly country nights continued to run in certain local venues.

What distinguished Liverpool's country music scene, perhaps, was the way that its decline was attributed not just to the introduction of new musical trends and developments, and to the ageing of the scene's participants and a decrease in the number of musicians involved, but also to Liverpool's economic decline. In fact, the city's economic problems were sometimes presented to us as the main or only reason for the decline of scene, and they had certainly hit particularly hard the venues, neighbourhoods and communities that had spawned the scene and helped to sustain it. Kenny Johnson told us, 'the man in the street hasn't got the money ... The Liverpool country scene compared to what it used to be is finished. It's dead' (in McManus, 1994a: 32). Similarly, Paddy Kelly remarked, 'Because of the recession there's no money in Liverpool ... The venues are closing down' (p.c.). Hank Walters told us:

> We went along the Dock Road last night, and when you see pubs, real established ale houses, always hives of activity, boarded up and closed up, then that really frightens you ... The scene has altered. The clubs are closing down and if they're not closing down they're putting other things on.

In a song called 'Progress', Walters used his music to challenge the port authorities and their vision for the future of Liverpool and its economy following the introduction of containerization in the mid-1950s, which encouraged the decline of the city's dockland activities and the reduction in the local labour force:

> When I went to the docks there was forty-seven thousand men going through the gates in 1953, and now there's roughly eight hundred men, so it's a bit frightening. And if you get some arsehole saying 'that's progress,' well, progress is a marvellous thing provided that you're not one of its casualties. So this is my observations in the song (p.c.).

Such narratives of decline were, however, accompanied by a struggle for renewal. It was clear from the journeys taken by followers of local country bands to see those bands perform, and from their physical and verbal responses to those performances, that they attended live performance events partly to demonstrate their support for the scene and their desire to help keep it going. Meanwhile the musicians harked back to the scene's golden age (when 'It was a magic scene', as Paddy Kelly put it, p.c.) in order to emphasize the importance of continuity, they also expressed a desire to attract 'new blood' to the scene in the form of younger musicians, one source of which was their own offspring. Walters explained that his desire to ensure the continuity of the scene was what had led to him to establish a band with his three daughters (Hank Walters and the Arcadian Ladies), and a couple of his fellow musicians made similar comments. John Neild's two sons, Paul and Darrren, had joined him in a country band named UK Country, while his nephew, Kevin McGarry, performed with The Hillsiders, and occasionally with UK Country, and had also performed with John in a band called the Tennessee Five.

The involvement of the younger generation was clearly something that older country musicians were proud of and actively encouraged, and it contributed to a strong sense of resilience within the scene: 'If there's any kids coming up we'll give them the push that they need. It'll never die – especially not in Liverpool' (Patsey Foley, p.c.). Local musician Kevin McGarry remarked: 'My greatest admiration is for our John because he's got his lads drumming and singing with him. He's the luckiest one of the whole family. When me, John and George [another uncle who was also a member of a country band] retire his kids will keep the chain going' (in Cohen and McManus 1991: 39). Finnegan (1989: 97) commented on country music in Milton Keynes, 'It was often assumed that teenagers were likely to be attracted to rock for a time, but that the general family commitment to and experience of country and western music would continue' (see also Peterson, 1997: 230). Country music's conventional emphasis on tradition encouraged that drive to preserve and sustain the music for future generations: hence the first Country Music Hall of Fame was founded in North America back in 1961 (Peterson, 1997: 223–4).

In 1998 Hank Walters and the Arcadian Ladies recorded an album entitled *City With a Heart* as part of a 'Regeneration Programme' which aimed to 'prevent the loss of Liverpool's own unique Country Music Culture and Heritage' by producing recordings of local country musicians.[25] The use of the term 'heritage' suggests a desire to legitimize local country music and the people and places that it was perceived as speaking for. The album was launched at Liverpool's Dockers' Club, and it included a couple of Jimmie Rodgers songs and several original songs that Hank and his daughters had written about Liverpool. The CD cover featured a rather poor sketch by one of the musicians featured on the album, in which a figure that is clearly meant to be Hank Walters gazes out over what appears to be a busy dockland scene. The producer of the album was the lively, enthusiastic and highly capable Pauline Walters of the Arcadian Ladies, and she travelled to the international music industry convention MIDEM to promote the album.[26] She presented us with a copy of it and explained it to us in terms of community, heritage and regeneration – terms that also feature in the CD's sleeve notes and promotional literature. Pauline had a background in community work, and the recording was funded by the National Lottery Arts Scheme as the first stage of a 'community project'.[27] One of the seeds for the album was an earlier 'community recording', which aimed to raise funds for the Everton Neighbourhood Council. Pauline's sleeve notes state, 'From there, Hank Walters and his family, who already had a growing concern for the continuity of Liverpool Country Music as a culture, decided to pioneer another community

---

25   www.mbus.com/bands/genadm/Hank.Walters.and.the.Arcadian.Ladies.htm, accessed July 2004.

26   She travelled with a small group of local music-makers, and their trip was partly funded by the Merseyside Music Development Association discussed in Chapter 5.

27   http://artists.iuma.com/IUMA/Bands/Hank_Walters_and_the_Arcadian_Ladies/comments-0.html, accessed July 2004.

recording. This time, as a pilot and foundation for the preservation of existing and future original work being produced' (CD liner notes, *City With a Heart*, 1998).

Pauline's sleeve notes thus describe the album as being about 'working with music as a community for a community'. Elsewhere in those notes, the local music journalist and broadcaster Spencer Leigh emphasizes the close affinity of country music to Liverpool: 'Country music might be mocked in a more sophisticated environment but because of the music's sentiments, because of its strong moral values, because of its pictures of working-class life, and because of its sheer bloody pubsingalongability, country music has a strong hold on the City with a Heart.' The album is dedicated by Pauline 'to the People of Liverpool, who we love, honour and respect.' Likewise, an autobiographical account of Hank Walters and the Arcadian Ladies featured on one website states that many of their songs 'depict their love for the City of Liverpool and paint a picture of a strong and caring community.'[28]–Notions of 'community', 'regeneration' and 'heritage' were thus connected through the album initiative, applied to local country music and extended to apply to the city as a whole.

Music and Alterity at the Heart of the City

Within Liverpool's country music scene there was thus a dual emphasis on, and tension between, two different perpectives on the country scene. They involved perceptions of that scene as marginal and in decline, but also a contrasting and parallel stress on renewal and on a sense of pride in local country, as illustrated by the celebration of country as the city's heritage and heart. There was also the tension between the cosmopolitan and the local that I highlighted earlier. I have so far explained these tensions largely in terms of the social and ideological conventions that distinguished country as a genre, including the conventional, ideological emphasis on community and home, tradition and continuity. In this final section of the chapter, I want to reflect upon the case of country music-making in Liverpool and the tensions that characterized it, and consider what it suggests about the two key themes of this book: how was the country scene affected by circumstances specific to Liverpool and by local social and economic change? In turn, how did country music and its specific genre conventions contribute to the production of local difference?

Music and Liverpool Identity

In Chapter 1 I explained how Liverpool's role as a port enabled the city to capitalize upon and pioneer the development of world trade and a newly emerging global economy, and to become a migrant city and cosmopolis. By contrast, Chapter 2 discussed the Liverpool of the 1980s and early 1990s and stereotypical references to the city as insular. This chapter, however, has suggested that during those same two decades cosmopolitanism and insularity coexisted, sometimes in a state of

---

28   http://stage.vitaminic.co.uk/main/walters/biography, accessed July 2004.

tension within the city, and it illustrated how that tension was mediated by country music and by the local country scene. The scene was produced through transnational routes and networks involving the movement of migrants, sailors, musicians and servicemen, and it was also produced through the mass mediation of country music sounds, images and ideologies that were globally disseminated following the growth of multinational capital and technology and the expansion of the world market for popular music products. Moreover, a core group of musicians involved with the scene emphasized the cosmopolitanism of country music and of Liverpool when explaining how the two became connected. At the same time, however, those musicians categorized, claimed and promoted country music as a Liverpool scene and sound and as Liverpool heritage. They thus connected their music to an 'elsewhere' but also to a 'here' – associating it with particular local groups and neighbourhoods. Country music offered them a sense of community, solidarity and continuity, and it encouraged fierce and proud attachments to the city and its dockside neighbourhoods and to the local past.

Country music also played a part in constructions of Liverpool as different; hence the patriotic claims within the local country scene on Liverpool as the original site of British country music. Yet the city's country scene was not unique in this respect, as illustrated in the previous chapter on the local rock scene. Moreover, others have likewise argued that Liverpool embraced American popular music earlier and more eagerly than other British cities. Shaw (1971: 85), for example, suggests that the first jazz heard in England came from the Dixielanders in Liverpool, and that 'no place in the UK welcomed ... ragtime as the Liverpudlian did'. Brocken (1996: 14) analyses the American popular songs that were covered by the Beatles early on in their career, and suggests that the Beatles were uninterested in contemporary British rock 'n' roll performers and developed instead a taste for comparatively obscure r'n'b and Motown music – a taste that was, he suggests, unique within a British context.[29] Du Noyer (2002: 62) claims that during the early 1960s the number of beat groups in Liverpool exceeded that in any other city, including London (whilst at the same time acknowledging that no one knows what the number actually was). Some have also proclaimed Liverpool to be uniquely musical. According to Du Noyer (2002), for example, 'Liverpool is a reason why music happens' (1); 'Creative individuals don't trickle out from Liverpool's edges: they explode from its very core' (3); 'Music, as we've said, is the heart of Liverpool' (10); 'Liverpool made more music than most cities, and made it more passionately, because it was in the personality of Liverpool to do so' (58). For Shaw (1971: 63), 'Unless you realise that we are all minstrel boys, or girls, in the "Pool" you cannot understand us ... To the world the Beatles may

---

29   Brocken argues that Liverpool's marginal position within the UK helped to explain the Beatles' attraction to 'the otherness' and 'the underground' that r'n'b represented, and that the Beatles appropriated and rearticulated these songs in order to draw attention to their own economically, politically and culturally 'marginal existence on the cultural outskirts of the British consciousness' (ibid.: 56).

have seemed a unique phenomenon. Not to us … We are all singers in Liverpool. Even if we can't sing.'

These comments suggest that country music contributed to a broader emphasis on local difference in Liverpool and Merseyside, a sense of difference from other cities and regions that has been the subject of much discussion and debate and has been described as 'swaggering, aggressive, and defiant' (Taylor, 1988: vii). But why did that emphasis on local difference appear to be so strong and what had encouraged it? Belchem (2000) argues that a sense of 'apartness' or 'otherness' has been crucial to Liverpool's identity, and that the city has always been exceptional within a British and English context: 'In the north of England but not of it, Liverpool (and its "sub-region" of Merseyside) was (and has continued to be) highly distinctive, differing sharply in socio-economic structure, cultural image and expression, political affiliation, health, diet and speech from the adjacent industrial districts' (ibid.: xi–xii). In terms of party politics, for example, Liverpool has always differed from that of other industrial cities in northern England (Belchem, 2000). Thus the Militants took over Liverpool City Council during a period of national Conservative rule, whilst during the 1960s and 1970s, and a period of national Labour government, the city council was Liberal. Before that the Conservatives were in power – partly because the city's Catholics voted Irish National Party (INP) whilst the Protestants voted Orange Lodge or Conservative, and partly because the politics of the Labour Party did not suit terribly well the political needs and aspirations of a city that was based on trade, entrepreneurialism and casualism and that lacked a stable workforce.

Irish migration also helped to make Liverpool 'the least "English" of the great Victorian provincial cities', and 'the victim of a long-standing English prejudice towards the Irish (Belchem, 2000: xiv; Nightingale, 1980: 75–6). Rogan Taylor, a football studies scholar at Liverpool University, has provided an example of that prejudice. He has pointed to similarities between the negative, post-Hillsborough reporting on Liverpool mentioned in the previous chapter, and the anti-Irish sentiments of leading articles about Liverpool in Britain's national newspapers of 1847 following the mass migration from Ireland to Liverpool.[30] Liverpool's sense of difference was further enhanced by the way the city 'defined itself against industrial Manchester and in rivalry with commercial London' during its Victorian heyday (Belchem, 2000: 38). Historical tensions existed between the mercantilist interests of Liverpool and the manufacturing interests of Manchester, tensions that were expressed in associated social distinctions and in the differing stances taken by the two cities towards slavery – the port clinging to the trade and the manufacturing city opposing it (Meegan, 1995: 69–71). Meanwhile, as Britain's second city, Liverpool resented London's 'monopolistic privileges and practices' (Belchem, 2000: 47) and sought during the nineteenth century to rival London in its commercial infrastructure, and to establish itself as a 'self-dependent financial centre' (ibid.: 37).

---

30   He was speaking on 11 August 2003, at a seminar held in Liverpool's Racquet Club Hotel and organized by the Liverpool Biennial.

Meegan (1995: 48) refers to Londoners' perception of Liverpool as provincial and uncultured, and to a quotation attributed to John Lennon (ibid.: 82):

> The north is where the money was made in the 1800s; that was where all the brass and the heavy people were, and that's where the despised people were. We were the ones who were looked down upon as animals by the southerners, the Londoners. In the States, the Northerners think that down south, people are pigs, and the people in New York think West Coast is hick. So we were Hicksville.

According to one Liverpool historian, 'This standing-up for our city, wherever we may be, tends, I fear, to make us disliked ... "Coming from Liverpool", said actor Norman Rossington, "is like belonging to a worldwide club, an exclusive clan"' (Shaw, 1971: 19). These quotations hint at a defensive Liverpool but also at northern pride and truculence:

> A northern upbringing frequently involves the inculcation of an unusually powerful set of attachments to place; a deep rooting in a particular physical, social and cultural environment. At the same time, however, those loyalties are strongly inflected, almost from the outset, by awareness of a questionable place within the larger social and political geography of England (Wrightson, 1995: 29, cited in Bailey, Miles and Stark, 2004: 62).

Music, Local Identity and Social and Economic Change

Collective identities are commonly reasserted and their symbolic boundaries reinforced in the face of threats of various kinds. The patriotic promotion of country music as Liverpool heritage helped to authenticate the local country scene and situate it at the heart of Liverpool culture and identity, offering scene participants a sense of cultural ownership, status and continuity. On the other hand, however, country music was constructed as Liverpool heritage because the scene was perceived by its participants to have been overshadowed and left behind, and to be shrinking and dying. It is perhaps unsurprising that claims upon country music as local culture, and the construction of local difference through country music, seemed to be particularly strong within the Liverpool of the 1980s and 1990s. Country music became a resource for the construction of local identity and difference at a time when Liverpool was becoming increasingly marginalized within a global and national context, and demonized in the British press. The tension within the local country scene between vulnerability and pride thus pointed to the symbiosis of culture and economy that was highlighted in the previous chapter,[31] as did the related tension between decline and renewal.

During the 1980s and 1990s de-industrialization encouraged narratives of decline within popular music culture in Liverpool, as illustrated by the fears of country musicians about the demise of the local country scene. It also encouraged an emphasis on regeneration, although Liverpool regeneration programmes had

---

31   See also Belchem (2000, Chapter 2) on the Scouse dialect.

already been under way since 1936 (Meegan, 2003: 56). Throughout the 1980s and 1990s the city experienced a particularly intense climate of regeneration involving local, regional, national and European agencies operating across public, private and voluntary sectors. Later chapters will illustrate how by the end of the millennium city officials had turned to culture and to cultural heritage as a focus for regeneration, yet the local country music scene remained largely invisible in relation to local regeneration initiatives. As a music of lament, loss and disempowerment, country appeared to speak to another more marginal and outdated Liverpool that was not that compatible with official city marketing and re-imaging strategies (see Chapter 7).[32] As indicated above, however, Hank Walters nevertheless presented through his music a critique of certain contemporary developments, and the *City With A Heart* album provided an alternative contribution to and perspective on the regeneration process. Whilst regeneration initiatives have led to huge improvements in Liverpool there remain large pockets of poverty, and by the end of the 1990s two areas of North Liverpool were officially categorized as the most deprived in the whole of Europe.

Country Music and the Production of Local Difference

Liverpool's country music scene was thus influenced by a long-standing emphasis on the city as different, and by specific social and economic changes within the city. How, then, did the specificity of country music as a genre, and as popular music, contribute to the production of local difference?

For the country musicians we met, country music was a mobile, cosmopolitan culture and a symbol of the city's transatlantic connections, and of cultural mixing, exchange and hybridity. When they explained their music to us they emphasized the sailors and migrant communities that had developed and shaped it, and the 'ordinary' working-class people that the music spoke to and for. The music thus helped to create a sense of solidarity and shared experiences, or 'families of resemblence' (Lipsitz, 1990: 136), and the musicians continually engaged with traditions and cultures from the past, including the local past. Following the dialogical approach of Lipsitz (ibid.: 159), the music could thus be described as a vibrant repository of collective memory inscribed with the buried narratives of the social groups that had created it. Elsewhere (Cohen, 1998) I have likewise discussed music's effectiveness in stimulating a sense of identity and preserving and transmitting cultural memory, pointing to the way that individuals and groups can use music as a cultural 'map of meaning', and draw upon it to locate 'themselves in different imaginary geographies at one and the same time' (as Hall has written of 'diaspora' – 1995: 207).

Country music was also closely connected to city neighbourhoods that had experienced so strongly the disruptions and uncertainties of migration, the comings and goings of local seafarers, the uncertainties of the dockside labour market, the

---

32   Robins (1991: 39) makes a similar point about the 'Andy Capp' image of other northern industrial cities in Britain – that is, as portrayed in the eponymous cartoon-strip in the *Daily* and *Sunday Mirror*.

upheavals caused by slum clearance and 1960s modernization, and the ravages of economic crisis. Such social and economic changes informed the claiming of country as Liverpool heritage, thus illustrating the description of popular music by Connell and Gibson (2003: 9) as: 'simultaneously a commodity and cultural expression. It is also quite uniquely both the most fluid of cultural forms (quite literally, as sound waves moving through air) and a vibrant expression of cultures and traditions, at times held onto vehemently in the face of change.' The previous chapter likewise situated the appropriation of rock as a 'Liverpool Sound' within a context of social and economic change. Within specific circumstances during the 1980s and 1990s, country and rock music had become a lament for the city, and both were haunted by the local past whilst speaking to present conditions. Yet the musical production of local difference is influenced by genre. Roger Hill described Liverpool rock music from a rather detached position of music critic and commentator, and as an observer of Liverpool rock culture. He described its 'riverine' tendency as the dreamy, reflective sound of Liverpool's grief and 'soul', and in terms of loss and abandonment; and his notion of the Liverpool Sound was shaped by the social and ideological conventions that distinguish rock as a genre. In this chapter, however, Hank Walters and his fellow country musicians defined country as Liverpool heritage in an effort to claim and promote it as their own and present it as the gritty, resilient and proud heart of the city. That production of country as Liverpool heritage was informed by social and ideological conventions that are specific to country music, including country's emphasis on tradition and community, nostalgia and home.

Conclusion

This chapter focused on country music in order to examine how a global popular music genre was claimed as the heritage of one particular city. The chapter considered the meaning of music heritage for country musicians in Liverpool, and the activities and circumstances through which that heritage was constructed. In doing so it highlighted the impact of social and economic change within the city on the local country music scene and, in turn, how the specificity of country as a scene or genre, and as popular music, contributed to claims upon the music as local, city culture, and to the production of local difference. Whilst country music emerged as a Liverpool scene through the global expansion of world trade and music and media industries, Liverpool's economic problems encouraged claims upon country as Liverpool heritage. Those problems affected particularly severely the groups and neighbourhoods most closely connected with the country music scene, and that combination of genre and locality produced tensions within the scene between decline and renewal; between the cosmopolitan outlook, influences and origins of the scene, and more insular notions of both scene and city; and between a sense of marginality and expressions of musical pride.

Chapter 4

Music as a City Business: Trial, Tribulation and Place in a Labour of Love

The Head of Communications at Cream, a contemporary dance 'superclub', is angry. We are sitting in a seminar room that has been hired for a consultation exercise organized by a partnership of public and private sector organizations.[1] The partnership has been given the go-ahead to redevelop a large area of Liverpool city centre, an area in which Cream is located. The consultation exercise is aimed at businesspeople, residents, community groups and public sector agencies that have a stake in the area, and we have been split up into seminar groups involving around 30–40 people. Three delegates have turned up to represent Cream. They include Cream's Head of Communications, who has a long and distinguished history of involvement with local music and performing arts that suggests tireless enthusiasm and creative energy. She is also known for her unique and individual style – a style that has undergone continual transformation and reinvention. Ten years previously, when I had first met her, she was closely associated with the city's post-punk scene and her head was shaved and her make-up dramatic. Today she looks smart and chic in a pinstriped suit and with a sleek and shiny red hairdo. Cream has achieved considerable commercial success with its 'superclub' and now, she complains, 'everybody asks, "what has Cream done for the community?" – but we *are* the community!' She launches into a long and impassioned speech in which she emphasizes what Cream has contributed to Liverpool, although she is also keen to emphasize that Cream 'is not a Liverpool club. Cream has never said it was a Liverpool club.' One of Cream's directors suggests otherwise, however, by stating 'we're a Liverpool organisation and we always will be' (quoted in Du Noyer, 2002: 195).

This chapter continues to examine the relationship between music and the city by focusing on the business of music in Liverpool. How did the local social and economic changes described in the previous chapter affect that business, and in turn

---

1   The seminar took place in the summer of 1997, and Abigail Gilmore and I participated in it as part of our research for a two-year study, 'Music Policy, the Music Industry and Local Economic Development'. This chapter draws upon case material gathered during that project, which ran from 1996 to 1998, but supplements it with interview and research data from other projects that I was involved with during the 1980s and 1990s (the projects are described in the Appendix and include a survey of music businesses on Merseyside conducted in 1989).

how did the specificity of music as a commodity, business and industry contribute to the production of the city? In order to address those questions the chapter draws upon illustrative case material on the production of rock and contemporary dance music. It begins by introducing two specific companies, one of which is Cream; it then positions those companies in relation to commercial music production in Liverpool and Merseyside, and global and genre-based business networks. The second part of the chapter draws upon that discussion to consider what it has suggested about the impact of locality and social and economic change upon music business activities, networks and discourses, and about how the local, urban setting of the music businesses mattered to the people involved.

The Business of Music in Liverpool

Two Liverpool-based Music Companies

Liverpool Music House (LMH) was a music production and management company. The company was housed during the 1990s in a large, red-brick building that had once been a laboratory, and was therefore referred to by those involved with it as 'The Lab'. The building was situated in a narrow, deserted backstreet in a quiet part of Liverpool city centre between the financial district and the northern docklands. It was flanked by a dark, gloomy old church and ghostly Victorian warehouses that were clad in rusted cast-iron fittings, and topped by spiky foliage that sprouted through broken roof slates. Directly opposite The Lab, behind the jagged segments of a broken brick wall, were the crumbled ruins of a deserted block of council flats. Yet behind The Lab's heavy wooden door there was always a hive of activity. In the large hallway music and recording equipment was usually piled up ready to be loaded onto a van or carried upstairs, and in the kitchen musicians and engineers would be chatting and making tea and toast. Sometimes LMH staff would be in the studio recording their own material and that of the artists they worked with, but usually the studio had been rented by another group of musicians and Carl from LMH would often act as engineer. Sometimes he was there all night and I would occasionally look in on him through the window in the door and see him sitting patiently at the mixing desk, listening carefully to the harsh and repetitive beat of a snare drum, and making slight adjustments to the settings on the desk in order to alter the quality and tone of the sound. In front of him, behind a large pane of glass, the drummer would slouch over his kit as he hit the snare whilst his fellow band members lounged around the desk looking tired and bored. The length of the time the recording session had already taken could be measured by the number and distribution of cigarette ends, sweet wrappers and empty plastic cups from the tea and coffee machine downstairs.

The directors of LMH, Colin and Gary, also worked long hours and late into the night, taking care of the building and business administration, or working on pre-programming and post-production. Frequently they were called back in the early hours of the morning to deal with a security scare – a faulty alarm or a rock band whose members had accidentally locked themselves out of the building. Both of them came from white, working-class Liverpool families, and both had worked in the past as professional, waged musicians and for various community music initiatives. When they first met in 1983 they were in their late twenties and had begun to dream of establishing their own business that would nurture and manage a group of songwriters and musicians and, with the help of their own in-house studio production facilities, help those artists to achieve creative and commercial success.[2] The following year they established Liverpool Music House (LMH) in a rented studio in an old city-centre building. The term 'house' suited the cosy, informal atmosphere they wanted to foster in the belief that it would facilitate collaboration and encourage innovation. They envisaged their business as a creative hothouse inspired by New York's Brill Building, where the songwriters of Tin Pan Alley had been based, and by PWL, a British company known for its stable of commercially successful pop songs and artists. Carl had been helping out the previous owners of the studio they rented and he joined Gary and Colin in their new venture. He was then only 14 years old but, like his older brother Darren, he had already been performing with rock bands for a few years.

Eventually, LMH was able to lease more spacious accommodation in The Lab. The building was knee-deep with industrial and chemical waste, so with the help of friends they completely gutted and renovated it before bringing in a studio designer; but the building and the studio required constant and ongoing attention and upgrading. The LMH offices were on the first floor, whilst the company's recording studio and 'live rooms' were at the top of the building. Other music businesses rented out space elsewhere in the building, including a company that specialized in the hire, sale and repair of audio-recording equipment, and a management company that looked after Space, a local band that had done well in the British rock/pop charts. For a while the producer Ian Broudie also had an office and studio in the building. By the time they moved into The Lab, Colin and Gary had gathered together a diverse and shifting group of artists that included pop singer-songwriters and 'indie' rock bands (including Carl's own band). They worked with those artists on the composition, rehearsal, recording and live public performance of original material, and on the development of their image. At the same time Colin and Gary also produced their own compositions to market to established artists and agents, publishers and media organizations. They supplied music for jingles to a couple of radio stations, for example, and were commissioned to compose and produce original music for a low-budget film. In addition, the LMH recording studio was regularly leased out on a commercial basis to local and visiting artists, radio stations and major record

---

2   I first met Colin and Gary in 1985 when conducting fieldwork in Liverpool for my PhD thesis. Eventually, Colin and I became personally involved, a relationship that has since continued. Colin and Gary were interviewed by my co-researchers for some of the projects described in the Appendix. This chapter draws upon those interviews but I have chosen LMH as a case study partly so that I can also make use of my own first-hand experience of the company.

companies. LMH also used the studio to run training sessions in sound recording and the music business for local community and educational organizations.

On the other side of Liverpool city centre, past the grand buildings that had once housed the offices of shipping and marine insurance companies and the cotton, fruit and corn exchanges, and past the city's central shopping district, was Cream, a company run by Gary's cousin James Barton. James established Cream in 1992 with his friend Darren. Both had been heavily involved with an electronically generated style of contemporary dance music played by 'artist-DJs' in clubs during the late 1980s and 1990s, which was sometimes referred to as acid house or rave culture.[3] Darren frequented dance clubs in Britain and America, while James ran his own club nights in various Liverpool venues. Together they started Cream as a new weekly club that initially attracted a few hundred customers. The club became connected to a nationwide moral panic that focused on contemporary dance culture largely because of its associations with youth and drug-taking, and because of the illegality of early rave events.[4] In spite of (and perhaps largely because of) this panic the club became increasingly popular, so much so that it eventually moved to Nation, a dome-shaped, 3000-capacity warehouse situated on the corner of Concert Square. On a Friday or Saturday night the square would be packed with young people, whilst crowds of lively revellers dressed for a night out would meander around it on their way to and from brightly lit bars, pubs and clubs. Bouncers dressed in uniform black jackets and trousers guarded the doorways of those venues, and police cars and vans patrolled by. At the height of Cream's popularity a queue of people would snake along the entire length of Nation and into the square, and the walls would throb from the rhythmic pulse of the music pounding inside.

The Breadth and Diversity of Local, Commercial Music-Making

How did LMH and Cream compare with other music businesses in Liverpool and Merseyside? Most of those businesses were also concentrated in Liverpool city centre, and most were small[5] and did not generate a significant profit or actively export their products overseas.[6] Cream was exceptional in this respect. The company

---

3   The music originated from black Detroit and Chicago house musicians who were influenced by disco, funk and German electro-pop (Laing, 1997: 129), and it soon developed into a complex variety of sub-genres.

4   See Thornton (1995) on club culture and moral panic.

5   Over 27 per cent had no full-time employees and many were run on a sole-trader basis (Music City report, 1991, Liverpool: Ark Consultants).

6   A 1992 report calculated the total turnover of Merseyside's music businesses as £9,267,525, the number of people working in them as 609, the number of businesses as 133 (with only two employing over ten people) and the average annual salary as £11,504 (Merseyside Training and Enterprise Council). In 1999 an economic profile of music on Merseyside stated that the value of the music industry to the region was almost £1.9 million, and the industry produced an aggregate turnover of £45.8 million, £6.5 million of which originated from the live performance sector ('The Hidden Economy: An Economic Profile of

achieved an unusual degree of commercial success, and the only Liverpool-based music organization with a larger number of employees was the Royal Liverpool Philharmonic Society. Most businesses, including Cream and LMH, were also run by relatively young white men who were not formally trained in business and were not represented by unions or other official organizations. Employment within local music businesses tended to be sporadic, voluntary and unpaid, and jobs were created rather than applied for. In order to run their businesses most local companies had to target or buy in services located outside the city and region.[7] What Liverpool lacked was businesses specializing in music publishing, distribution and manufacture and in the provision of specialist financial and legal advice. During the 1990s this was typical of provincial British cities because in Britain, as indicated in Chapter 2, most major music companies were concentrated in London, including recording and publishing companies, unions, representative bodies and rights-collecting agencies. Pressing facilities and equipment manufacturers were also located outside of Liverpool and Merseyside.

The local business of music was nevertheless a broad and diverse field of activity. Like LMH there were companies that specialized in artist management and promotion, the composition and recording of musical works and the post-production, promotion and marketing of music recordings. Like Cream, there were companies that specialized in club culture and the public performance of recorded music. There were also companies that provided space and equipment for music rehearsal and organized live music performance, and those that specialized in the retail of music instruments and recordings. Many of those involved with the running of these businesses were or had been musicians, even in cases where the business was not directly involved with the creative aspects of music-making; or they managed and promoted musicians in addition to running their business. Meanwhile, various support services for musicians and music businesses were supplied by local commercial and non-commercial organizations, particularly in the areas of music information, training and education. This diversity of businesses involved with music has led some commentators to refer to music industries in the plural, distinguishing, for example, industries based around recording, live performance and the production of specific music genres.[8]

Yet distinctions between and within such industries tended to be blurred. LMH was a rock/pop management and production company whilst Cream was generally perceived as a dance club, but the activities of both nevertheless cut across industry sectors. This can be illustrated with the case of Cream, which diversified rapidly

---

the music sector on Merseyside in 1999', produced by the Merseyside Music Development Agency).

7   Almost 25 per cent of businesses surveyed spent nothing on local goods and services (Music City, 1991).

8   Although many music-makers and scholars misleadingly refer to 'the music industry', when what they are really discussing is the recording industry (Shank, 1994: 204; Williamson and Cloonan, 2004).

following its initial focus on the club. Since young people were flocking to the club, the company established a membership scheme and a national network of individual members who were paid on commission to arrange for coachloads of dance fans from their local area to visit the club. A senior manager at Cream told us, 'I think this week there is probably about 1200 people coming on coaches on Friday night and 1600 on Saturday night … but then there'll be a lot of people who will travel in cars.' Some have thus suggested that Cream became the first Liverpool club to attract a 'travelling audience', likening it to Britain's 'all-night' Northern Soul events that dancers travel some distance to attend (Du Noyer, 2002: 202). A Cream 'feeder bar' was set up that Cream customers could visit en route to the club, and a Cream shop where they could purchase clothing and accessories that signalled their affiliation to the club (Cream merchandise could also be ordered from a mail order company). During nights of the week when the club was not so busy, Cream rented out space within Nation to other organizations that staged a variety of music events there, including salsa nights and rock gigs. Meanwhile regular Cream nights were held in clubs across the UK and overseas. These included, most famously, club nights on the island of Ibiza, but also those in Ireland, Latin America, North America, the Far East and mainland Europe. Cream fans were encouraged to travel to such events, thus helping to promote Cream as a significant player within contemporary dance tourism.[9]

At the same time, by releasing compilation CDs of music played at these Cream events and distributing them through licensing deals with major record labels and retail chains, the company was also able to target audiences that were too young to attend the clubs. DJs helped to promote those recordings and related Cream merchandise in the clubs in which they performed. However as club culture became popular with wider audiences Cream had to bid against other clubs to keep the best-known DJs, and the company was subsequently accused by the music press of spearheading a cult of notoriously high-paid 'star' DJs. Cream therefore established its own resident DJs and a DJ agency, which by 1997 represented and promoted around 26 top British and North American DJs, including Pete Tong, Seb Fontaine, Judge Jules, Danny Rampling and Paul Oakenfold. This increased Cream's status within contemporary dance and club culture since major British clubs had to book those DJs through the company. In 1996 Cream launched Creamfields, an outdoor dance festival that was run on an annual basis in Liverpool, where it attracted 50,000 participants, but was also staged in other cities and countries along with one-off Cream events. Cream was booked, for example, for the China/Hong Kong handover party, and on New Year's Eve, 1998, 'Cream' events were held simultaneously in London, Newcastle, Manchester and Liverpool, catering for thousands of dance fans. Reports in the national music press dwelt upon the fact that Cream DJs were flown from city to city in a specially chartered plane. At the turn of the millennium Cream began to develop interests in television, radio and record production, establishing a youth-oriented radio station

---

9   See Connell and Gibson (2003, Chapter 10) for a discussion on this kind of tourism.

in partnership with Absolute Radio UK, and a television production company that broadcast Creamfield shows and a television series based on the company's activities in Ibiza. The company also launched the first of a new chain of bars, named BabyCream.

The activities of Cream and LMH thus bridged different sectors of the music industry, and they also crossed over into industries that were closely or only loosely related to music, including mass-media industries (hence the synergies with film, TV, radio and internet) and industries based upon design, fashion and beverages. This integration was by no means unusual. The UK recording industry emerged from the Anglo-American electrical goods, hardware and publishing industries during the late nineteenth century, whilst the 1990s saw high-profile mergers between music, telecommunications and IT industries. Liverpool-based music companies also operated across commercial, public and voluntary sectors. The training schemes of LMH were funded by the European Union, for example, whilst the Merseyside Trade Union Community and Unemployed Resource Centre was a subsidized organization that offered advice, training and facilities for unemployed musicians, but also ran a music venue called the Picket on a partly commercial basis (see Chapter 7). In addition, many companies were involved with various music genres. The LMH studio, for example, was hired by music-makers involved with country and classical music as well as rock and pop, and Cream promoted both rock and dance music through its club, festivals and radio station. One of the main aims of the Creamfields festival, according to one Cream director, was to 'bridge the gap' between dance and rock music: 'it will start off as a dance festival and bring the Liverpool bands old school side into it. And if that works I think that will be a great fusion' (p.c.).

Commercial Ambition and Global Production and Distribution Networks

I have described the breadth, diversity and complexity of the music business in Liverpool, and I now want to consider how those involved went about promoting their products. First, however, it is important to emphasize that a vast amount of local music-making was not aimed at the commercial marketplace. Colin and Gary, for example, produced recordings that had little to do with LMH and were largely for their own enjoyment and artistic development. Others were involved with music as a business, yet making a profit was not one of their primary concerns. They included independent, 'micro' record labels that specialized in alternative rock and were usually operated from private homes by sole traders who worked full-time in professional jobs unrelated to music (Strachan, 2003). The performance of cabaret music, involving cover versions of well-known songs, also generated a substantial amount of revenue and provided a source of income for musicians, many of whom were not (or no longer) that bothered about releasing records or even about making a career in music.

At the same time, however, much popular music-making in Liverpool involved, as Toynbee puts it (2000: 29), 'an extraordinary anticipation of commerce' and a quest for seemingly elusive 'jack-pot' success. In order to promote their products, those with commercial ambitions tried to tap into national and transnational production and distribution networks, including genre-specific networks. The director of a contemporary dance label in Liverpool explained to us:

> the Indie rock approach has always been London based ... all the deals come from London. All the A&R men get on the train to come up and see the latest indie band and then get off again ... Cast are a good example because they're here and they're now. It won't be long before they get off towards the South ... their managers have already spoken about getting London offices because there's no real need for them to stay here ... if they want work towards worldwide success they're going to have to go to where it is for them, and that's the South for every level.

One manager told us that all of the rock musicians he looked after were Liverpool-based, whilst their record companies, publishers and press offices were all in London. A London-based artists and repertoire (A&R) manager described to us the 'insularity' of the London-based industry and thus the importance of having a London base. Similarly, a Manchester-based music-maker stated, 'the location of all the major record labels, music publishers, magazines and media in London creates something of a glass ceiling: "In the end you're going to be shagged if you're not in London"' (quoted in Haslam, 2000: 268).

This movement of local music-makers to London was commonplace and was highlighted in Chapter 2. London was part of what has been referred to as an interlinked network of 'hub' cities that also included New York, Tokyo and Los Angeles: cities that occupied a central position within global networks of finance and capital, trade and distribution, media, communications and information (Sassen, 1991). Located within those cities were the headquarters of multinational record companies that were part of an oligopoly of multinational conglomerations. During the 1980s and 1990s those conglomerations came to represent, through a process of government deregulation and business integration, synergy and convergence, a global media and 'information' economy and telecommunications-computer infrastructure. The global recording industry became concentrated in the hands of just five (now four) such conglomerates, which were able to distribute standardized products over expanding geographical markets. The directors of LMH were therefore concerned to present their artists and songs to affiliated London-based record and publishing companies that would be in a position to offer substantial financial investment, and the resources to market and distribute those products nationally and internationally. They were thus dependent upon, and in constant contact with, the A&R divisions of those companies, because that was the division responsible for identifying and signing new talent. Occasionally they organized special 'showcase' performances of LMH artists in venues thought to be more convenient for the companies to visit, including those in London.

LMH did secure a major publishing deal for Carl, but many of their artists and engineers eventually left the company and moved south to further their careers. They included two producers and songwriters who arrived at LMH in their teens and later worked in London with well-known pop acts such as S Club 7; two songwriters who left LMH in order to take up a deal with Sony and had short-lived success with the band Halo James; and a sound engineer who moved from LMH to work with Radiohead and David Bowie, and produced an album by Busted. Ian Broudie, who was not part of LMH but achieved considerable success with his band whilst based in The Lab, also eventually moved to London. Carl stayed with LMH and continued with his band, eventually signing a record deal with Peter Gabriel's Real World label. Nevertheless, there were many musicians and managers who bypassed London and promoted themselves directly to major companies located elsewhere. They included composers at Parr Street Studios – who produced music for the moving image and were responsible for the soundtracks of some major Hollywood films – and a rock band managed by LMH and promoted to record companies in New York and Los Angeles. The band was eventually enticed away from LMH by one of the producers brought in to work with them and they relocated to America; but they returned to work with Colin and Gary several years later.

The trend towards concentration and centralization within the global recording industry had been accompanied by a parallel trend towards decentralization, dispersal and diversification, a trend that some have described as 'post-Fordist'.[10] (Others have described music as *the* 'post-Fordist' industry because it is so flexible, specialized, design intensive and knowledge-based, and have argued that it thus provides a template for post-Fordist economies (Lash and Urry, 1994: 123).) During the 1970s the increasing availability and lower cost of music technologies enabled the emergence of music industries in some of the world's smaller countries, and the geographical dissemination of local music styles (Wallis and Malm, 1984). It also enabled British musicians of the 1980s and 1990s to record and produce music themselves in their own homes, a trend boosted by the development of new information and communication technologies. This encouraged the emergence of independent production and distribution networks operating on a local, national or transnational basis. As Connell and Gibson point out (2003: 256), 'Media and technology giants like TimeWarner and Sony aim to wield global power, yet the dynamics of south and south-east Asian cassette cultures, or even the Christian and New Age music industries … demonstrate that their influence is not universal.'

Similarly, Hesmondhalgh (1998: 234) describes the UK dance music industry as 'relatively decentralised' and 'made up of large numbers of "independent" companies'. During the late 1980s small, specialist and independent dance labels proliferated across Merseyside, assisted by the widespread availability of new digital technology and relatively low costs of promotion. Those labels composed music digitally, mastered from digital audiotape (DAT), pressed vinyl in relatively small numbers, and tapped into regional networks of specialist DJs, clubs, radio

---

10   Negus (1992); Abercrombie, Lash, Lury and Shapiro (1992); and Hesmondhalgh (2002) suggest various ways in which the music industry has been transforming along 'post-Fordist lines', including the changing organizational structure of major music companies and the way that they have increasingly sub-divided and sub-contracted to small and medium-sized firms, whilst maintaining centralization in terms of administration and promotion.

stations, magazines, record retailers, pluggers and distributors. Their records usually had a shelf life of only a few weeks, and prestigious for a while were so-called 'white label' records that did not feature the name of the artists involved: 'this lack of a star system meant that small record companies did not have to spend time and money building up a profile for a new artists. There was no need, for example, for the promotional videos and live concert tours which rock and pop artists need to break through into a wider market' (ibid.: 240). Other music-makers in Liverpool also relied upon relatively cheap and independent means of production and distribution. As discussed in Chapter 3, for example, many country musicians promoted their music through recordings they had produced themselves, as did many rock musicians. In terms of retail and live performance there were local record shops and venues that also operated on an independent basis, in addition to those connected to major, London-based chains.

The Struggle for Commercial Success

As well as finding ways of tapping into or forging networks of music production and distribution, local companies specializing in the production of rock and contemporary dance music had to cope with the challenges posed by a market that was notoriously unstable and unpredictable, and that was driven, perhaps more than other industries, by a quest for novelty in terms of its final products (Scott, 2000: 36). Commercial music-making was thus characterized by struggle, and by risks and costs that often heightened competitiveness and divisions amongst local music-makers (Toynbee, 2000: 17). I now want to illustrate that struggle with reference to the case of Cream and LMH.

In order to spread the risk of commercial failure across a large range of products, the recording industry was characterized by consistent overproduction in relation to consumer demand (Toynbee, ibid.: 16). Jones (1998) thus describes it as an industry based on the production of failure. Even businesses that fiercely desired to maintain their independent status often ended up forging deals with major music companies, either because they wanted to reach wider audiences, or because they could no longer survive without such investment. So, despite the proliferation of decentralized, independent music companies, in order to achieve sustained commercial success local businesses had to forge relations with major companies and distinguish their products by investing in branding. Dance producers, for example, had to cross over into more commercial markets in order to achieve substantial sales, sustained success and greater economic capital, even though in doing so they risked a loss of cultural capital leading to a decrease in long-term sales (Hesmondhalgh, 1998: 240, 241). Those crossovers were achieved through partnership agreements with larger companies (ibid.: 244), including licensing, distribution, ownership and financial deals, and they were accompanied by strategies designed to maintain 'credibility' and 'underground' as opposed to 'mainstream' status (Thornton, 1995).

3Beat Records was a Liverpool-based dance label, record shop and mail order company that had chart success during the 1990s with acts such as K-Klass and

Oceanic. The company was established by university graduates, who started it off by selling their record collections in Quiggins, a downmarket, youth-oriented flea market in Liverpool city centre. They began to release their own white label dance records and eventually forged deals with major record companies and released more commercial and mainstream material. One of the company's directors told us

> We fucking hate this kind of poppy dance crap, but it sells and it's a fact of life. If we can sell a few million copies of these types of records, and get our own shit together, we can put a studio together and do the kind of stuff we're into. And that kind of stuff needs money spent behind it in getting it perfect and then actually selling it to people.

By 1997 3Beat generated a turnover of around half a million pounds and employed seven full-time staff. However, as one of the directors explained to us, a large percentage of the company's profits went to London-based companies: 'we still have to rely on London for our marketing and distribution, our publishers, the pressing plants, most radio promotion companies, most DJ mail-out companies. In fact, 90 per cent of the calls from us are going to 0171, 0181 [former London dialling codes], so we still rely heavily on London infrastructure for our success.' At the same time, however, he suggested that the company's northern location was a distinctive advantage and offered them credibility and thus cultural capital: 'with dance music you can have very regional differences in music taste, and I think one of our advantages is being based in the north. We can very easily find out from the DJs who come in the shop from the clubs in the area what the big tunes are up here.'

Cream was exceptional as a Liverpool-based music company in terms of its dramatic expansion, global notoriety and commercial success. Along with Gatecrasher in Sheffield and the Ministry of Sound in London, it pioneered a new kind of 'superclub' – a global multimedia corporation that played a central role within local, national and transnational dance scenes. The company was nevertheless engaged in a continual struggle to maintain that success, and also its credibility as a company, and this involved a heavy emphasis on promotion, diversification and legitimization. To begin with, the company expanded its market by promoting products through a geographically dispersed network of affiliated local companies, and much of Cream's business was also conducted via London. One of its directors worked for the London-based record label through which Cream released its compilation albums, and the company's DJ agency was also based in London. 'As we get more successful,' Cream's Head of Communications told us, 'it's harder to keep things in Liverpool because the expertise is not here … there will be bits which will have to move out because we can't get the people to move to Liverpool.' Cream thus came to symbolize the corporate face of contemporary dance culture, and was described by one journalist as epitomizing 'everything that had gone wrong with club culture … a betrayal of the original anti-Thatcherite values of rave culture' (*The Guardian*, 25 July 2002). Such views annoyed those running Cream, who responded by emphasizing the innovative nature of the company: 'the main difference is now we make more money, but we still book the same DJs and still have the same ideas' (p.c.); 'Cream is still considered to be at the forefront, breaking new ground. Where Cream goes the other clubs will follow' (p.c.).

Nevertheless, Cream was perceived by many Liverpool music-makers as having a dominant and controlling influence on local and global contemporary dance scenes. The directors of one local dance label described it to us as a 'mini empire': 'without Cream there would be no club culture in Liverpool, it is very important. It can make or break records.' Smaller local dance clubs and labels began to move away from house music, partly as a reaction to Cream and to the corporatism and homogenous 'mainstream' that house music had come to represent. In turn, Cream differentiated itself from smaller local clubs by claiming superior status as a trendsetter that introduced the city to new musical styles (Gilmore, 2004: 121). There were thus shifting relations of dominance and subordination amongst the businesses involved with the contemporary dance scene in Liverpool, although Toynbee (2000: xxiv, 149) describes contemporary dance music as produced through a network that was alternative, flat and democratic.

A vast amount of Cream's profits was spent on branding. That involved advertising the company through micro or niche media, flyers and specialist magazines, national and international mass media, and the Cream website where Cream products could be sold and the notion of a Cream 'community' encouraged. At the same time the company was forced to legitimize its activities, hence the appointment of a Head of Communications who described her job to us as 'dealing with the perception of Cream in the outside world'. She helped the company to establish close relations with policy-makers, and to successfully lobby for a change in the local licensing laws so that Cream could extend its club opening hours. Reflecting on her appointment one of the company's directors told us:

> it's the best move we've made in terms of filling in our understanding of how things really work within Liverpool ... You're almost out on your own because of how people perceive the club, in that it's full of drug-crazed lunatics, and it's still hard to break that mould and get the powers that be to come to recognize its importance really.

Consequently, Cream launched a series of PR campaigns. In August 2000, for example, it announced the employment of an in-house doctor following a high-profile drug-related death within the club.

By 1997 Cream employed large numbers of part- and full-time staff[11] and had an annual turnover of £3–4 million, much of which was earned through overseas promotional activities. Five years after its launch as a weekly event in a city-centre backstreet, Cream had become a global multimedia brand with a logo that represented a distinctive lifestyle. In 2002, however, shortly before Cream's tenth anniversary, the Cream 'feeder bar' closed and the company announced the temporary closure of its Liverpool club so that its future could be reviewed. Its press release attributed this to 'a shift in dance trends from nightclubs towards large-scale events and festivals',

---

11   There were 110 part-time and 52 full-time staff according to one director (p.c.).

although there had also been a parallel shift towards smaller clubs.[12] The press release emphasized Cream's deepening involvement with TV, radio and record production, explaining that the company had sold more albums during the first six months of 2002 than during the whole of 2001. Cream's tenth birthday celebrations went ahead as planned and the Creamfields festival continued, but the closure of the club led to media speculation about 'the death of the superclub' (*The Guardian*, 25 July 2002).

The story of Liverpool Music House is quite different but can likewise be characterized in terms of struggle. When they started the company, Colin and Gary had no money to invest in it, so they had to raise initial funding for studio equipment, which they then rented out. Their financial planning was complicated, however, by the difficulties they experienced in retrieving payments for studio bookings. If payment was demanded up front they would have lost a considerable proportion of their clientele, many of whom were unemployed or employed only on an occasional basis. Much time and effort was thus devoted to debt collecting, a task that they found both draining and demoralizing.[13] Earnings lost during the company's first year of business had to be recouped during subsequent years. None of the company's staff were able to draw a salary from the business, and the constant effort to keep the business afloat left little time for more creative concerns. Colin, Gary and Carl were thus forced into a combination of survival strategies that was familiar to other local music-makers. For a short time, for example, they raised money for the business by performing together in local pubs and social clubs, playing cover versions of other people's songs. They also spent a lot of time renovating and decorating The Lab so that they could become landlords and sub-let rooms to other businesses: 'You can't keep the whole thing going on just studio hire alone', one of them told us, 'and having a big building helps'.

Colin and Gary did not sign contractual agreements with LMH artists, partly because they wanted to establish relationships based upon trust; partly because they could not afford the legal costs of establishing contracts or taking artists to court for breach of contract; and partly because, like others involved with similar businesses at that time, their attention was perhaps naively diverted away from a central focus on the acquisition of and trade in music rights (including rights in the recording, broadcasting and performance of musical works), and towards a concern with facilities and resources. The company's business relations were thus largely informal and involved a barter economy whereby, for example, the services of photographers, accountants and T-shirt manufacturers were paid for with studio time, and a freelance programmer and arranger occupied a room in the building rent-free in exchange for the loan of his equipment. In addition, Colin and Gary courted particular individuals who they thought might invest in the company, and they continually submitted applications to other sources of private funding as well as applications for bank loans and grant aid. They encountered, however, a general wariness of and lack of experience of the music

---

12   'Cream of Clubs set to abandon Saturdays', *The Guardian*, 24 July 2002.
13   Other local companies also ran on credit, including, for example, local rehearsal studios.

business on the part of banks and public sector agencies, a problem commonly faced by other music-makers.[14]

LMH eventually secured a bank loan through personal guarantees, and it was matched by investment from a Manchester-based venture capitalist and a small building grant and rent rebate from Liverpool City Council. That funding package almost collapsed, however, when the council withheld its contribution because LMH had an outstanding rates bill. It proved impossible to persuade the council to arrange for the money to be transferred internally from the department dealing with the rebate to the one dealing with rates. There were further delays due to another bureaucratic technicality, which meant that LMH had to re-submit the grant application to the council. The funds were eventually secured but by that time large commercial recording studios were beginning to struggle to survive financially following the move to digitization and home recording, and in Britain the recession was biting hard and interest rates were running high. Almost half of the company's income was spent paying off the interest on their loan and the lease on the building. Colin and Gary tried to purchase The Lab at a time when the building was worth the equivalent of just four years of the rent they were paying, but none of the banks they approached would grant them a mortgage. Gary and his partner eventually sold their house to keep LMH going, and the re-mortgage for their second house acted as a new guarantee against the company's loan. During the late 1990s, however, the company's activities were scaled down as the debts continued to mount, and in 2000 the decision was taken to strike off LMH and put the company to bed. By then, however, the area surrounding The Lab had been developed and new loft apartments and office spaces built. The property value of The Lab had consequently escalated. The company was nevertheless forced to pass the building on to others and try to pay off the remainder of its bank loan, a loan for which the directors were personally liable.

It was not usual for those running local businesses to discuss their financial difficulties and business affairs with each other, or with other organizations (in fact it was more conventional for them to present their businesses as thriving or as poised on the brink of major success). 'Local music businesses like to keep their cards close to their chest', one of them told us; whilst a bank manager who had a professional association with local music businesses said, 'there's always been a sort of secretive side to it – "don't tell anybody what we're doing", you know' (p.c.). Yet despite its problems LMH kept going for 14 years at a time when the lifespan of most local music businesses was far shorter, and many LMH artists went on to achieve successful careers in music. The difficulties faced by the company were familiar to other local music companies; hence we encountered many similar stories of trial and tribulation. Businesses were involved in a precarious daily struggle to balance creative and commercial concerns, to maintain control over their music-making and musical output and to simply stay afloat. According to one report, over 90 per cent of

---

14   N. Wilson, D. Stokes and R. Blackburn, 'Banking on a Hit: The Funding Dilemma for Britain's Music Businesses'. Small Business Research Centre, Kingston University, for the UK Department of Culture, Media and Sport, 2001.

British music businesses could be defined as small or medium-sized enterprises, and they 'face distinct problems which hinder their ability to grow';[15] yet at the same time the music industry was one of Britain's most economically successful industries.[16]

Creativity and the Culture of Production

Before moving on to relate the above discussion more closely to the key themes of this book, it is important to emphasize that the music business in Liverpool was not just an economic sector but a way of life. It offered an opportunity for creativity and social interaction, and businesses had social and symbolic as well as economic significance.

Whilst dance music has been categorized as a peripheral sub-sector of the music industry,[17] Cream's Head of Communications insisted that Cream DJs were 'artists' who aimed to 'educate' their audiences and take them on a 'musical journey', and that the production of innovative music was Cream's primary concern:

> people question, is it about music? And it *is* about music. Dance music is real music ... At the end of the day, music is the thing that the lads [Darren and James] care about ... and every so often if it starts to lose its way a little bit, which it will occasionally, it's like 'Pull it back', and the point that you pull it back to is the music and the credibility of the music, and is it new, and is it breaking ground, and once you start asking those questions, it puts you right back on track. (p.c.)

Within Cream's Liverpool club a mix of house and handbag styles was usually played in the main room, whilst more experimental and hybrid styles of funk, disco, trance and drum 'n' bass were played in the smaller annexe.

Other Liverpool music-makers also resented any suggestion that their businesses might be a peripheral concern and situated themselves at the core of music production. Colin and Gary from LMH frequently stated that music managers played a central role within the industry, because it was they who represented musicians to a range of industry sub-sectors and were thus positioned at their intersection. The editor of the regional music magazine *Groove* suggested that his publication played a central role because it represented local music-making to the industry, and to a wider public, and thus helped to develop it (p.c.). The owner of Crash rehearsal studios described his company to us as the 'backbone of the industry'. 'We have about one hundred bands a week whereas recording studios may only have ten', he added, explaining that Crash was not just a rehearsal studio but also helped to promote local bands to

---

15   Banking on a Hit.

16   For details of jobs and earnings relating to the British music industry see 'Banking on a Hit' and 'Overseas Earnings of the Music Industry', a report by British Invisibles, 1995: 28.

17   See, for example, Feist, D.C. and Laing, D. 1996. *The Value of Music: A National Music Council Report into the Value of the UK Music Industry*. National Music Council and University of Westminster.

record companies, and to repair their equipment.[18] Meanwhile musicians described live performance venues as the 'heart' of local music-making because they were a focal point for social gatherings, and because the experience of performing live was so highly valued. The social and symbolic significance of local venues such as the Cavern, Erics and the Picket was evident in the groups and initiatives mobilized to lobby (unsuccessfully) against their closure. Other music companies, particularly independent record shops such as Probe Records, which had been running since 1971, also acted as social hubs. They provided a meeting place and networking opportunity for local music-makers, introducing them to particular recordings and sounds and offering them information on local music events and scenes. It was at Probe Records that I first met the rock broadcaster Roger Hill, and I spent many hours sitting in the offices of rehearsal studios such as Vulcan and The Ministry, chatting to and observing musicians who were there not necessarily to rehearse, but just to hang out. Others hung out at the offices of management companies or in recording studios.

Some of the individuals involved with the running of such businesses had become well-known figures within the local music business, and they acted as a focal point for information and advice on local music-making. In addition, many individuals who were originally from Liverpool and Merseyside had taken up employment in London, where they had managed to establish successful careers in the music industry. They included London-based record producers, record label and publishing executives, artist and repertoire managers and radio broadcasters. Together, they were referred to by one local musician as the 'ex-pat Scouse Mafia'. Those individuals provided local music-makers with another important source of information and advice, and with a useful social network that was drawn upon by those organizing speakers and panels for Liverpool-based music business seminars and workshops. The individuals concerned were usually happy to help out their home city and could also use such occasions as an excuse to visit family and friends.

The business of music thus involved a lifestyle and social networks that could be difficult to break out of. Those involved with LMH regularly got together in the pub to discuss business matters and strategies away from the pressures and pace of life in The Lab, but they also exchanged anecdotes and jokes about everyday LMH occurrences. The pub gatherings did not simply provide a break and an opportunity for informal meetings, but also reinforced the social bonds between those involved and helped them to motivate and psyche each other up to keep the business going day after day. Boundaries between amateur and professional business activities were blurred, and domestic and working lives became interdependent. Older entrepreneurs in particular had become used to self-employment, and irregular working hours enabled some to work in non-music occupations during the daytime or to mind children. Most were prepared to work long hours on a voluntary basis for little or no financial reward primarily because of their love of music. The business of music offered them a chance to make a living doing what they felt passionate about and to be

---

18   See Cohen (1991a) for other similar examples.

involved with something pleasurable and creative. Moreover, the business was fast-changing and unpredictable, challenging and full of possibility. There was always the chance of creating or discovering an innovative new artist or sound, or a hit song, or attracting the interest of a journalist, broadcaster or record company. In fact I was struck by the overwhelming confidence and optimism of local musicians and music entrepreneurs, their belief in their creative abilities, and their certainty that their talents would eventually be recognized and their hard work would pay off.

Liverpool in the Music Business

The case material on Cream and LMH has highlighted the breadth and diversity of the music business in Liverpool during the 1980s and 1990s, and its position within local, national and global networks of production and distribution. It has also suggested that the business was characterized by tension. It encouraged collaboration amongst those involved and offered them a sense of autonomy and the possibility of creative and commercial success. Yet it also involved a day-to-day struggle for survival that generated frustration, division and a sense of dependency. Despite exceptional cases of commercial success, most businesses were precariously poised between success and failure. These tensions were partly produced by the specificity of the music businesses and the peculiar commercial pressures and constraints involved; but how was the business of music influenced by its local and urban setting, and by social and economic change within the city?

Spaces, Clusters and Cliques

To begin with, the national recession and poor state of the local economy had certainly hindered music business development. Funding was difficult to acquire and interest rates were high ('I keep the bailiffs in business', the owner of Probe Records told us). Local clients had less money to pay for studio hire or to spend on music clubs and events: 'every band and every manager I know is unemployed and have probably been unemployed for a long time' (recording studio owner, p.c.); 'we have about 100 bands a week … 90 per cent of our customers are unemployed and we set our rates around them' (rehearsal studio owner, p.c.). Yet at the same time the city's economic problems had in certain ways enabled commercial music-making. De-industrialization had left an abundance of vacant industrial and commercial buildings, providing spaces that were relatively cheap and thus accessible for music businesses. Some parts of Liverpool city centre subsequently became known for their musical vibrancy, although the appropriation of disused city buildings (often for limited periods of time) by music-makers, and particularly by those involved with alternative or bohemian cultures, has been a common and long-established tradition in Europe and North America. Zukin (1989), for example, describes how during the 1980s artists transformed late nineteenth-century industrial buildings and districts in New York, and how the industrial landscape of those districts consequently came to have symbolic significance and to be connected with notions of authenticity. In Manchester, warehouses and factories left over from cotton manufacturing and other local industries were appropriated for use as nightclubs, bars, record shops, cafes and restaurants. They included The Hacienda Club, which opened in 1982 and played a central role in the city's post-punk scene (Haslam, 2000).

In Liverpool the Cavern Club was launched in 1957 as a jazz venue in the cellar of one of Mathew Street's storage warehouses (see Chapter 7). Other music clubs and venues, as well as local rehearsal and recording studios, were likewise housed in industrial warehouses. When LMH took over The Lab building it had lain empty for some time; whilst the area in which Cream's club and headquarters were located was characterized by decaying warehouses left over from rope-making and other port-related industries. Many of them were occupied by cultural producers, including an old tea factory that housed a number of music businesses. More recently the area has been a central location for alternative scenes based on electronica, punk, avant-garde and experimental music. The musicians involved with those scenes have performed in spaces that have included the cellar of a print works, a boarded up fish and chip shop, disused garages and empty warehouses, all located within a few streets of each other (Strachan and Cohen 2005).

The accessibility of such spaces helped to facilitate the development of clusters of interconnected music businesses within particular buildings and geographical locations, and most music entrepreneurs spoke of the benefits of working in close proximity to others involved in related activity. Some argued that despite recent developments in communication technologies, nothing could better face-to-face interaction. LMH had close dealings with many music businesses in Liverpool, but particularly with those based in The Lab. One business, for example, supplied equipment for the LMH recording studio, and in turn LMH supplied that business with personnel; Carl sang backing vocals on a Lightning Seeds album and in turn the Lightning Seeds loaned equipment to LMH. Similarly, Cream established close connections with bars, retailers and music businesses operating around Concert Square. In 1989 the property developer Tom Bloxom renovated an old furniture warehouse in Concert Square for use by small cultural businesses. Known as the Liverpool Palace, it housed the offices of Cream, the management company of Rob Swerdlow, 3Beat Records, a design company and the editorial offices of *Groove* magazine. The Palace acted as a meeting point for music-makers and Bloxom emphasized to us the synergy that the initiative had created, and how it had encouraged 'a tremendous amount of trading' between the businesses involved and had also provided them with local role models:

> you can see the people next door making it work, making it happen and you've got all the resources there to do the labels, get someone to press it, get it reviewed next door. And working like that adds something to the business. If you're working from an office or a small house it's very isolating; it's soul destroying.

These business clusters thus comprised dense networks of social relationships characterized by reciprocity and exchange. They were a focal point and resource for business support, collaboration and trade; the daily, face-to-face sharing of advice, expertise, contacts and technology; and the circulation of rumour and stories of local successes and failures. They provided a reservoir of specialist information and knowledge, and through them local music-making traditions and conventions were reproduced, and the profile and productivity of individual companies was often enhanced. Scott (2000: 33) likewise describes geographical concentrations of cultural producers in London and Los Angeles as, 'not just foci of cultural labor in the narrow sense, but also active hubs of social reproduction in which crucial cultural competencies are maintained and circulated.' Hall (1998: 299) cites the work of other scholars to suggest that such clustering helps to foster innovation and competitive success in advanced-technology industries, and that cities provide the most favourable conditions for clustering because they are 'adaptable, flexible and diverse'. That clustering was characteristic of the music industry, which was dominated by a few large, multinational corporations that were horizontally and vertically integrated and covered a whole chain of processes, but depended upon a multitude of small, interdependent companies.

In Liverpool, however, clustering had long been a characteristic of the local economy, which was largely based upon trade, and it has been suggested that 'local (urban and regional) traditions, norms and sensibilities actively shape the structures and strategies of business operations in the cultural economy and the design of final outputs' (Scott, 2000: preface). The Jewish-run tailoring workshops described in Chapter 1, for example, comprised, like music, a specialist trade based upon small businesses and dominated by fashion. Such trades encouraged a tradition of entrepreneurialism and self-employment within the city, as did the casualized nature of the dockside labour market. Cream's Head of Communications associated Cream's directors with that tradition when she described them to us as, 'young entrepreneurs. James [Barton] used to sell socks in the school playground. They are Liverpool lads who know how to earn a buck ... he is a very very sharp, working class Liverpool lad James.' Her emphasis on a local, canny, working-class entrepreneurship differs from, but can be connected to, Du Noyer's reference to James as 'a Liverpool entrepreneur in the tradition of its top-hatted Victorian merchants' (2002: 195). Barton's father had been one of the 'Cunard Yanks' – described in Chapter 3 – who, in addition to his duties on board ship, wrote music reviews for an American journal and accumulated an impressive collection of American r'n'b and soul music.[19]

Competition, Creativity and the Local Economy

The diversity and clustering of local music companies, in addition to local economic circumstances, enhanced perceptions of commercial music-making in Liverpool as collaborative but also cliquey, which suggested another tension within local music-making produced by the dual emphasis on collectivity but also division.

---

19   A film, *The Cunard Yanks*, is currently being made by Souled Out Film Productions in Liverpool (see also Chapter 3, note 21).

From the mid-1980s when I first started to research rock music-making in the city, those involved described it to me as highly competitive and factionalized. At times it seemed like a simmering cauldron, a field of activity shrouded in suspicion and intrigue, gossip and secrecy. Those involved with contemporary dance music represented it in similar ways. In fact, one of Cream's directors suggested to us that the local dance scene was even more factionalized than the rock scene, and emphasized how careful Cream had to be in terms of the businesses they chose to establish relationships with. A music business plan listed 'infighting, jealousy and self-destructive attitudes' as some of the key weaknesses of the music sector on Merseyside,[20] and during the late 1990s a couple of our interviewees even compared the business of music in Liverpool with the Bosnian conflict, which was at that time hitting the national news headlines. A few argued that working alongside other music businesses did not necessarily lead to collaboration or mutual support. A director of 3Beat Records, for example, told us that another record label, 'would probably never play our records and would probably diss them as being no good ... And we're based next door!' The music entrepreneurs we spoke to in Manchester and Sheffield tended to characterize the music business in those cities in similar terms, which suggests that competition and divisiveness was characteristic of the music industry in general and not specific to Liverpool. Nevertheless, some believed that those characteristics were more intense in Liverpool and they attributed this to the poor state of the local economy. An arts consultant told us that local music-makers 'don't think that they can afford to share'; whilst a band manager explained: 'Liverpool is very cliquey ... it is the kind of town where people get into little huddles and snipe at each other ... part of the problem is that when you have scarce resources things get very competitive.'

The city's economic problems thus appeared to have encouraged negative perceptions of the local music business. On the other hand, however, as mentioned in Chapter 2 it was also commonly believed that those problems had increased the amount of music-making in the city, made the city more creative, and sharpened the entrepreneurial skills and commercial ambitions of those involved:

> Liverpool has always been musical ... there's always been a bit of an unemployment thing here even in the good days. And the more there is a no-hope situation, the more music comes out. The more affluent places you go to, the more reserved people get, and the more they expect people to entertain them rather than entertain themselves' (band manager, pc).

> Liverpool is a busker, deep down. When you've no job, nor any income to speak of, you look to what talent you do possess, and put the hat on the pavement. When all else fails – and sometimes it does – this town will sing for its supper (Du Noyer, 2002: 254).

---

20   'Business Plan: September 2000 to August 2003'. Merseyside Music Development Agency (MMDA). May 2000.

Similarly, a local rock promoter, referring to Liverpool, spoke of 'musical genius arising from poverty', whilst Haslam (2000: 278) writes: 'in Manchester, like Liverpool, Detroit – other places with similar problems of poverty and crime – music has given the city a voice, broken the silence, woven itself into the fabric of life.'

This linking of poverty with music-making and musical talent can be connected to a familiar romantic ideology of creativity typified by the image of the starving artist at work in their garret. It suggests a rather unsettling celebration of unemployment, when for most of the musicians and music entrepreneurs that I got to know unemployment was a demoralizing and usually demotivating experience, but it nevertheless suits various scholarly theories. For Gardner (1993), creative individuals tend to be socially marginal (whether through gender, class, ethnicity or nationality) and 'at the edge' (cited in Hall, 2000: 642–3) – a theory that could potentially be applied to young unemployed musicians and music entrepreneurs in Liverpool. For Turner (1982: 44), those music-makers might count as socially 'liminal', a state that involves 'the liberation of human capacities of cognition, affect, volition, creativity etc, from the normative constraints incumbent upon occupying a sequence of social statuses'. For Hall (1998: 289), structural instability produces feelings of discomfort and uncertainty that make some cities more creative and innovative than others.

Yet 'creativity' is a fuzzy, complex notion defined and used in many different ways, and it needs to be explained, as Hall (ibid.) acknowledges, in terms of a combination of factors arising at particular times and within particular circumstances. Cities have been associated with innovation because they are places of migration, mixing and dense social interaction, and they are therefore open to new ideas and cultural exchanges (Connell and Gibson, 2003: 103). This is particularly the case with port cities, such as Liverpool and New Orleans, and cities that are situated at the crossroads of routes of migration, trade and capital, such as Memphis and Chicago. For Hall, migrant cities are places of transition and transformation. This can produce a clash or disjuncture between old and new orders, 'experienced and expressed by a group of creative people who feel themselves to some important degree outsiders: they both belong and they do not belong, and they have an ambiguous relationship to the seats of authority and power' (ibid.: 284–5). Great, serious art, according to Hall (ibid.: 285, 286) is produced by outsiders and is in some way subversive. Yet the argument that major metropolitan areas are places of migration, and therefore more creative than other places, seems rather vague and generalized and also counter to the notion of creative isolation that is often celebrated by musicians and music critics, including Roger Hill in his description of Liverpool's 'riverine sound' (Chapter 2). Elsewhere (Cohen, 1994: 125) I have quoted Liverpool musicians who insisted that rock bands on the fringes of the city were more 'creative' than those in the city centre, and various scholarly theories have likewise linked geographical remoteness with musical innovation. Glasgow (1987: 251), for example, argues that innovation in jazz has come from outside city centres (see also Connell and Gibson, 2003: 96).

Haslam's explanation of musical 'creativity' in Manchester (2000) highlights the 'edginess', cosmopolitanism and entrepreneurialism of that city, and its collisions of class and culture. Yet a remarkably similar combination of factors has been used to explain Liverpool's reputation as a 'music city' and the success of the Beatles: hence the references of the country musicians in the previous chapter to Liverpool's cosmopolitanism, and to the entrepreneurialism and non-conformism of local sailors, and Du Noyer's reference to Liverpool as 'edgy' (2002: 8). Particularly important, however, are the social networks, spaces, events and chance encounters that provide a catalyst for music-making at a micro level. Chapter 1, for example, described the musical encounters within the clubs of Liverpool 8 during the 1950s and 1960s. During the late 1970s and early 1980s the owners of the club Erics promoted an eclectic mix of musical sounds and styles, and the club consequently attracted audiences drawn from a mix of social groups that was unusual for the city at that time. Erics thus became an important meeting point and catalyst for the city's post-punk scene, which has been described as 'creative' and 'innovative' (Cooper, 1982). Those who met and formed bands through the club included members of Big in Japan, Wah!, Orchestral Manoeuvres in the Dark, Teardrop Explodes and Echo and the Bunnymen.

Whilst unemployment alone cannot account for musical or entrepreneurial creativity in Liverpool, unemployment benefits did provide income support for local musicians and music entrepreneurs. The directors of LMH, for example, supported themselves and many of the artists they worked with through an intricately balanced and timed rotation of government unemployment schemes as well as financial contributions and loans from family and friends: 'At the start of 1986,' one of them explained, 'I was unemployed for a year and then on Enterprise Allowance the year after, and then unemployed for another year and then back on Enterprise Allowance after that. And it was all just trying to keep, you know, your head above the water, and we spent that time just developing the business from absolutely nothing' (p.c.). In addition, whilst unemployment was generally inflicted upon local musicians rather than something they consciously chose to experience, some musicians believed that if they truly wanted success then they needed to follow the example set by the Beatles in the 1960s and devote themselves to music-making on a full-time basis. This was not something specific to Liverpool, however: hence the debates about rock music-making and unemployment that hit the British news headlines in the late 1990s following the launch of a new unemployment training scheme by Britain's new Labour government. The scheme was criticized by several high-profile rock musicians and managers, who argued that it was because they did not have to work that Britain's most successful rock bands of that time (most notably Oasis) had been able to learn their craft.

Music Branding and the City

Social and economic change had thus produced conditions in the Liverpool of the 1980s and 1990s that enabled rather than determined music-making and entrepreneurialism, but that encouraged representations of the city as uniquely and musically creative. One city marketing campaign drew upon Liverpool's name and its reputation as a creative city to promote the city as a 'pool of talent'.[21] A development plan for Merseyside music listed as one of the sector's key strengths: 'National/International established brand name based on consistent flow of music talent over four decades'.[22] Despite regular complaints by local musicians about their difficulties in attracting industry attention (see Cohen, 1991a), Liverpool's reputation for commercial and artistic success had made it a focus of attention for the music industry. The city thus attracted regular visits of journalists and A&R personnel from London-based music companies, and those companies cultivated a network of Liverpool-based informants who could report back to them on local developments, including local DJs, journalists and promoters who had access to musicians and knowledge of local music scenes. During the early 2000s a joint venture was established between Sony BMG and Deltasonic, a Liverpool-based independent record label associated with the rock band The Coral. That investment into a regionally based label by a major London-based company was unusual for the time, and it provided further evidence of decentralization within the music industry. All Deltasonic record releases were distributed and marketed through the Sony BMG network. In turn, Sony BMG had a major stake in Deltasonic, was able to buy into the credibility of a local label and gained access to local talent at a relatively early stage in its development.[23]

The association of Liverpool with musical talent and creativity also influenced the attitudes, practices and identities of local musicians and music entrepreneurs. It became part of 'how we are', 'what it is like here'; it attracted to the city musicians and music fans from elsewhere who contributed to the development of local scenes and sounds; and it gave local music-makers confidence in their music-making and heightened their commercial and creative ambitions and expectations. Colin and Gary established LMH in order to nurture local talent, but the name of the company also reflected a desire to build upon the city's positive reputation for rock and pop and use it as a marketing opportunity: 'we called the company Liverpool Music House for a reason,' said Gary, 'it had Liverpool in front of it because we knew that probably everywhere outside of the city people would look at it and go "Aha, I can equate music with Liverpool"' (p.c.).

At the same time, however, the above-mentioned development plan listed as one of the key weaknesses of Merseyside's music sector, 'negative regional/national perceptions of Merseyside', and those perceptions had an impact on local music-making. One of Cream's directors, for example, tried to defend the company from accusations of corporatism by claiming, 'We need to be commercial due to being in Liverpool. You need to work twice as hard to get people into the city.'[24] A director of 3Beat told us that he and his colleagues encountered 'a real snobbishness towards Liverpool' when they tried to promote bands; whilst a band manager mentioned

---

21   The campaign was launched by The Mersey Partnership in 1995.

22   Merseyside Music Development Agency draft business plan, 2000.

23   See also Rose (2005) on Deltasonic, the music industry and post-industrialism.

24   James Barton speaking at the annual 'In the City' music industry convention held in Glasgow in 1995.

the reputation of Liverpool music-makers for 'bad credit' (p.c.). In addition to such attitudes, local music-makers also had to confront common media representations of Liverpool as not simply musically creative, but also as a city that was burdened and haunted by its musical past and had lost its creative and innovative edge. Whilst many local musicians and music entrepreneurs celebrated and embraced the city's musical traditions, many others deliberately worked against them and tried to create something totally different. There were thus musicians who admired and were inspired by the Beatles, but also those who set out to sound as different from the Beatles as they possibly could.

One of Cream's directors, Darren, explained to us that they deliberately tried to set up Cream as something different from other local clubs, and that the Cream bar, Mello Mello, was 'deliberately set up not to be a typical Liverpool kind of bar'. According to the company's Head of Communications, 'Cream's pitch has always been that it is a Liverpool-based company that works world-wide. It is not a Liverpool club'. Thus, whilst the branding of Liverpool Music House sought to build upon the city's positive reputation for rock and pop music, those at Cream were anxious to distance the company from what they regarded as typical Liverpool dance and club culture, and to promote it as a global brand. This contrast appears to confirm the argument of Straw (1991), who suggests that alternative rock scenes are insular and closely tied to the local, whilst contemporary dance scenes have a cosmopolitan outlook that is more attentive to developments elsewhere. Yet those involved with the production of contemporary dance music also drew upon the local to develop, market and promote their products. House music, for example, was marketed through labels such as Detroit techno, Chicago house and 'Scouse house' – a style of contemporary dance music that was connected to Liverpool and Cream, and has been described as particularly 'tuny' in 'a curious echo of the city's rock'n'roll traditions' (Du Noyer, 2002: 203). Moreover, those working at Cream certainly connected their company to the local when it suited their interests to do so. One of the company's directors, for example, said:

> We're big ambassadors for Liverpool ... I have a London office now but we're a Liverpool organization and we always will be. We love the story and we've refined it over the years: how two kids with no money started this thing, and everyone came to support it. It's a Liverpool story ... (ibid.: 195) ... the fact that I was born and bred in Liverpool, that Cream was started as a love affair, with very little investment, and grew and grew ... Stories like that can only come from places like Liverpool (ibid.: 205).

Global Ambitions and Local Concerns and Obligations

Thus for companies such as Cream and LMH, their Liverpool urban setting provided them with accessible spaces for music-making and for the development of business clusters, and with a set of local cultural and creative traditions that could be worked with or against depending upon the specific circumstances involved. Hence those at Cream could describe the company as Liverpool-based and not a Liverpool club, but also as a Liverpool organization and a typical Liverpool story. Moreover, as Chapters

5 and 7 will discuss, Cream became celebrated by Liverpool policy-makers as a local rags-to-riches success story and as a new model of local entrepreneurialism, despite the fact that the development of the company was a familiar example of capitalist expansion and was hardly alternative or progressive.[25] This was partly because Cream's management began to emphasize the company's contribution to the city and to local tourism, regeneration and economic development. Cream was thus presented by its management as a company that could, following that familiar slogan, 'think global, act local'.

Nevertheless, one of Cream's directors told us that the company had been the victim of a local backlash because of its success:

> Liverpool's a funny place for success, you know what I mean? It kind of treats it very strangely. It doesn't always pat it on the back, sometimes far from it – the opposite ... there's a clique within Liverpool that follow you when you're small and underground and give up when you're not. But I think that might be true of every city, I don't know. It's especially true of Liverpool.

At the planning and consultancy workshop referred to at the start of this chapter, and also in conversation with us, Cream's Head of Communications attacked those who suggested that Cream was somehow separate from the city ('the community') because of its success. She explained how seriously Cream took its role in relation to Liverpool: 'For us it's like really really serious that it is done properly ... it's about the image of the city, it's not about making a quick buck and moving on.' She emphasized the number of local people that Cream employed and how the company had improved the physical environment around its club. She also dwelt upon her own personal involvement with local schools and community groups, and on the fact that she had stayed in the city when a lot of her friends (who included some well-known rock/pop musicians) had left. Cream, she argued, had shown how you could both stay and be successful.

The experiences of Cream thus suggested that the business of music in Liverpool was characterized by additional tensions between global ambitions and local concerns and, as evident in the city's rock culture, between leaving and staying (Chapter 2). During the 1980s and early 1990s, as Liverpool's population shrank and its media image worsened, local sensitivity over the departure of commercially successful musicians and music entrepreneurs for London was particularly high. It was exacerbated by deepening economic and political divisions within Britain between the provinces and the capital, and between north and south. One article in a national British newspaper stated: 'No one in Liverpool has any respect for anyone who actually stays here out of choice. Indeed, they think there must be something intrinsically wrong with him.'[26] Another stated of Liverpool, 'No city in Britain is

---

25   Hesmondhalgh (1998: 248) also makes this point in relation to the institutions that were central to contemporary dance music, contrasting them with the post-punk companies that preceded them.

26   Stanley Reynolds, *The Guardian*, 18 December 1997.

losing its population so fast. It's a place people are very proud to *come from*. But they don't stay there.'[27] Given such distorted and grim representations of the city it was hardly surprising that one music entrepreneur told me that Liverpool sometimes seemed to him to be like a 'prison'. When Cream announced the closure of its Liverpool club some interpreted it as a depressing signal that Cream was to move to London – like a typical Liverpool success story. A local Cream fan accused Cream's director, James Barton, of betraying the city and being disloyal to his Liverpool roots (cited in Gilmore, 2004: 123).

At the same time, however, the city's economic problems encouraged expressions of local pride and loyalty (as illustrated in Chapter 3), a sense of obligation and commitment to the city, and a desire to stay and try to help out. Hence the emphasis on what Cream had done for Liverpool. Similarly, a director of LMH spoke to us of the enormous impact that the Beatles had on him when he was a young boy – particularly since they were from his own city – and how he had toured Britain with bands during the 1970s and met people who responded warmly to him because they regarded Liverpool as an exciting and creative place. Consequently, he explained, it was such a shock to find only a short while later that Liverpool and its residents had become so loathed and denigrated. He told us that he and his business partner had originally envisaged their company as being not just *in* but *for* Liverpool. He remembered the Conservative government minister Michael Heseltine saying:

'The only thing that can change Liverpool is the people of Liverpool.' It was down to you to make things happen and start that process. He didn't say the future lay with Liverpool City Council or with the Merseyside Development Corporation. At the time there was nobody trying to establish that kind of relationship between the city and, you know, its music, so it [LMH] was obviously an attempt to achieve that, you know, whatever we thought of Heseltine and however naff it sounds.

Paul McCartney explained, 'everyone had said "You'll never make it, coming from Liverpool." Which angered us a bit, so we stayed up in Liverpool a lot. We didn't just all move down to London, we tried to prove ourselves from Liverpool' (cited in Du Noyer, 2002: 22). Yet the Beatles left Liverpool for London relatively early on in their career and never returned to live there or to perform there as a band. Echo and the Bunnymen, on the other hand, have been referred to in Liverpool as an example of a successful local band that has stayed in the city. The band's lead singer, Ian McCulloch, has been mentioned as an example of a musician who has remained loyal to his roots and thus retained credibility: 'he has lived in Liverpool all his life and has no intention of leaving' (cited in Connell and Gibson, 2003: 111, and taken from Sheddon, 2001: 17). This may help to explain why McCulloch has on occasion been sought out by the local media to comment on events of local and

---

27   Paul Barker, *New Statesman*, 7 February 1997. 'Liverpudlians are very proud of their heritage.'

musical significance.[28] Stahl (2001: 104) highlights the existence of a similar rhetoric within the rock culture of Montreal[29] and suggests, 'For those who choose to stay, this choice often necessitates the employment of certain heroic narratives, survival myths evincing what Bourdieu has called "the prestige of romantic triumph".' Toynbee (2000: 37) argues that cultural production may anyway be an altruistic affair, suggesting, 'In popular music, perhaps more than any other cultural form, musicians claim to act on behalf of the community and for the collective good.'

During the late 1990s, as Liverpool's economy began to improve, local music-makers began to comment more frequently on examples of well-known musicians and entrepreneurs who had decided to keep the city as their base, and the discursive tension between leaving and staying became less obvious: 'the Liverpool economy is a lot better, there's more for them to spend their money on, I suppose, so they don't need to go away as much. Because we did go through a really bad time, didn't we? And it wasn't that pleasant to go out, but that's changed now' (manager of Parr Street Recording Studios, p.c.). At the same time local music scenes and businesses were invigorated by a dramatic increase in the number of students attending Liverpool's two main universities.

Commerce and Creativity, Centres and Margins

Local social and economic circumstances and changes thus affected music businesses in Liverpool. But if the city, both real and imagined, influenced commercial music production then how, in turn, did the specificity of music as a business contribute to the production of the city?

Straw (1991) draws attention to the replication of popular music scenes across different localities and argues (2003), 'Of all the media industries, popular music has often been depicted as exceptional in terms of its periodic capacity to nurture and sustain active and innovative local spheres of production.' In this sense therefore, the local was a product of the music industry and its drive for profit, and Liverpool's musical clusters and scenes could be described as a 'reservoir' of talent and unwaged musicians and music entrepreneurs that the music industry could dip into and exploit (Toynbee, 2000: 26). Companies such as LMH, Cream and 3Beat thus drew upon the local as a source of credibility and cultural capital, whilst at the same time developing talent on behalf of the industry and supplying the industry with product. In Chapter 2, however, I illustrated a common perception amongst Liverpool music-makers that the London-based music industry existed in opposition to the local, and threatened and exploited local musical creativity. This is a familiar perspective: hence Bianchini (1993: 4) describes Liverpool as endowed with indigenous cultural talent, but as

---

28   In 2004, for example, he was interviewed as part of a BBC TV North West news report about his views on Liverpool's success in its bid to become European Capital of Culture 2008.

29   Interestingly, Montreal shares certain characteristics with Liverpool, including its role as a port and its former 'second city' status.

traditionally exploited by London-based commercial cultural industries.[30] Yet by associating the local with creativity, and distinguishing it from the commercial, such perspectives end up romanticizing and fetishizing the local.

Alternatively, Street (1997: 113) highlights the symbiotic relationship between London and the regions, pointing out that 'the pop industry still remains dependent on the regions, both as a source of talent and as a way of constructing the cultural significance attached to its production and consumption.' Music-makers within Britain's provincial cities depended upon the industry to promote their products, and were closely monitored by and networked into the industry so that cases of innovation or potential commercial success could be quickly co-opted. In turn, however, those cities were depended upon by the industry for music product, and major music corporations could not completely control local music-making but were challenged by its breadth and diversity, and by the unpredictability of local musical trends. Hence Toynbee usefully describes local music scenes as relatively autonomous 'proto-markets' (2000: xxi).

Conclusion

This chapter began by introducing two Liverpool-based companies. It positioned those companies within local, national and global networks of production and distribution, and examined their efforts to access such networks. In doing so it highlighted the range and diversity, flux and unpredictability of the music business, but also described it as a way of life and labour of love for those involved. The chapter also considered various ways in which their Liverpool setting had influenced the commercial networks of local music-makers and their music- and business-related practices. The city's highly mediated cultural traditions provided strong creative models that local music-makers could work with or against, using them as a source of inspiration and as a marketing opportunity, or as a basis for the construction of something new and different. Meanwhile the city's economic difficulties had not diminished or dampened local musical creativity; and to a certain extent they actually helped to motivate local music-makers, fuel their commercial ambitions and hone their entrepreneurial skills. The demise or departure of industry from Liverpool had also left in its wake a wealth of physical spaces that enabled the development of music business clusters. Moreover, music-makers commonly attributed the strength of local creative and commercial activity, and some of its key characteristics, to the poor state of the local economy and high levels local unemployment. Yet at the same time the city's economic problems hindered the development of local businesses and heightened concerns and debates about the relationship of music-makers to the

---

30   See also articles in the music press, such as 'Liverpool's Second Coming' (*Melody Maker*, 24 July 1976), which referred to 'the tragic waste that characterised London's musical rape and pillage of the city in the Merseybeat boom and the sudden, petulant desertion of the City by a music scene which had discovered "progressive music"'.

city, and about the relationship between local music-making and the London-based music industry.

The discussion pointed to various sets of tensions within the music business in Liverpool that were fuelled by the specificity of music as an industry and by local social and economic change. The local music business was creative and collaborative but also competitive and divided. It offered those involved a sense of autonomy and the possibility of creative and commercial success, and it encouraged collaboration. Yet at the same time the risks and costs of the business encouraged competitiveness and division, and produced a common, day-to-day struggle for survival and a sense of frustration and dependency. At the same time within the local music business there was also a preoccupation with leaving or staying in the city that can be connected to the poetics of loss and abandonment described in Chapter 2, and to the tension between marginality and pride described in Chapter 3. These tensions and preoccupations will be explored further in the following chapter, which builds upon the discussion of commercial music-making and the urban 'creative milieu' in this chapter. It explains how Liverpool Music House, Cream and other music-related businesses and organizations, including my own, became implicated in the efforts of the local state to categorize and develop music as a city or regional industry.

Chapter 5

Music as a City Industry: Haemorrhage, Debt and the Politics of Music Policy-Making

The two consultants stood beside a large, white flip chart in a grey city council office on a dull February afternoon. My first meeting with them had taken place a decade earlier in 1985 when both were working for the regional association Merseyside Arts. According to my field notes one of them was on that occasion dressed in battered jeans and had long, wavy hair; but he now wore a three-piece suit and had a short, stylish hairstyle, whilst his colleague was dressed smartly in grey. Twelve of us were seated in a semicircle facing the flip chart. All were involved with music in one way or another (some also had a history of involvement with Merseyside Arts) and I was more or less familiar with everyone. Roger Hill was there from Radio Merseyside, as was a solicitor who specialized in music, and four people who worked for subsidized, community or public-sector organizations. Colin from Liverpool Music House (LMH) was also there, sitting alongside three managers (of a rehearsal studio complex, a live music performance venue and a well-known local rock band). Lastly, there were two of us from higher education: myself from Liverpool University's Institute of Popular Music, and a woman from the Liverpool Institute for Performing Arts (LIPA).

The consultants began the meeting by explaining that they had been commissioned by a partnership of public-sector organizations to conduct a survey into Merseyside's 'arts and cultural industries sector', and produce a report that would help to inform the funding process. We were there, one of them explained, to provide him and his colleague with information on the music 'sub-sector'.[1] He then picked up a fat felt-tipped pen and drew a large black triangle on the chart to represent, pyramid style, the structure of the music industry, and he asked us to identify sub-sector strengths and weaknesses that he could mark up on the triangle. This clearly irritated the four businessmen amongst us. One of them accused the consultants of duplicating research that he and others, including 'most of those seated around this table', had already conducted for the recently established Merseyside Music Industry Association. He also questioned the role of the consultants by suggesting that those who were actually involved with music-making were best placed to assess their own 'sub-

---

1   In the letter of invitation to the meeting the participants were described as 'key players' within the sub-sector.

sector' needs and report on them directly to the funding agencies. Another angrily questioned whether those present could really represent the music sub-sector given that he had only just found out about the meeting and had come along without even being invited. A third businessman agreed that other music companies were being excluded. These interventions annoyed the consultants, who pointed out that they had only allocated one hour for the meeting and time was fast running out, but tensions escalated and the meeting was eventually dissolved.

The consultants subsequently wrote their final report, which became accepted as a policy document by the Government Offices on Merseyside (GOM) in March 1995. However, one of my colleagues at the Institute of Popular Music, who also happened to be Chair of the Merseyside Music Industry Association, was appalled by its representation of the music industry, and he specified his criticisms in a personal letter sent to GOM, which also called into question the consultants' competence.[2] Given that I was at that time directing an ethnographic research project on local music policy-making based at the Institute of Popular Music, my role as an ethnographer suddenly appeared more complicated than I had originally envisaged. The letter caused consternation amongst policy-makers who were concerned about its potentially damaging effects on public funding for the region (although one senior civil servant at GOM told us that the letter did contain some important points that the consultants had since taken on board), and the episode reinforced my impression of civic music policy-making as a battlefield involving groups with conflicting interests in music.

This chapter is about that policy-making,[3] and it focuses on policy initiatives aimed at the business of music in Liverpool and Merseyside during the 1980s and 1990s.[4] The aim is not to assess the success or local impact of such policy-making. Rather, the chapter aims to examine the impact of social and economic change in the city on music policy-making, and in turn the distinctiveness of popular music as a focus for civic policy, and how that affected the production of music as a city industry. The first part of the chapter presents some background to the meeting described above, and explains how music came to be targeted by the local state as a new industry for Liverpool and Merseyside that would contribute to local economic development. It illustrates the kind of initiatives that this spawned, the

---

2   He was not the only one to criticize the report. One City Council officer, for example, suggested to us that the report had not been based on extensive consultation and it excluded certain cultural activities: 'I wouldn't like to see it become a yardstick for judging every single funding application that goes through'.

3   For the purposes of this chapter I have defined music policy as direct or indirect intervention into, and support for, music practice by local, national and international governing bodies based on conceptions of music's social, cultural or economic significance.

4   The chapter draws upon ethnographic research conducted for several different projects. In particular, however, it is informed by a two-year project entitled 'Music Policy, the Music Industry and Local Economic Development' (1996–98), that involved myself, Adam Brown, Abigail Gilmore and Justin O'Connor (see Appendix for further details on the project and the pilot study that informed it).

groups and interests involved with those initiatives, and the conflicts and debates that the initiatives gave rise to. The second part of the chapter examines the notion of music as a city industry. It considers how initiatives aimed at the development of that industry promoted particular images and ideas about the city and were affected by the specificity of music as an industry.

Music Industry Policy-Making in Liverpool

The Music Industry and Local Economic Development

In September 1988 I joined a delegation from Liverpool on an official visit to Sheffield. On board our minibus were several council officers, a couple of arts consultants, the manager of Amazon Studios and the manager of a couple of well-known local bands who had also been co-owner of the music club Erics. A few years earlier, Sheffield City Council had appointed a Cultural Industries Officer who had co-ordinated a local economic development strategy that focused on music and film industries, and was for some time widely regarded as innovative and successful. Our visit to Sheffield had been organized with the aim of bringing together music- and policy-makers from both cities in order to facilitate an exchange of ideas and experiences. Upon our arrival in Sheffield we were met by the leader of Sheffield City Council, various council officers and members of the Human League, a Sheffield band that had achieved considerable success in the British rock/pop charts. We were taken to see the recording studio that the Human League had built in Sheffield's newly developed Cultural Industries Quarter (CIQ), and during a guided tour of that quarter we were shown how an area that had recently housed a concentration of derelict industrial warehouses had been transformed into a conglomeration of subsidized facilities for local music and film businesses.[5] This kind of 'cultural quarter' was partly inspired by the kind of creative 'clusters' discussed in the previous chapter, and a belief in their potential economic benefits.

During the early 1980s, following the rapid decline of its steel industry, Sheffield had become the first British city to seriously connect the 'cultural industries' with local economic development. Sheffield, like other industrial cities in Europe and North America, had been badly affected by the economic recession and de-industrialization that followed the crisis in the global, Fordist regime of accumulation and mass production. This provoked efforts to restructure the economies of those cities. They involved a turn to more flexible and casualized, knowledge- and design-intensive industries that were targeted at specialized or niche markets, and the development of new economies based on culture and creativity (Zukin, 1995; Lash and Urry, 1994; Bianchini and Parkinson, 1993). Cultural and economic policy thus became

---

5   The meeting was not a great success, much to the dismay and irritation of its Sheffield-based organizer, who complained to us later that apart from the manager of Amazon Studios the Liverpool visitors appeared to be inexplicably unforthcoming about their own cultural projects and plans.

more closely connected, and in Britain that connection was initially forged by city governments rather than by central government (Frith, 1993; Street, 1997). Traditionally in Britain, government subsidy and support had been reserved for the 'high' arts cultivated by a social elite and regarded as having educational, aesthetic and moral value and a significant role in the construction of national culture. During the general economic recession however, which led to substantial cuts in government arts subsidies, the left-wing Greater London Council (GLC) broadened its definition of the arts to include popular culture and the 'cultural industries'. The latter were defined as industries that 'produce and disseminate symbols in the forms of cultural goods and services, generally, although not exclusively, as commodities': industries that were thus central to 'the transmission of meaning' (Garnham, 1987: 25). They included industries based around film, the performing arts, broadcasting, advertising, publishing and music. They were identified as new growth industries that generated employment and income and made a positive contribution to the image and quality of life of Britain's urban areas, thereby helping to revitalize them and attract to them visitors and other investment. The GLC thus argued that in order to counter widespread economic recession and changes in patterns of employment, the arts and cultural industries should be invested in and developed strategically rather than merely subsidized and preserved.

Various British cities, particularly northern cities that had suffered most severely from the effects of de-industrialization, took up the GLC's ideas and launched 'arts and cultural industry strategies'. Those strategies were influenced by the culture-led regeneration initiatives of North American and Western European cities,[6] and they were supported by high-profile research that emphasized the local economic impact of the arts and cultural industries, and close connections between tourism and the arts.[7] They depended upon the argument that cities had a peculiarly close connection with the arts and cultural industries:

> In analyses of the changing functions of cities and in speculations about the future role of cities, the opinions consistently expressed are: That cities are by their very nature uniquely equipped to generate and sustain artistic activity, and that this role is closely related to the cities' continued economic vitality. By virtue of their substantial capital investments in arts facilities, their providing the necessary concentration of the artists themselves, their centrality in large-market areas, and their proximity to related entertainment and leisure opportunities, many cities have in the arts a substantial asset and a significant opportunity to employ this asset to generate additional economic activity (McNulty, 1988: 266).

By the late 1990s policies connecting culture with economic growth had become 'a common feature of the modern city' (Street, 1997: 106), with even quite small cities 'aggressively seeking to play the cultural economy card as a way of promoting local business and job growth' (Scott, 2000: 210). Hall (2000: 640) writes that in cities across Europe culture and the cultural industries are, 'now seen as the magic

---

6   See Bianchini and Parkinson (1993) and Landry and Bianchini (1995: 40).
7   See, for example, Meyerscough, 1986, 1988; Bianchini, 1989.

substitute for all the lost factories and warehouses, and as a device that will create a new urban image, making the city more attractive to mobile capital and mobile professional workers.' As part of their arts and cultural industries strategies, local authorities in various British cities invested in facilities and resources, training schemes and support mechanisms aimed at commercial music-making (Street, 1993). At the same time similar initiatives emerged in North American cities such as Austin (Shank, 1994) and New Orleans (Atkinson, 1997). Nevertheless, the definition of 'cultural industries', and the formulation and implementation of arts and cultural industry strategies, were in many ways locally specific. Some cities prioritized city marketing and prestigious 'flagship' projects intended to act as symbols of rebirth,[8] while others focused on developing facilities and support mechanisms to assist small-scale cultural production; some cities concentrated on high culture, whilst others were more concerned with the popular; and some city councils, as in Sheffield, adopted a proactive stance with regard to cultural policy, whilst the approach of others was more laissez-faire (Brown, Cohen and O'Connor, 1998).

Cultural Policy in Liverpool

So how did Liverpool fit into such developments? Culture-led urban regeneration seemed an obvious focus for Liverpool in view of the city's severe economic problems and its reputation for cultural and creative achievement, but it was not a priority for Liverpool City Council between 1983 and 1987 when the Labour Party had majority control. The party was dominated by a Trotskyist faction, the Militant Tendency, which was rooted in trade unions and in traditional working-class areas of the city. The Militants emphasized production and manual work and did not develop close networks with the city's business sector. They prioritized local taxation and housing policies, regarding art and culture as peripheral concerns: poor or 'soft' replacements for 'proper' local industries and distractions from urgent housing and welfare needs. Liverpool City Council thus had a Department of Arts and Libraries but no specific cultural or arts policy. Support for arts and cultural activities was channelled through the regional authority (Merseyside County Council) and the regional branch of the national Arts Council (Merseyside Arts) before both organizations were dismantled by the central Conservative government during the mid- to late 1980s.

Various factors combined, however, to push the arts and cultural industries to the centre of Liverpool's political and economic agenda. Liverpool City Council had consistently been at the forefront of opposition to aspects of Conservative government policy, and in 1986 it threatened to bankrupt the city unless the government gave it more money, and it borrowed from foreign banks to support an extensive public housing programme. The council was consequently disqualified from holding office by the House of Lords, and its leaders expelled from the Labour Party. This paved the way for the rise of the New Left, and the city's newly elected

---

8   Glasgow is an oft-cited example of a city that managed to reinvent itself through culture and city marketing initiatives (see Boyle and Hughes, 1991).

council began to involve a wide range of organizations in policy-making, and to develop partnerships with Liverpool-based central government and private-sector agencies. It also responded to the insistence of central government that funding from its urban programme be directed less at social welfare and more at initiatives with a clearer economic orientation. In 1987 the council published its Arts and Cultural Industries Strategy, which aimed 'to maximize the contribution that the arts and cultural industries make to the economic and social well-being of the city',[9] and to create local facilities for cultural training, production, management, distribution and marketing (Parkinson and Bianchini, 1993: 162–4).

In order to implement the strategy, the council established an Arts and Cultural Industries Unit within its Department of Arts and Libraries. A few years later that unit was transferred to the council's Economic Initiatives Department, thus signifying the increasing attention paid to the economic aspects of culture. These developments were initiated by a few young council and arts officers who had a professional interest in the arts, although during the 1980s and most of the 1990s the council generally lacked a well-planned and co-ordinated cultural strategy. Nevertheless, during that period the council did instigate, or become involved with, a series of initiatives aimed at culture and at local economic development, and they included two kinds of initiatives aimed at the music business. The first involved the development of 'cultural quarters' and is discussed in Chapter 7. The second involved the planning or launch of new institutions and agencies to facilitate and co-ordinate local music business development, and I will now outline the main initiatives involved in that process. In doing so I want to show what a small world music policy-making was in the city at that particular time, and how it involved efforts to make music fit a policy agenda. They included efforts of the local state to use popular music as a glamorous 'hook' for economic development; efforts of consultants to map local music onto a triangle or 'template', reduce it to a series of neat statistics, and monitor and regulate music bids for public funding; and efforts of music-makers to represent local music for policy-making purposes.

The Liverpool Institute for Performing Arts (LIPA)   On a bitterly cold January afternoon in 1995 I queued in a courtyard along with the Director of the Institute of Popular Music and other shivering guests invited to attend the launch of the Liverpool Institute for Performing Arts (LIPA), a grand, high-profile initiative that had been spearheaded by Paul McCartney (soon to become Sir Paul) and was housed in his old school.[10] The start of proceedings had been delayed due to a security alert, so we stayed where we were while hordes of uniformed security guards scampered around us with walkie-talkies. Crowds of Beatles fans waited anxiously outside the courtyard's perimeter fence, cameras at the ready, their faces pressed against the iron

---

9   'An Arts and Cultural Industries Strategy for Liverpool'. Liverpool City Council, November 1987.

10   McCartney also backed Liverpool's bid to the central government 'City Challenge' funding programme during the early 1990s.

railings, eager to catch a glimpse of McCartney himself. After a long wait we were finally allowed to enter the institute. The grand neo-Gothic building had been gutted and beautifully renovated, and we were taken on a tour of its impressive new facilities, including state-of-the-art recording and dance studios and a swish café and bar. We were then led into the grand and plush auditorium that had been modelled on an old-style theatre, to listen to performances by LIPA's first student cohort and speeches by a succession of dignitaries, with McCartney himself appearing on stage for the finale. McCartney's support for the project had been secured by the private, London-based company that had developed LIPA. The initial model for the institute had been music-focused, with an emphasis on community provision and collaboration with the city's existing music organizations; but that emphasis subsequently shifted and LIPA became an international 'centre of excellence', offering higher degrees in the performing arts validated by Liverpool John Moores University and boasting its own high-quality, in-house resources. The institute received funding from local, national and European government agencies as a major city 'flagship' that would attract outside investment, help to regenerate part of Liverpool city centre, and improve the city's image and create local jobs and businesses in the arts and cultural industries. A marketing officer at LIPA thus described the institute to us as, 'a symbol, if you like, of regeneration and the role of popular music and popular culture within that regeneration.'

Music City The initial proposal for LIPA had been developed under the auspices of the Music City Study, which was launched by Liverpool City Council to assess the current state of Merseyside's music industries, identify their training needs and establish key areas for effective public and private investment. David Horn and I from the Institute of Popular Music contributed to that study, conducting the survey of music businesses referred to in the previous chapter, contributing to the initial feasibility study for LIPA and compiling a study on the local provision of music information. The resulting Music City Report,[11] written and produced by the director of the Music City study, emphasized the importance of an integrated cultural industries development strategy for Merseyside linked to the development of physical infrastructure, and it suggested ways of maximizing the contribution of the music industry to the region's economy. In addition to a partially developed proposal to establish a Liverpool Institute for Performing Arts, it advocated the development of a Music Information Centre and a major international music festival. However, the report received little response from Liverpool City Council, which had (against the advice of the director of Music City) become centrally involved with the staging of the 1991 John Lennon Memorial Concert. This was a major international event

---

11   'Music City'. Produced by Ark Consultants for Liverpool City Council in March 1991.

intended to raise Liverpool's profile and lay the foundation for similar events in the future, but it was surrounded by controversy and resulted in substantial debts.[12]

City Beat   Whilst LIPA had been advocated by the Music City study, in turn that study had emerged out of an earlier Liverpool City Council initiative entitled City Beat.[13] I first read about that initiative in an article in a national newspaper, which was accompanied by a photograph of the council officer who was the driving force behind the initiative. That officer later commissioned the Music City report before becoming a key consultant for LIPA, whilst the City Beat report was co-authored by one of the consultants at the meeting described at the start of this chapter. City Beat was a bold initiative that helped, along with some innovative film schemes, to launch and publicize Liverpool City Council's new Arts and Cultural Industries Strategy. The City Beat report proposed that the council establish a Liverpool-based and council-run music production and management company that would develop and commercially exploit local music talent in order to generate revenue for the city. The company would be non-profit-making and would have a limited liability status, with profits reinvested in the company and in related cultural industries initiatives. The proposal was criticized, however, by local music-makers. Some expressed doubts about the council's ability to run such a company and were concerned that the company's existence would be threatened when a new council was elected. Others suggested that the proposal lacked knowledge and understanding of the music industry, and they criticized the council for proposing a scheme that duplicated or competed with existing private-sector businesses, and for not consulting them about the initiative. A couple of those critics were subsequently invited to join council officers and consultants on the minibus trip to Sheffield. One of them (the ex-owner of the club Erics) was later appointed director of the Music City Study, which was initiated by the council following the abandonment of the City Beat initiative.

The Merseyside Music Industry Association (MMIA)   Concerns about a perceived lack of consultation of local music-makers over music industry policy initiatives nevertheless resurfaced, and they encouraged the launch of the Merseyside Music Industry Association in 1993. The association aimed to give those involved with local music-making a voice within the policy-making process, and it was approved at a meeting of around one hundred or so music-makers. I was struck by an atmosphere of excitement and enthusiasm at that meeting, as were friends and colleagues who also participated. Consequently, Colin from Liverpool Music House (chapter 4) was

---

12   As documented in the national newspapers: 'MPs ask why music gala cost £2,000 a minute' (*The Independent*, 13 September 1993); 'Instant Bad Karma by the Mersey: Michael Gray went to Liverpool for Saturday's John Lennon Tribute Concert, but the event was a musical disaster, out of tune with his memory' (*The Times*, 7 May 1990). Moreover, few local musicians were invited to participate in the event, a fact that prompted the organization of an alternative and simultaneous event named Liverpool Now!, which became an annual showcase of local musical talent aimed at London-based record companies.

13   'City Beat'. Report for Liverpool City Council, August 1987.

elected as Secretary, whilst one of my colleagues from the Institute of Popular Music was elected as Chair. The rousing calls for solidarity and support amongst local music-makers were echoed in the association's first leaflet:

> What's happening to music on Merseyside? Liverpool is famed throughout the world as a centre for popular and orchestral music. So why does the local picture so often seem fragmented and stagnant? We have the talent, facilities and contacts to build a thriving music industry here ... With your help we can all put Merseyside back on the map!

The MMIA was established as a democratic body with statutes, an elected working committee and regular open meetings. Its membership consisted of music-makers from the public and private sectors, and its committee tried to make the association as inclusive as possible but worked on a voluntary basis and without funding. The committee nevertheless met weekly and organized a series of music business seminars to provide a public forum for discussion and debate about local music. It eventually produced a development plan for music on Merseyside that it circulated to policy-makers.[14] The plan outlined collective strategies for improving the region's music industry, primarily through the centralization of information and training and investment in businesses and services. It took into account the needs of different music genres and a broad range of music activity, from community music to business enterprise. Amongst other proposals it advocated the establishment of a staffed Music Industry Resource Unit and the post of Music Officer within Liverpool City Council (the council already employed a Film Officer). The manager of the city's Royal Court music venue said of the plan, 'I think that it fulfils most of the aims of the music industry ... there has been a lot of time and effort put into it and I think that if people come behind that plan and say this is what we need there are then opportunities to funnel through the resource centre' (p.c.).

The Merseyside Music Development Agency (MMDA) The Merseyside Music Industry Association and its development plan were overtaken, however, by a new music initiative directed at European funding. In 1994 Merseyside was awarded Objective One status, which is the European Union's highest funding category reserved for its poorest regions. This was the first time that an area of Britain had been categorized as such, and it meant that £1.25 billion of EU and UK central government funding was to be spent on Merseyside between 1994 and 1999 in order to encourage sustained growth and job creation and enhance the region's competitiveness in the global marketplace.[15] Specified within the region's Objective One plan was the role

---

14   'MMIA Music Industry Development Plan', November 1994.

15   The funding was directed at developing new rather than existing structures, and it was to be distributed via a partnership involving the EU, UK central government, the five local authorities responsible for the Merseyside region, and various training or development agencies and community or voluntary groups. Private businesses were not allowed to apply for funds directly but could apply through 'eligible bodies', although initially there was much confusion over how such bodies should be defined.

that culture, media and leisure industries could play in economic development.[16] Objective One thus presented Merseyside with a unique opportunity to develop cultural policy, and it illustrated the growing influence of EU funding on British arts and cultural industries development. The MMIA tried to assist its members in bidding for Objective One funding by summarizing in lay terms the Objective One planning document. In addition to this the association submitted its own Objective One bid that highlighted a compatibility between MMIA's development plan for local music and the aims and objectives of the Objective One programme. However, local arts and cultural businesses appeared to face particular problems submitting Objective One bids.[17] Two consultants were therefore commissioned by a partnership of public-sector bodies, including Liverpool City Council and the Government Offices on Merseyside (GOM), to investigate the region's arts and cultural industries sector, monitor Objective One funding bids and prepare a report and strategy relating the sector to Objective One principles, objectives and criteria. The report was intended to help GOM make informed decisions about the sector, and to help those within the sector gain access to Objective One funding. The consultants divided the arts and cultural industries sector into separate sub-sectors (moving image, radio, design, music, visual arts, theatre, events and festivals) and organized a series of meetings to discuss sub-sector strengths and weaknesses, which included the music meeting described at the start of this chapter.

Following those meetings and the submission of their final report, the consultants were commissioned to draw up a template for a series of 'enabling agencies' that would develop and distribute funds to each arts and cultural industries sub-sector. They were also commissioned to prepare an Objective One bid for an overarching agency that would co-ordinate the entire sector. They did so with the help of another arts consultant who had been centrally involved with earlier music policy initiatives, including City Beat, Music City and LIPA. Consequently, a series of lengthy and sometimes difficult meetings took place involving consultants and music-makers, which were designed to discuss and prepare the Objective One bid for a Merseyside Music Development Agency (MMDA). The bid was successful: the MMDA was launched in July 1998 at the House of Commons in London and was awarded a total of £1,120,000 during its first year. The MMDA's main aims were to attract inward investment to Merseyside from the music industry in order to lever down matching public funding from the European Union and other sources, and to create a network of initiatives that would develop and support the region's music industry and thereby attract further investment. The MMDA board comprised a group of music-makers from public, private and voluntary sectors. The board worked on a voluntary basis and

---

16   *Single Programming Document: 1994–1999.* Directorate General for Regional Policies: European Commission. ERDF no: 94.09.12.001. ARINCO No. 94.UK.16.001. 18 November 1994.

17   In the first round of the Objective One bidding process all of its five 'drivers' were greatly oversubscribed to, except for the one that specifically related to the culture, media and leisure industries.

organized public meetings with other music-makers. During its first couple of years the MMDA was able to pay for its own premises and the board met there weekly, but the agency later moved to LIPA. This followed a change in the membership of the board after unfounded allegations of corruption targeted at specific board members appeared in the city's main newspaper, the *Liverpool Echo*.[18] Due to a shift in its funding the MMDA later began to focus more on the provision of business advice and on initiatives targeted at local youths and minority groups.

Participants in Music Industry Policy-Making

Music industry policy-making thus emerged as a response to social and economic change in Liverpool, and it involved a series of initiatives aimed at developing music as a local industry. Those initiatives did not conform to any pre-existing plan, but unfolded in a more unpredictable and sometimes haphazard manner and generated a confusing array of acronyms. The initiatives were formulated and implemented by a few key players drawn from particular occupational and interest groups, and I will now briefly introduce the three main groups involved. Broadly defined, they consisted of government officials or policy-makers, consultants and music-makers.

Policy-Makers and Consultants   To begin with, the initiatives involved government officials representing various local, national and European public sector organizations, including Liverpool City Council. Few of them had specialist knowledge of the arts and cultural industries, so they employed consultants to inform and advise them on those industries and develop particular initiatives. In fact in Britain the growing interest of policy-makers in the arts and cultural industries had given rise to a new tier of professional consultants (and 'cultural intermediaries') with expertise in those areas. Some consultancy organizations had rapidly become leaders in the field, assisting and advising on the arts and cultural industry strategies of a number of different cities, and specializing in the production of 'impact'/'feasibility'/ 'mapping'/'scoping'/'SWOT' studies that supported cultural policy initiatives. The quality and reliability of such studies was variable, partly because the economic impact of cultural activity was notoriously difficult to assess, measurement criteria varied and those working in the arts and cultural industries had little experience of justifying their work in terms of economic development. Nevertheless, the studies generated statistics that helped to raise the profile of local arts and cultural activity, and measurement models gradually became more sophisticated.

One striking feature of Liverpool cultural policy-making during the 1980s and 1990s was the central and continuous involvement of a small and close-knit group of consultants. Unlike cultural practitioners and scholars who were occasionally employed by public or private organizations to research and develop particular

---

18   One of those board members consequently resigned from the board but brought a legal case against the newspaper, whose editors subsequently printed a correction and agreed to settle out of court.

projects, these were professional consultants who specialized in the broad field of arts and cultural industries and enjoyed close connections with public sector agencies. Some of them had lobbied for the introduction of cultural policy in Liverpool, helping to break down divisions between high art and popular culture and promote arguments for the economic significance and impact of the arts and cultural industries: 'We are recognizing,' one of them told me during our journey to Sheffield in 1988 to visit its Cultural Industries Quarter, 'that the creative industries ... are not like any other industry but are actually a model for the future'. Several of those consultants had pursued similar career paths, moving from an involvement with community arts, the Arts Council and other public sector bodies, to become freelance consultants and professional funding bidders employed for their knowledge of the intricacies of public and EU funding. They also socialized together and were collectively referred to by several policy- and music-makers we interviewed as the local 'Arts Mafia', the 'Garden Party Network' and 'Champagne Socialists' – descriptions that hinted at a shared perception of them as an influential and middle-class clique. Two of them had been Labour city councillors and both had acted on separate occasions as Chair of Finance and Policy at Liverpool City Council. One former Labour government minister associates them with a particular social group: 'University-educated, mostly from out of town, and mostly based in the south end of Liverpool, they became known as the "Sainsbury set" on account of their apparent tastes in food and wine' (Kilfoyle, 2000: 215). His wariness of them becomes clearer when he suggests that by moving into consultancy and advising on Objective 1 funding these former councillors made use of 'the expertise gleaned on the council and elsewhere'(ibid.: 256).

Music-Makers   The music-makers involved with music industry policy-making generally had a background in rock/pop music and current or previous experience of the public sector and its funding mechanisms. Their interest in policy-making also stemmed from a long-standing involvement with local music-making and a concern that it should receive appropriate support or investment for the benefit of those working in it and of the city as a whole. A member of the MMIA Working Committee told us of her belief that the right kind of policies, strategically targeted and properly implemented, could have an enabling potential, helping to create an appropriate environment in which music-making could flourish. Another committee member said that he wanted to enable music-makers to have an influence on policy-making (p.c.). Colin from Liverpool Music House (LMH) told us that it was his often frustrating experience of running a business that had prompted him to get involved with such policy-making. He wanted to try to strengthen networks and collaboration between local music-makers in order to promote the profile of local music, and increase its potential for growth and investment.

Cream was not directly involved with the music industry development initiatives outlined above, but the company made efforts to forge links with policy-makers, particularly after the appointment of its Head of Communications, who had previous experience of working with public sector agencies, and after the appearance of one of its directors in a televised debate on urban regeneration.[19] As a club, Cream was particularly concerned to influence local licensing regulations, but the company also owned properties within the city centre and had an interest in city-centre regeneration (see Chapter 7). Cream joined the Chamber of Commerce and the quasi central government organization Merseyside Partnership: 'Now, at last,' one of its directors told us, 'there's a massive, massive interest in Cream by people like the Merseyside Development Trust and a lot of other bodies I don't even remember the names of.' In 1997 Liverpool newspapers announced the results of a survey carried out by Liverpool John Moores University, which suggested that 70 per cent of the university's new students had chosen to study in Liverpool so that they could attend Cream. Whether any such survey was actually carried out has been questioned (Du Noyer, 2000: 206, reports that Cream's Head of Communications made it up), but again it drew attention to Cream's impact on Liverpool's image and economy. A city marketing official at Merseyside Partnership told us, 'I've been pushing Cream ... There has to be something there if students will come for three years just because of it.'

Despite the cases of Cream and LMH, most music entrepreneurs and most musicians were simply not interested in policy-making, or felt alienated by it. Many of those entrepreneurs suggested to us that what they really wanted was not music policy but a physical environment in which they could operate more effectively. The local authorities, they believed, should therefore devote their attention to the removal of litter from city streets rather than trying to interfere with a business they did not understand. Some also tried to convey to us how frustrated, baffled or disempowered they felt in relation to civic policy and the funding processes involved. They complained, for example, of difficulties in gaining information and advice on application procedures and in finding time to complete the relevant documentation. Most could not afford the consultants or administrative back-up employed by larger organizations and despaired over the maze of procedures and paperwork involved. A property developer who had worked with a number of local music businesses told us, 'The general impression is that there is a mass of money about but it's impossible to get hold of it'; whilst a director of Crash rehearsal studios said, 'we've heard that there's grants available. All we can seem to see is there's a mountain of red tape to get through' (p.c.).

Changes in the language and structures of cultural policy throughout the 1990s (including a shift in terminology from 'cultural' to 'creative' industries) generated additional confusion, and in recognition of this the MMIA tried to help its members by, as one committee member put it, translating policy terms into 'music speak'. A bank manager who sat on the committee and had close ties to local music-making told us, 'most artists find it very difficult to work with the financial sector and the grants and local authorities and officialdom generally'. Merseyside's Objective One

---

19   He was invited to appear on the programme after another guest speaker from outside the city happened to mention to a Liverpool policy-maker that his daughter was a big Cream fan (Cream's Head of Communications, p.c.).

status, for example, had been launched with much publicity and hype[20] but initially it gave rise to much rumour, confusion and disenchantment on the part of those in competition for funds, administering funds or advising on the whole process. We were told, for example: 'Even for experienced practitioners this is a completely new process, and rules and requirements are changing as we go along. Inevitably that breeds, even in the Council, some degree of cynicism' (senior manager, Central Policy Unit, Government Offices on Merseyside); '95 per cent of people don't understand Objective One, it's a very opaque, very difficult funding mechanism to understand' (the local Director of European Affairs); 'The only people who are getting anything out of it are the people who know the system' (arts consultant).

Other Participants   Besides the government officials, consultants and music-makers there were others who had a more marginal or occasional involvement with music industry policy-making. They included a couple of solicitors and a bank manager who had a close professional involvement with local music-making, as well as individuals employed in higher education. Amongst the latter were members of staff at the Liverpool Institute for Performing Arts (LIPA), an institution that had been funded partly to occupy a strategic position as a channel for the development of local arts and cultural industries (Peck, 1993), and at Liverpool University's Institute of Popular Music (IPM). A couple of staff at LIPA became members of the MMDA board and the association eventually occupied an office at LIPA. The Development Officer of the IPM helped to facilitate initial meetings designed to discuss the development of a Merseyside Music Development Agency at the university, which was generally perceived to be a relatively neutral location, and eventually became an MMDA board member, whilst another colleague acted for a short period of time as Chair of the Merseyside Music Industry Association. More recently, undergraduate and postgraduate students at the IPM have become involved with MMDA and related music-policy initiatives. The IPM also produced the first annual Merseyside Music Industry Directory, based initially on information gathered for the survey of music businesses conducted for the Music City study. In addition to this and other invitations to produce 'useful' research findings, IPM staff were once or twice called upon to express an 'expert' opinion in the local media on particular policy initiatives, and to act as advocates for local music-makers with whom we had professional and personal associations. Yet at the same time we also tried to maintain our interest in music industry policy-making as a field of academic study.

    The involvement of the IPM and LIPA in music industry policy-making was by no means unusual, and increasingly other scholars in other cities have played a similar role. They include colleagues from the Manchester Institute of Popular Culture (MIPC) who were involved with cultural policy-making in Manchester, and popular music scholars such as Cloonan, Williamson and Frith (2004) who were employed as consultants by policy-makers in Scotland because of their interest and

---

20   As illustrated by articles in the *Liverpool Echo* with titles such as 'Mersey set for £690m spree', 'Euro Pot of Gold', 'Euro millions will help whole of Merseyside'.

experience in popular music research, but also because they could be presented as 'objective' interpreters with no obvious stake in either legislation or the market. However, the role played by these scholars has not gone uncriticized. Negus (1995), for example, accuses music-policy researchers of colluding with either legislators or with the market, whilst Cloonan et al. (2004) provide an illuminating account of the efforts of both music- and policy-makers to discredit their research on the Scottish music industry.

Music Industry Policy-Making as a Contested Process

Music industry policy-making involved individuals from these broadly-defined social and occupational groups in numerous plans and ideas, and it generated excitement, commitment and enthusiasm. At the same time, however, it also provoked confusion, bitterness and disillusionment. Reading over transcripts of interviews with those involved I was struck by the mistrust with which some of them viewed one another, and the extent to which initiatives were informed by gossip, rumour and misinformation. Music policy-making was thus by no means straightforward or consensual but was a politicized and contested process.

The City Beat proposal, for example, generated much scepticism; the Music City report was largely ignored by the policy-makers who had commissioned it; the MMIA, as I will discuss below, was also ignored by policy-makers and consultants; and MMDA board members were deliberately discredited. LIPA was also contentious. Questions were raised, for example, about the institute's contribution to local economic development, with some music-makers expressing scepticism as to whether, as promised, LIPA graduates would indeed stay and establish businesses in the city: 'What's the use of training them in Liverpool for them to then get off and take their talents to London' (director of 3Beat Records, p.c.). There were also concerns about the hiring out of LIPA's in-house music facilities on a commercial basis, and whether this would undercut related local businesses; about whether performing arts establishments helped or hindered musical creativity and innovation; and about LIPA's prominence within the policy-making process.

These and other concerns were expressed not just by music-makers but also by policy-makers and local community and voluntary sector organizations. Liverpool City Council's Arts Officer told us, 'I've no objection to anybody saying, "I want a school to immortalize me" as long as they put the money into it. What I object to is an extension of the ego that is being subsidized by the public.' He added that he was annoyed by the lack of community consultation over LIPA, the lack of community access to the school and by 'the hype', and he thought the 'arts community' should lobby against it. The Head of Corporate Sponsorship at Liverpool City Council explained to us:

> The criticism of LIPA is that it was conceived as this big 'Paul McCartney gives something back to the community event'. Loads of public money has gone in, and when it's materialized there's no local kids there. It's international rich kids ... You can understand

why there is a lot of political ill-will in the city towards LIPA, because they renovate a beautiful building and it looks nice from the outside. They spend a fortune of local public sector money, most of which comes from local council tax payers. So you've a situation where very poor families whose kids can't even get on the YTS [government-funded training] scheme have been asked to fund this international school for young people whose parents are probably richer than the entire street.

Meanwhile, the arts consultant who put together LIPA's business plan and helped to raise its public funding told us: 'We knew with McCartney's name we could get to places no other arts organizations could', and he described local opposition to LIPA as 'begrudgery'.

Music industry policy-making thus generated tension and debate, but it also involved a struggle for control over the policy-making process, and over the representation and monitoring of music for policy-making purposes. Street (1997: 111) suggests that for music-policy initiatives to work there needs to be 'a degree of sympathy between lobbyists and politicians, a sense of a shared culture', whilst Shank (1994: 215) illustrates how music industry policy initiatives in Austin, Texas, benefited from a strong collaboration between music-makers and the local business community. Such relationships were not well established in Liverpool. Moreover, music industry policy-making in that city depended upon the continuous involvement of a small network of consultants and music-makers, and this contributed to an entrenchment of political and personal rivalries. One particular source of tension was the role played by consultants in the initiatives that I have described. The consultants clearly exerted considerable influence over cultural policy-making in the city. They defined what the cultural industries were; categorized them into various sub-sectors; represented them to policy-makers; monitored and controlled funding bids; and basically tried to make music fit their policy-making agenda and the cultural industry models and templates that they devised and promoted. In addition to this, they issued invitations to key policy meetings and, as illustrated by the meeting described at the start of this chapter, they tended to invite those who shared a similar background or social network to themselves. One of the consultants who organized that meeting later complained to us: 'We called together focus groups of people that I knew, and knew were operational, and that group was somewhat hijacked in the meeting.'

In order to gain employment, the consultants had to promote themselves as cultural experts and 'intermediaries', and sell their knowledge of and expertise in the arts and cultural industries sector, and their ability to deploy that knowledge for policy-making purposes. One consultant described his role, and the role of his fellow consultants, as that of providing a 'bridge' between policy-makers and music practitioners (p.c.), but some music practitioners described it as more of a barrier:

> I find it objectionable really, if the money is available for that project, that you have to then pay somebody either a percentage of what you get or a fee to put the package together in order to get at the cash. They're leeching on the system. They go and get people to act as the intermediary ... but they're probably failed artists or something in the first place. Or not failed necessarily but would like to have been but couldn't cut it on their own, so they

now get fat salaries for being terribly important (bank manager and MMIA committee member, p.c.).

There seems to be a growth in consultants who are making applications for people and, as part of a small group of people who do actually know about Objective One, are cleaning up (manager of the Royal Court music venue, p.c.).

Members of the MMIA's Working Committee believed that those working within the industry knew that industry best and understood its needs, and that it was therefore they rather than the consultants who should be representing the industry directly to policy-makers. They also questioned the role that the consultants were playing in advising upon and monitoring funding bids from the cultural sector, including Objective One bids relating to music:

> The only people who know about the music industry are those people in it, not the planners and the strategists who at present seem to be pulling the strings. This is why MMIA is a separate entity, which will freak people out. It seems ludicrous to me to have to pay consultants to draw up the [Objective One] proposal, when the thinking, methodology and everything else about it was developed and delivered by the original instigators of it. The people who motivated it, did the runnings for it and carry on running, they should have the ball (community music worker and MMIA committee member, p.c.).

> MMIA has defined who's involved in the local music industry, and if anyone else has got any other thoughts on it they can tell us, but as far as we're concerned we know what industry we're in (music manager and MMIA committee member, p.c.).

Many of the music-makers we spoke to also accused the consultants of lacking specific expertise in music and lacking understanding of its specificity as a cultural industry. The consultancy reports referred to earlier, for example (including the Objective One and City Beat reports), were criticized for, among other things, relying on an industry model that excluded the exploitation of music rights, which was perhaps the industry's most profitable aspect. At stake was not just the accuracy of such reports, but also competing claims to knowledge about the music industry and competing efforts to influence its development. In turn, the consultants described music as the most fragmented and divided of all Merseyside's arts and cultural industries. This was evident, for example, in the Objective One consultancy report that was based on meetings like the one described at the start of this chapter. Within a brief analysis of the region's music 'sub-sector' the report pointed to 'hostility between people and organisations who should naturally be partners', and stated that this presented a barrier to development. It also stated that there was an absence of 'leadership' within the sub-sector, which presented problems for local economic development.[21] In conversation with us, one consultant described music as the most 'difficult' sub-sector to deal with, whilst another referred to music's 'begrudging little turf wars'

---

21   'Objective One: Arts and Cultural Industries Study'. Submitted to the Government Offices on Merseyside, March 1995.

and described the music sub-sector as, 'insular, unpleasant, under skilled ... and that's the subsidized aspiring bit. It's a mess. It doesn't make anything. It makes very little.' The breakdown of the music sub-sector meeting described at the start of this chapter may have contributed to such perspectives. It had certainly irritated the consultants involved, and other consultants were obviously aware of what had happened. The businessmen present had challenged the consultants' plans and procedures, thus threatening the policy-making process.

In response to the consultants' report, MMIA committee members pointed us to normal and healthy differences of opinion (rather than hostility) amongst local music-makers, and to increasing collaboration and co-operation, partly due to the work of the association itself. (It is possible that the adoption of the term 'industry' in the singular by the Merseyside Music Industry Association helped the association to present local music-making as coherent and integrated.[22]) Yet one of the consultants who organized the meeting described at the start of this chapter criticized the MMIA for trying to create a large democratic body in order to imitate government policy-makers and gain their support, and suggested to us that policy-makers 'would see through this straight away' (p.c.). Ironically, therefore, when music-makers tried to convince the authorities that they represented a respectable, well-organized industry, they were perceived as being too bureaucratic and businesslike, and not creative, entrepreneurial or dynamic like the music industry was supposed to be. Another consultant, referring to the MMIA, criticized 'organizations that purport to represent people and never actually meet', but also said 'I'm not into representation I'm into effectiveness' (p.c.). Consequently, although MMIA committee members tried to publicly demonstrate to consultants and government officials their willingness to help co-ordinate a package of complementary Objective One music bids, the association attracted little support from government officials and arts consultants. Apart from the Music Officer of the regional Arts Board, and the Arts Officer of Liverpool City Council (who was in fact a member of the MMIA committee), none of them attended MMIA meetings and seminars, despite regular invitations. They also did not respond to the MMIA's Development Plan, although a senior civil servant at the Government Offices on Merseyside told us that the plan 'should be something that we're aware of and take on board'.

Unsurprisingly, therefore, many of the music-makers who had been persuaded to become directly or indirectly involved with music industry policy-making subsequently found themselves excluded and marginalized, which generated a sense of frustration and disillusionment, and of shattered hopes, plans and ambitions. At the same time, it must be remembered that only a small minority of music-makers became involved with such policy-making in the first place, and that the business of music in Liverpool also did not appear to be equally accessible to everyone. Hence

---

22   This possibility is underlined by Williamson and Cloonan (2004), who suggest that the reference to a music 'industry' in the singular 'disguises conflict *within* the industries. It assumes the common interest of musician and label, of promoter and venue, and of organizations which are in daily competition with each other.'

the difficulties experienced by local black music entrepreneurs (Chapter 1), and the fact that local music businesses were predominantly run by men (Chapter 4).[23] In fact, Toynbee (1996) argues against the building of music industries in Britain's provincial cities because he believes that the skilled and the entrepreneurial benefit from such policies whilst the poor and minority groups don't. Nevertheless, whilst access to the cultural industries was a neglected or sidelined issue in terms of Liverpool's early music policy documents and initiatives, later initiatives did raise consciousness and debate about that issue, and provoked further initiatives aimed at marginal and minority groups. The committees of the MMIA and MMDA, for example, considered the issue of access at great length, partly because some of them had a background in community arts or identified closely with minority groups, and partly because of the increasing emphasis on social inclusion within the European Union. In order to fulfil its European funding criteria and become more locally embedded, LIPA also introduced various schemes aimed at local community and minority groups and at enabling access to music and other cultural industries.

Liverpool in Music Industry Policy-Making

In the Liverpool of the 1980s and 1990s, a period of intense social and economic change and restructuring thus encouraged the local state to think of music as a local industry, and to launch or support initiatives aimed at developing that industry. Despite the similarities in the music industry policy-making of several British and North American cities during the 1980s and 1990s, the ways in which it was formulated, implemented and responded to were nevertheless locally specific, reflecting distinctive characteristics of the cities concerned. Bianchini and Parkinson (1993: 155) describe cultural policy in Liverpool during the 1980s and early 1990s as a 'tale of missed opportunities'. They discuss the way that it was hampered by local economic and political circumstances, including communication problems between council departments, a lack of financial resources and a lack of commitment to cultural policy on the part of the local authorities. According to Bianchini (1991: 19), the implementation of Liverpool's 1987 arts and cultural industries strategy was not a sufficiently high priority within the local authority and was never properly phased or funded. One arts consultant who was centrally involved in all of the music initiatives outlined above described the strategy somewhat cynically to us as: 'a complete fuck up ... officers weren't good enough, councillors didn't care enough, including this one. The Arts and Cultural Industries Unit was a complete and utter waste of space. I've got no views on it at all these days. I'm just like a whore – If you pay me I'll work, if you don't I won't.'

If music industry policy-making reflected social and economic circumstances within the city then how, in turn, was the city produced through that policy-making?

---

23   The history of popular music-making has been described as accessible and 'structurally democratic', but at the same time a 'history of exclusion: of African-Americans and Caribbeans ... of women' (Toynbee, 2000: xi, xii; see also Frith, 1983: 17).

I will now address that question by first considering how support for music as a local industry was mobilized, and how the city was imagined through that process; and second, how specific characteristics of the music business affected efforts to develop and think about music as a local, city industry.

Music as a City Industry

Increasingly during the 1990s, political and funding priorities encouraged music industry policy initiatives to adopt a regional perspective, and this helps to explain the growing emphasis on music as an industry for Merseyside. Nevertheless, there was still a tendency for Liverpool to dominate discussions about that industry. This was due to a combination of factors, including the concentration of music businesses within the city (see Chapter 4); the city's dominance within the social, cultural and economic life and image of the region; and the way that music activity outside of the city was often ignored or marginalized by those living and working within it. Hence music was thought of most often as a city industry, a notion that had popular appeal amongst the key groups involved with the policy initiatives that I have described.

It thus became increasingly commonplace for local rock musicians and entrepreneurs to refer to a local music 'industry' rather than, or as well as, a local 'scene', references that had been relatively uncommon during the mid-1980s when I first started to conduct research on rock culture in Liverpool. Support for the notion of music as a city industry, and for initiatives aimed at developing such an industry, was mobilized by the rhetoric of loss, abandonment and marginality that was highlighted in earlier chapters, and by the tensions that informed that rhetoric. Hence the departure for London of successful Liverpool musicians and their earnings was a starting point for Liverpool's early cultural policy documents, and a concern raised by all of the policy initiatives I have described. One statement that appeared in a number of documents, for example, concerned the rock/pop band Frankie Goes To Hollywood, who attained considerable commercial success during the early 1980s: 'It is estimated that in their first year of success, sales of their records and ancillary products generated £200 million in revenue income. Not a single pound of this revenue went to Liverpool.'[24] Similarly, music-makers who attended the public meetings organized by the MMIA, most of whom were involved with rock or pop music, made comments such as: 'Liverpool is good at producing good artists and product which we then send to London'; 'We've got to stop the haemorrhage'; 'keep success local'. As the manager of a large music venue put it:

> the main thing, as far as the music industry is concerned, is to stop the flow of talent away from the city ... if anyone is successful within six months they are on their way down to London. If we can encourage people not to leave the city then that will help the

---

24   Report entitled 'Arts in Inner Cities', commissioned by the Ministry of Arts and cited in Mitchinson (1988).

infrastructure ... the general feeling in the community is that they don't want successful people to leave.

A London-based A&R manager who was originally from Liverpool and participated in one of those meetings proclaimed, 'Liverpool has produced some very successful people but they are now elsewhere. They all move away. It is ironic that a lot of people who are still here have not been very successful. Success leaves.'

In conversation with us, a couple of those music-makers suggested that the need to pursue activities and lifestyles necessitated by success explained the departure of some musicians from Liverpool, but others censured such musicians for being greedy and for 'deserting' or 'selling out on' the city. The notion of 'selling out' took hold within 'independent' or 'alternative' rock culture following the emergence of punk in the 1970s and its 'do-it-yourself' aesthetic, which promoted the credibility of independent record labels and adopted an anti-commercial stance. 'Selling out' was thus usually an accusation aimed at music-makers who were perceived to have compromised their credibility and artistic integrity for commercial gain by engaging in financial dealings with major rather than independent music companies. In the Liverpool of the 1980s and 1990s, however, the notion of selling out was also commonly interpreted in spatial terms. Similarly, musicians were often accused of leaving Liverpool without having 'paid their dues' to it. Exactly what that payment of dues should involve was rarely spelt out, but it was a notion that carried much weight, as illustrated by one young rock musician planning a move to London who felt obliged to tell us that he refused to feel guilty about leaving Liverpool, adding: 'I think I've paid my dues here.'

The relationship of 'successful' musicians with Liverpool was intensely scrutinized and lines of debt and accountability more tightly drawn. As discussed in the following chapter, this was particularly the case with the Beatles. A local businessman with a key interest in music told us:

> [The Beatles'] fame is because of the world outside and not because of Liverpool and while everyone wants to hang on to the relationship and say they are Liverpudlians, 'aren't we good and aren't we clever for producing them?' I think we must not be greedy. We must not claim these people and associate them with Liverpool as if they owe it to Liverpool. I don't think they do owe it to Liverpool.

Meanwhile, local newspapers reported on what well-known local rock/pop performers were supposed to have said about Liverpool or to have done for the city. In the early 1980s the manager of the Liverpool rock band Echo and the Bunnymen was questioned in the music press about his forthcoming move to London offices, and about the accusation that by moving he was 'selling out and deserting Liverpool'.[25] A few years later the *Liverpool Echo* devoted its front page to a comment that a member of Echo and the Bunnymen was reputed to have made to a national music paper in which he referred to Liverpudlians as 'scum'(Cohen, 1991a: 11). A member

25   *Melody Maker*, 4 April 1981.

of Frankie Goes To Hollywood is quoted as saying, 'Where you're from does make you what you are ... But do you owe it to that place? It's like this whole thing of turning your back on it: "Oh, you've moved to London now". I dunno, they lay on this really weird guilt trip' (quoted in Du Noyer, 2002: 173).

Such debates about the way that local musicians related to the city often involved the drawing of distinctions between the musical life of Liverpool and that of nearby Manchester, as illustrated by the following quotations:

> The music industry does need central resources but not a central profit stream. Liverpool earns money but it doesn't come back here. In Manchester money moves around, but in Liverpool ... money doesn't come back (London-based A&R manager, speaking at a music business seminar in Liverpool).

> Merseybeat ripped the heart out of Merseyside. They all left, so by the time I got involved in the 70s there was no real infrastructure left here. They had all gone to London with their skills, but that hadn't happened in Manchester because Manchester wasn't as successful, so more of them stayed in Manchester (rock band manger, p.c.).

> There's that sort of tradition of people coming to Manchester with an idea and it succeeding without them having to sell out. Whereas in, say, Liverpool there's like, well, even the Beatles and Frankie Goes To Hollywood, Liverpool groups, had to go to London to make it. The groups that were left just seemed sad. It's like a bitter circle. Once Frankie Goes To Hollywood go to London, then the interest moves away from Liverpool, you know, whereas in Manchester, because New Order and the Stone Roses and Happy Mondays were identifiably still in Manchester, even though the Stone Roses were technically obviously on a London label, it was still as though, er, Manchester could renew (Manchester-based DJ and writer, p.c.).

Similarly, the Music City report stated, 'Liverpool, unlike its neighbour Manchester, seems to have established a trend for its successful bands not investing in major projects in their city.' It suggested, however, that Paul McCartney's plan to establish an Institute for Performing Arts in his old school building 'set a valuable precedent'.[26] LIPA thus became a focus for debates about the relationship between the Beatles and Liverpool. A well-known Manchester music promoter and broadcaster repeatedly drew contrasts between Liverpool and Manchester musicians regarding their commitment to those cities. He argued: 'If The Beatles had done to Manchester what they did to Liverpool, the people there would have been furious. No one has put anything back into [Liverpool, which has] a history of leaving and not reinvesting.' Paul McCartney's recent LIPA initiative had come, he suggested, 'too late'.[27] The Head of Corporate Sponsorship at Liverpool City Council told us:

> McCartney only did LIPA because it was getting to the stage where the Beatles were receiving so much media stick from Merseyside for playing on their city's connections yet fucking off to the south-east [of Britain] and beyond. In the end, Paul McCartney had to

---

26   'Music City', 1991, p5.
27   Anthony H.Wilson, speaking at Liverpool University in 1990.

put his name to something, otherwise he couldn't have come back to Liverpool again. And if he'd had that slur on his personality – that he'd been false to his roots and abandoned the city, he would not have got that level of recognition that people can look forward to at this stage.

Liverpool music industry policy initiatives of the 1980s and 1990s thus encouraged a rhetoric of loss, abandonment and marginality. That rhetoric promoted images of a bounded and weakened city that leaked talent like a faulty container, and that bled like a wounded body. Moreover, as discussed in the previous chapter, Liverpool music was commonly portrayed as being implicated in a colonial relationship with London. There were thus punning references to a local 'pool'[28] or 'stream'[29] of musical talent, and a sense that this talent was seduced and lured away, poached and exploited by the London-based music industry – described by one local musician as 'the glittering bright lights at the end of the motorway' (p.c.). There was therefore much discussion about how to develop a local music industry that would help to persuade 'local talent' to stay and invest in the city and its wider region, and would 'put Liverpool back on the map'. A local newspaper suggested that the MMIA was putting out a call to all Liverpool musicians who had 'made it' and moved away to 'return home'.[30] A participant at a public MMIA meeting suggested that one successful local musician should be applauded because he had not only chosen to stay in Liverpool, but in doing so he had also attracted other 'stars' to visit the city and record in local studios. At that same meeting a local musician and youth worker argued in favour of greater investment into community music in order to help prevent the city from 'losing all our kids'. The head of the City Technology College urged those present at the meeting to ensure 'that product stays in the region rather than traipses off to London: Why have to go to London? Why not Liverpool again?'

This kind of rhetoric was to a certain extent shaped by factors specific to Liverpool, including the unprecedented notoriety of the Beatles, the severity of the city's economic problems and the strong emphasis on local difference that was discussed in Chapter 3. However, a similar rhetoric was also a feature of other music industry policy initiatives that we studied in Manchester and Sheffield, and of those in Norwich (Street, 1995) and Austin (Shank, 1994). According to Shank (ibid.: 189), for example, those involved with music industry policy initiatives in Austin believed, 'that the only way to protect Austin musicians, and those businesses that lived off the efforts of those musicians, from the cycles of pop fashion and the vagaries of

---

28   In 1995 the Merseyside Development Corporation launched an expensive image campaign under the slogan 'Liverpool: A Pool of Talent'.

29   Music was thus portrayed as a natural local resource. We noted similar metaphors during our research on music policy in New Orleans (see Appendix), where music was promoted as something that could be 'tapped into' to replace the city's collapsed oil industry. Likewise, Shank (1994: 216) refers to an Austin newspaper article which 'utilized the now common natural resources metaphor about musicians – calling them a "cool-flowing natural spring"'.

30   *Merseymart*, 7 April 1994.

adolescent desires, was to establish in Austin the infrastructure of a "music industry".' This highlights the aptness of Frith's (1993) comparison of cities such as Liverpool and Sheffield with small countries such as Sweden. Those countries have likewise used cultural policy to try to promote local music within a global marketplace, but also to protect their musical cultures and industries in the face of increasing international competition and foreign imports (Wallis and Malm, 1984; Robinson, Buck and Cuthbert, 1991).

Many of those involved with music industry policy-making in Liverpool and Merseyside recognized the parochialism implicit in this rhetoric, and were at the same time engaged in practical discussions about how to develop local music-making given the centralization of the national recording industry, and how to access increasingly global networks of music production and distribution. They also recognized the futility of the calls to challenge the London-based industry or bring it to Liverpool, and instead advocated more realistic ways of capitalizing on and promoting local talent. It could be suggested, therefore, that the public rhetoric that I have described was strategically deployed for political purposes and to further the interests of the groups involved. It served the interests of the local state, for example, because it helped to promote local integration. It also encouraged expressions of local identity that helped to generate support for policy initiatives promoted by the local state. The rhetoric served the interests of arts consultants because it helped to convince policy-makers of the need for policies aimed at developing the local arts and cultural industries, and thus for their own particular expertise. It served the interests of the local media, which were anxious to encourage a sense of local allegiance and to be seen to represent the city's interests and act as its main voice. It also served the interests of ordinary music-makers who simply wanted the opportunity publicly to voice their complaints about various injustices that they believed hindered them and their music-making. Finally, the rhetoric served the interests of those self-selected music-makers who were concerned to lobby policy-makers for greater recognition and support, and to mobilize other music-makers to join them in such efforts.

Making Music Fit a Policy Agenda

Support for music industry policy initiatives in Liverpool, and for the notion of music as a local industry, was thus mobilized by a rhetoric of the local. But how were efforts to categorize and develop music as a local industry affected by distinctive characteristics of that industry and by its difference from other arts and cultural industries? One music entrepreneur criticized consultants and the local state for the way that they 'lumped together' the music industry with other arts and cultural industries, 'as if it could be compared with bead-makers', and he suggested that they did not appreciate, or take into account, the uniqueness of music as a cultural industry (p.c.).

Popularity and Public Relations   To begin with, why did popular music and the music industry become a focus for civic policy-making in Liverpool? Commercially successful local musicians, such as the Beatles and Frankie Goes To Hollywood, were certainly perceived as being able to generate a huge amount of income that could potentially be harnessed for the benefit the city, although some policy-makers regarded the music business as so successful that it was best left alone. As one arts consultant put it, 'There is no problem convincing them that there is an industry. The problem is convincing them that they should invest in it because all they see is the top end – the Elton Johns and Paul McCartneys, making shitloads of money' (p.c.). Popular music was also valued by policy-makers for its glamour and PR potential. The City Beat initiative, for example, was aimed partly at attracting maximum publicity for Liverpool City Council's new Arts and Cultural Industries Strategy. One manager of local rock bands suggested that Liverpool music-making was 'blessed with a very sexy profile. It is very media friendly, so it tends to get more attention paid to it than other industries' (p.c.). Policy-makers may also have focused on popular music because of its public appeal. The rhetoric that characterized music industry policy-making in Liverpool pointed to the special significance of music and musicians. The director of LIPA told us: 'I don't see any reason why musicians should be treated any differently from architects, dentists, lawyers, physicians, biologists … they're allowed to go anywhere and encouraged to apply for jobs, but why is it that musicians all of a sudden are in a special kind of category? They are not allowed to leave Liverpool.' In Britain, as Toynbee suggests (2000: x), 'The popular musician … is exemplary just because s/he comes from the people and cleaves to popular values. Musicians have to "pay their dues" and "stay in touch with the roots", even (perhaps especially) in genres like independent rock which set themselves up in distinction to purportedly commercial sorts of music.'

Risk and Illegality   Yet despite this interest in popular music and the music industry on the part of the local state, many music- and policy-makers were against the notion of any kind of government intervention in commercial music-making. There were policy-makers, for example, who regarded the music business as financially too risky for the local state to get directly involved with, although some of them suggested that the state could nevertheless play more of an indirect and enabling role. Other policy-makers told us that they were wary of the music business's associations with illicit or disreputable activity,[31] and to some extent the industry itself promoted such associations and represented itself as 'an oppositional, resistant form' (Bennett et al., 1993: 9). The Director of European Affairs at the Government Offices on Merseyside told us, 'The problem with popular music is … it tends to be structurally self employed, halfway between legality and on the black, and organizations without proper company structures. To find a method of how to build that up as an industry is quite difficult.' One of Cream's directors believed that it was harder for those involved

---

31   See Frith (2002) for a fuller discussion of popular music's disreputable associations.

with dance music to get 'the suits' to listen to them because dance was regarded as even less respectable than 'old school' rock or pop.[32]

Conflict and Division   In addition, many of the music- and policy-makers we spoke to in Liverpool, and also in Sheffield and Manchester, argued that the music industry was fundamentally incompatible with civic policy-making because they perceived it as being uniquely competitive and divided. Some pointed to the lack of well-established, representative bodies for local music-making. A local bank manager and MMIA committee member told us that music-makers 'don't like being organized at all', and added, 'the music industry is years behind the rest. There's a Liverpool cartoonist association and they meet regularly to talk about the problems of the industry, but until MMIA the musicians didn't talk together and I'm not altogether sure whether they do now really! I think a lot of people said, what a load of crap.' Haslam (2000: 267) sums up the feelings of many of the Liverpool music-makers we spoke to when he writes, 'many artists are by nature born mavericks, not readily given to joining groups or gangs, or committees … In a city with long traditions of independence and nonconformity, many creative people in Manchester have become mavericks in a maverick city.' Similarly, Jim Dickson, who played drums on the recorded music at Stax records, has been quoted as saying:

> The Memphis sound is something that's produced by a group of social misfits in a dark room in the middle of the night. It's not committees, it's not bankers, not disc jockeys. Every attempt to organize the Memphis music community has been a failure, as righteously [sic] it should be. The diametric opposition, the racial collision, the redneck versus the ghetto black is what it's all about, and it can't be brought together. If it could, there wouldn't be any music' (quoted from Werner in Connell and Gibson, 2005: 161).

Similar comments were made by music-makers in Liverpool, where it was also suggested to us that collectives and committees did not work because of the competitive, egotistical and maverick nature of music-making. This was clearly something that some music-makers revelled in and boasted of, but it could also be a source of considerable frustration. During a conversation about the MMDA one of the three directors of 3Beat records suggested:

> because of the nature of this industry people aren't going to be in one room at the same time … Making records is going to be artistic and on any artistic level there's going to be disagreement about what's a good way of progressing. There's probably not a time where we'd get our heads together and work jointly on anything, and that goes for a lot of the industry. It's quite a backstabbing sort of … There's always fall-outs. I mean, it's difficult to pin it down, but without tapping people's phones you'll never know what people are saying about you, or what people are trying to do to you (p.c.).

Another 3Beat director explained,

---

32   A local dance producer suggested to us that dance music was excluded from policy-making because those involved believed that 'it's not a real music'.

It's just not feasible to get bands, musicians and labels together and try and expect them to be one voice. It would be absolutely brilliant if everyone could do it, but it won't happen. Part of the problem with music is that musicians see themselves as artists and there's just too many individuals pulling all the time (p.c.).

These views were shared by the editor of *Groove* magazine:

Music – it kind of comes from the heart doesn't it? You're dealing with egos and you're dealing with emotions. It isn't a straight cut and dry business. You can't tell a band that their songs are no good. You'd have them saying, 'what are you doing, like?' you know, 'this is my life,' you know what I mean? 'You've just slagged me off!' and they take it really personal. And that's where the problem lies, trying to make it a business, trying to bring everything together and make a music infrastructure, trying to offer services and everything is quite difficult when you start talking, at the end of the day, with bands and individuals and people who have pride and egos and things (p.c.).

The Urban Policy Co-ordinator of Liverpool City Council described the local music business to us as a 'ruthless sector' that was difficult for the public sector to relate to: 'I've dealt with five or six different groups, and it might be to do with the entrepreneurial nature of the thing but there's often a lot of tension there.' Similarly, the consultants who produced the Objective One report on the local arts and cultural industries criticized local popular music-making for its 'messiness' and 'fragmentation'. At the same time, however, it could perhaps be suggested that the breadth, diversity and interconnectedness of local music scenes and business sectors (Chapter 4) complicated and frustrated their efforts to pin music down as a sub-sector, and to monitor and represent it for policy-making purposes.

Such negative representations of local popular music-making were challenged by some of the music-makers we spoke to. Cream's Head of Communications, speaking at an MMIA meeting, argued that policy-makers were just scared and nervous of dealing with popular culture, stating 'The city doesn't understand the product and probably never will.' The Arts Officer for Liverpool City Council told us that in his experience public funding bodies were simply biased against popular music and were more interested in classical music, and to a lesser extent jazz. Moreover, whilst music-makers commonly described local music-making as highly factionalized (see Chapter 4), some argued that this was in fact a positive characteristic because it indicated a high degree of individual creativity, independence and ambition. A Manchester-based DJ and writer told us:

Fragmentation is, in fact, a sign of health that we all want to do our own thing and that everyone has got enough of a brain to reject a whole lot of scenes in favour of one, or go off and do their own ... fragmentation also doesn't harm the music industry because it means there's niche marketing ... if you've got a good enough handle on what each of those fragments is about, why they're like that, what they've rejected, or what they've accepted in order to have that identity, then you can cater to them.

Likewise, a well-known Manchester-based music entrepreneur suggested that the music industry involved a healthy, Darwinian struggle for the survival of the fittest, and it should therefore be left to its own devices:

> It's very difficult to put money into this kind of industry – how do you help? It's like building a municipal rehearsal room, you know – fuck it! The argument being, if you can decide which ten bands out of the one thousand deserve the rehearsal room, don't be a councillor be a fucking record company because you'd be a millionaire. Because, you know, the whole point of music is that everybody does it, and therefore it's impossible really to do anything. You know, one of the strange things, since the music industry comes from by and large … from the radical left or whatever … one is aware of pop music's Darwinian inheritance in that it succeeds and it's as if you have to have that winnowing out process. You know, you have to believe in what you're doing, to actually struggle and to get the equipment, gigs, find a manager (p.c.).

Some music-makers in Liverpool agreed that commercial music-making was competitive and ruthless, and they too suggested that because of this any involvement of the local state would do more harm than good.

Industry Centralization and a Labour of Love   There were also music- and policy-makers who questioned the notion of music as a *local* industry. We spoke to people employed by London-based music companies, for example, who thought that it was unrealistic to think of music as a local industry given the centralization of the national recording industry, the concentration of major music companies and organizations in London, and the absence within Liverpool and Merseyside of such key elements of the industry as publishing and manufacturing. Meanwhile, a couple of city policy-makers questioned whether music was an industry that ought to be promoted by the local state given that (as described in Chapter 4) it depended upon unpaid or poorly paid and part-time employment, and upon the commercial exploitation of music-making as a labour of love. McRobbie (1999: 28–9 makes a similar point when she questions the emphasis of Britain's new Labour government on employment schemes targeted at the cultural industries:[33] 'How can we begin to develop a strategy for employment in this sector where, in some parts of the country such as Liverpool or the North East, being a musician means more or less being on the "rock and roll" for life?'[34]

The Value of Music   Finally, some Liverpool music-makers were also critical of, or opposed to, music industry policy-making because it emphasized the economic value of music-making rather than its social, artistic or educational value. The assessment criteria for various public funding schemes, for example, required local

---

33   Such as the much criticized 'New Deal for Musicians'. The government has since continued to launch local, regional and national schemes aimed at developing creative and media industries.

34   Rhyming slang for 'dole' – state unemployment benefit.

music organizations to justify themselves in economic terms and in terms of their contribution to local tourism. Likewise, the emphasis of the reports connected to the music industry policy initiatives described above was largely on music's economic value; on music as an 'industry' rather than a 'scene'; on music businesses rather than on musicians; and on major commercial success rather than on alternative and more progressive music-making. Haslam (1999: 268) highlights the irony of the phrase 'the creative industries' by pointing out that in terms of Manchester's music-makers, 'many of the truly creative voices in the city don't want to be part of an industry. They may be idealistic, unrealistic or cynical, but they don't want their work filtered through a marketing process, and don't want to be commercial in a way an industry demands.' In response to such views, the MMIA's Working Committee suggested to its members that it was important to link music strategically with local economic development in order to acquire public funding before it was spent on another sector. It adopted the slogan 'Music, the New Industry for Merseyside' largely in order to emphasize to policy-makers and potential investors that music should be recognized as an industry just like any other. Nevertheless the association's development plan emphasized the importance of an integrated approach to the development of local music, and took into account the cultural, educational, community and business aspects of local music-making.

Conclusion

This chapter began by explaining how economic restructuring during the 1980s and 1990s encouraged claims upon music as a local industry, particularly in port and industrial cities of Britain and North America that had a strong reputation for popular music. In Liverpool a series of initiatives was launched, aimed at developing such an industry and increasing music's contribution to the local economy, initiatives that were formulated and implemented by a few key interest groups. Support for those initiatives, and for the notion of music as a local industry, was mobilized partly by the rhetoric of loss and abandonment highlighted in previous chapters, which was a cultural response to social and economic change within the city. Nevertheless the initiatives provoked various conflicts, struggles and debates. The linking of cultural and economic policy gave rise to a new group of consultants who specialized in the arts and cultural industries, and were able to exert considerable influence and control over the policy-making process, and over the ways in which music was defined, categorized and represented for policy-making purposes. This generated a sense of frustration amongst many of the music-makers involved, who found themselves excluded or marginalized from that process. Moreover, the specificity of popular music and the music industry both encouraged and challenged the notion of music as a local industry and policy initiatives targeted at that industry. As a local business, popular music attracted the local state because of its economic and public relations potential, as well as its popular appeal. Yet there was also a perceived lack of fit between music and civic policy. This was because the music business was regarded as overtly commercial, uniquely competitive and dependent upon maverick and egotistical musicians who were unlikely to take an interest in or conform to policy-making procedures. It was also associated with risk and illicit activity, and with an industry that was centralized in London to an unusual and problematic degree. Furthermore, consultants employed to investigate the local music 'sub-sector' represented it as fragmented, divided and lacking in organization and leadership, and as the most difficult of all the arts and cultural sub-sectors to monitor and regulate. The following chapter continues to discuss music in relation to cultural policy and the cultural industries by focusing on music and tourism in Liverpool.

Chapter 6

Music and City Tourism: Respect, Betrayal and the Haunting of the Beatles

It is a wet Thursday afternoon and my co-researcher Connie and I are on our way to the Cavern pub to meet fans of the Beatles who are arriving in Liverpool for Beatle Week 1996 and the annual Beatles Convention. Weaving our way through the shoppers and street traders we eventually reach Mathew Street, a short, narrow street lined with bars, restaurants and shops. The Cavern pub is situated near the far end and as we approach it we pass a lone busker singing a song by the British rock band Oasis, and a man setting up a stall of Beatles T-shirts. A hot-dog stand has appeared opposite the entrance to the Cavern Club, where a small crowd has gathered in the rain to watch a Samba band dressed in bright green and yellow. An enormous papier-mâché head is propped up against a nearby wall, and a deckchair, parasol and potted yucca plant have been placed on top of a small pile of sand at the club's entrance to announce an afternoon of performances by Brazilian Beatles tribute bands. The Cavern Club was made famous by the Beatles, who performed there on a regular basis between 1961 and 1963, but it was demolished in 1973; so what we are looking at is a replica club that has been built on the same side of the road as the original and only yards from where it once stood. Those working in Beatles tourism recount a familiar story of how the club's owners had tried to build the replica to the same specifications as the original using thousands of the original bricks.

We enter the Cavern pub, which lies directly opposite the club, and adjust our eyes to the long, darkened room. Glass frames and cases are mounted on its low-vaulted brick walls, displaying items of music memorabilia – including instruments and newspaper cuttings – connected to the Beatles and other Merseybeat musicians. Apart from a small group of men standing by the bar almost everybody in the pub appears to be visiting Liverpool for Beatles Week and the Beatles Convention. Leaning against table legs are plastic bags featuring the familiar logos and slogans of the local Beatles shop, museum and tourist information centre. In a back corner of the room, wedged between a jukebox and a cigarette machine and almost hidden from view, I come across Marianne, a shy, 20-year-old from Mexico. It is the first time she has ever journeyed outside of Mexico and she has travelled alone. She nervously watches other fans as they greet each other with hugs and shouts of recognition and delight. She has been a Beatles fan since she was a young child, and with tears in her eyes she tells me how terribly excited she is be in Liverpool, and how it is her 'dream to be here'. The pub is becoming crowded and I introduce Marianne to Patrick, a 36-year-old freelance writer from England who is attending the convention for the 14th time; but he is soon distracted by the arrival of a married couple who first met at the 1995 convention and are now proudly showing off their newborn son. There is much cooing and ahing as the couple work their way round the room. Two Italian teenagers enter the pub bearing enormous rucksacks, their long hair dripping with rainwater. They have been backpacking around Europe and are in Liverpool just for the afternoon. They are 'big Beatle fans' they declare, and they plan to visit local Beatles sites but stay in the pub instead, sheltering from the teeming rain and soaking up the cheerful, friendly atmosphere.

A couple of local musicians have been performing familiar pop songs and they now start to play Beatle songs and invite members of their audience to join them on stage. Accompanied by cheers from the crowd a tall, large man introduced by one of the musicians as 'Australian Jack Daniels' strides up to the microphone, dressed from head-to-toe in black leather, a cowboy hat, sunglasses and sporting a long beard. He then proceeds to sing and play guitar enthusiastically along to 'Please Please Me'; he is followed by Toru from Japan, who leaps around the stage whilst singing an excellent version of 'Twist and Shout' in an impressively accurate Liverpool accent. A lively group of young Scottish women join in from the back of the room, singing and clapping. Most of them have attended previous conventions but they tell us that they have recruited a few more friends to join them this year. Some familiar local characters arrive, including Alan Williams, the Beatles first manager, and Charlie Lennon – the elderly and frail-looking uncle of John – who walks with a stick, wears a sailor's cap and poses for photographs with Beatles fans. A pony-tailed 'Ringo Starr' sits in the midst of another group of young women, passing around drinks with bejewelled hands and smiling beneath dark glasses, whilst a couple of thin and pale 'John Lennons' with long straggly hair and little round glasses hover nearby. More convention-goers arrive, streaming in from the rain, and by the early evening the musicians are still playing Beatles numbers; to my surprise I am still there, sitting in that steamy Liverpool pub holding hands with Marianne from Brazil and Franco, an Italian backpacker, and singing 'Hey Jude' along with a densely packed, swaying crowd. The damp humidity, collective singing and general warmth of feeling combine in a seductive manner to make the music, the place and the moment take on a special significance.

This chapter continues the investigation of cultural policy and local economic development that was launched in the previous chapter. It focuses on Beatles Week 1996, and on Beatles tourism in Liverpool, in order to examine how through tourism popular music was claimed as local culture and connected to the city and local economic restructuring.[1] The first part of the chapter discusses Beatles tourism in

---

1   The chapter draws largely on research conducted for a two-year project entitled 'Popular Music, Tourism and Urban Regeneration'. The project ran from 1995 to 1997 and involved ethnographic research conducted by Connie Atkinson and myself (see Appendix for further details).

Liverpool as a response to local and global social and economic change. It begins with a description of Beatles Week in order to give some sense of the kind of activities involved, and it introduces the groups and interests that were implicated in it. The second part of the chapter examines the production of Liverpool through Beatles tourism, examining how through tourism connections between Liverpool and the Beatles were forged but also contested. The chapter ends by considering how the specificity of popular music as a tourist attraction contributed to the production of Liverpool.

Beatles Week 1996

I first visited Liverpool's annual Beatles Convention in 1986 when I was conducting fieldwork in the city as part of my doctoral studies. The event was held on an August bank holiday in the Adelphi hotel, and in my field notes I described it as a rather miserable affair, involving largely male and middle-aged Beatles fans studiously rifling through Beatles merchandise stacked in boxes across a series of stalls. Over subsequent years, however, the event expanded. By 1996 it attracted between 200 and 300 visiting Beatles fans, in addition to some local fans, and had become a central part of a week-long programme of activities and events labelled 'Beatles Week'. That week involved live performances by Beatles tribute bands at various local venues, from small to large. Lenny Pane from Sweden, for example, performed at the Royal Liverpool Philharmonic Hall with their mini orchestra and managed to perform the entire *Abbey Road* album before the interval. Evening performances such as this were followed by parties at the Adelphi where some performed on a more informal basis. On Saturday the annual auction took place, and for hours on end a peculiar mix of Beatles-related memorabilia was paraded in front of us, including concert tickets and autographed photographs, but also Beatles curtains, stockings and even toilet roll holders.

The convention proper took place on the Sunday. Stalls had been set up in the Adelphi's grand entrance hall and adjoining rooms, which had high, elaborately painted and sculpted ceilings and ornate mouldings and alcoves. On sale were Beatles books, postcards, posters, T-shirts, records, CDs, original artwork and other assorted memorabilia. The rooms were packed with people selling, buying and browsing. A few stalls had been hired by local artists, writers and Beatles-related organizations, including the local Beatles museum and fan club. In one room guest speakers were interviewed by local Beatles 'experts', whilst other rooms had been reserved for exhibitions and live music. The largest of those featured a raised stage with video screens and an adjoining bar. Performing on that stage between midday and midnight were 12 Beatles tribute bands from Argentina, Russia, Ireland and elsewhere, and we managed to sit through eight or nine versions of 'She Loves You', spurred on by the infectious enthusiasm of the crowd, the impressive musicianship and the contrasting approaches to performing or being the Beatles.

Throughout the week special coach tours had been organized and I joined 'The Fifth Beatle Tour'. Our guide was a lively young woman named Jackie. She introduced the tour by stating that certain individuals had played such an integral part in the Beatles success that they could be awarded the honorary title of 'fifth Beatle', but that others would also like to claim that title. They included, she added, 'the man in the pub who will claim that he played guitar with the Beatles and should therefore be entitled to fifth Beatle status', but she explained that our tour was to visit sites connected with the more serious contenders. The tour began with places associated with the Beatles first drummer, Pete Best, and later moved on to the managers of the Beatles and their former bass player, Stuart Sutcliffe. Throughout the tour Jackie laughed and joked with the Beatles fans on board and with the bus driver, and exchanged stories and anecdotes about the band. Some of the fans appeared to know more about the Beatles than she did, and they often corrected, elaborated or expanded upon her narrative. Occasionally the coach stopped so that we could all troop out and take photographs, and Jackie did her best to prevent us from being run over, shooing us out of the paths of drivers as well as pedestrians. At various points during the tour Jackie emphasized the breadth and depth of the Beatles connections with Liverpool and argued that the city should be doing a lot more to preserve its 'Beatles heritage', pointing to buildings whose Beatles connections had yet to be officially recognized and marked. Towards the end of the tour, as the coach headed back to the Adelphi, Jackie began to dwell upon the Beatles relationship with Liverpool and the importance of Liverpool's Beatles heritage for the city, before revealing, for the tour's finale, that the real fifth Beatle 'will of course always be the city of Liverpool'.[2]

Beatles Week concluded with the Mathew Street Festival, a free one-day event that took place in the area around Mathew Street, which had been blocked off to cars. A few beer tents and mobile fast food outlets had been set up, as well as a small funfair. During the morning the weather was unsettled – with bursts of heavy rain interspersed with sunshine – but the streets were busy with people obviously intent on enjoying a day out. Musicians carrying guitar cases made their way to or from over 40 indoor and outdoor festival stages. Most of the stages were devoted to Beatles tribute acts and 1960s rock'n'roll, but there were also stages for contemporary rock and pop bands and one for tribute acts based on other well-known artists, including Madonna and the Who. Connie, my co-researcher, had volunteered to help man the phones at the festival headquarters, and this gave us a good vantage point from the upper floor of a Mathew Street building. During the afternoon we watched as the crowds swelled and the queues of people trying to get into the pubs and bars snaked along the pavements. Live rock'n'roll music blared out of open doors and windows,

---

2   In later years Cavern City Tours, the company that organized the tour, was able to promote this argument on its website: http://www.cavern-liverpool.co.uk/company_profile2. htm, accessed December 2004. Du Noyer (2002: 31) writes, 'Liverpool itself has often been called the fifth Beatle. The character and traditions of the city were so influential upon the Beatles' personalities that the assertion is perfectly valid.'

and bouncers had been employed to control the flow of people in and out. Here and there bar staff could be spotted sneaking in friends and acquaintances through a back door. By mid-afternoon Mathew Street was jammed with people, and when someone accidentally set off the fire alarm in the Cavern Club the fire engine got stuck and police had to block off the street to try to ease the crowd along.

Later in the day it started to rain heavily, creating rivers and pools of water on streets and pavements. A few outdoor performances were called off, and small groups of festival-goers huddled in shop doorways or under umbrellas; but the rain didn't dampen the enthusiasm of others. Amongst the small crowd gathered around one outdoor stage were those who removed shirts and tops and danced or sprawled on the ground, letting the rainwater stream over them. By 6pm the crowds had thinned and the rain had eased, although the sky was dark. A band was still performing on one of the main outdoor stages, with occasional flashes of lightning providing a dramatic backdrop. In front of the stage a crowd of people danced, and several middle-aged and elderly women in plastic macs flourished their umbrellas as they jived rock'n'roll style. Around them scantily dressed youngsters splashed in a state of blissful, drunken abandonment, whilst beneath their feet swirled soggy fast food wrappers, empty beer cans, bottles and white polystyrene cups. Above our heads a line of small young boys kitted out in the Liverpool football strip perched on the dangerously narrow window ledge of a tall office building. By 9pm there were still small groups of people wandering around the streets, and bands were still performing at some of the indoor venues. Meanwhile, back at the festival headquarters cheques were being signed, instructions were meted out for the dismantling of outdoor stages, and damp signs bearing the names of commercial sponsors were stacked up.

On the last afternoon of the convention there was a final party at the Cavern Club with live performances by Beatles tribute bands and recorded Beatles music played by a local DJ who was enthusiastically kissed goodbye by young girls who shouted 'next year!' as they left. By the evening many convention-goers had already left the city or were packing and resting in their hotels, but a few gathered in the Cavern pub where a local cabaret band played. Sitting in a corner were some exhausted looking convention organizers and tour guides, and a 'Ringo Starr' and 'Paul McCartney' leaned against the bar gazing at two young female convention-goers who were dancing together in the middle of the room, dressed, sixties style, in back and white mini-dresses and knee-length patent leather boots. A Liverpool grandmother of ten smiled as she watched them and told us that they reminded her of the fashions she had worn in her younger days. She was a Beatles fan during the early 1960s and she tried to attend convention events every year. The young bar manager pulled people up off their chairs, urging them to join in the dancing, but soon the handshaking and waving began in earnest as people said their goodbyes.

Beatles Tourism in Liverpool: Development and Organization

Beatles tourism in Liverpool took different forms and involved overlapping social, occupational and interest groups. I will now focus on three broadly defined groups: public sector policy-makers, private sector tourist entrepreneurs and Beatles fans.

Beatles Tourism and the Public Sector

In 1997 Beatles Week was recognized by the Merseyside Tourism and Conference Bureau as the region's second most important annual tourist attraction after the Grand National horse-race, and the Chair of Leisure and Tourism at Liverpool City Council declared, 'By the year 2000 Liverpool will have become a "shrine" to the Beatles.'[3] For some years it had been commonly reported in the British media that the Liverpool authorities were exploiting the city's Beatles connections to the hilt.[4] Yet despite increasing emphasis on the potential contribution of the Beatles to the local economy, local public sector organizations had not always been that convinced about the merits of promoting the Beatles as a tourist attraction, and their views on it diverged and were sometimes contradictory or ambiguous. Moreover, throughout the 1980s and 1990s, Liverpool lacked a coherent tourism policy and also 'co-ordination between the many agencies responsible for marketing Liverpool' (Parkinson and Bianchini, 1993: 171). Nevertheless, as mentioned in Chapter 1, Liverpool had long been a place that tourists had visited, largely due to its grand architecture and waterfront and its notable cultural, entertainment and musical traditions.

Music and tourism have always been connected (Connell and Gibson, 2005). Visitors have been lured to particular places by music scenes and sounds and music compositions and events – whether the classical and operatic concerts aimed at the leisured and travelling elite of nineteenth-century Europe, or the carnivals and festivals of contemporary or traditional music. Music is also commonly represented in tourist literature and marketing campaigns. Over the past few decades the world's tourist industry has expanded dramatically due to various factors, including developments in transportation, the availability of cheaper and more accessible forms of travel, and increasing affluence and leisure time in the West. These developments have contributed to the growth of urban tourism involving visits to cultural attractions within cities and the promotion of city culture as 'heritage': 'Cities are sold just like any other consumer product ... Each city tries to project itself as a uniquely wonderful place to visit, where an unceasing flow of events constantly unfolds' (Fainstein and Judd, 1999: 4).

According to Ron Jones, who had been Tourist Officer at Merseyside County Council, the idea of promoting Liverpool as a tourist attraction seemed laughable during the late 1970s and early 1980s in view of the city's severe social and economic

---

3   He made those comments during a public presentation at the University of Liverpool in March 1997.

4   See, for example, *Music Week*, 22 January 1994.

problems and poor media image: 'Tourism wasn't in the dictionary of the city fathers', according to the director of the local Beatles museum.[5] Despite this, Ron opened Liverpool's first information office and launched a 'Discover Merseyside' campaign, which, he told us, attracted a lot of publicity 'because everyone thought it was an absolute hoot'. He also began to develop Beatles tourism largely under his own initiative and without his colleagues' knowledge or approval. Ron was a Beatles fan and he knew of other fans who were keen to visit Liverpool because of the Beatles, yet there was little information available to them on the city and its Beatles connections. Ron therefore produced a Beatles souvenir pack entitled 'The Beatles: from Liverpool to the World', and launched a Beatles Walk, Beatles package weekends and a bus tour with official Beatles guides. In the meantime he visited Beatles conventions in North America in order to try to improve the Liverpool-based convention, which was run by local Beatles fans and associates on what Ron described as an 'amateurish' and ad hoc basis. The convention was taken over by the county council in the mid-1980s,[6] but the council was dissolved by Britain's central government in 1986.

By that time local tourist attractions had begun to be developed by Liverpool-based government agencies. A couple of high-profile 'flagship' initiatives emerged, including the Albert Dock visitor attraction, developed by the Merseyside Development Corporation, that was modelled on North American dockland development schemes and combined tourist, retail and leisure facilities with private accommodation and historically significant dockland and waterfront buildings. Such initiatives reflected an increasing emphasis on the development of cultural tourism in the port and industrial cities of Britain, Europe and North America as a replacement for traditional industries that had declined or disappeared. In Britain this encouraged the growth of a commercial heritage industry that transformed urban industrial sites into heritage centres that aimed to bring the past to life in an entertaining manner, and to contribute to local economic development. Gradually, official notions of heritage broadened to incorporate the popular and more recent cultural past.

These developments increased pressure on Liverpool City Council to develop cultural and tourism policies, as did widely disseminated studies highlighting strong links between tourism and the arts and the potential benefits of both for local economies (particularly Myerscough, 1986). Tourism thus began to be taken more seriously by the local state, although at that time it was still the responsibility of the council department that dealt with sports, libraries and festivals rather than the one responsible for economic development and urban regeneration. The interest of the local state in tourism was encouraged by the launch of European Union funding initiatives that also connected culture and tourism to local economic development,

---

5   Quoted at http://www.washingtonpost.com/ac2/wp-dyn/admin/, accessed December 2004.

6   The first convention had been organized in the 1970s. From 1981 it became an annual event – http://www.cavern-liverpool.co.uk/company_profile2.htm, accessed December 2004.

and in 1993 the council employed its first ever tourist officer, who told us that his brief included an investigation into Beatles tourism and its potential for the city. 'The city council wasn't Beatle-minded in 1988,' the director of the local Beatles museum told us, 'but they've now opened their eyes and are thinking they can make money out of the Beatles.' A city planning official told us, 'the city council are beginning to realize now that the Beatles are something to capitalize upon'. A series of reports, feasibility studies and proposals emerged for Beatles and popular music initiatives, from a 'Beatles village' to various museums of popular music and culture. Most never amounted to much, but at the start of the new millennium Liverpool's Speke airport was officially renamed 'John Lennon Airport'. Moreover, official bids submitted for Liverpool to become World Heritage City 2007 and European Capital of Culture 2008 (see Chapter 7) symbolized how strongly the authorities had come to embrace cultural tourism and heritage as part of their programme of economic restructuring.

At the same time national tourism and heritage organizations also began to take more of an interest in popular culture and the Beatles. In 1998, for example, the English Tourist Board published a guide to places that had inspired British popular musicians.[7] In 2000 English Heritage unveiled a plaque on the former Liverpool home of John Lennon. The organization was launched in 1983 to offer advice and give grants for the preservation of historically important buildings, and it had established a scheme that involved displaying blue plaques on the front of buildings deemed to have significant cultural heritage. Until the Lennon plaque this had been a London-based scheme, and with regard to music it had only involved buildings associated with classical musicians and composers, apart from one plaque erected in 1998 on the former London residence of rock guitarist Jimi Hendrix, which generated considerable controversy.[8] Meanwhile, Britain's National Trust purchased the former Liverpool homes of Sir Paul McCartney and John Lennon and developed both into visitor attractions (the first opened in 1998, the second in 2003). The Trust is a registered charity, founded in 1895 to act as 'a guardian for the nation in the acquisition and protection of coastline, countryside and buildings threatened by the impact of uncontrolled development and industrialisation'.[9] It is a notoriously conservative institution that had hitherto shown little interest in popular culture.

The interest of public sector organizations in Beatles tourism was encouraged by broader developments connecting popular music and tourism. During the 1980s and 1990s popular music heritage publications, tours, trails and museums involving a range of musical styles, from jazz to techno, began to emerge in other cities (Connell and Gibson, 2003, 2005). Some emerged in cities that were not so well known for their music, or in those with no obvious connection to the heritage concerned (hence Beatles tourism initiatives arose not only in Liverpool, London, New York and Tokyo, but also in Prague and Lithuania). However, other port, industrial and

---

7   Entitled *Rock and Pop Map of Britain: One Nation, One Groove.*

8   Dissenting voices within English Heritage were highlighted in a BBC2 documentary about the plaque, entitled *Picture This*, which was broadcast on 5 June 1999.

9   http://www.nationaltrust.org.uk, accessed December 2004.

so-called 'music cities' provide a more obvious comparison with Liverpool. It was because of their shared reputation for popular music that Liverpool was twinned with New Orleans in 1989 and with Memphis in 2004. New Orleans attracted visiting jazz fans from the early 1940s when it had a reputation as a 'city of sin', a place for jazz but also for drinking, gambling and prostitution. From the early 1990s, however, jazz began to be promoted seriously by the city's tourist authorities, which sought to overcome its negative connotations, and by newly established organizations such as the Arts and Tourism Partnership. Their interest was prompted by the sudden collapse of the city's oil industry and the decline of port activity during the mid-1980s, and by the success of the New Orleans Jazz & Heritage Festival established in 1968. By the mid-1990s an official tourism economy had developed around music, involving the establishment of jazz venues, museums and monuments, live jazz performance, and proposals for jazz theme parks and a black music hall of fame. Memphis, meanwhile, was promoted as the birthplace of rock'n'roll and the home of rhythm and blues, soul and Elvis Presley. Music venues in Beale Street, which had been the hub of that music-making, were demolished or left to decline following the race riots of the1960s and the recession of the 1970s, but they were later renovated or rebuilt as part of official efforts to reverse the recession. A broad range of visitor attractions developed, including Gracelands, Elvis's former home, and Elvis Week, which became a model for Beatles Week in Liverpool and involved performances by Elvis tribute artists.[10]

Beatles Tourism and the Private Sector

Despite the growing interest in Beatles tourism on the part of the local state, throughout the 1980s and 1990s it was largely developed and promoted by a small and generally close-knit group of private sector tourist entrepreneurs,[11] and whilst it had emerged from the informal activities of Beatle fans, it gradually became organized on a more professional and commercial basis. The entrepreneurs involved related to us the same familiar stories, anecdotes and arguments about the development of Beatles tourism in the city. All of them described the murder of John Lennon in 1980 as a turning point in that development. One told us that Lennon's death had 'put a full stop at the end of an age', whilst another said that it had triggered a desire on the part of many Beatles fans to travel to Liverpool, and showed people within the city how deep interest in the Beatles still was (p.c.). An employee of the Beatles Shop mused, 'Memphis and Elvis and that. It's only in the 80s when the poor buggers started

---

10   Connell and Gibson (2005: 91) point out that such performances are a characteristic of Elvis tourism elsewhere. This was certainly borne out by a visit to Brisbane, Australia, that I undertook in the summer of 1997, when I spent a curious day at an 'Elvis Picnic' in the city's central park observing the antics of hundreds of Elvises – from Elvis brass bands and magicians, to flying Elvises that parachuted into the park from an aircraft hovering above.

11   The Beatles themselves were not involved but their record company, Apple, sponsored the occasional event connected with Beatles Week, and demanded the right of approval over the use of Beatles images.

dying off, and people say, "hold on, this isn't going to last forever. Oh my god, that's my past dying", sort of thing' (p.c.).

The Beatles Shop was established in 1982 selling Beatles merchandise, but the dominant player in local Beatles tourism was Cavern City Tours (CCT), the main organizer of Beatles Week and Liverpool's only city-based tour operator of the 1980s and 1990s. One or two entrepreneurs expressed to us their resentment of what they regarded as CCT's monopolization of Beatles tourism, but at the same time they gave the company credit for what it had achieved. CCT was launched in 1983 and the company worked hard to rapidly expand and diversify its interests not only in tourism but in leisure and entertainment more generally. It took over ownership of the Beatles convention when the county council was disbanded, and it established a daily 'Magical Mystery Tour' of local Beatles-related sites involving a brightly painted bus identical to the one used in the Beatles 1967 film *Magical Mystery Tour*. The tour passed by the former homes of the Beatles and involved scheduled stops at Penny Lane and Strawberry Fields, places that had inspired Beatles songs and whose names featured in the song titles (the words Penny Lane were painted onto a wall because the street sign had been stolen so often, whilst the gates to Strawberry Fields were covered with scribbled messages from Beatles fans). Later, CCT became a ticket agent for the John Lennon Memorial Concert and other events; it took over the tenancy of the Cavern Club and pub; it developed its own range of Beatles souvenirs; and in 1993 it launched the first Mathew Street Festival.

During the late 1990s CCT struggled to progress plans for a Beatles themed hotel and restaurant, and recruited a special promotions manager for the Cavern Club. On 14 December 1999, Paul McCartney performed at that club for the first time since 1963. The event was a huge coup for CCT and the local media emphasized the positive worldwide publicity that it had given to the city (whilst at the same time providing publicity for McCartney's new album). By that time other commercial Beatles-related initiatives had emerged in Liverpool. The Beatle City museum opened in 1984, only to become bankrupt a few years later,[12] but in 1990 The Beatles Story museum was launched as 'a £1m visitor attraction which provides a lasting and permanent tribute to the Fab Four' (*Merseymart*, 26 July 1990). At the end of the 1990s the Jacaranda coffee bar that the Beatles had frequented during the 1950s was renovated. Murals painted in the bar by members of the Beatles had been restored, and it opened as a visitor attraction and as the headquarters for another tour operator running private Ticket To Ride tours. A gallery also opened specializing in the art of John Lennon.

Other commercial businesses also benefited from Beatles tourism but were not directly involved in it. They included the hotels that hosted the convention and convention visitors, and the cafes, bars and pubs based in and around Mathew Street.

---

12   Its location had never been ideal, too much money was spent setting it up, the entrance fee had been relatively expensive and initial estimates of its trading potential had been overly optimistic (Appendix D. 'Pop Music Hall of Fame'. Pre-Feasibility Study prepared for Merseyside County Council, August 1985).

The manageress of the Lucy in the Sky cafe described herself to us as a humble, working-class woman who played a central but unacknowledged role in local tourism. She displayed her own collection of Beatles-related objects around the cafe and every day she placed flowers on the Eleanor Rigby statue in a nearby street and cleaned it – not because she wanted to, she said, but because she was ashamed that no one else bothered. She also sold postcards featuring a drawing of the cafe, and she told us that she always made an effort to talk to city visitors who came to her cafe and suggest places for them to go. In 1990 a Liverpool Beatles fan club named Beatlescene was established, which, when it eventually went online, promoted itself as 'the only Beatles information service based in Liverpool, England – where it all began'.[13] One of the club's organizers told us, 'We act like a tourist office really. We are very conscious of the image of the city and we try our best to include in our literature items about what's going on in the city.' In turn, it was in the interests of Cavern City Tours, a company that aimed to turn fans into tourists, to operate rather like a fan club. In fact in 1995 a spokesperson for CCT announced plans (that never materialized) to launch at the Mathew Street Festival 'the first official world-wide Beatles fan club' and related newsletter, as a joint initiative with Liverpool City Council.[14]

Beatles Fans and Visitors

When they described their clients to us, CCT distinguished between the 'fans' who visited Liverpool on a 'once in a lifetime' Beatles 'pilgrimage', the 'fanatics' who visited Liverpool repeatedly from all over the world and the 'general interest' visitors who visited the city for other reasons besides the Beatles. During the 1990s the company made increasing efforts to target their activities at the latter because the fans and fanatics represented a more limited market. It was nevertheless an important market, and it included local and visiting fans – amongst them musicians and Beatles tribute artists, and fans who specialized in the collection or trade of Beatles memorabilia, or who produced Beatles fanzines. Liverpool's Beatles attractions were visited throughout the year, but Beatles Week attracted visitors in larger numbers.

The 1996 Beatles convention attracted roughly equal numbers of male and female fans[15] who comprised a striking mix in terms of nationality and age. They included many who were under the age of 20,[16] and groups from Western Europe, America

---

13   http://come.to/liverpoolbeatlescene, accessed December 2004.

14   Half of the newsletter was to be dedicated to information on the Beatles, and the other half to tourist information on Liverpool ('City Launches Beatles Club'. *Liverpool Echo*, 24 August 1995).

15   Although, according to the organizers of the Liverpool Beatles Fan Club, 70 per cent of their members were female.

16   Many of the older fans we spoke to expressed surprise at the notable increase in younger fans attending Liverpool's Beatles Convention. They attributed it to the 1995 release of the Beatles anthology, the mid-1990s revival of interest in 1960s fashions and styles or

and Japan, where CCT worked with local tour operators to help them recruit visitors. They also included those who described themselves to us, or were described to us by others, as not 'real' fans at all, but who had attended the convention largely in order to accompany a friend or relative who was a fan; those who described themselves as just 'casual fans' and said that their interest in the Beatles was not that intense; and those who said that they 'lived and breathed the Beatles every day' and planned much of their lives around Beatles-related activities and events. Dave from Devon travelled with an album that featured photographs of his vast collection of Beatles-related memorabilia and the security system that had been specially designed to cater for it. Steve had left his wife and children at home in Lincolnshire to indulge his passion for the Beatles, as he did every year, and he pulled up his sleeve to show us a large tattoo on his forearm featuring intricate and intertwined portraits of all four Beatles. Val from Swansea booked annual holidays for herself and her family that were designed to coincide with the date and location of live concerts by members of the Beatles, or musicians closely connected to the Beatles. Peter from Birmingham closely scrutinized the activities and routes of McCartney and regularly turned up for events at which McCartney was due to appear (he had been one of the many fans crowded around the courtyard at the launch of the Liverpool Institute for Performing Arts (LIPA) described in the previous chapter). Many had participated in previous conventions in Liverpool and elsewhere, a fact that they acknowledged with pride, and they thus referred to themselves and each other as 'returnees'.

Throughout Beatles Week distinctions between fans were the subject of considerable discussion and debate. Older British convention-goers, for example, complained to us about younger and usually female ones, suggesting that they weren't proper fans but were there only because the sixties were currently fashionable and because they simply wanted to dance and be entertained. A group of young women from Leeds who were attending the convention for the first time ran around in an excitable state throughout the week, daring each other to drop lumps of ice down the backs of eligible-looking men and chatting with the 'lovely Scouse policemen' who let them try on their helmets. A gregarious and giggly group of female 'George fans' from Portsmouth explained that they had indeed attended the convention 'to dance and have a good time', but pointed out that they had all attended the convention over previous years, and complained that it now attracted too many people, including those who weren't proper fans because they didn't 'let themselves go and sing and dance' but attended 'just for the pose' (p.c.). Thus whilst many described convention participants (and Beatles fans in general) to us as one big happy 'community' or 'family', others moaned that although this used to be the case the convention had since become too big and impersonal.

---

simply to the 'timeless' appeal of the Beatles. Meanwhile some of the younger fans attributed their interest in the Beatles to the record collections of parents and other relatives, the use of Beatles songs in English-language classes at school, to Beatles films and to a recent broadcast on British television of a medley of Beatles songs by the popular British boy-band Take That.

The convention-goers we met were interested in attending in order to indulge their interest in the Beatles and engage in discussions about the band and their music. They also wanted to meet and interact with other fans and establish and maintain friendships and social networks. Many continued to communicate with each other in between conventions, exchanging news and gossip through printed Beatles fanzines and newsletters, letter-writing, the internet and through face-to-face interaction at Beatles-related concerts, fairs and conventions, and at private social gatherings. They were clearly well aware of popular and often negative stereotypes of both fans and tourists, and tried to distance themselves from them.[17] Some refused to be labelled as 'fans' because they felt that the way that fandom was generally perceived did not match their own experience, and some also disliked being referred to as 'tourists': 'I'm not a tourist, I guess. I'm here because of the Beatles and if I don't have the time to visit any tourist sites then too bad, they'll have to wait until another time' (David from Chicago, p.c.). As in other parts of the UK, local policy-makers tended to use the term 'visitor' rather than 'tourist' – partly to escape such negative stereotypes, but also to broaden out from the narrower implications of 'tourist' and encourage those travelling to the city on business, or to see family and friends, to visit city attractions.

Liverpool in Beatles Tourism

Beatles tourism thus brought together public and private sector interests, and connections between the Beatles and Liverpool meant different things to those involved. For many it was an emotional connection: the Beatles meant a lot to Beatles fans, for example, and had played an important part in their lives. For the tourist entrepreneurs it was also a business connection, and the success and status of that business depended on their ability to become an authority on the Beatles and demonstrate Beatles-related knowledge and expertise (Kaijser, 2002). Meanwhile public sector officials were increasingly interested in what the connection could contribute to the marketing and economy of Liverpool. Beatles tourism developed in response to social and economic change and was shaped by local circumstances, and also broader, global trends. Yet Beatles tourism did not simply reflect the city but also produced it, and connections between Liverpool and the Beatles were not simply 'there' to be marked, celebrated and used, but were actively forged. How was this achieved, and was it a straightforward process? How were the Beatles made into Liverpool culture through tourism, and how was Liverpool shaped and thought about through that process? I now want to address those questions by examining the claiming of the Beatles as local, city culture, and the tensions and debates that this provoked, focusing on debates concerning the ownership, evaluation and representation of local culture. The discussion will highlight the impact of those claims, tensions and debates on the city and on how the city was imagined. They

---

17   See Cavicchi (1998) on perceptions of fans and fandom.

indicated, for example, the kind of city that people wanted Liverpool to be but also what they feared the city might become.

Claiming the Beatles as Liverpool Culture

> They were ours, they were Liverpool's, they belonged to us … We felt a bit deserted … Why did they have to go and leave us? … We lost them to the world … After they'd gone, after they'd made it, I didn't go to any of their concerts, I didn't buy any of their records.[18]

Tourism has commonly raised debates about cultural ownership and Beatles tourism was no exception. During and in the run-up to Beatles Week there emerged competing claims on the Beatles. Before examining such claims it is important to note that the Beatles connected *themselves* to Liverpool and were perhaps the first rock band to make their local origins a part of their commercial success. They wrote nostalgic songs about the city, for example, and Liverpool locations featured as a backdrop in some of their videos and films. They also emphasized their Liverpool origins and identity in media interviews, and their local dialect was a feature of their singing style as well as their speech. The Beatles' Liverpool connections are thus discussed in the varied and extensive literature on the band, and they are a topic of interest for Beatles fans:

> part of the success of the Beatles is attributable to their city of origin; being from Liverpool authenticated their music as fresh and original, coming as it did from a northern provincial city (in opposition to supposedly bland southern pop), to then create a storm of critical and commercial success in London, New York and elsewhere. The Beatles were always known in relation to Liverpool. It grounded the band in place, gave them roots amid 'authentic', working class, Scouse-accented, masculine youth culture, and added to the mythology of the band as it went on from success to success (Connell and Gibson, 2005: 44-45).

> The Beatles brought a whole image with them which is so firmly rooted in the place. Even though by early 1964 none of them lived here any more, they had all moved down to London, they still showed a certain love for the place. They were still singing about the place. And the other groups that came out of here and were big at the time also associated themselves with Liverpool really. 'We come from Liverpool. We like the place. This is us. If you like us then we'll bring the city with us'. Groups from other places didn't do that at all (Steve from the Beatles Shop, p.c.)

Throughout Beatles Week connections between the Beatles and Liverpool were also actively forged through the activities of fans, tourist entrepreneurs and those working for public sector organizations. The daily Magical Mystery Tour, for example, mapped out a particular Beatles Liverpool, connecting the Beatles to a selective and nostalgic social history of Liverpool that focused on the 1950s and did

---

18   A young female Beatles fan speaking on a programme about the Cavern Club entitled *Celebration*, broadcast on Granada TV, August 1993.

not mention the city's subsequent social and economic problems (Kaijser, 2002).[19] Liverpool was thus represented in specific ways through the narratives of tour and exhibition guides, the stories related by guest speakers at the convention and in the local Beatles fanzine. One of the fanzine's editors explained, 'because we are from here we can give them stories about Liverpool from people who knew them, or used to sit in the pub and drink with them, or lived next door to them. We try to include that and that's why we think that we have been so successful' (p.c.).[20] Connections between the Beatles and Liverpool were also forged through the promotion of familiar slogans announcing Liverpool as the birthplace of the Beatles; the mounting of plaques on buildings that had a Beatles significance; the sale of postcards and souvenirs connecting the Beatles with visual images of Liverpool; the distribution of tourist brochures promoting Liverpool as a major influence on the Beatles; and the organization of special events. (The latter included a church fete staged in a Liverpool suburb in July 1997 that re-enacted the fete held in the same place 40 years previously at which John Lennon and Paul McCartney had first met, and was designed to 're-capture a great moment in history'.[21]) Such connections were also forged through the act of visiting Liverpool on the part of Beatles fans.

Visiting Liverpool was not necessarily the main motivation of those who registered for the annual convention, yet many of them told us that they were interested in learning more about Liverpool as the 'birthplace' of the Beatles, and the place that had influenced and inspired the band and their music. In addition, for many fans it was its Liverpool location that made that particular convention so special. We talked to fans who had travelled to Liverpool in order to see for themselves the place 'where it all began' and to actually 'be there', experiencing the environment the Beatles grew up in and the kind of people they grew up with: 'To imagine these to be the streets and pubs and clubs where the Beatles actually hung out is a dream to us … It's difficult to explain, but reality doesn't always come into it. Being in Liverpool is a dream come true' (Denise and Mike from North Carolina). Thus for some, being in Liverpool was an important part of being a Beatles fan and establishing a deeper sense of connection to the Beatles, and it also served as a public demonstration of their fandom. Hence tourism is one means of performing fandom (Connell and Gibson, 2005).

---

19   The tour was thus compatible with the conservative heritage industry that emerged in Liverpool during the 1980s and 1990s, and was related to a golden, pre-1960s age (Belchem, 2000: 53).

20   On various occasions we heard people refer to the Liverpudlian keen to claim some sort of personal connection with the Beatles (as Jackie did in her introduction to the Fifth Beatle Tour), such as the taxi drivers who regaled city visitors with tales of their schooldays with John Lennon – a stereotype familiar to locals and visitors alike. Du Noyer (2002: 16) writes of the 'old associates from Beatle days' who sit in the bars around the Cavern Club, 'their anecdotes worn smooth as pebbles in a stream'.

21   According to a co-organizer of the event, quoted in the *Liverpool Echo* (7 July 1997).

It was clear, however, that many of the fans we spoke to and observed not only sought a closer connection to the Beatles, but felt that they had a particular claim on the band. Such fans had invested a great deal of time, effort and emotion in the Beatles and were keen to tell us and each other stories about how much the Beatles meant to them, how they had encountered and grown up with the Beatles, and the central role that Beatles music had played at key moments in their lives. It is perhaps unsurprising, therefore, that several regular convention-goers expressed resentment at the presence of so many locals and 'non-fans' at the Mathew Street Festival, and told us how irritated they were to have been unable to gain access to some of the festival's overcrowded indoor venues. One said that he felt it was as though the fans' own 'special event' had been 'invaded'. Yet local fans felt that they had a particularly close connection with the Beatles, and they expressed a clear sense of ownership and pride in the Beatles as Liverpool culture. 'They were the greatest and they were our band and let people from all over the world know it', one of them told us.

Claims on the Beatles as Liverpool culture were problematized or challenged, however, by the band's phenomenal commercial success and mass mediation, and the fact that Beatles music had reached and touched all sorts of people from all over the world. The Beatles had consequently become promoted not just as Liverpool heritage but as national heritage, and as a symbol of global culture: part of everyone's heritage and the ultimate 'Music of the Millennium'.[22] During our 'Fifth Beatle' coach tour, our guide had bemoaned the loss of Beatles memorabilia ('our heritage') from Liverpool, and complained about the fact that items that had once been displayed in Liverpool's Beatle City museum had since been 'lost' from the city and 'sold off to the Americans'. As illustrated in Chapter 2, however, there existed different and competing claims on music as Liverpool culture, and shifting relations between central and marginal music heritages. The Beatles and country music, for example, were implicated in a struggle to determine what the city's culture and heritage actually was, and country music was defined as local heritage in relation to the dominance of Liverpool's Beatles heritage, just as Beatles heritage had been constructed in relation to the city's more established, 'high culture' tourist attractions.

Claims on the Beatles as Liverpool culture were also problematized by the fact that Beatles had become a focus for the local tensions that I discussed in previous chapters. On the one hand the Beatles were a symbol of local pride and of Liverpool's uniqueness, creativity, cosmopolitanism and global significance. On the other hand they were commonly drawn into narratives of local decline. The Beatles thus represented local success and resilience, but also loss and abandonment. Hence in British media reports the Beatles were often referred to in order to juxtapose the city's golden era with its subsequent downfall and failure, and Beatles tourism was portrayed as an example of the city's needy desperation or obsession with its own past. Such tensions began to recede as the city's economy showed signs of improvement. They nevertheless put a different slant on the proud slogans familiar to

---

22   The title of a British Channel 4 television series broadcast in 1998, during which the Beatles were voted by viewers as the ultimate 'Music of the Millennium'.

Beatles tourism – such as 'From Liverpool to the World', 'four lads from Liverpool who shook the world' and 'Liverpool, the 5th Beatle' – and they complicated efforts to re-image the city and contributed to an ambiguity concerning the development of Beatles tourism on the part of the local authorities. These tensions should not be interpreted as evidence for British media claims that Liverpool was obsessed with the Beatles and with the local past;[23] but they do illustrate that, despite their physical absence, the Beatles nevertheless had a strong and in some ways haunting presence within the Liverpool of the 1980s and 1990s.

Throughout the course of our research on Beatles tourism we were told of a reluctance to promote the Beatles as a tourist attraction on the part of the city's authorities and residents. The directors of Cavern City Tours told us that most Liverpool residents were disinterested in Beatles tourism and were generally unaware of the activities and events involved; and that Beatles fans and Liverpool residents were two separate markets and the local market was 'extremely difficult to reach'. They also mentioned a strong feeling amongst locals that it would not be appropriate to promote Liverpool through the Beatles because the band had left or 'deserted' the city. The leading article in the first issue of the local Beatles fanzine was entitled 'Did the Beatles turn their backs on Liverpool?'[24] Similarly, the CCT website states:

> 'What have The Beatles ever done for Liverpool?' This is a question journalists and even locals have often asked over the years and it is only recently that local businesses and councillors have realised what a valuable asset The Beatles are to the City ... There are 94 people directly employed in The Beatles industry. These are real permanent jobs in a growth industry. But still some Scousers say: 'So what? They left Liverpool in 1963. The Beatles themselves have never done anything positive to help this area.' This betrayal theory is alarming for the simple fact that it is just not true.[25]

During the early 1980s one Liverpool councillor said of the Beatles, 'I agree, as quite a number of the committee have said, that once they left Liverpool that was it. They haven't put a penny back into this city that they've taken their living out of.' Another commented, 'In my long life of public work I come across people who I think statues should be erected to far more than the Beatles – people who have really contributed to the city.'[26] By the mid-1990s, however, when our research on Beatles tourism was conducted, we did not come across anyone who promoted such views, but we did speak to many local residents who were supportive of or indifferent

---

23 Despite the often rather parochial celebration of the Beatles and Liverpool in the city's main newspaper, the *Liverpool Echo*.

24 *Across the Universe: Liverpool Beatlescene's Own Newsletter*. Liverpool: Liverpool Beatlescene, Autumn 1993.

25 http://www.cavern-liverpool.co.uk/company_profile2.htm, accessed December 2004.

26 Both comments were broadcast during the programme *Dancing in the Rubble* (Radio 4, 29 October 1982).

to Beatles tourism in Liverpool. Nevertheless that 'betrayal theory' was mentioned to us over and over again as an explanation for the character and development of Beatles tourism in Liverpool:

> There are two views: the camp who feel that the Beatles turned their backs on the city as local lads-made-good, and those who feel that Liverpool shouldn't have to rely on four lads because there's more to it than that … The city council's view has been very much against exploiting the Beatles over the years, and only in recent months have they caught up (Head of Merseyside Tourism and Conference Bureau, p.c.).

> The Beatles, of course, people have really disregarded them for a long long time and seen them as having nothing to do with Liverpool, and it's crazy but that's how it's been (Liverpool City councillor, p.c.).

Evaluating Connections between the Beatles and Liverpool

> The Beatles are to Liverpool what the Pope is to Rome and Shakespeare to Stratford (CCT director, p.c.).

Beatles tourism generated tensions and debates concerning not only the claiming and ownership of the Beatles as Liverpool culture, but also their value. Again, different images of and ideas about Liverpool and Liverpool culture emerged through such debates. The value of the city's Beatles heritage for Beatles fans was indicated by the religious terminology that many of them adopted in order to discuss it. Whilst one or two fans referred to Beatles fans in general as a Beatles 'congregation', visits to Liverpool were commonly described as a 'pilgrimage'; and for some fans Liverpool was clearly almost a sacred place, and their visit to the city an emotional experience that offered them a spiritual connection to the Beatles. An organizer of the local Beatles fan club told us:

> They feel as if they're coming home, you know? One woman, who had never visited England before, boarded a train and said, 'I just knew I was coming into Liverpool. I felt as if I was coming home'. She was from New Zealand, but she just knew. An American woman got off the train at Lime Street station and said to her husband 'I am home' but she'd never been here before. 'I am home,' she said, 'this city is in my soul'.

Some fans claimed that there were moments in Liverpool when they felt the presence of the Beatles quite strongly. A Japanese Beatles fan wrote: 'Being in Liverpool gives "all" the Beatles' songs a striking resonance; like many ineffable mysteries in life, you'll actually perceive this aura of meaning through some sense beyond the five normal ones. It's almost as if their former presence here has transferred some sort of core-deep understanding to you.'[27] A fan from Florida clasped her chest and sank to her knees as a Lennon tribute artist took to the Cavern Club stage, as if he were a ghost from the past.

---

27   Saki at http://www.dmac@math.ucla.edu, accessed June 2003.

Cavicchi (1998) points out that religious terms are used by fans not because they believe that fandom is a religion, but in order to highlight parallels between fandom and religion; whilst Stokes (1999: 150) highlights the way that tourism has commonly been connected with pilgrimage and 'framed in a religious idiom'. Yet Beatles fans were often represented in Liverpool as obsessive, religious fanatics. Thus one newspaper article about the auction of a local barber's shop mentioned in the Beatles song 'Penny Lane', quotes the shop's owner describing it as 'a mecca for Beatles fans from across the world'. He claimed that it attracted 'about 100 people per day visiting the shop purely through the Beatles connection. And we also get people picking away at the window frames to get a souvenir ... They believe the spirits of people are trapped in the fabric of the building' (*Merseymart*, 30 January 1997).

Given how highly they valued Liverpool's Beatles heritage, the fans we spoke to were keen to ensure that it would be preserved, and some of them viewed the demolition of the original Cavern Club as a prime example of the city's disinterest in, and lack of respect for, that heritage. According to the local Beatles fanzine, 'For many years the one thing that has dismayed Beatles fans more than anything else has been the way that The Beatles heritage has been neglected ... There has certainly been a reluctance by the city authorities to maintain the legacy we have.'[28] Alan from Kent told us, 'I don't know for certain whether the city fathers are interested or not, but as an outsider it doesn't appear so. They've got to stop relegating happenings like the Beatles to the margins of history.' Beatle fans had for years been lobbying Liverpool City Council to support plans for Beatles statues or motorway signs. They were supported in this by Beatles tourist entrepreneurs, who continually complained to us that they had been fighting what one CCT director described as an 'uphill battle to get Liverpool recognized as Beatle City' (p.c.). They bemoaned what they perceived to be a lack of local interest in Beatles heritage – especially on the part of the city council – and a lack of local recognition, funding and support for their efforts to develop Beatles attractions and market the city as a tourist destination. They commonly referred to Beatles tourism as a 'missed opportunity' on the part of the public sector, and described the demolition of the original Cavern Club as a typical example of the city 'shooting itself in the foot' (p.c.). The tourist official for the dissolved Merseyside County Council, who had helped to pioneer local Beatles tourism, complained to us, 'Liverpool, being Liverpool ... missed the boat and has been missing the boat – on the Beatles, on pop music heritage ever since.'

Beatles tourism thus generated tensions between tourist entrepreneurs and state officials, although it has been suggested that the interests of both should closely converge (Holcomb, 1999: 69). Cavern City Tours became the main driving force behind a lobby on the part of Beatles tourist entrepreneurs to convince the local authorities of the commercial potential of Liverpool's Beatles connections. The company's directors regularly updated their clients (Beatles fans) on their campaign for public sector support, a campaign that some fans were actively engaged with. The

---

28   *Across the Universe*, fanzine of the Liverpool Beatles Fan Club, Autumn 1993.

above-mentioned 'betrayal theory' provoked Beatles entrepreneurs to emphasize as part of that campaign what the band had contributed to the city and could contribute. At public meetings organized to discuss local music, CCT directors argued that the Beatles could be used as a 'hook' or 'tool' to improve Liverpool's image and attract interest in the city. They stated that for many people, particularly those based outside the UK, 'Liverpool was synonymous with the Beatles',[29] and they insisted that the city had to 'cash in' on the Beatles and be 'packaged on the back of The Beatles', because it simply could not afford to do otherwise: 'If there is one thing that sells this city world-wide then it's The Beatles. The Beatles are here forever whether we like it or not, and we should milk it ... They sell Liverpool every day and it costs us nothing and we benefit' (CCT director, p.c.). The directors also promoted their arguments through the company's reports and media interviews, and they later reproduced those arguments on the company's website: 'The Beatles mean originality, genius, talent, humour, and Liverpool. We must capitalise on our direct links with the most important and successful entertainment phenomenon the modern world has ever witnessed.'[30]

In their efforts to attract public sector support Beatles tourist entrepreneurs also argued for the cultural value of the Beatles and their potential longevity as a tourist attraction: hence the comparison illustrated above between the Beatles and Shakespeare, a comparison that was repeated to us by tourist entrepreneurs, tour guides and fan club organizers. Similarly, a businessman trying to develop tourism around Liverpool's Penny Lane told us that local residents 'don't seem to be aware of what a gold mine they are sitting on. The Beatles are going to become the classics. Ultimately, obviously after they die, they will go down as the equivalent of Beethoven or Mozart.' Elsewhere, similar strategies were adopted in order to promote popular culture as heritage. Moore (1997: 90), writing about the Rock and Roll Hall of Fame in Cleveland, Ohio, states that the museum 'marks a deliberate attempt to raise rock and roll to high culture'. He quotes a newspaper article that said of the building in which the collection was based: 'There's little doubt that the building marks an impressive statement about the artistic credentials of rock'n'roll. It suggests, by using the architect who designed the Louvre expansion, that the artifacts of rock'n'roll are every bit as important as the art of Picasso.'

In addition, Beatles tourist entrepreneurs sought public sector recognition and support by describing themselves as Liverpool's 'Beatles industry', which helped them to argue that Beatles tourism was a distinct economic sector within the city and should be recognized and invested in like other local industries:

> We want the council to recognize what exists, and what has existed, without council support; to recognize that there is a Beatles industry and that we have an international market. We've proved it with the convention. What we can't do is maintain it at its present

---

29   A statement supported by media reports on the city. Hence the article entitled 'Think Liverpool and you immediately think The Beatles' that appeared in *Music Week* (22 January 1994).

30   http://www.cavern-Liverpool.co.uk/company_profile2.hmt, accessed December 2004.

level, because the amount of time we spend dealing with the press and media ... We are subsidizing what is perhaps a public sector thing and we need help from the public sector (A CCT spokesman speaking at a forum on the Mathew Street Festival).

It was suggested that the Mathew Street Festival was launched by CCT 'as a last ditch attempt to rescue dwindling audiences at Liverpool's annual Beatles convention'.[31] However, the company's directors told us that they had launched it in order to provide further proof of the impact that Beatles events could have on Liverpool's image and economy, and to organize an event that would appeal to locals as well as visitors, and that would entice the convention-goers and their spending out of their hotels and into the city centre. The first festival, according to one estimate, attracted around 30,000 participants as well as media attention, and it boosted the earnings of Mathew Street pubs and bars and helped CCT to increase their local status and expand their sphere of activity. It grew in size over subsequent years,[32] and following the 1996 festival CCT threatened to withdraw from organizing the event in the future unless they received more financial support from the city.[33] CCT, the city council and the regional tourist board each made their own attempt to measure the local economic impact of that festival, sending out young recruits with clipboards and questionnaires to interview participants. There was, however, considerable variation in the resulting assessments. As Fainstein and Gladstone point out, 'The criteria for evaluating the impact of tourism and the relative costs and benefits of public investment in tourism versus other industries are uncertain and contested' (cited in Holcomb, 1999: 69).

Consequently, at the end our research on Beatles tourism we organized a large forum at Liverpool University to discuss the future of the festival. The event was launched by the Mayor of Liverpool and brought together tourist entrepreneurs, state officials, Beatles fans, musicians, brewers and hoteliers. The forum highlighted conflicting views on the value of Beatles tourism for Liverpool. Some officials questioned whether the festival was good value for money given the shortage of available public funds, the organizational challenges involved, the threat posed by factors outside of the city's control (including the weather) and the fact that the festival attracted a lot of local people and therefore didn't bring much new money into the region. They also pointed out that in general Beatles tourism depended largely on day trippers rather than overnight visitors, which made it less profitable. (Research by the regional tourist board stated that by 2000, the Beatles contributed £20 million to the local economy.[34] Official figures also indicated that whilst the Beatles accounted for just under 10 per cent of the tourism income pouring into Liverpool each year, they nevertheless helped provide a spark for other investment.[35])

---

31   *Liverpool Echo*, 27 June 2005.

32   Liverpool City Council estimated that 70,000 participated in the 1995 festival (Tourism and Leisure Development Officer at Liverpool City Council).

33   The 1997 event was scaled down following a decrease in funding from the city council.

34   http://www.merseyside.org/research/tourism_faqs.html, accessed December 2004.

35   http://www.washingtonpost.com/ac2/wp-dyn/admin/, accessed December 2004.

Privately, a couple of officials expressed to us their concern that further public sector support for the festival would assist the commercial expansion of CCT and that of other private businesses that benefited from the festival but contributed little to its funding (including large city-centre stores). They were also critical of the fact that CCT employed services from outside the region to help run the festival. In turn, Beatles tourist entrepreneurs emphasized the potential for the expansion of the city's Beatles industry, and the immeasurable contribution of the Beatles and the festival to local pride and to the city's image. Tensions between CCT and the council concerning the festival and its organization have since continued to surface.

Beatles Tourism and the Transformation and Representation of Liverpool

> There is no doubt that if Penny Lane was in the States there would be a whole Disneyfied cottage industry around the area. I would hate to see anything tacky. Maybe a plaque in the area to commemorate the Beatles link would be appropriate (Beatles tourist entrepreneur, p.c.).

Beatles tourism raised not just debates about the ownership of local culture and its value for the city, but also concerns about how the city's Beatles connections were developed and represented and the impact of this on the built urban environment. Those concerns highlighted the way that Beatles tourism was characterized by a tension between authenticity and commerce. Most of the Beatle fans we spoke to were interested in authenticity, and felt it was important that stories about the Beatles told through tourism should be historically accurate and factual accounts of what really happened (as in the notion of 'telling one's story' rather than the notion of 'story' as a fictional account). Participating in Beatles Week, for example, were fans who called out to Beatles guides in order to flesh out or correct their narratives, and those who raised questions about the authenticity of Beatles items up for auction or on display. Some fans were also irritated by the tribute artists and told us that they would have preferred to have had more opportunities to see 'real' performances by the 'real' Beatles on video. There were also concerns about the authenticity of local Beatles sites. Some fans were clearly upset about the demolition of the original Cavern Club and the fact that its replica had been rebuilt in the 'wrong place'. Beatles tourist entrepreneurs sympathized with such views and were concerned to address and cater for them. The director of the Beatles Story museum told us, 'If I came to Liverpool I would like to see the Cavern, the original Cavern, not the new one with its clean bricks, its air conditioning or whatever.' An assistant at the Beatles shop said:

> People come in the shop and say 'where's the Cavern?', and I say 'it's up the road, on that side, by the car park'. 'Is that the real one?' 'No, we knocked it down.' And they all go 'WHAT!?' 'Yes, it was knocked down. Yes, that was a bit of a mistake by the council or whatever. At the time no one cared.'

Yet there were also fans who accepted that stories about the Beatles were selectively constructed and based on a combination of fact and fiction, and that tourist attractions would not necessarily be authentic. Some told us that if they couldn't see the original Beatles or Cavern Club then reconstructions were the next best thing, helping to fill the absence left by the original and make them feel closer to the Beatles. They rated tribute bands according to how well they physically resembled the original Beatles, or how accurate they were in their mimicry of Beatles performance styles and sounds, or in capturing a flavour or essence of the original band. (Five teenagers from Argentina who called themselves The Beat stole the show at the convention. One audience member said, 'they have the energy of the young Beatles, that restlessness that people liked', whilst another commented, 'they don't try to imitate but they have the feel'.) Some fans clearly enjoyed pretending, in 'postmodern' fashion, that reconstructions *were* the real thing (during Beatles Week 1996 this tended to be the younger, female convention-goers), and were either unconcerned about authenticity or actually enjoyed the inauthentic (tourism based on the inauthentic and kitsch has been long-established – Las Vegas and Disney World being obvious examples). The 'George fans' from Portsmouth screamed at Beatles tribute bands and queued backstage for autographs. With much fluttering of hands and rolling of eyes they told us how excited they had been to meet members of one particular band, how they had repeatedly asked 'George Harrison' to demonstrate his stage moves, and how they had argued with another convention-goer who questioned the merits of the band ('He obviously wasn't a George fan').

Many of those we met, however, expressed concerns about the commercial development of Beatles tourism in Liverpool. Whilst that tourism was in various respects modelled on music tourism initiatives in North America, it was also frequently contrasted with Disney World or Gracelands, both of which were used as familiar symbols of Americanization and the service economy, and of the commercial and inauthentic. This is illustrated by the following remarks made by four Beatles tourist entrepreneurs: '[Penny Lane] can't just be like Elvis's Graceland because that is a manufactured concocted place after he was famous. When I talk to tourists about the Beatles I actually feel the hair stand up at the back of my neck because you can feel, you're telling them *this is it*'; 'You can overdo things – the Americans are good at that. You don't want a Mickey Mouse city'; 'If Penny Lane was in the US it would be a theme park by now'; 'what people want is not to see Penny Lane as a big tourist attraction like Graceland, they want to see it as a working community which has really not changed very much.' Some fans expressed surprise but also pleasure at how undercommercialized (and underdeveloped) Beatles tourism and tourism in general were in Liverpool. Manfred from Stuttgart said 'It's strange, because if the Beatles had come from Stuttgart the city would have promoted them 24 hours a day, 7 days a week.'[36] David from Colorado told us, 'If it all got rather too big then where's the magic? I like to think that I'm part of something that is a little quirky ... I quite

---

36   Similarly, the CCT website states with regard to popular music tourism in Detroit: 'The Americans had left us standing in terms of presentation, selling, promotion and impact.

like the idea that people walking past the Adelphi don't really know what's going on inside.' At the same time, however, we overheard conversations between fans who felt inconvenienced by the fact that Liverpool was, in their view, not terribly tourist-oriented, and wanted Beatles events to be better organized and catered for in terms of local facilities and resources. In addition, several fans suggested that Liverpool was in desperate need of any income or positive publicity that it could possibly generate, and should therefore make as much of the Beatles as it could.

Yet throughout Beatles Week we also heard fans grumbling about the commercial aspects of the event. A group of British fans complained of being 'ripped off' by memorabilia sellers, hotel staff and tourist entrepreneurs. They nevertheless distinguished between individual entrepreneurs who were 'cashing in' on the Beatles, and entrepreneurs who were 'real' fans who demonstrated 'respect' for the Beatles and for Beatles fans, and were thus involved with Beatles tourism for the 'right reasons'.[37] This notion of respect may have been used strategically by fans in order to avoid having to deal with or worry about the commercial transactions that were taking place, but it was central to fans' discussions about Beatles tribute artists. Artists were criticized if it was felt that they were performing purely for profit or career purposes and were not showing due respect for the Beatles, or that they believed they really were the Beatles because of the 'superior attitude' they adopted toward fans on or off stage. There were similar debates amongst Beatle fans about the British rock band Oasis, who had attracted considerable media attention during the months leading up to Beatles Week. Oasis were described as just another Beatles tribute band, criticized for being a poor imitation of the Beatles or praised for publicly demonstrating their debt to the Beatles and their respect and admiration for them.

Tourism, the Beatles and a Musical Production of the City

Beatles tourism in Liverpool thus generated debates about cultural value and ownership, and debates and tensions between authenticity and commerce and between representation and the real. These debates have typified cultural tourism and informed people's understanding of what it is.[38] Concerns have been typically been raised over whether cultural events aimed at tourists are genuine and authentic, or contrived and artificial and merely a show staged for profit (Stokes, 1999). Cultural tourism has been seen to involve a quest for authenticity (MacCannell, 1976), or an acceptance that 'there is no authentic tourist experience' (Urry, 1990: 11). Cultural heritage has been described, following Hobsbawm and Ranger (1983), as

---

One wonders at the exploitation or utilization of the Beatles had they been born elsewhere.' http://www.cavern-Liverpool.co.uk/company_profile2.hmt, accessed December 2004.

37   The manageress of the Lucy in the Sky cafe was also critical of those who had 'cashed in' on the Beatles, but argued that she was different because she had 'dedicated' herself to the Beatles.

38   See, for example, Connell and Gibson (2005) who discuss such debates in relation to other forms of music tourism.

the 'invention of tradition' (Kong, 1998; Kneafsey, 2002), a conspiratorial 'false-history' (Hewison, 1987; Boniface and Fowler, 1993: 16), and a form of 'strategic inauthenticity' (Connell and Gibson, 2005: 158, 267). It has been feared, for example, that tourism based around traditional and 'world' music would end up destroying local music traditions, staging authenticity and inventing tradition. Yet such tourism has also been welcomed as a means of preserving local music traditions, promoting local identity and pride and contributing to local economies. In New Orleans, bars in the city's French Quarter hired bands to play in a Dixieland style that enchanted a lot of visitors, but that many traditional jazz fans considered to be hackneyed and clichéd (Atkinson, 1997; Connell and Gibson, 2005: 142). Likewise, for some the Liverpool Sound represented by the Beatles was a tourist cliché, while for others it was an authentic expression of 1960s Liverpool.

If, however, Beatles tourism illustrated trends and debates that were typical of cultural tourism, then how did the distinctiveness of popular music-based tourism contribute to the production of the city? I will end this chapter by reflecting on that question, and highlighting certain aspects of Beatles tourism as music and as popular music.

Popular Music as Tourism and Heritage

the Beatle who joked 30 years ago about smoking marijuana in the Buckingham Palace toilets, went back to see Queen Elizabeth today to collect a knighthood for helping to revolutionise pop music. The impish lad from Liverpool, one of the most successful songwriters in history, became Sir Paul in a centuries-old ceremony of pomp and solemnity … 'it's a long way from a little terrace in Liverpool' he told reporters (Reuters, 11 March 1997).

During the mid-1990s Beatles tourist entrepreneurs clearly felt compelled to try to justify investment in popular music as a tourist attraction, hence their efforts to legitimize the Beatles and elevate them to 'high culture' status. Yet the notion of rock music as tourism and heritage sat uneasily with conventional rock ideology – through which music was associated with the contemporary as opposed to the past – and with the authenticity of 'the street' as opposed to the museum. Hence some rock music-makers, particularly those involved with alternative rock, were appalled by the development of Beatles tourism in Liverpool, and suggested that music should be about 'spontaneity' and 'the magic of the moment' rather than about trying to recreate what has 'been and gone'. 'Sod the heritage,' shouted one musician during a public speech by CCT directors, 'let's move on to the future not look at the past'. In response to such views the Cavern Club's promoter pointed out that other cities were developing tourism around events and sites of ancient historical interest, but the Beatles were only very recent history so shouldn't really be thought of in terms of conventional notions of heritage (p.c.). Another CCT spokesman proclaimed, 'It is time we had some serious recognition of the power of our pop heritage. But pop is about style and rebellion, not museums. Let's hope we keep it fun.'[39]

Throughout the 1980s and 1990s, however, the development of Beatles tourism contributed to a growing institutionalization, legitimization and canonization of rock and pop music that mirrored similar developments involving jazz and classical music earlier in the twentieth century. Back in 1970s Britain there had been little general interest in the Beatles as a credible rock classic – particularly given the notoriety of hard rock and punk music – and this contributed to the lack of official support for the promotion of the Beatles as Liverpool heritage. The 1980s, however, witnessed the promotion of rock 'classics', a process encouraged by major record companies anxious to exploit the newly introduced CD format by plundering and recycling their back-catalogues (Beatles Week 1996, for example, attracted newcomers due to the 1995 release of the Beatles anthology). Increasingly, major auction houses held high-profile events designed to help them sell off particular rock/pop collections, attracting not just private buyers but public sector museums that had become more interested in popular culture (and the everyday) as part of local and national 'heritage'. A national newspaper article of 1996 referred to a battle between London and Sheffield to establish a national rock museum: 'Forty years after it first blasted its way across the Atlantic from the US, rock'n'roll is now so old and powerful that it is to get its own British museum. North and South are fighting each other for the honour.'[40]

Music, Affect and Experience of the City

> Ya hear so much about the Beatles and Liverpool and when you actually get to come here it's like living the music … it's that extra bit to being a Beatles fan (Dave from Atlanta, p.c.).

Beatles Week thus highlighted the distinctiveness of popular culture, and particularly popular music, as tourism. It also drew attention to the way that music and the city are not just represented and interpreted through tourism, but also experienced and felt. Whilst I have examined efforts to consciously claim music as Liverpool culture, fix music to the city and forge connections between music and city, music has physical and emotional effects, and a city can emerge in and through music. Many of the Beatles fans we spoke to who participated in Beatles Week 1996 insisted to us that the most important thing about the Beatles was their music. They elaborated on this by trying to convey in words what the Beatles music had meant to them and had done for them, and more often than not they ended up resorting to familiar and tired clichés – pointing, for example, to the music's ability to transcend international boundaries and unite people, or to the way that it had helped them to overcome personal crises.

---

39   Quoted in the *Liverpool Daily Post*, 24 June 1997.
40   John Harlow in *The Sunday Times* (21 July 1996).

Yet these fans were clearly saying something important about the music and how it made them feel, something that could not easily be put into words.

Some fans told us that the music of the Beatles had inspired them to travel to Liverpool and had given them a sense of the city before they had even visited it:

> It's written from the heart. It's somebody writing about something that means something to them. It is not just words. It's like I can feel this place because I lived there … If you are sincere about something and are honest about it then it will shine through and that is what comes through with all the Beatles songs. And Penny Lane in particular, and Strawberry Fields. They honestly and truly felt something about the place and it is there, it's in the song and you can feel it (Robert from Seattle).

A Beatles fan from Japan told us that Liverpool had sounded 'bigger' to him through the Beatles music, so he was somewhat surprised when he first visited the city. During Beatles Week music was performed and broadcast at various events and it shaped visitors' experiences within the city, thus questioning the conventional emphasis on the tourist 'gaze' (Urry, 1990; 1999). Sometimes the music was barely noticeable or rather irritating. During the Fifth Beatle bus tour, for example, a tape of early Beatles music was played but the volume was turned down so that we could hear the tour guide, and the tape recorder produced a distractingly tinny sound. In Mathew Street the sound of Beatles music emanating out of a couple of bars contributed to a general cacophony of noise, but nevertheless served to mark out the street as a tourist space within the city. At the convention and festival some of the performances by the tribute bands were impressive and enjoyable, some slick and uninspiring, some not that good.

On a couple of occasions, however, the music seemed to take over, producing a kind of musical place that could be entered into and enveloped by. This chapter began by describing a reunion of Beatles convention-goers in the Cavern pub. The event produced a general hubbub of noise punctuated by shouts of greeting, cheers of applause and playful heckling. As newcomers arrived, people began to bump and jostle against one another; but there was a strong feeling of goodwill and the air seemed heavy with excitement and anticipation. The teeming rain outside, combined with the humidity inside, appeared to bind us together in that low-ceilinged, darkened room, like travellers welcomed in from a storm, and to seal us in and steam things up. In the midst of the room the musicians skilfully worked with their audience and through their set, orchestrating the crowd and gradually encouraging us all to join in. Although I did not consider myself to be a Beatles fan and was attending the event for other reasons, I was touched by the collective singing, by the close interaction between relative strangers and by how meaningful those songs obviously were for those present. An American woman I had been talking to previously leaned towards me and stopped singing for a moment to shout in my ear: 'This is what it's all about,' she explained, 'This is why we're here.' During the rendition of 'Hey Jude', which inspired a linking of arms and hands and swaying of heads and torsos, the social situation and material setting combined with the music to produce, for me at least, a sense of attachment, belonging and immersion that caught me by surprise. The venue and its city setting seemed momentarily transformed.

DeNora draws on the work of Victor Turner to point out that music is something that we can be caught up in, awakened by or find ourselves in the middle of (2000: 159). She thus describes music as 'a way of happening'. In this sense, 'music is not "about" anything but is rather a material that happens over time and in particular ways. Music is a medium, *par excellence*, of showing us how happening may occur' (ibid.: 158). But how do we account for what happens in music, and for music's ability to move people, transform place and produce something or somewhere quite different? To begin with, various musicologists have highlighted the way that music creates its own time, space and motion, taking people out of 'ordinary time' (Tagg. 1979; DeNora, 2000: 158). Blacking (1976: 51) states, 'We often experience greater intensity of living when our normal time values are upset ... music may help to generate such experiences.' Scholars have also highlighted the texture, grain and tactile quality of musical sound (Shepherd, 1987) because music's vibrations travel not just to us but also within us. We can listen to music and hear the body in the voice and in the physical movements of the accompanying musicians, and also witness music's effects on the bodies of its listeners. Moreover, as music fills and structures space within and around listeners it can also appear to envelop them. As sound, music can thus be described as 'a wrap-around medium' with no equivalent of the 'frontal' and 'side on' angle (Van Leeuwen, 1999: 14). It is because of music's physical presence, writes Shepherd (1987: 158), that music 'brings the world into us and reminds us of the social relatedness of humanity ... it makes us aware of our very existence. Symbolically, it is our existence.' This may make listeners forget that music is culturally and socially produced, and encourage a sense that experience is unmediated by culture, that it is direct, individual and non-cognitive (DeNora, 2000: 159).

It may be suggested, therefore, that music has a peculiar ability to produce place, although this ability is dependent on the specific social situations and contexts in which music is performed and heard. Morton (2005: 338-9) suggests that music and place can become intertwined through performance, and states, 'the messy spaces of performance allows us to understand place as more dynamic, embodied and expressive. This makes more sense to me than a representation which only tells me that we are missing the life which it failed to pin down, the life that is excessive: the spark of living that got away.' Stokes (1994a: 3) goes so far as to suggest 'The musical event, from collective dances to the act of putting a cassette or CD into a machine, evokes and organizes collective memories and present experiences of place with an intensity, power and simplicity unmatched by any other social activity.'

Conclusion

This chapter has examined Beatles tourism in Liverpool and the people, practices and interests involved. The first part of the chapter explained how Beatles tourism emerged in response to social and economic change, contributed to local economic restructuring, and reflected local circumstances. The second part showed how, in turn, Beatles tourism contributed to the social and symbolic production of the city. It generated claims on the Beatles and tensions and debates concerning the ownership, evaluation and representation of Liverpool culture. It also provoked concerns about authenticity and commodification of the city and its culture. The chapter ended by considering the specificity of popular music as a tourist attraction and its contribution to the production of the city. First, Beatles tourism and heritage illustrated the increasing institutionalization and legitimization of popular music as Liverpool culture. Second, through the music of the Beatles the city was not just consciously reflected upon, represented and made meaningful, but also experienced and performed in specific ways. The discussion on music, tourism and cultural policy is continued in the following chapter, which focuses on the physical regeneration of the city and the development of cultural and heritage 'quarters'.

Chapter 7

Music as a City Quarter:
Brands, Noises and Regeneration

It was a grey January morning and my co-researcher Connie Atkinson and I were in Mathew Street, a short narrow street situated towards the north end of Liverpool city centre, linking the city's financial and shopping districts. At one end of the street a crowd of people had gathered around a raised platform. It was positioned in front of a large black curtain that hung from a metal rig. At the back of the crowd a cluster of international news reporters equipped with cameras and tripods, booms and zoom lenses perched precariously on scaffolding. On either side of them curious catering and bar staff in white hats and black and white uniforms leant out of the windows of nearby cafes, craning their necks to see what was going on. We huddled in a nearby doorway to try to escape the bitter cold air and waited for something to happen. It was the 40th anniversary of the Cavern Club, and we were standing alongside council officers, musicians, journalists and Beatles fans to witness the unveiling of a 'Cavern Wall of Fame' directly facing the club, a wall that had been commissioned by Cavern City Tours (CCT).

Eventually, the mayor of Liverpool appeared on stage to tell us that the Cavern was 'the most famous club in the world' – the place where, as legend has it, 'it all began', and that Liverpool was very proud to have it. He described the wall as a 'great step in the development of Liverpool tourism, and yet another major attraction for tourists to visit', but he added that it was of course important for local people as well and that CCT should be thanked and congratulated on behalf of Liverpool for all their hard work in promoting the city. Two Liverpool-born musicians – Gerry Marsden from the Merseybeat band Gerry and the Pacemakers, and the jazz singer George Melly – then gave brief speeches, joked with fellow musicians in the crowd and released the curtain. A wall of bricks was revealed, each carved with the names of those who had performed at the Cavern Club. We all applauded, although for me, the impact of the unveiling was somewhat marred by a new life-size, though not terribly lifelike, statue of John Lennon situated in front of the wall, the head of which was later replaced in an effort to improve it. A rather dowdy poster was displayed in a window above featuring the words 'death', 'illness' and 'accident' in large, bold print, and advertising the services of an insurance company that had helped to sponsor the wall.

The speech-givers posed for photographs while a small group of musicians scanned the wall intensely, searching for the brick that featured the name of their band. The rest of us filed into the Cavern Club for a complimentary lunch, and as we queued to get in two city councillors solemnly shook their heads as they discussed the day's depressing news announcement that there was to be a loss of 3,000 jobs at Merseyside's Ford car factory. Among the guests inside were musicians who had performed at the Cavern Club over the previous four decades. They included Hank Walters and other members of the Dusty Road Ramblers, and rock'n'roll musicians who still sported impressive quiffed hairstyles and passed round photographs of themselves and their bands in their younger days. Some of them were accompanied by their grown-up sons and daughters, and many of them performed during the afternoon and evening. The performances included a session by the original members of the Wall City Jazz Band, the Merseysippi Jazz Band and The Ralph Watmough Band – three bands that had featured on the bill at the Cavern Club's opening night 40 years previously.

This chapter uses the Cavern Club as a starting point for an examination of popular music's role and significance in the construction of urban 'quarters', and in a politics of culture and regeneration.[1] The first part of the chapter explains how the Cavern Quarter (see Figure 3) emerged as a response to economic and social change within Liverpool, and describes the development of the quarter and how popular music was used as a theme and brand for the physical regeneration of one particular urban area. The second part of the chapter discusses the rhetoric through which that and other cultural quarters, and culture-led urban regeneration more generally, were promoted. It critically examines that rhetoric in relation to the impact of those quarters on the musical life of the city. The discussion highlights the tensions and debates that such initiatives generated and the concerns they raised about the city and its development. The chapter ends by considering what the specificity of popular music contributed to the regeneration and re-imaging of the city, and the claiming of music as a local culture.

Music and Regeneration in Liverpool

The Cavern Quarter

The story of the Cavern Club has been told and retold and I do not want to repeat it here. Nevertheless, aspects of the club's history, recounted to us by those based in and around Mathew Street,[2] help to illustrate a familiar process of culture-led urban regeneration, and the contribution of music heritage to the physical development and marketing of the city.

---

1   The chapter draws on research conducted for the two-year project on popular music, tourism and urban regeneration mentioned in the previous chapter, and the two-year project on music policy, the music industry and local economic development mentioned in Chapter 5 (see Appendix).

2   They included musicians, music entrepreneurs and music fans, tourist entrepreneurs and other businesspeople and professionals.

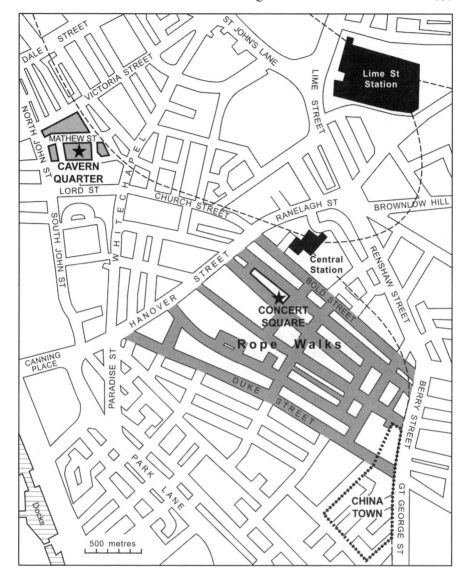

**Figure 3   Map of Liverpool showing the Cavern Quarter
and the RopeWalks © Sandra Mather**

The Cavern and Bohemian Culture   In 1957, when the Cavern Club first opened, Mathew Street was a dark and dingy backstreet. The club was housed in the barrel-vaulted cellar of one of the street's Georgian warehouses, which had previously been used to store fruit and other goods imported through the docks. It was launched as a jazz club by a local Jewish entrepreneur and modelled on a club on the Left Bank of Paris, which was part of that city's 'underground' culture. The Cavern became very popular, particularly with local youths into bohemian culture. Eventually, country and skiffle groups began to perform at the club alongside the jazz groups, and by the beginning of the 1960s rock'n'roll had arrived and the club had become a key venue in the so-called Merseybeat scene. In 1966, however, the club closed after experiencing financial difficulties. Its members fought to revive it and organized an appeal fund and a march to protest against the closure, and later that year the club was officially reopened under new management by Britain's then Prime Minister, Harold Wilson. It subsequently hosted live performances by internationally renowned musicians, but it was nevertheless still beset by financial problems, and on 27 May 1973 the club closed its doors for good and was demolished – largely to make way for a railway ventilation duct, which was never actually built. The Cavern stage was broken up and sold in pieces for charity, and the site eventually became a car park.

Throughout the 1970s Mathew Street nevertheless remained a popular haunt for Beatles fans, nearby office workers and young music enthusiasts. They frequented Mathew Street's pubs, a nearby coffee bar, Rushworth's musical instrument shop (which was situated next door to where NEMS record store run by the Beatles manager Brian Epstein used to be based) and Hessy's music shop, which had been established by the Hessleberg family in 1935 and was for some time frequented by the Beatles. A small flea market was established in Mathew Street incorporating second-hand clothes and record stalls, art exhibitions and a coffee bar that was frequented by local rock musicians.[3] Known initially as Aunt Twacky's, it was renamed The Liverpool School of Language Music, Dream and Pun, and a bust of the psychologist Jung was erected on the building featuring the inscription 'Liverpool, pool of life'. The venue was popular with young people interested in bohemian culture, and at one point Mathew Street also had its own short-lived performance art festival. An independent record shop called Probe opened at the main entrance to the street. Further along the street the Zoo record label was launched, as was a club called Erics that ran for three years. Erics featured live performances by nationally renowned punk and reggae artists, and became a focal point for the development of an alternative, post-punk music scene that spawned several nationally and internationally known rock bands, most notably the Teardrop Explodes and Echo and the Bunnymen. In Mathew Street, therefore, as illustrated in Chapter 4, buildings connected to the port and related industries provided relatively cheap and accessible spaces for popular music-making, and this helped give the street a cultural vibrancy. Erics closed in 1980, largely due to financial problems, although a march took place to protest against the closure. Thus by the time that I arrived in Liverpool in 1985, Erics and The Liverpool School of Language, Music, Dream and Pun no longer existed, but amongst the musicians

---

3   The bar was singled out in a *Melody Maker* article entitled 'Liverpool's Second Coming' (Geoff Brown, 24 July 1976).

and music fans I spoke to they had already become the stuff of myth and legend, and Mathew Street's bohemian scenes and atmosphere were fondly remembered.[4]

During the early to mid-1980s several of Mathew Street's empty warehouses were bought up cheaply by developers but were left to deteriorate. Other buildings were also in a poor state of disrepair, including a small 'McCartney's Bar' that had a gaping roof, rotting façade and windows that had been crudely boarded up with wooden planks. I visited the street frequently to interview or hang out with musicians in the Armadillo tea room, the White Star pub and Hessy's and Probe music shops, making my way past the young, spikey-haired punks and goths who clustered in black around the front steps of Probe. At the Grapes pub I was first introduced to the Jactars and Crikey It's the Cromptons, two indie rock bands that became case studies for my research on the city's rock culture (Cohen, 1991a). Just around the corner I regularly met with musicians in the Ministry Rehearsal Studios, a large warehouse in which bands regularly rehearsed and socialized, and also in Brian's cafe. This was a small, shabby but welcoming cafe run by ex-boxer Brian and his wife Joan. It had featured in a Channel Four television programme about the local band Echo and the Bunnymen, and rock performances took place there on an occasional basis. The cafe's walls were adorned with posters advertising local gigs (one of which featured a comical and affectionate sketch of Brian and Joan) and postcards from regular customers and well-wishers.

The Cavern as Beatles Heritage   Mathew Street had been a meeting point for local Beatles fans and had acquired a couple of rather quirky Beatles statues, and from the early 1980s the street and the Cavern Club became a focal point for the development of Beatles heritage and tourism. When John Lennon was murdered in 1980 the site of the original Cavern Club became a shrine of mourning adorned with written messages and prayers, and bunches of flowers stuck in bottles and taped to concrete posts. Within the following three years a statue of Eleanor Rigby was unveiled, sitting on a bench overlooking Mathew Street. The Beatles Shop also opened in the street featuring another Beatles sculpture over its doorway, and just across the street the local tour operator Cavern City Tours (CCT) established an office. Meanwhile work began on the Cavern Walks shopping complex, a large redevelopment project that was supposed to incorporate the restoration of the original Cavern Club, but too much of the club had been destroyed so a replica was built. Cavern Walks also contained small fashion and specialist shops, offices, a pub called Abbey Road, a cafe called Lucy in the Sky and a large statue of the Beatles.

A few years later another replica of the Cavern Club was built within the Beatles Story museum as part of a reconstruction of Mathew Street that included the original sign from Hessy's music shop. It involved an attempt to recreate the experience of the street from the early 1960s:

---

4   They are also mentioned in biographies and autobiographies of some of the music-makers involved (see, for example, Cope, 1994; Cooper, 1982).

Window shop in Hessy's music store and then stroll up Mathew Street – again faithfully reproduced from old photographs of the area. Hear the sound of laughter from the Grapes pub as you approach the famous Cavern Club. And don't forget to breathe in – many of the displays come complete with appropriate smells. Step inside one of the highlights of the Beatles Story – the Cavern Club. Rest your feet as you sit on one of the old wooden chairs (yes they used to sit in the Cavern). Take a trip back in time as the commentary outlines the group's appearance at the club' (*The Merseymart*, 26 July 1996).

The launch of the Mathew Street Festival helped to promote Mathew Street as the hub of Beatles tourism in Liverpool, and later on CCT unveiled the Cavern Wall of Fame and progressed their plan to establish a Beatles-themed hotel at the top of the street. In 2001 a new pink and gold wall of fame was erected at the Cavern Club entrance, featuring 53 gold discs representing all of the records by Liverpool artists that had reached No.1 in the national charts since 1952.

The Cavern as an Urban Quarter and Brand   From the mid-1990s the Cavern Club inspired the emergence of an urban quarter and was promoted as a local brand. Popular music thus became a symbolic frame for the development and marketing of the Mathew Street area. In 1993 a group of professional businessmen based in or near Mathew Street had got together to discuss ways of improving the area. They decided that the way forward was to create and market a distinctive and cohesive image for it, so they launched the Cavern Quarter Initiative (CQI), which involved regular meetings attended by representatives from Liverpool Stores Committee and City Centre Partnership, Liverpool City Council, Merseyside Police and some of the area's businesses. The chairman of CQI was a prominent local solicitor. Thus, as its name suggests, the CQI tried to capitalize on the musical vibrancy of Mathew Street's past in order to attract new investment, which was why dance club Cream's Head of Communications (see Chapter 4) described musicians and other cultural producers as the 'foot-soldiers' of urban regeneration. The CQI's chairman told us that all those involved with the initiative 'see the area branded with the musical tradition'. The focus, however, was on the Beatles. A CQI newsletter explains how the name of the initiative was decided upon: 'in the end the answer was obvious. The area included the world's most famous club, the Cavern, mecca for hundreds of thousands of Beatles fans every year; Beatles connections abound, and are the area's most high-profile assets' (*The Cavern Quarterly*, 5 December 1996).

The first CQI newsletter, drawing on terminology popular with policy-makers at that particular time, described the initiative's aim to 'transform the district … into a centre of excellence', whilst its chairman, speaking at a CQI meeting (9 July 1996), declared that the aim was to develop the quarter into something that could be 'held up as a model for the entire city'. Some of Mathew Street's old buildings were renovated and the CQI decorated the street with wrought-iron archways, flags featuring the Cavern Quarter Initiative logo and a banner proclaiming 'Welcome to the home of the Beatles'. The CQI also initiated the pedestrianization of the street, investigated the cost of hanging flower baskets and commissioned new public artwork to try to give the quarter a physical identity and coherence and provide visitors with something to look at and photograph, thus encouraging them to stay longer in the area. The artwork comprised four chairs made of wood and metal with various musical and Beatles symbols incorporated into their design. The CQI planned to encourage more restaurants and pavement cafes within the quarter, as well as residential areas, and to create what they described as 'a truly 24-hour village environment' (*Liverpool Echo*, 17 March 1997). This, along with a relaxation of local licensing laws, encouraged a number of new cafes and bars to open up in Mathew Street, including Retro, Rubber Soul, the Lennon bar and the Cavern pub. The street thus became more animated during the evenings, and Beatles tourism became integrated with a wider-ranging entertainment sector.

Parts of Mathew Street also became more gentrified. An upmarket hairdressing salon and a couple of designer fashion shops opened, and the Armadillo tea room – where so many rock musicians had once congregated – transformed itself into a rather expensive restaurant. One fashion retailer gradually expanded its site to dominate a whole corner of the quarter alongside Hessy's instrument shop and opposite Probe, whilst directly behind Probe a department store built an extension that backed onto the quarter. By 1996 the *Liverpool Echo* (7 November) was describing the Cavern Quarter as 'a high-class fashion mecca' and likening it to London's Carnaby Street, but the CQI preferred to describe the quarter as Merseyside's 'Covent Garden' (*Liverpool Echo*, ibid.). The distinction is an interesting one – the youthful, musical and hippy associations of Carnaby Street contrasting with the more upmarket image of Covent Garden.

Musical Quarters and Culture-Led Urban Regeneration

The role played by culture in regeneration has become familiar and commonplace, and the Cavern Quarter reflected broader trends in urban regeneration. During the 1980s and 1990s similar quarters emerged in industrial and port cities within Britain, Europe and North America, transforming areas that had become disused and had fallen into decay. Whilst the term 'cultural quarter' was not consistently applied to such areas (it was not usually applied to the Cavern Quarter for example) it did, as I shall illustrate later, become more commonly used. Such quarters were intended to act as focuses for city-wide development, and thus as 'motors of economic and physical regeneration' (Bell and Jayne, 2004: 6).[5] As illustrated by the above quotes from the CQI, terms like 'village' and 'garden' were commonly used to connect the quarters with cosy and romanticized images of gentrification.

Some quarters were public sector led, were created in areas that had not previously been sites of cultural activity and were focused on cultural production (including Sheffield's Cultural Industries Quarter mentioned in Chapter 5). They were aimed at providing a physical base for the kind of clusters of interrelated cultural businesses described in Chapter 4, and at creating an environment conducive to cultural 'creativity' and economic growth. More common, however, were quarters

---

5   See also Parkinson and Bianchini (1993); Brown, O'Connor and Cohen (2000).

like the Cavern Quarter that focused on cultural consumption and were based in areas that had been or still were sites of cultural activity. They aimed to revitalize those areas by improving their appearance, image and evening economy, and thereby attract visitors, including tourists. As Fainstein and Judd point out (1999: 6), 'The constant transformation of the urban landscape to accommodate tourists has become a permanent feature of the political economy of cities.' Some quarters were based around a heritage theme and were initiated by the private sector[6] or by public–private partnerships (Liverpool's first heritage quarter was the Albert Dock development scheme, launched in 1984 and referred to in the previous chapter, that now incorporates the Merseyside Maritime Museum and the Liverpool Tate Gallery). Yet many were aimed at a mixed usage, involving the development of heritage, leisure and tourism, but also residential areas and occasionally facilities for cultural production.

These quarters help to illustrate profound changes affecting not just Liverpool but other port and industrial cities across the UK, Europe and North America. As numerous scholars have noted (including Harvey, 1990; McGuigan, 1996; Robins, 1991; Miles and Hall, 2003), such cities have been remodelled as part of a wider process of social and economic restructuring governed by the politics and economics of neo-liberalism. City planners and policy-makers have been rethinking and rebranding those cities as centres of consumption; attracting investment into them from corporate capital and property developers, in addition to the spending of young, middle-class professionals; encouraging the development of city-centre living and the night-time economy; and using the arts and cultural activity as a stimulus for the physical regeneration and marketing of cities (hence Landry's creative cities 'toolkit' aimed at city planners and policy-makers – 2000). British local authorities have had to adapt to such developments and to a gradual undermining of their powers by central government since the early 1980s. Their central concerns have consequently shifted from an emphasis on social welfare provision to the pursuit of an entrepreneurial approach to urban development involving the development of partnership schemes with the private sector and encouragement of outside commercial investment. Culture and cultural heritage have been used as a focus for the revival of decaying city centres and to promote new and positive city images that professionally package cities as different in order to enable them to compete with each other for visitors, private investment and public funds.[7] Considerable amounts of money and effort have been invested in re-imaging Liverpool, for example, through a series of costly campaigns involving the promotion of images and slogans that attempted to counter,

---

6   Organizers of the Cavern Quarter initiative complained of a lack of public sector support, and they criticized Liverpool City Council for neglecting even the most basic of services and the general upkeep of the area. At the same time, however, they were proud of the successes that they had achieved without public sector assistance.

7   See Massey (1999: 122); Robins (1991: 38); Short (1996: 432–3); Holcomb, 1999: 54). Glasgow has often been cited as a city that managed to improve its image through its status as European City of Culture 1991 and slogans such as 'Glasgow's Miles Better', and to transform itself from an industrial city into a service sector and retail city.

override (and even send up in one case) earlier negative images of the city. The aim has thus been on marketing Liverpool not just as different from other cities, but also as different from the Liverpool of the past.

Liverpool in Music and Culture-Led Regeneration

The Cavern Quarter thus emerged as a response to social and economic change in Liverpool, and to broader trends in culture and regeneration; but what impact did this and other similar Liverpool-based initiatives have on the city and its popular music culture? The CQI's promotional literature characterized the Cavern Quarter as distinctive and colourful, vibrant and mixed, pointing to its 'bustling network of narrow streets with a distinctly European feel' and describing it as 'city life in all its rich variety, drawing people together', 'a little pool of creativity' containing 'something for everybody' (*The Cavern Quarterly*, 5 December 1996). The emphasis was thus on promoting the quarter as inclusive, diverse, distinctive and creative, and I will now critically examine each of these themes in turn in order to consider how this marketing rhetoric compared to actual events within the quarter.

Social Inclusion

By describing the Cavern Quarter as a place that 'drew people together' and contained 'something for everybody', the CQI represented it as socially inclusive, thus tapping into the emphasis on social inclusion within the European Union's early 1990s urban regeneration agenda. 'We value this area', said one CQI member, 'and wanted to promote retail, business, tourism, leisure, the Beatles and its culture while creating an attractive and safe environment for residents, the people who work there and visitors' (*Liverpool Echo*, 7 November 1996). The quarter, which covered only a small area (see Figure 3), was certainly used by a variety of social groups. Young shoppers inspected the designer labels while middle-aged and younger rock musicians congregated with other regulars in the Grapes and White Star pubs. Office workers grabbed sandwiches from the Cavern Walks shopping centre while Beatles fans photographed a nearby statue. Students and music enthusiasts on their way to live music events at the Cavern Club or Flannagans brushed shoulders with large groups of young men or women who had taxied in for the evening to cruise the street's new bars and celebrate a hen or stag night. Zukin (1995) illustrates, however, that despite the language of inclusion that might be associated with culture, the reality is that culture is not always the unifying force that some might like it to be. The CQI's emphasis on social inclusion certainly rang hollow for some music-makers, and the quarter thus generated tensions between inclusion and exclusion.

In North America, Britain and elsewhere concerns have been raised about the role of the local state and its encouragement or enabling of urban planning proposals and development schemes that typically serve the interests of city elites and commercial investors lacking in local accountability. As Low and Lawrence-Zuniga point out

(2003: 20), such concerns tend to be well justified, and like similar cultural quarters in other cities, the CQI sought to regenerate the Mathew Street area in order to appeal 'to the consumption practices of the emerging nouveau riche of the professional, managerial and service classes' (Bell and Jayne, 2004: 1). The initiative prompted a rise in rent and rates within the area and the subsequent exodus or exclusion of those who could no longer afford to be based there. They included musicians and music businesses, despite the fact that music had helped to make the area a focus for development in the first place.[8] Groover Records, for example, was a small, independent shop that traded in Mathew Street and specialized in contemporary dance music. Following the rise in rent and rates, however, the shop was forced to close. Stories like this have become an all too familiar aspect of the regeneration process, and even a cliché. The same sequence of events has arisen in connection with culture-led regeneration within other British and North American cities, and it is described in Zukin's seminal *Loft Living: Culture and Capital in Urban Change* (1989). Gibson and Homan (2004: 74) highlight a similar process in Sydney, where rising land costs and redevelopment forced the closure of landmark music venues.

In addition to its goal of gentrification, the CQI was concerned to develop and unify the Mathew Street area around a coherent image and to discourage activity that did not suit those plans. In this sense the CQI could be seen as an initiative that aimed to control and manage the area partly in order to protect and foster the professional and commercial interests of its members. The young music fans that hung around Probe were already not welcome in the closely monitored space of the Cavern Walks shopping complex, and could probably not afford to shop there anyway. Moreover, Probe record shop and label were situated at the main entrance to Mathew Street, and the owners of both insisted to us that they weren't invited to CQI meetings, and were 'forced' out of the street by the initiative because the shop and its clientele did not suit the area's new image; they allowed their building to be fly-posted, for example, and had painted it in bright colours. 'They can't handle someone like me or my style of doing things', the owner of Probe record label told us, 'I have always have been an outsider.' His partner at the record shop said, 'Some fellas came along and they said we were downmarket. And they got rid of us really. The rents were too much. They didn't like us in that "prominent place".' In 1995 Probe moved out of Mathew Street after being based there for almost 20 years.

At the same time the CQI enabled the commercial growth of some of the area's larger companies, hence the owner of Groover Records complained to us about the quarter's 'fat cats' who 'trampled upon the little guys below'. Some fashion retailers based in or around Mathew Street were encouraged to expand and to buy out smaller ones, and Hessy's musical instrument shop was bought out by one of them after 30 years in business (Rushworth's music shop also closed down following financial difficulties). Also

---

8   As the case of Liverpool Music House (Chapter 4) illustrated, the vast majority of music businesses in provincial cities do not own the properties in which they are based and survive on a short-term lease, which leaves them particularly vulnerable to shifts in the property market. Such music businesses are generally small and notoriously unstable.

prominent were the cafe-bars and breweries that were quick to take advantage of positive encouragement for night-time economies through the granting of liquor licences. They encouraged the expansion along Mathew Street of a thriving drinking culture. Haslam (2000: 265) describes a similar process in Manchester, and argues that it led to a decrease in demand for music clubs and to an emphasis on drink rather than on music.

Cultural Diversity

It seems ironic that Probe and other music businesses should complain of being evicted from, or priced out of, the Cavern Quarter when the CQI promoted the quarter as 'mixed', and as 'city life in all its rich variety'. The description suited the growing emphasis on cultural diversity within local, national and European government policy; hence during the 1990s Liverpool's public sector organizations strove, like those in other British and North American cities, to adopt more democratic, inclusive and pluralist perspectives on local culture. Yet the rhetorical emphasis on diversity also rang rather hollow given the narrow, thematic focus on the Cavern and the Beatles in the branding of the quarter. The quarter thus illustrated a tension that existed within Liverpool between a drive to capitalize on the city's notoriety for the Beatles and a drive to emphasize instead that the city was more than the Beatles and forward- rather than backward-looking. That tension manifested itself in various ways. The CQI, for example, did not want the musical symbols incorporated into the design of the quarter's musical chairs artwork to be focused entirely on the Beatles, and instructed the designers to produce something more ambiguous. The designers thus talked us through their efforts to come up with a design that was not 'too Beatley', but nevertheless had an obvious Beatles connection so that it would appeal to Beatles visitors and conform to the quarter's Cavern theme. The Blue Meanies and other Beatles symbols were pretty prominent within the final design. Similarly, one issue of the CQI newsletter urged businesses based in the quarter to gather information on the history of Mathew Street's buildings and their musical connections; yet the questionnaire they subsequently distributed concentrated on Beatles connections.

Meanwhile, Cavern City Tours supported the recommendation of the Music City report that Liverpool should launch an international, multicultural music festival by suggesting that the Mathew Street Festival could act as the 'seed' for such an event. The 1996 festival, which was described in the previous chapter, promoted rock'n'roll and country music as well as local rock bands performing their own original compositions, and it also incorporated a world music stage. Yet the organizer of the local salsa band that performed at the festival complained to us, 'I didn't see any jazz down there; I didn't see any Latin down there; I didn't see any African music down there; I didn't see any Indian music down there. Chinatown has nothing on and why not? It should be part of the whole thing.' Over subsequent years commercial pressures seemed to outweigh any interest in cultural diversity, and despite the efforts of the Music City study and the Merseyside Music Industry Association (Chapter 5), attempts to incorporate the festival and Beatles tourism into a more coherent and inclusive music policy were unsuccessful. The number of sponsored outdoor festival stages decreased – although bars and pubs still hosted their own indoor stages to entice festival-goers in as customers – whilst the number of mobile fast food outlets and funfair rides expanded.

At the same time the festival became increasingly focused on cabaret and tribute bands (as opposed to musicians performing their own original material), particularly those specializing in rock'n'roll and the Beatles, and also on visiting musicians.[9] One local rock musician told us, 'Most of the time it's just bands who are Beatles bands', but he added that, realistically, 'without the Beatles at the top of the page it wouldn't be much of a festival. I don't think you would get half the crowd'. Another said of the festival and the Cavern Club, 'They're no use to us bands are they? The bands that play there are Cabaret bands – old hits. That's what you get … They won't pay us. They think punters don't want to hear new stuff' (p.c.). Johnson and Homan (2003: 40) suggest that in Sydney the decline of small to mid-size venues staging live performances by bands performing their own original rock music was partly due to 'The dominance of cover/tribute bands perpetuating and even homogenizing established internationalist styles [which is], a response to general client demand.'

Yet the Cavern Club did not just cater for tribute and cover bands but opened up the venue for bookings by other local groups and organizations. Local 'indie' rock bands also performed there on occasion, for example, and the indie band The Coral had a residency at the club during the early 2000s. Likewise, although Du Noyer (2002: 15) writes of 'the piped music of tourist shops [and] theme pubs' in Mathew Street, the Cavern Club and Pub, and also the Irish theme pub Flanagan's, regularly promoted live music aimed not just at tourists but also at locals and students. They included performances that were diverse in style and occasionally surprisingly quirky or radical; hence the venues provided a space in which the unexpected could, and sometime did, emerge. Nevertheless, for many the Cavern Club and Mathew Street had come to symbolize a predictably tacky kind of tourism, and also the dominance of particular cultures, heritages and social groups. Local jazz and country musicians resented the way that those genres had been omitted from popular narratives about Mathew Street and the Cavern Club (Chapter 3). Yet to a certain extent the Cavern Wall of Fame represented an attempt to broaden out from the Beatles and highlight the diversity of musical genres and styles that the club had promoted over the years. For some local black musicians, meanwhile, the Cavern was a 'site of whiteness' (Doss, 1999: 195).[10] They challenged the claim that the Cavern was 'the place where it all began', suggesting that the roots of Merseybeat had more to do with the black clubs and communities of Liverpool 8, and with the black American

---

9   Connell and Gibson (2005: 126–7) highlight a similar situation in other tourism locations.

10   One musician, for example, described the Cavern Club to us as 'a shiny beacon of apartheid.'

musicians who had influenced the Beatles and other Merseybeat musicians.[11] The editor of the 1960s local music magazine *Mersey Beat* agreed, insisting 'The Liverpool scene was NOT created at the Cavern. Liverpool has a musical heritage that goes back much further.' With reference to local black musicians of that period he added, 'These were the people who felt for the music, who created something that the audience knew was real. With the Cavern it was just trendy, pastiche, gimmicky.'[12]

As indicated in earlier chapters, many local rock musicians also felt excluded by the dominance of the city's Beatles heritage, and were irritated by the way that they and their music were continually situated and judged in relation to it. Newspaper articles about Liverpool's contemporary music scenes carried headlines such as 'The Curse of the Beatles' and 'In the Shadow of The Beatles';[13] hence the existence of a local contemporary rock music festival entitled 'Liverpool Now!' (Chapter 5). A spokesperson from the Liverpool Institute for Performing Arts told us 'It is quite difficult to give the future and present the profile that it deserves because you are always competing with the past. It [the city's Beatles legacy] ties us to the past in a sense that nothing else compares, and it is really quite difficult to get away from that.' That burden of history was certainly revisited again and again in media reporting on the city, and it was a media construction that had local effects, influencing local perceptions of the city and almost demanding some sort of response from local musicians. A feature on the first Liverpool Now! event in the city's main newspaper suggested,

> At last Liverpool music is fighting back against the dominance of Manchester and against its own history. While most of the city went nostalgia mad last week, the Liverpool Now festival proved that there is still music being made here for the future ... If the city can afford nearly half a million pounds towards a tribute to John Lennon, why is there no money available to encourage the Lennons of the future? (*Liverpool Echo*, 12 May 1990).

Creativity and Distinctiveness

The Cavern Quarter thus generated tensions between inclusion and exclusion within local popular music culture, and also between homogeneity and heterogeneity. The

---

11   *Who Put the Beat in Merseybeat?*: documentary broadcast on Britain's Granada Television in 1996, and based on interviews conducted by researchers at the Institute of Popular Music, Liverpool University. Moreover, whilst jazz has been promoted as a tourist attraction in the French Quarter, the 'second line' street parades of the city's black, inner-city neighbourhoods have been ignored; hence Regis writes that, 'the minstrel-like appropriation of black cultural tradition by the city's elites and the tourism industry proceeds without any acknowledgment of the popular black street based tradition on which it is based' (cited in Connell and Gibson, 2005: 253).

12   Speaking on the *Who Put the Beat in Merseybeat?* documentary (ibid.), and quoted in the *Liverpool Echo* ('The Real Merseybeat', 1 March 1996).

13   *Haaretz Weekly Supplement*, Israel, 2 September 1994.

Cavern Quarter Initiative promoted the quarter as a place that was not only culturally diverse but also distinctive, and this emphasis on distinctiveness reflected a broader concern with the professional packing of cities as different. Yet global capitalism, as many scholars have pointed out, produces a dual process of, and tensions between, difference and sameness, heterogenization and homogenization.[14] The local, Frith suggests (1993: 23), 'is now equated with the different not by reference to local histories or traditions but in terms of a position in the global market place'.[15] Thus whilst cultural quarters played a part in the marketing of cities as different, they nevertheless pursued dominant regeneration models that made them in some ways more and more alike.[16] For some of the city visitors we spoke to the Beatles were distinctive to Liverpool and representative of 'real' Liverpool culture, yet they also perceived Mathew Street as a generic tourist space. With its bars, restaurants and retail developments, tourist attractions and souvenir shops, the Cavern Quarter shared certain similarities with tourist sites elsewhere, such as Beale Street in Memphis. There were also similarities concerning the historical development of Beale Street and Mathew Street. Connell and Gibson (2005: 162–6) draw upon the work of various historians to describe how Beale Street had once been a black, creative and highly politicized space, but was demolished during the 1970s as a consequence of neglect and racism on the part of the city authorities and for the purposes of urban renewal. During the 1980s the street was renovated, rebuilt and officially promoted as 'The Birthplace of the Blues' and as a major tourist and heritage attraction.

The owner of Groover Records described the Cavern Quarter to us as 'Sterile-ville', complaining: 'You want individuality. You want not designer labels but something where you'd say, "yeah, that's typical of Liverpool".' The owners of Probe record shop and label, both of whom had frequented the Cavern in their youth, were annoyed that the musical history of Mathew Street was being exploited by those trying to 'cash in' on it. They described the street's Beatles-oriented bars as 'sordid', 'opportunist' and 'highly embarrassing'. For the label-owner, Mathew Street had been transformed from a place that was musically 'arty', 'zany', 'wild', 'hard' and 'special' into what he described as:

> bloody Disneyland theme heritage shit. I hate it all. It always comes too late. They fuck it up all the time. They do things to actively discourage it, stop it, and then when they see a few bob in it or something ... they come in with all of this crap. You can see it not just in the Cavern Quarter, you can see it replicated all over ... it's plastic (p.c.).

---

14   See, for example, Wade (2002: 106–7); Wallis and Malm (1984); Zukin (1995: 268).

15   In Britain, concerns about the homogenizing effects of regeneration have provoked a recent emphasis by central government on the character and sense of place; hence reports such as 'The Historic Environment: A Force for our Future' (UK Government Department of Culture Media and Sport, 2002) and 'The Power of Place: The Future of the Historic Environment' (Historic Environment Review, 2000, London: English Heritage).

16   For further evidence of this see Stevenson (2004: 120); Bell and Jayne (2004: 254, 255); Fainstein and Judd (1999: 12).

The quarter was likewise described as 'phoney mop top tourism' by a local pop songwriter who had once been a Beatles guide, and as 'repellent' by one journalist, who wrote 'Liverpool has turned Mathew Street ... into a garish, pedestrianised Beatleland' (*The Guardian*, 28 November 1997).

The Head of Communications at Cream, who had been closely involved with the post-punk scene centred around Mathew Street's Erics club, also bemoaned the fact that a street that had been such a creative space had become so 'sanitized' and 'turned into some mini Disneyland' (p.c.). The chairman of the CQI had proclaimed that he intended the quarter to be a model for the entire city, and the CQI promoted the quarter as 'a little pool of creativity'. The managers of Cream, however, described the Cavern Quarter to us as a model of what *not* to do, and as the antithesis of the musical creativity of the Beatles, who had made the Cavern so famous, and of the post-punk bands associated with Erics. Similar debates were provoked by the music heritage quarters of other cities. Connell and Gibson, for example, describe the restored Beale Street as 'antiseptic and saccharine' as opposed to 'a continuing space of lived black culture' (2005: 166). They also (ibid.: 142) borrow a quotation from the New Orleans clarinet player Michael White, who said:

> In the French Quarter are the tourist traps where a ghastly parody of New Orleans jazz is inflicted night after night on the unsuspecting public. It is an irony that you stand a better chance of hearing New Orleans jazz, a genuine attempt at the real thing, like it was, in Tokyo, London or Madrid that you do in New Orleans itself.

Hence, Haslam (2000: 279) suggests that: 'leisure and pleasure have become big business. The power of commercial forces in our society is massive. Even the most creative underground activity is eventually assimilated, taken from the streets, neutered and fenced off, and then sold back to the populace as product.'

A City of Culture and Quarters

The Cavern Quarter was thus perceived in terms of the ideological opposition between creativity (and authenticity) and commerce that was described in the previous chapter. It is important to emphasize, however, that the quarter meant different things to those involved and was perceived in different ways, whether as a wonderfully kitsch or miserably tacky tourist spot, a memorial and a sacred site for Beatles pilgrimage, a place in which to have a drink or see a band, work or shop. Moreover, the history of popular music has shown how even those musical styles regarded as the most commercial, derided and 'mainstream' (disco for example) can be a focus for the construction of alternative identities and experiences. Nevertheless, developments within the Cavern Quarter raised important concerns about commercial expansion, social inclusion and cultural diversity. As I shall now go on to explain, those concerns intensified during the late 1990s and early 2000s, and debates over culture-led regeneration became increasingly polarized.

The RopeWalks   Du Noyer's chronological history of Liverpool rock and pop music is subtitled From Cavern to Cream (2002). Around the mid-1990s, however, both Cream and the Cavern were simultaneously celebrated as commercially successful city brands, and both were a focal point for the promotion of cultural quarters and culture-led urban regeneration. Mathew Street and its surrounding area was not the only heritage or cultural quarter in Liverpool. The Albert Dock development was mentioned earlier and was promoted by central government during the early 1980s; but there was also the RopeWalks area where Cream was based.

During the late 1980s the newly elected and reformist Liverpool City Council launched its Arts and Cultural Industries Strategy and sent some of its officers to visit Sheffield's Cultural Industries Quarter (Chapter 5). At that time the council already had plans to establish a cultural quarter in a specific area of Liverpool city centre. The area was regarded as strategically important because it lay between (and could thus help to connect) the city's central shopping district, two universities and student residences, Chinatown and the Albert Dock. Much of the area had become run-down and derelict but it contained restaurants, cafes and shops; Georgian residences; many listed buildings; Victorian factories and warehouses left over from rope-making and the shipping industry; and small businesses based around design, media production and music, including clubs and live music performance venues.[17] During the mid-1980s, based in one tall Georgian building on the perimeter of the area, was a second-hand clothes shop, Pink Moon record shop and, up in the loft, the combined Acorn Gallery and cafe. The latter had a homely atmosphere. The food was baked on the premises in a tiny kitchen leading off a large room that contained a few tables and chairs and had the appearance of a rustic artist's studio. The wooden floors were bare and creaky. In one corner, perched on a raised platform close to the beamed and angled roof, was the owner's bed. Similar galleries, cafes, arts and craft shops and artists' studios and co-operatives were housed in other buildings in neighbouring streets.

In 1989 Liverpool City Council sold off its freehold interest in the area for an astonishingly low sum of money (reportedly around £7 million) to a private, London-based property development company that had stated its willingness to work with the council to develop the area as a cultural quarter. The company went bankrupt before any work could begin and buildings in the area were subsequently bought up cheaply by other private developers, who left them to decline while they waited for an upturn in the property market. In 1993, however, properties around Concert Square, which was situated at the core of the area, were renovated by the Manchester-based property development company Urban Splash. This involved the creation of some loft apartments, three youth-oriented bars that also operated as art galleries, and combined office and retail spaces, including those rented by music businesses and youth-oriented designers and fashion retailers. The flea market Quiggins also

---

17   According to a survey conducted in the 1990s and cited by Gilmore (2004: 115), 82 of the 400 businesses in the area were music-related, and 12 of them were performance venues.

opened, containing second-hand and alternative clothing and furniture stalls, and later on a cafe and art galleries. It attracted hordes of young people, including groups of goths who spent their Saturdays sitting around the steps outside. The area thus had a contemporary cultural feel and vibrant nightlife, and a student culture that thrived following a dramatic rise in the number of students registered at Liverpool's two main universities during the mid-1990s. Probe moved to the area following its alleged eviction from the Cavern Quarter.

Eventually, the city council backed a new regeneration scheme for the area. A consultancy report was produced, documenting ambitious plans for culture-led development, but nothing much happened. During the late 1990s, however, an alternative initiative was launched by a public/private partnership (English Partnerships) and the area was renamed the RopeWalks. This followed an intensification of the climate of regeneration in Liverpool, fuelled by an increase in European funding for the Merseyside region and by the election of the Liberal Democrats, who took over the council in 1997 and brought with them a new emphasis on urban entrepreneurship and culture-led regeneration. The RopeWalks was granted a large package of public/private sector funding and was officially launched in 2002. It was envisioned as a 'distinctive and diverse quarter of the City, building on its history and heritage, working towards Liverpool's new economic future'.[18] The RopeWalks Action Plan flagged up the significance of the creative and cultural industries, and consultancy reports were produced on the night-time economy and on the potential for digital networking.

Cream owned property within the RopeWalks and was therefore interested in the development of the area as a cultural quarter. Representatives from Cream invited English Partnerships to visit the club and they attended planning workshops for the quarter, as did Abigail Gilmore and myself as part of our research on music policy, the music industry and local economic development (see Appendix). Hardly any other music entrepreneurs or music-makers attended besides Cream; nor were they targeted for consultation, although leaflets inviting local businesses to attend the planning workshop had been distributed within the area. The subsequent RopeWalks Action Plan referred to the way that Cream had raised the profile of the area, attracted visitors and new businesses to it and helped to generate employment. It also identified a 'Cream Zone' and announced plans for the expansion of Cream's activities, including the establishment of a Cream Hotel (plans that help to further illustrate the parallels with Cavern City Tours and the Cavern Quarter). Cream had been promoting itself as a central player in the development of local tourism because its club attracted coachloads of visitors from outside the city who stayed overnight in city hotels, and because the Creamfields festival had become the region's third most popular paid admission event. A 1998 publicity brochure produced by Cream stated that the company was recognized by Liverpool City Council and the Merseyside

---

18   'RopeWalks Supplementary Planning Document: Consultation Draft'. Produced in partnership with Liverpool Vision and with the assistance of the consultants Jones Lang LaSalle and BDP, April 2005.

Tourist Board as having played an important role in the economic regeneration of Liverpool, and that thanks to Cream a whole area of the city centre that had once been desolate was now thriving. According to Cream's Head of Communications, Cream was responsible for instigating 'the beginnings of a cultural quarter.'[19]

Cream closed its club not long after the launch of the RopeWalks, and the quarter was beset by various problems (Gilmore, 2004). Nevertheless, there were some striking developments and the area became a curious mix of urban renewal and industrial decay. Cobbled paving was laid on one street and old warehouses were converted into luxury flats and loft and office accommodation. The Jacaranda cafe that the Beatles had frequented in the early 1960s was renovated and turned into a bar and tourist attraction. High-profile flagship projects were launched. A Chinese arch was erected at the entrance to Chinatown, which was ornately decorated with Chinese designs and calligraphy and promoted as the biggest Chinese arch outside of Asia. FACT opened in 2003, a sophisticated centre for film, art and creative technology and for cutting-edge exhibitions and cultural events. There was also a proliferation of new chromed bars and trendy cafes and restaurants – a development encouraged by Liverpool City Council through the designation of European funding, relaxation of the licensing laws to allow the selling of alcohol until 2am, and liaison with key figures within the private sector. Juxtaposed with these shiny new symbols of renewal were pockets of dereliction containing empty buildings, some of which offered haunting reminders of the past and were temporarily and unofficially appropriated for performance events by those involved with local alternative music scenes (Strachan and Cohen, 2005).

Capital of Culture and World Heritage Site

The RopeWalks initiative exhibited the typical hallmarks and jargon of culture-led urban regeneration, and at the same time other areas of Liverpool were also targeted for development. Numerous articles appeared in the local press announcing the launch of, or plans for, specific cultural or 'arts quarters', as well as a 'Media Factory', a 'Cultural Corridor', a 'Cultural Campus' and various cultural 'Districts' and 'Villages'. The city's embrace of culture as a tool for urban regeneration was symbolized in 2004 when Liverpool was awarded the title of European Capital of Culture 2008. Moreover, in 2005 the city was officially awarded the title of World Heritage Site, a site that encompassed parts of the RopeWalks area.[20] These awards provoked a new flurry of announcements proclaiming a dramatic turn in Liverpool's fortunes, and the city's rebirth or renaissance as a modern, European

---

19   Speaking at the 'Cultural Impact' conference held at the Liverpool Institute for Performing Arts on 30 July 2002.

20   'A cultural World Heritage Site is an historic monument, site or group of buildings, which has outstanding universal value to the whole international community, provided that it satisfies certain criteria specified by the United Nations Educational, Scientific and Cultural Organization.' http://www.liverpoolworldheritage.com/index.asp, accessed February 2005.

city characterized by culture, architecture and creative enterprise. 'The dark days are over,' declared Sir Bob Scott, champion of Liverpool's 'Capital of Culture' bid.[21] The *Washington Post* proclaimed:

> These days Liverpool is staging a rousing comeback. After decades of economic decline and social unrest, this proud, prickly and distinctive city is undergoing a full-scale revival that is cultural as well as financial. And tourism is at the heart of the boom ... What's equally important, city leaders contend, is the revival of Liverpool's spirit ... Liverpool has been designated as the European Union's Capital of Culture for 2008, and it is wasting no time in claiming the title. No place fell farther or faster than Liverpool, and none has climbed back with quite the same spirited and self-conscious determination. 'We're seeing a renaissance, and it's very infectious,' said Mike Storey, head of the city council.[22]

Following the announcement of Liverpool as European Capital of Culture 2008, the number and variety of local organizations staking a claim on cultural knowledge and expertise began to expand – a process that was evident even within my own university as certain departments began to launch initiatives directed at culture and regeneration when they had previously shown little interest or involvement in either. Official definitions of culture appeared to broaden, and culture became not only something through which to sell the city, but also an umbrella under which various goals were pursued simultaneously and a variety of urban problems were tackled. It became a facilitator for the promotion of local creativity and distinctiveness, for economic and community development, for cultural diversity and social inclusion. (In Britain, the emphasis on social inclusion intensified following the election of the 'New Labour' government in 1997, and local regeneration companies aimed for Liverpool to be an 'inclusive European Renaissance City by 2010' – Meegan, 2003: 66.) Liverpool's bid for Capital of Culture 2008 was thus promoted through the same kind of official rhetoric that was used to promote the Cavern Quarter and the RopeWalks. Its slogan, for example – 'The World in One City' – was designed to represent and celebrate the city as socially inclusive and culturally diverse. According to members of the panel that judged the bid and those of the other shortlisted British cities, Liverpool won not just because of its many notable cultural attractions and achievements, but because of the emphasis the bid placed on inclusion and community participation. The head of that panel declared, 'above all Liverpool had 'a greater ... sense that the whole city is involved in the bid and behind the bid'.[23] The leader of Liverpool City Council stated, 'the reason we won is because we were the people's bid' (cited in Jones and Wilks-Heeg, 2004: 342). The bid also involved a familiar emphasis on local distinctiveness, although to a certain

---

21   Quoted on http://www.savethepicket.com/newdirections.html, accessed December 2004.

22   *The Washington Post*, December 2004. http://www.washingtonpost.com/ac2/wp-dyn/admin/, accessed February 2005.

23   SirJeremyIsaacs.http://www.culture-routes.lu/php/fo_index.php?lng=en&dest=bd_ar_det&id=00000071, accessed July 2005.

extent cities tended to be promoted through similar themes, images and initiatives. Hence one newspaper report on the six cities shortlisted for European Capital of Culture 2008 described how all of the cities were 'falling over themselves to prove that not only are they keen on culture, but that they are culturally diverse'.[24]

Social Polarization and the Culture Killer

Despite this emphasis on inclusion and diversity, cynicism and opposition towards culture-led regeneration increased, as did confusion over the definition and role of 'culture' in the regeneration process. The Capital of Culture award intensified a local politics of culture and regeneration, and debates became increasingly polarized – particularly given the early failure of certain high-profile flagship projects that had been planned for 2008, and the diversion of funding previously earmarked for voluntary and community sector organizations. I now want to discuss how popular music was implicated in all of this, and consider its social and symbolic significance.

The RopeWalks and the Cavern Quarter illustrate how city centres have been deregulated to assist corporate investment, yet the increasing privatization of urban space has resulted in greater regulation and in social and spatial control over cultural and leisure activity. In Liverpool, as in other cities, this process has involved the introduction of surveillance cameras and gated dockland communities, which have been a focus of recent scholarly literature. In addition, a new scheme was introduced for the licensing and regulation of street musicians,[25] and there was a clampdown on fly-posting and graffiti, which were perceived as a nuisance by city officials in charge of promoting and regulating the RopeWalks.[26] Yet many music venues depended on fly-posting as their main source of advertising, even though it was often in breach of the law and the local authorities had increased penalties against those who broke that law. In 2003, shortly before the panel of judges for Capital of Culture 2008 were due to visit the RopeWalks and FACT, efforts were made to remove fly-posters from the RopeWalks area in order to clean it up. This, as Gilmore (2004: 128) illustrates, provoked the pasting of further posters in the quarter stating 'This is Culture'. The posters featured a subtext that encouraged people to make copies of the posters and distribute them throughout the city.

As with the Cavern Quarter Initiative, the RopeWalks also contributed to a rise in rents and property values, and although the 'creative industries' had been prioritized in the planning process for the quarter, no specific cultural production strategy was

---

24   'Bright Lights, Big City', *The Guardian*, 29 March 2003.
25   See http://www.catalystmedia.org.uk/issues/nerve7/licence_to_busk.htm, accessed June 2005, for a discussion on this.
26   'With 2008 approaching the city is determined to become a lot cleaner, greener and safer for all who live, work and visit by sending out the message that we will not tolerate anti-social behaviour like fly-posting' (local councillor commenting on 20 successful prosecutions against illegal fly-posters by Liverpool City Council in *The Merseymart*, 20 January 2005).

produced. Gilmore (2004: 117) describes how one building, which had been used as a low-cost rehearsal space during the 1990s by the Farm, the La's and other local rock bands, was taken over for private development by a brewery. It was later announced that the Palace – a building situated at the heart of the RopeWalks and rented at low cost by small, independent cultural producers and clothing retailers – was also to close. Likewise, the Jump Ship Rat was forced to close to make way for another commercial development. Run by an arts collective, it had been established in a disused garage set back from a narrow side street, its corrugated iron front daubed with graffiti and its entrance obscured. I visited it on a few occasions and inside the venue was basic and surprisingly large. Beer was sold through a small gap in one wall, and huge metallic artworks dangled from the walls and ceiling. On one occasion, in a gloomy, smoky, cavernous space at the back of the venue, local indie musicians performed by candlelight in the midst of a horde of young people who sat on the floor or stood around the walls in heavy jackets and overcoats, a huddle of dark shapes and shadows and pale, flickering faces.

Particularly controversial was the closure of the Picket, a professional and subsidized live music venue connected to a community recording studio. It had been in operation since 1983 and was situated in the Merseyside Trade Union Community and Unemployed Resource Centre, which was close to the perimeter of the RopeWalks. Staff involved with the Picket had established an open door advisory service for local unemployed rock musicians, the Liverpool Now! annual showcase of local rock bands and a series of rock gigs targeted at local youths under 18 years of age. In 2004, however, it was announced that the centre was to close and the premises were put up for sale. A long and well-publicized but ultimately unsuccessful campaign was launched to try to save the Picket. At the final farewell concert on 30 April 2004, three generations of local rock musicians performed – including the notorious Pete Wylie, who introduced his band as, 'for one night only', The Luxury Flats. The manager of the venue emailed a message to everyone who had supported the campaign:

> To see the whole thing end like this has been very upsetting. What a contrast with the emotions I experienced whilst listening to the announcement … on the 4th June 2003. 'The European Capital of Culture for 2008 is … LIVERPOOL'. I jumped out of bed, ran down stairs shouting to my wife 'We have won'. I hugged my kids, punched the air, and exclaimed, 'Yes, yes, yes'. It felt great; it was good news for Liverpool. I welcomed those comments, felt proud of 'our' achievement and was optimistic about the future. I believed that the Picket – our 20 years of work – had contributed in its small way to securing the Capital of Culture award. I expected that the Picket's community music facilities along with other indigenous arts and cultural organisations would benefit from the accolade … How wrong I was.[27]

---

27   A copy of the message is also printed on the Picket website http://www.savethepicket. com/newdirections.html, accessed June 2005.

By that time another campaign was also under way to support Quiggins, a flea market within the RopeWalks which was to be demolished to make way for a major retail development. The venue was a magnet for musicians, music fans, artists, writers and various youth cultures, and events were organized to protest against its closure at which T-shirts and badges were distributed proclaiming 'I am Culture'.[28]

Efforts were made to relocate the Picket and the Jump Ship Rat within the Independents 'cultural district', which had been situated within a cluster of deserted streets and derelict dockland warehouses close to Liverpool city centre. The district was launched in 2002 to host exhibitions as part of the Liverpool Biennial contemporary arts festival, and a few buildings within it had been bought by a charitable arts trust for use by independent artists and arts organizations. For a while the trust was represented by Cream's ex-Head of Communications, who explained,

> When I was growing up in the city there were a lot of artists with studios in Mathew Street, which was then a derelict area. Then the developers came in and we moved to Slater Street [in the RopeWalks] where the same thing happened. We want to secure as much property as possible so this won't be able to happen.[29]

At the time of writing, however, the work of the trust appears to have stalled and the future of the Picket, Quiggins and the Independents District remains in doubt.[30]

For many of those working within the city's 'alternative' cultures, Quiggins and the Picket thus became totems of resistance, and as such they provided a contrast to the cultural flagships that were officially promoted as symbols of urban renewal. They fuelled a cynicism towards the official, celebratory rhetoric connecting culture and regeneration and those promoting that rhetoric. It was a cynicism informed by a long legacy of poor planning and regeneration initiatives within the city, initiatives that loomed large in local collective memory (as indicated in Chapters 1 and 3).[31] The song 'Who Killed Clayton Square', by the Liverpool rock band Shack, addresses the demolition of one part of Liverpool city centre, which had housed a popular theatre, to make way for a new shopping centre:

---

28   See Jones and Wilks-Heeg (2004: 341) for further discussion of Liverpool's alternative culture and the Capital of Culture initiative.

29   *Liverpool Daily Post*, 14 January 2003. http://www.liverpoolculture.com/get-news-and-events/news_detail.asp?pid=47&ID=118, accessed June 2005.

30   In fact the 'new' Picket was eventually relaunched in Liverpool's Independents District during the summer of 2006.

31   See also Du Noyer (2002: 9–10) for a brief discussion on this.

There's a bulldozer around
And it's in your street
Bringing Clayton Square to the ground
Could've sworn it was there last week[32]

'Clayton Square', explained one of the band's members, 'was like where the gay community lived. Now it's been demolished, just like that; taken out of the city and replaced with a new shopping centre. Clayton Square was beautiful.'[33]

Throughout the 1980s and 1990s I accumulated a large collection of newspaper articles on Liverpool culture and regeneration taken from the local and national press. Looking through them recently I noted common trends that emerged. In the local press, for example, there was continual reflection on the city's image and internal and external perceptions of the city, a sort of self-examination that only occasionally suggested belligerence. At the same time there were constant references to a backdrop of local political infighting, instability and crisis and long-running dock disputes; yet there was also a major emphasis on renewal involving regular and grand announcements of new funding schemes (of which Capital of Culture was only the latest), related initiatives that promised to transform the city and declarations of a local renaissance.[34] I was struck by the optimism and enthusiasm of such announcements and by the energy and imagination of those behind all the plans and initiatives. With hindsight, however, it was also clear that many initiatives had never amounted to much, provoking an alternative impression of empty hype, wasted opportunities and promises unfulfilled, and of haphazard developments that were poorly managed and co-ordinated.

Cynicism was certainly expressed by a lot of the musicians I regularly met up with and spoke to about regeneration within the city, particularly but by no means only those involved with the city's alternative music cultures. For many of them, capital and culture were perceived in terms of opposition, and Capital of Culture was nothing but a blatant economic initiative that had little to do with culture as they saw it, and was more about the culture of capital. They suggested that 'culture' was being 'hijacked', threatened and exploited to legitimize a continued expansion of commercial retail and corporate leisure based on a capitalist ideology of economic growth rather than on social justice. They were angered by the apparent disjuncture between their experiences of local developments and the official rhetoric of cultural diversity, social inclusion and participation through which culture and regeneration were promoted. Further criticisms of culture-led regeneration were raised by local

---

32   http://perso.wanadoo.fr/chambermettes/nouvelle5.htm, accessed March 2005.

33   http://www.shacknet.co.uk/interviews-shack-sounds-03-88.htm, accessed March 2005.

34   They included local and national newspaper articles with headlines such as 'Predicting a Bright New Future for the City' (*Liverpool Echo*, 6 April 1979), 'The Tide is on the Turn for Liverpool' (the *Daily Telegraph*, 19 October 1993), 'Mersey Turns the Tide' (*The Independent on Sunday*, 3 May 1992); and descriptions of Liverpool as, for example, 'a city risen from the dead' (*Liverpool Echo*, 25 October 1993).

supporters of various organizations (including Friends of the Earth, The World Development Movement and People Not Profit), and opposition was expressed in public forums and on various websites (for example indymedia, the Independents District website and *Nerve* newsletter, which gives examples in its fourth issue of various small businesses within the RopeWalks that were forced to close in 2005 due to rent increases or compulsory purchase orders, including art galleries and a second-hand bookshop). One BBC news item described regeneration as 'the culture killer'.[35] Citing the conclusions of a report by the Royal Institution of Chartered Surveyors (RICS) and the independent think tank Demos, the item stated that 'The flood of franchised businesses which often follow regeneration projects can turn buzzing areas into bland ones.' It also quoted Louis Armstrong, the chief executive of RICS, as saying 'Cities are often guilty of killing the goose that laid the golden egg by allowing the creative heart of a city to be smothered by commercial development.' The launch of large theme bars within Liverpool's RopeWalks was mentioned as a particular cause for concern.

More importantly, there was increasing concern that cultural quarters, and culture-led urban regeneration more generally, would contribute to the production of a socially and spatially polarized Liverpool, and there was considerable evidence to justify that concern. Various scholars, for example, have concluded that cultural quarters and culture-led regeneration help to create a regenerated and increasingly privatized core and a disadvantaged and marginal periphery.[36] Predictions and hopes that high-profile city-centre regeneration initiatives would have an economic impact that would eventually 'trickle-down' to outlying regions have been questioned or challenged.[37] In such circumstances, certain culture-led regeneration initiatives have come, unsurprisingly, to symbolize urban inequality for some local residents. Furthermore, Liverpool's Capital of Culture was promoted through bold and often overstated claims for what culture could do for the city and its economy (Jones and Wilks-Heeg, 2004: 346) – claims that are questioned by an extensive, comparative study of 29 previous European Capital of Culture city designations that was commissioned by the European Union (Palmer/Rae Associates, 2004). The study concludes that such cities rarely realized their potential despite unprecedented investment, that sustainable long-term change was ignored in favour of short-term benefits and that community regeneration was overshadowed by physical development.

In the face of such evidence it is perhaps not surprising that one critic proclaimed, 'Real urban renewal is hard-won, and is more about jobs and health and homes than the comparatively cheap, vaguely defined stuff of "culture". I'm left wondering whether art plays the part of midwife in Liverpool's mooted rebirth or is merely an

---

35   'Regeneration: the Culture Killer'. http://news.bbc.co.uk/go/em/fr/-/1/hi/entertainment/arts/2963356.stm, accessed July 2005.

36   See, for example, McGuigan (1996); Robins (1991); Haslam (2000: 269–70); Stevenson (2004: 122); Garcia (2004: 115); Gotham (2002).

37   See, for example, Robins (1991); Boyle and Hughes (1991); Evans and Foord (2003); Loftman and Nevin (2003); Zukin (1995: 283–5).

epidural.'[38] Cultural policy has likewise been described as a 'carnival mask' that deliberately diverts attention away from social inequality, polarization and conflict within cities (Harvey, 1989). Meanwhile, the transformation of industrial buildings and areas into cultural heritage has been described as an ugly product of social failure (Hewison, 1987). For Liverpool, Belchem (2000: xii) writes:

> the great days have gone, an absolute decline rendered more painful by relative comparison. Manchester has usurped regional capital and second metropolis status. Other 'Atlantic' cities like Glasgow and Bristol have successfully 're-branded' themselves. Liverpool is left with its past. Packaged as heritage, history is becoming its main 'trade and source of attraction, the last hope of regeneration for the shock city of post-industrial Britain'.

Zukin (1995: 273) points out that culture-led urban regeneration is 'often a worst-case scenario of economic development' that suggests (ibid.: 274) 'the utter absence of new industrial strategies for growth'.

Regeneration, Cultural Enrichment and Economic Development

The cynicism and criticism that developed amongst certain local groups in response to Liverpool's cultural quarters and its status as European Capital of Culture 2008 highlighted serious concerns about culture-led regeneration and some of its more harmful effects, and raised important questions about its economic benefits. At the same time, however, the polarization between the official rhetoric and the 'grass roots' opposition to it tended to obscure some of the complex struggles and productive initiatives that were taking place under the general umbrella of culture-led regeneration, and the way that some regeneration schemes were helping to support and enable local cultural activity.

On the one hand there were the concerns of musicians and music entrepreneurs over the fate of the Picket, Quiggins and other music-related venues and projects. On the other hand, however, other musicians and entrepreneurs were engaged with innovative and exciting initiatives aimed at cultural activity, regeneration and widening participation. They included music projects funded through the newly launched 'creative communities' scheme connected to Capital of Culture; neighbourhood- and community-based regeneration targeted at art and cultural activity, such as those in the Garston and Speke areas of Liverpool, and those targeted at the city's most recent immigrant groups; and initiatives that sought, through creativity and the performing arts, to give voice to differing local perspectives on the regeneration process, including those targeted at residents of a run-down and almost entirely abandoned North Liverpool street and of high-rise tower blocks in Kirkby. Some of these and other similar projects were supported by local cultural flagship organizations, including FACT, the National Museums of Liverpool, the Liverpool Tate and the Liverpool Biennial (a contemporary arts festival). Individuals

---

38   Tom Morton. *Frieze* magazine review of Biennial at www.frieze.com/review_single/asp?r=2073, accessed May 2005.

working for other public and private sector agencies described their struggles to balance community initiatives with the parallel emphasis on entrepreneurialism and large-scale commercial developments, including residential, retail and tourism developments. They expressed a keen desire to learn from past mistakes and to curb the more harmful effects of global capitalism whilst also reaping its rewards. Moreover, as illustrated by Urban Splash, commercial and private sector developments were not always or necessarily a threat to alternative culture, and initiatives like the Cavern Quarter promoted some well-intentioned schemes – such as the CQI public art initiative, that was not wholly self-serving but also meant to benefit the city as a whole.

At the Liverpool Culture Company, which was responsible for delivering and overseeing the city's Capital of Culture celebrations, one official informed me of new plans to celebrate but at the same time broaden out from the Beatles and promote the city's more recent and contemporary music scenes. Yet a slight tension or ambiguity concerning these two aims nevertheless remained. The supporting literature for the city's Capital of Culture 2008 bid stated: 'Mention Liverpool, almost anywhere in the world, and it's recognised straight away – "Beatles" and "Liverpool or Everton FC" or more recently "Cream" are the quality brands that the people of the world associate with our city' (Gilmore, 2004).[39] Soon after the success of the bid the Culture Company established a 'Music and Beatles Industry Group'. A post in 'music and tourism' was subsequently advertised,[40] but a local newspaper reported, 'Liverpool is to appoint a Beatles officer to exploit the worldwide potential of the Fab Four for the city.' The article quoted the head of Liverpool City Council as saying: 'The Beatles are important to this city and I don't think we realise the relevance they have to this city and region. We should be more positive in the development of the Beatles because people flock to Liverpool from all over the world. Other cities would give anything for this opportunity' (*Liverpool Echo*, 27 July 2005). At the same time, however, within Liverpool's Capital of Culture bid popular music and the Beatles were notably underplayed. Following the announcement of the bid's success it was reported that 'Liverpool successfully shed its Beatles stereotype to prove to the judges that there is more to the city than the fab four.'[41] An 'action plan' for Liverpool produced by Mersey Partnership stated, 'The world already knows about the Beatles and the City's famous football teams. The title will enable the City to tell a more complete story, encompassing everything from the Tate in Liverpool to the many events of the Liverpool festivals.'[42] In 2005 a second Mathew Street festival, featuring live performances by the Stranglers and the Buzzcocks, was launched by Liverpool City Council and scheduled to run alongside the original festival with

---

39   'Liverpool: the World in One City', bid document for UK Capital of Culture 2008, produced by the Liverpool Culture Company.
40   Liverpool City Council, 22 June 2005.
41   http://www.bbc.co.uk/capitalofculture/winner_liverpool.shtml, accessed June 2005.
42   An Action Plan for the City Region 2002–2005, November 2001

its Beatles tribute bands. The Larks in the Park festival that had once featured performances by many of the city's post-punk bands was also relaunched.

Despite the tensions surrounding the Beatles and those raised by culture-led regeneration, it was clear that Capital of Culture was helping to raise the profile of local cultural activities and achievements and generate new cultural activity. It also provided a welcome public platform for debate about culture and regeneration and their significance for the city, for alternative visions of Liverpool and for competing claims upon local culture. In addition, although the award generated apathy and confusion – and a struggle on the part of many individuals and local organizations to try to find out what was going on and what the implications might be – there were those who welcomed it as an opportunity rather than as a threat. Moreover, also in many ways the award clearly helped to inspire local confidence and encourage a sense of anticipation and excitement, and to make many people feel better about the city, tapping into a deep, long-standing pride in Liverpool culture and identity (Chapter 3).

Undoubtedly, there have been many positive changes in Liverpool over the last decade or so, partly due to government grant aid – much of which has been directed at improving the city's infrastructure – and partly due to improvements in the national economy. There has been an increase in local jobs and a growth in the local economy. Port activity has continued with smaller sized docks and a considerably reduced labour force;[43] in 2004 it was reported that for the first time since the 1930s there had been no annual decrease in Liverpool's population; and reporting on the city in the British media has become more positive, particularly following the declaration of Liverpool as Capital of Culture 2008. In addition, there has been a growth of employment in the banking, finance and insurance sectors, although the biggest increase has been in services and the distribution, hotel and restaurant sectors. As Meegan puts it (2003: 70), Liverpool 'is becoming more and more a city of consumption', with a renaissance built upon leisure and entertainment. The pace of regeneration has also intensified, with the demolition or renovation of many sites and a commercial boom in the construction of new buildings, including hotels and restaurants and large-scale retail developments that threaten to transform and dominate the entire city centre. Yet whilst there have been huge improvements, there nevertheless remain large pockets of poverty. As Meegan points out (ibid.: 72), the local economy remains weak and the city still tops various league tables of deprivation, with 19 of the city's 33 wards now featuring in the 10 per cent most disadvantaged wards in Britain (ibid.: 158). The city also continues to be plagued by racism and other instances of social injustice. There are thus, as Ben Tovim argues (2003), challenges as well as opportunities ahead, and a need for an improvement in civic leadership and the adoption of a more strategic and co-ordinated approach to local development.

---

43   The Mersey Docks and Harbour Company employs only 800 in its Liverpool operations (Meegan, 2003: 68).

Music Making a Noise

I have highlighted the way that popular music was implicated in culture-led regeneration in Liverpool and in a fierce politics of culture and regeneration. Music-makers, along with other city residents, had to grapple with the implications, effects and paradoxes of the neo-liberal policies that I have described; but what did the specificity of popular music contribute to the regeneration process?

As the brief historical account of the musical life of Mathew Street and the RopeWalks indicated, musicians and music entrepreneurs appropriated particular spaces within Liverpool city centre and helped to revitalize them. In doing so they and the music they produced transformed those spaces into distinctive places that were associated with cultural vibrancy and youthful entrepreneurialism. Their music activity also helped to produce commercially successful global brands in the form of the Beatles, the Cavern and Cream. Popular music thus became an obvious starting point for culture-led regeneration, and a useful 'hook' upon which to physically regenerate and re-image particular urban areas and reel in visitors and commercial investment. At the same time, however, popular music also presented a unique challenge to that process

Within the Cavern Quarter the music of the Beatles was often heard during the daytime and it served to mark out the boundaries of the quarter as a tourist space. Yet musical sounds could also transgress boundaries and invade space. In Liverpool, as in other cities, popular music contributed to increasing concerns about noise pollution, which had become a top public health issue.[44] The manageress of the Lucy in the Sky cafe in the Cavern Quarter complained to us that she used to play Beatles music in the cafe until occupants of the newly built offices nearby objected. Residents in the new loft apartments within the RopeWalks had initially been attracted to the idea of living in an area known for its nightlife and cultural vibrancy, but some soon complained about the volume of the musical sounds emanating from nearby music venues and about the noise of the people entering or leaving those venues.[45] Residential developments and office spaces in 'mixed use' urban areas were thus marketed on the basis of their proximity to sites of cultural consumption and associated lifestyles, yet that proximity produced conflicts of interest.

Similar conflicts have been mentioned in relation to Manchester (Haslam, 2000: 264–5); whilst Gibson and Homan (2004) examine the decline in live music venues in the suburbs of Sydney following gentrification and stringent noise legislation. They conclude, 'Live music presents an ongoing challenge to the regulatory

---

44   Johnson and Homan (2003) and Gibson and Homan (2004) discuss this in relation to the performance of live music in Sydney.

45   Those complaints were reported on local television news and referred to in the 'RopeWalks Supplementary Planning Document: Consultation Draft', produced in partnership with Liverpool Vision and with the assistance of the consultants Jones Lang LaSalle and BDP, April 2005: p21.

balancing act that accompanies the new emphasis upon the "24-hour city"' (ibid.: 74). Furthermore, Gilmore writes, 'In terms of urban cultural life, popular music audiences have previously been portrayed as a necessary evil – going to see bands and visiting nightclubs are the prerogatives of youth, and can bring into the public domain problems which need to be contained, such as alcohol, noise, litter and violence.'[46] Within the RopeWalks and the Cavern Quarter popular music was also associated with noise or mess in a visual sense. The owners of Probe complained that they were evicted from the Cavern Quarter because their customers and their brightly painted building did not suit the planned gentrification of the quarter. Meanwhile music-related fly-posting and graffiti were perceived as a nuisance by officials in charge of promoting the RopeWalks. On occasion, some musicians also made a noise through their musical compositions and performances in order to protest against the negative effects of particular regeneration initiatives.

To a certain extent the Cavern Quarter Initiative helped to generate audiences for musicians and to allow for, if not actively encourage, live music performance, whilst depending on Cavern City Tours and other local businesses to organize them. Yet at the same time the Cavern Quarter and also the RopeWalks had a negative impact on small music businesses operating within their boundaries. Certain music-related businesses and venues had for some consequently become symbols of resistance to urban entrepreneurship and the commercial developments involved. Within the RopeWalks, musicians involved with the city's alternative music scenes were at the forefront of campaigns to protest against the closure of Quiggins and the Picket. Their live music performances provided a public platform, focus and broadcaster for dissent, helping to mobilize support for those campaigns and involve people in collective protest. Some musicians also expressed such concerns through their lyrical compositions. Haslam (2000: 208) likewise highlights the noise that popular music can make in cities such as Liverpool and Manchester, albeit in unhelpfully romanticized and generalized terms: 'The bad vibes are slamming the ghettos shut. But someone, somewhere is getting up, not giving up. The corporate merchandisers, the so-called experts, the planners, the politicians can't stifle the desire to break the silence, to be heard, to make some noise.'

The city's popular music culture was thus centrally implicated in the emergence and development of cultural quarters and in culture-led urban regeneration; but also in the critical response to that process. Paradoxically, however, the city's popular music culture was also relatively hidden. In the planning and development of the RopeWalks, for example, there was considerable emphasis on the need to respect and maintain the distinctive character of the area, yet the focus was on the quarter's material and built environment, as in much of the literature on culture-led urban regeneration (see, for example, Zukin, 1995). There was little recognition of or discussion on how places might be distinguished in more intangible ways, and

---

46   'City beats' – local popular music and cultural policy. *The International Journal of Urban Labour and Leisure* 3(1). http://www.ijull.org/vol3/1/000018.htm, accessed December 2004.

through an urban soundscape as well as material landscape. Whilst concerns about noise pollution intensified, there was no official discussion or documentation on how musical sounds and experiences might contribute to and characterize urban space in more positive ways.[47] Furthermore, music-makers were not prioritized for consultation about either the Cavern or the RopeWalks initiative, and a music and cultural production strategy was not pursued for the RopeWalks despite early plans for one. Stokes (1999: 146-7), writing on music and tourism, suggests that even in the case of states that have made much of music in their packaging of tourist destinations, 'there is virtually no recognition on the part of tourism development boards that a marketable musical profile or image relies on a complex and fragile world of music making.'

Conclusion

This chapter began with the unveiling of the Cavern Wall of Fame. To some it might have seemed a rather ordinary wall with some names etched onto it. To others it might have been a monument to local musical creativity, or symbolic of a tacky and overly commercial tourist expansion. I have tried to look beneath the surface, however, and expose the tensions and struggles that the bricks and mortar concealed. The Cavern and the RopeWalks illustrate how claims upon popular music as local culture and heritage became the basis for the development of urban 'quarters,' and a focus for culture-led urban regeneration; and I considered the groups, practices and interests involved with their development. Both quarters emerged in response to economic and social change within the city, and to more general trends within the global political economy. They were promoted through a celebratory marketing rhetoric that concealed the tensions, and urban inequalities involved and provoked opposition, generating debates that had come to characterize culture-led regeneration and had, in Liverpool at least, intensified and become increasingly polarized. Popular music nevertheless contributed to the development of these quarters, and to the regeneration process more generally, in particular ways. It had widespread appeal and pulling power, and by appropriating urban areas popular musicians, audiences and music entrepreneurs helped to revitalize them and transform them into distinctive places that generated, for some residents and outsiders, a sense of identity, belonging and attachment. Popular music thus became a useful seed or hook and symbolic frame for the regeneration of such areas. Yet at the same time it presented a unique challenge to that process, and musicians were centrally involved not only in the development of these initiatives, but also in opposition to them. Music recordings and live performance events provided a public platform that helped to promote that opposition and mobilize support for it.

---

47   Although at one CQI meeting (12 March 1997) a local solicitor had raised the question of how to bring in street entertainers to liven up the quarter. The subsequent discussion was brief and focused on how best to invite local music students to perform – a further example of the kind of regulation and control of urban space that such quarter initiatives encouraged.

Conclusion

This book has explored the relationship between popular music and the city using one particular city as a case study, and it has had two interrelated aims. First, it has aimed to examine the impact of social and economic change within the city on its popular music culture, focusing on the impact of de-industrialization and economic restructuring during the 1980s and 1990s. Second, and in turn, it has aimed to consider the specificity of popular music and its impact on the city. To conclude the book I want to relate those two aims to the book's key findings and its two main arguments.

Popular Music, Cities and Local Difference

The book examined popular music culture within a 'post-Fordist' context, relating it to topical debates and pressing issues concerning 'post-industrial cities' and their social and economic restructuring, a process governed by the politics and economics of neo-liberalism and involving an emphasis on culture-led urban regeneration. The book's first main argument concerned the symbiosis of culture and economy. In the Liverpool of the 1980s and 1990s de-industrialization and economic restructuring encouraged an emphasis on local difference that was influenced by social, cultural and economic factors specific to Liverpool – including local relations of class, gender and ethnicity. Within those circumstances popular music became a resource for the production of local difference. This involved efforts to represent and develop popular music as Liverpool culture and promote the city and its music as distinctive. Those efforts were directed at different aims and objectives and they took on different forms according to the particular social situation and context involved, but also according to the music genre involved and the social and ideological conventions that distinguished it. I examined a few examples of such efforts. They included grass-roots efforts to pin country and rock music down to one definitive and distinctive Liverpool sound and to local roots and origins, and to claim country music as Liverpool heritage and connect it to patriotic notions of local difference. They also included more institutional, public and theatrical efforts to promote Liverpool as distinctive within a global marketplace through the branding of music businesses and urban quarters, and initiatives aimed at developing music as a Liverpool industry and tourist attraction.

The book thus focused on the production of a city *through* popular music rather than just on popular music *in* the city, showing that precisely within a notoriously transnational or global culture, place and the local continue to be significant. Yet the discussion did not celebrate or romanticize the local as a site of resistance or authenticity. Rather, it showed how the production of the local is tied to developments in global capitalism, and how the local is a contradictory site of resistance but also compliance, of messages and images that are progressive but also regressive, and of struggle and tension. Efforts to turn popular music into Liverpool culture were fraught with tension and were also contested. I illustrated some of the different voices and perspectives involved, showing how popular music was embraced, appropriated and manipulated to serve a range of often conflicting interests and agendas. Popular music was thus implicated in a politics of place that involved a struggle for identity and belonging, status and prestige. But how was Liverpool shaped, represented and imagined through this process, and exactly what kind of tensions did it involve?

Marginality, Renewal and Local Pride

First, I highlighted a dual emphasis on decline and renewal within popular music culture in Liverpool, and a sense of marginality juxtaposed with expressions of local attachment or pride, a juxtaposition that I characterized in terms of tension.

Musicians involved with local country and rock music scenes connected rock and country music to a poetics of place, loss and abandonment, so that within certain circumstances the music became a lament for the city. The country scene (Chapter 3) was perceived by its participants to have been overshadowed and marginalized by various local events, and to be ageing, shrinking and dying. Concerns about the decline and vulnerability of the scene prompted some of the musicians involved to promote country music as Liverpool heritage in an effort to revive the scene. In doing so they expressed a gritty resilience and sense of pride in the scene and the city as a whole, and fierce attachments to particular dockside neighbourhoods and communities. Country music was thus a focus for a nostalgic, patriotic and sometimes rather insular emphasis on local difference. That emphasis jarred against the cosmopolitan outlook of the musicians involved, and their embrace of the American origins of country music and also the transatlantic crossings that had shaped and disseminated the music and the multicultural influences within it.

Similarly, rock culture and commercial music production in Liverpool involved a tension between 'heroic narratives' and a 'rhetoric of weakness and suffering' (Stahl, 2001). The music-makers involved raised concerns about the exodus of musicians and music entrepreneurs from Liverpool to London, where the national music industry was based – concerns that were not simply connected to familiar notions of 'selling out' (Chapters 3, 4 and 5). Through their descriptions of local music-making the city was represented as a creative pool or stream of talent, but also as a wounded city from which talent 'haemorrhaged', a city that had been left behind and was consequently isolated, grieving and introspective. That rhetoric was strategically deployed by consultants, music- and policy-makers and the local media to help mobilize support for the notion of music as a local industry, and for initiatives aimed at developing such an industry; hence the departure of commercially successful musicians (and their earnings) from Liverpool was a starting point for early cultural policy documents and debates (Chapter 5). Meanwhile Beatles tourist entrepreneurs suggested that the departure of the Beatles from Liverpool was perceived locally as a 'betrayal' of the city. Hence in their lobby for public sector support and recognition those entrepreneurs, in association with Beatles fans, emphasized what the Beatles 'had done for the city' and how much they had contributed to the city's positive image and worldwide reputation (Chapter 6).

The concern with leaving provoked a parallel concern with staying and with loyalty to the city. That concern that was evident in debates about the activities and obligations of successful local musicians and music companies, and in the questions that were raised about whether they had 'paid their dues' to the city (Chapter 5). It was also evident in the stance taken by music companies that adopted Liverpool as a brand, not just as a commercial strategy but also as a sign of their commitment to the city and its future development (Chapter 4). Liverpool's economic problems had in some ways hindered the development of those companies. They had also heightened concerns about the marginality and exploitation of local musical creativity and entrepreneurship by the London-based music industry. At the same time, however, de-industrialization had left in its wake a wealth of physical spaces in Liverpool that enabled the development of music-business clusters. Economic hardship was also widely perceived as an explanation for local musical creativity, and as motivating and sharpening music entrepreneurship, thus helping to distinguish Liverpool from other British cities.

Commerce, Creativity and Local Authenticity

These tensions between marginality and pride fuelled a second set of tensions evident within particular music-related scenes, events and situations. They took the form of a familiar ideological distinction between commerce and local creativity and authenticity.

Rock/pop music-makers, for example, struggled not only with the severe local effects of economic crisis but also with the risks and costs of the notoriously unpredictable music market that was driven by a quest for novelty (Chapter 4). This, in addition to 'the ideology of folk in rock' (Frith, 1981), encouraged them to perceive local music-making in terms of an opposition between commerce and local creativity and authenticity. Hence the Liverpool rock sound was commonly described as authentic and distinctive to the city, but it was also widely acknowledged that the sound was misrepresented by music and media industries, which promoted local authenticity and alterity as part of a commercial strategy designed to increase sales. Moreover, many music-makers were preoccupied with a brutal juxtaposition of commercial success and failure. They tended to equate Liverpool and the local and provincial with creativity, and London, the capital, with commerce, seeing London-based music and media industries as a threat to local creativity even whilst being also an opportunity. Paradoxically, that tension between creativity and commerce emerged too in characterizations of local music-making, which was described as creative and collaborative but also as uniquely commercially-orientated and competitive, cliquey and factionalized.

Tensions between commerce and local difference, creativity and authenticity were at the same time fuelled by aspects of the regeneration process. For example, the efforts of public sector tourist officials and private sector entrepreneurs to develop Beatles tourism in Liverpool and make it more professionally organized suited the interests of Beatles fans who wanted Liverpool's Beatles heritage to be recognized, preserved and made accessible to fans (Chapter 6). On the other hand, entrepreneurs and fans worried about the overcommercialization of Beatles tourism and the damage that it might do to the authenticity and distinctiveness of Beatles Liverpool. Hence fears were expressed that parts of the city would become increasingly bland and 'Disneyfied'. Those fears were fuelled by commercial developments in Mathew Street and the Cavern Quarter, which were based around a Beatles theme and sought to capitalize upon the fame and vibrancy of the Beatles and the club in which they had regularly performed (Chapter 7). For many music-makers those developments had turned Mathew Street into the antithesis of the musical creativity that it had once represented, so that the street consequently bore little relation to authentic Liverpool culture.

Concerns about the threat that commercial, property-led developments in the city posed to authentic Liverpool culture and creativity intensified during the late 1990s, when Liverpool City Council adopted a new emphasis on urban entrepreneurialism and culture-led urban regeneration (Chapter 7). Liverpool's success in its bid to become European Capital of Culture 2008 provided a focus for such concerns. In the first place it offered a unique opportunity for new cultural and regeneration initiatives, and a range of interesting, innovative and worthy projects were launched – from small-scale and experimental projects to larger and more costly initiatives. It also offered an opportunity to raise the profile of local cultural activities and achievements, and it provided a welcome public platform for debate about culture and creativity and their significance for the city. At the same time, however, those debates became increasingly polarized following the early failure of certain high-profile flagship projects that had been planned for 2008; the diversion of funding previously earmarked for voluntary and community sector organizations; and intense and well-publicized controversies surrounding large, commercial, property-led developments and their negative impact on small businesses. For many music-makers – particularly those involved with alternative music scenes and independent or 'grass-roots' music initiatives – capital and culture became perceived in terms of opposition, and the city's status as Capital of Culture was regarded as little more than a cynical economic and marketing initiative. The official rhetorical emphasis on creativity and local difference was thus challenged, and concerns were raised about the regeneration process and how it might end up destroying the authenticity and distinctiveness of local culture and ultimately 'killing' culture and creativity.

Popular Music and Urban Inequality

Claims on music as local culture were thus characterized by tension and conflict. They were also contested on unequal terms, and they exposed and generated certain urban inequalities, related to developments in global capitalism, that affected the city's popular music culture.

To begin with, the representations of Liverpool as marginal, abandoned and lagging behind highlighted the uneven effects of de-industrialization across cities: as a consequence of shifts in global trade Liverpool's economic problems were severe even in relation to those of other cities in Britain's northern regions. They also highlighted the uneven effects of de-industrialization within Liverpool itself. Country music, for example, spoke to and for working-class groups and urban neighbourhoods that had suffered particularly severely from the decline of Liverpool's port-related industries (Chapter 3). Considerable efforts were made to tackle urban deprivation, and I referred to a number of music initiatives aimed at providing services, events and training that would help to promote social inclusion. Nevertheless the city continued to be plagued by racism and by the persistence of deep social and spatial divisions, and to appear at or near the top of league tables designed to measure and chart levels of urban deprivation across Britain. In addition to this, questions were raised about the long-term benefits of culture-led regeneration following evidence that it contributed to local social and spatial polarization within cities. In Liverpool, cultural and musical 'quarter' initiatives encouraged inward investment and large-scale commercial developments, but they also resulted in the increasing privatization of urban space and a rise in rents and property values (Chapter 7). Inevitably, in what has become a familiar cliché, this resulted in an exodus of certain groups and 'misfits' or 'undesirables' from those areas, including small independent music businesses and groups of young musicians and music fans.

The vast majority of music businesses were also disadvantaged by certain public funding initiatives, as illustrated by the application process for Objective One European funding, which favoured larger organizations that had previous experience of dealing with public sector agencies, administrative assistance to cope with the extensive paperwork involved, and the resources to hire consultants who could advise them on how to proceed (Chapter 5). At the same time, however, the emphasis on culture as a motor for urban regeneration and economic development led to the rise of a new group of professional consultants who specialized in the arts and the cultural or creative industries, and who were employed by public agencies to act as their 'bridge' to the local cultural sector. Yet those consultants were able to exert considerable influence and control over the policy-making process, and over the ways in which music was defined, categorized and represented for policy-making purposes. This generated frustration amongst many of the music-makers involved with music-industry policy-making, who found themselves subsequently silenced, marginalized or excluded.

The tensions and contestations surrounding claims on popular music as Liverpool culture also exposed some of the inequalities that characterized commercial music production and music tourism in Liverpool. Whilst local music scenes and markets had a certain degree of creative autonomy, they were at the same time monitored, penetrated and capitalized on by multinational music corporations, which depended upon them as a source of and incubator for musical talent and creative entrepreneurship (Chapter 5). Music-makers struggled to access major music corporations and national and global music industry networks, and they commonly and simplistically characterized relations between the city and the music industry in terms of local, provincial creativity exploited and colonized by London-based music corporations. Nevertheless relations of domination and subordination also existed amongst Liverpool-based music businesses, hence the ability of a company such as Cream to dictate trends within the city's contemporary dance scenes (Chapter 4). The dominant position of a music organization and global music brand like Cream was enhanced by the way that it was celebrated and promoted by public and private sector bodies, and prioritized in media representations of local popular music culture (Chapter 5). Likewise the Beatles were invested in as a local heritage attraction by tourist entrepreneurs and were used to brand and market a city quarter and encourage commercial investment into it (Chapters 6 and 7). This provoked concerns about narrow and misleading representations of Liverpool's musical history, and initiatives aimed at promoting excluded or marginalized music heritages. It also provoked frustrated efforts to broaden out and promote the city as 'more than the Beatles'. The discussion thus pointed to the political and ideological aspects of music, heritage and regeneration.

The Musical Production of the City

I have described various efforts to connect popular music to Liverpool, and the tensions and inequalities involved. They raise important questions about the changing role and significance of popular music for 'post-industrial' cities, and its social, cultural, economic and aesthetic contribution to urban life and to the future development of those cities – questions that have as yet been little explored within popular music studies and cannot be resolved here. I have nevertheless tried to consider what such efforts to connect popular music to Liverpool suggest about the specific role and significance of popular music as urban culture. Each of the book's chapters illustrated how particular characteristics of Liverpool influenced its musical life, but in turn how music also shaped and produced that city, contributing to its distinctiveness as well as its 'cityness'. This brings me to the book's second main argument, which was that popular music's specific or unique role and significance in urban life (and perceptions of it as specific and unique) helps to explain why it was a focus for the production of local difference, and for tensions related to that process. At the same time the book exposed major contradictions in the way that popular music was perceived and valued within the city, and it illustrated ways in which the specificity of popular music challenged as well as encouraged efforts to categorize and claim it as local culture. So how was popular music valued and what was so contradictory about that process? What kind of challenge did popular music present to the production of local difference? Furthermore, if focusing on one city can illustrate the disinctiveness of popular music as urban culture, then what can the focus on popular music suggest about the specificity of cities as a particular kind of place? I will now address each of these three questions in turn.

The Value of Popular Music as Urban Culture

For a specific period of time during the 1980s and 1990s popular music became the focus of a poetics of place, loss and abandonment in Liverpool, and for initiatives aimed at local economic restructuring and urban regeneration. Clearly, connections between popular music and the city were held dear and were fiercely protected, debated and fought over; and popular music was no longer simply demonized or ignored by the local state but became, on specific occasions, a focus for cultural and economic policy. But why did popular music matter and why was it valued so highly?

When I first started working on my PhD thesis in 1983 I was based at a postgraduate college at Oxford University, where I benefited from contact with fellow students from many different countries researching a variety of topics, particularly those concerned with international relations and the political economies of Eastern Bloc and Middle Eastern countries. When individual research topics were first mentioned at social gatherings polite interest would usually be expressed and a few questions asked; but when it came to my research on amateur rock bands in Liverpool there was usually a pause, during which this unexpected piece of information was absorbed. Then, more often than not, people would express an opinion and offer me information and advice. I was later invited to advise upon a museum exhibition about Liverpool popular music; yet at the initial planning meeting with those responsible for putting the exhibition together it was clear that for many of them this was an opportunity to work on a project that really meant something to them personally, and each of them therefore had their own strong views about what should be included and how it should be presented. On this and on many other occasions I was struck by how knowledgeable people were about popular music, by the strong feelings and opinions that it provoked, and by how important popular music seemed to be to people's sense of self and their individual and collective identities. This may help to explain why popular music was a focus for competing claims on local culture and for expressions of *local* identity.

Beatles fans participating in Liverpool's Beatles Week 1996, for example, recounted to us their lives and their personal experiences and past relationships through references to the music of the Beatles (Chapter 6). For them and for other listeners just one simple musical phrase could evoke a private world of memory, sentiment and desire; but those fans also suggested to us that the music had provided a common language for people across the world and had created a transnational Beatles 'community' or 'family'. Similarly, country musicians explained to us the roots of their music and the working-class and migrant communities and seafarers that had developed and shaped it (Chapter 3). The music helped to create a sense of solidarity and shared experiences, and a dialogue with the past, embodying collective memories and traditions that took on a particular significance in a context of social and economic change. At the same time, however, both Beatles fans and country musicians connected Beatles and country music to Liverpool, and for many of them the music distinguished that city and inspired a sense of attachment or belonging to it. Elsewhere (Cohen, 1998) I have likewise discussed music's effectiveness in stimulating a sense of identity, preserving and transmitting cultural memory, transporting listeners to different imaginary locations and providing a map of meaning.

Yet music does not just play a part in the production of meaning but also structures emotion, as illustrated by one particular musical event at Liverpool's Cavern Club (Chapter 6). For Stokes (1994: 3), music evokes and organizes experiences of place 'with an intensity, power and simplicity unmatched by any other social activity'. For DeNora (2000: 169), 'The temporal dimension *(of music)*, the fact that it is a non-verbal, non-depictive medium, and that is a physical presence whose vibrations can be felt, all enhance its ability to work at non-cognitive or subconscious levels.' It is perhaps not surprising, therefore, that music appears to have a peculiar ability to capture the imagination and transport listeners from real to virtual places, and that people often turn to music to express sentiments that they find difficult to put into words, and to convey their ideas about the essential character or truth of a place. This helps to explain descriptions of rock and country music as the 'soul' and 'heart' of Liverpool (Chapters 2 and 3), although the idea that cities and other geographical places have souls and that music is best placed to express them is fairly commonplace.

The music discussed in this book thus helped to make the city meaningful and construct local identity, but also to structure emotion and experience within and relating to the city. As popular music, however, it was at the same time mass mediated and industrially produced, and therefore ubiquitous and accessible. It was commonly heard in both public and private spaces within the city, and it was relatively easy to make in the sense that educational and financial barriers to popular music-making were not as high as those to classical music or film-making (to give just two examples). Local music-making was thus an exceptionally broad and diverse field of cultural activity. Most importantly, popular music-making and listening tended to bring people together and encourage participation, collaboration and social interaction (whilst also marking and encouraging social divisions and rivalries), and this enhanced the music's popular appeal (Chapter 1). In addition to this, popular musicians were widely regarded as having a special connection to the city, hence their relationship with the city was closely scrutinized and subjected to critical attention (Chapter 5). Toynbee (2000: x) likewise highlights the popular appeal of musicians, describing the popular musician as 'exemplary just because s/he comes from the people and cleaves to popular values'. Similarly, Finnegan (1989: 333) points to the 'special value' and 'deep significance' attached to music in our society. She suggests that music is 'perhaps a unique and distinctive mode through which people both realize and transcend their social existence' (ibid.: 339), and that it is, 'among the most valued and, it may be, most profoundly human of [cultural] practices in our society' (ibid.: 341).

It was the music's popular and commercial appeal that attracted the interest of the local state during the late 1980s, as it turned to the arts and cultural industries as part of its programme of economic restructuring, and also the interest of private sector companies involved with urban regeneration (Chapters 5, 6 and 7). Whilst attitudes towards popular music varied considerably across both public and private sectors, it was nevertheless generally recognized that popular music had unique pulling power, and that it had helped to revitalize urban areas and transform them into distinctive and vibrant places. Popular music thus became a useful hook for city marketing initiatives, and a seed and symbolic frame for physical regeneration and the development of city 'quarters'. Some of the people behind such initiatives also recognized that popular music had a certain glamour and a peculiar ability to attract attention and generate controversy: hence its usefulness for public relations purposes and again as hook for the development and promotion of cultural policy. Above all, however, popular music was valued for its commercial and income-generating potential and for what it might contribute to the local economy. Moreover, for some, the music industry was particularly suited to the new 'post-Fordist' global economy because it was entrepreneurial, flexible, casualized and knowledge-based – hence Lash and Urry (1994: 123) describe music as *the* 'post-Fordist' industry.

The Challenge of Popular Music

The specific social, symbolic, sensual and economic value and appeal of popular music encouraged efforts to connect it to the city, and to categorize, claim and promote it as local culture. At the same time, however, the specificity of popular music did not just encourage those efforts but also challenged or undermined them.

Claims upon popular music as a local scene or sound and as local heritage were challenged, for example, by its mass mediation and its popular appeal, and by the fact that it is a 'travelling culture' (Clifford, 1992) and a global industry. Hence musical sounds, images, commodities and ideas were disseminated to and from cities through various global routes or 'scapes' (Appadurai, 1996) (Chapter 1). In fact some scholars suggest that music is 'the most global aspect of our global village' (Burnett, 1996: 1), and 'the most fluid of cultural forms' (Connell and Gibson, 2003: 9). Thus the Beatles were claimed as Liverpool heritage, but they were at the same time a symbol of global culture and they were also adopted as the heritage of other peoples and places (Chapter 6). Interpretations of particular musical sounds and structures as meaning the local were also challenged by the fact that cultural texts can invite alternative readings, and that music is again fairly specific in this respect given the abstract nature of musical representation, which can make music particularly open to interpretation (Chapter 2). The specificity of music as a commercial practice and industry posed additional challenges. The efforts of consultants and music-makers to categorize, unite or regulate local music-making as a single local 'industry' or 'sub-sector' were complicated by the breadth and diversity of local music-making (Chapter 5). Their efforts to promote music as a local industry, and to promote the local in music branding and within global networks of production and distribution, were also frustrated by the notoriously risky and unpredictable nature of the music market, and by the domination of that market by a few major and multinational corporations that were concentrated (to a degree that was relatively unusual across the cultural industries) in a few of the world's 'hub' cities (Chapter 4). At the same time the efforts of city planners, developers and policy-makers to use music to regenerate, distinguish and brand particular urban areas or 'quarters' were challenged by the visual and aural 'noise' that music could make (Chapter 7). Moreover, musicians had been at the forefront of local opposition to those regeneration initiatives, with music recordings and live performance events providing a public platform that helped to promote that opposition and mobilize support for it.

Meanwhile, efforts of the local state to develop and promote the music business within the city were challenged by a perceived lack of fit between the music industry and civic policy on the part of both policy-makers and music-makers (Chapter 5). Whilst popular music was prioritized by certain community and welfare initiatives directed at youths and at social inclusion, its incorporation into strategies aimed at economic restructuring and city marketing was contentious given that for many policy-makers it was still considered to be trivial or 'low culture'. Moreover, some policy-makers referred to the music industry's reputation for disreputable and illicit activity, and for being ruthlessly and uniquely competitive. They also associated the industry with the images and mythologies commonly promoted through the media of maverick, egotistical and unruly groups of working-class, male musicians, most of whom would be unlikely to take an interest in, or conform to, policy-making procedures. In addition to this, consultants hired to investigate and report on the local music 'sub-sector' for policy-making purposes represented it as fragmented, divided and lacking in organization and leadership, and as the most difficult of all the arts and cultural sub-sectors to monitor and regulate.

These examples highlight various contradictions concerning the value and status of popular music as urban culture. Although popular music was commonly regarded as special, it also tended to be taken for granted as part of the mundane and everyday (Chapter 1). Furthermore, despite the significant cultural status of commercially successful popular musicians, most musicians and music entrepreneurs were generally lacking in social and economic status, and were not prioritized for consultation over particular policy initiatives. Thus an association formed by musicians and music-makers to promote the interests of the music 'sub-sector' was marginalized and generally ignored and unsupported by policy-makers and the consultants that they employed (Chapter 5). Within those circumstances music-makers were thus high in cultural capital, to adopt the terminology of Bourdieu, but low in social and economic capital. At the same time the local state increasingly emphasized the economic value of music, which diverted attention away from its social and aesthetic value; whilst for city planners popular music was generally regarded as a 'hook' to hang other things on to rather than as significant in its own right (Chapter 7). Hence it provided a public platform for city marketing but was at the same time ignored, marginalized and devalued, thus remaining relatively 'hidden' (Finnegan, 1989). Moreover, whilst popular music was perceived as an opportunity for urban regeneration it was in some ways also perceived as a threat.

My post at a university Institute of Popular Music helped to bring home to me the contradictory views of popular music as socially, culturally and economically significant, but also as something of little cultural or educational value that public sector organizations (including universities) should not help to fund or promote. The latter view nevertheless diminished slightly over the 20-year period that this book focused on. The incorporation of popular music and culture into cultural and economic state policy became much more acceptable. At the same time the academic study of popular music proliferated both in Britain and abroad, and this eventually led to the appointment of popular music scholars as professors in British university music departments that had traditionally focused on classical music alone. When I first arrived in Liverpool in 1985 seeking information and advice on local rock music my initial key contacts were music broadcasters and journalists. If I had arrived 20 years later I would have been able to consult a wealth of relevant information available on the internet, and visit Liverpool University's Institute of Popular Music and the Liverpool Institute for Performing Arts, and those running degree programmes in popular music at Liverpool John Moores University, Hope University and Liverpool Community College. I could have looked up the Merseyside Music Business Directory and numerous consultancy reports on the local music business sector commissioned by a broad range of public sector organizations. I could also have contacted the Merseyside Music Development Agency and the regional association for Arts, Culture and Media Enterprises. For information on local popular music history I could have visited both private and public sector museums. The 1980s and 1990s thus witnessed an increasing institutionalization and legitimization of rock/ pop music.

Popular Music as Urban Culture

Through its focus on one particular city the book has thus highlighted contradictions and changes in the way that popular music has been valued as urban culture, and the specific challenges that it has posed to the production of local difference. In turn, however, what has focusing on popular music suggested about the specificity of cities as a particular kind of place, and about changes to cities and city living?

The global routes through which popular music is consumed, produced and disseminated show how the city is a nodal point within wider networks and flows, and a place of intense social interaction and mixing (Massey, 1999). Cities are also centres for the development of the social, business and entertainment infrastructures that enable music production. The book's focus on popular music also pointed to the vibrancy and creativity of cities and the breadth and diversity of music activity within them, and it showed how music influences social behaviour and social interactions within the city. Finnegan (1989: 324) suggests that the multiplicity of musical 'pathways' within towns and cities matches the characteristic density and heterogeneity of urban life, and 'the many-sided situational, often changing lives that people lead in towns today.' In this book, however, the focus on popular music has also shown cities to be sites of tension, turbulence and contradiction. At the same time it has shown cities to be sensual places and sites of affect and theatricality, and also socially and symbolically significant. Popular music thus influences how cities are perceived, experienced and made meaningful. Through popular music Liverpool was a focus for ideas and sentiments, and it was represented in various ways using a variety of metaphors, including organic metaphors. The city was a former 'gateway' to Empire with a contemporary popular music culture that was globally connected and cosmopolitan in outlook; yet it was also represented as a city that was insular and bounded but wounded, a city that had a heart and soul and that bled, wept and grieved.

Popular music thus helped to highlight the dynamism of cities and show that cities are never static but continually changing. Certain changes in Liverpool reflected broader trends affecting cities and their role and significance within the global economy. By the time that I arrived in Liverpool during the mid-1980s, de-industrialization had affected the physical settings for musical practice, the activities and infrastructures of local music scenes, and the way that music and the city were thought about and reflected upon. Yet there was also a parallel and long-standing emphasis on economic restructuring and urban regeneration, and over the following 20 years I witnessed a gradual and ongoing transformation of Liverpool into a city of consumption. Large amounts of funding from British government and European Union sources, combined with other notable developments,[1] resulted in dramatic transformations in the city's built environment and obvious improvements not only to the material landscape of particular inner-city areas, but also to the city's outskirts. They also led to significant and innovative schemes aimed at tackling urban deprivation and promoting social inclusion. The local economy began to show signs of improvement, as did the city's image in the national media, and in 2004, for the first time since the 1930s, the decrease in the city's population was halted. Meanwhile the city's popular music culture has continued to develop and thrive, and to produce a broad and diverse range of new and often innovative music scenes and sounds. The narratives of decline and the rhetoric of loss and abandonment that I described in this book – and that took on different forms and nuances according to particular social and cultural contexts – have, for the moment at least, been pushed into the background.

As I write the city centre is in turmoil due to ambitious schemes aimed at improving its transportation systems and redeveloping and repositioning its central retail district. Roads are being dug up, cranes have become a familiar feature of the city skyline and massive building developments are under way. There is a sense of déjà vu, of an urban landscape that is again being ripped up and torn apart – perhaps with the same devastating consequences of earlier initiatives and post-war slum clearance – and a concern that mistakes of the past will be repeated and that urban

---

1   These include, for example, a dramatic rise in the number of students in the city and an upturn in the national economy.

deprivation and social inequalities will not just continue but maybe even worsen. Yet there is also a sense of optimism and anticipation. With the extensive scaffolding, bollards and plastic sheeting it is as if the city as a whole is currently wrapped up like a cocoon and no one seems quite sure what kind of city will eventually emerge.

People commonly turn to music to provide metaphors for the city. They do so in order to say something about cities and urban living that cannot easily be put into words (Chapter 2), and because 'music provides a fund of materials that serve as paradigms, metaphors, analogues, hints and reminders of activity, practice and social procedure' (DeNora, 2000: 159). Cities, like music, are too messy, changeable and intensely experienced or felt than metaphors or representations can allow for, but music has helped to convey the rhythms and grooves of everyday life within the city and its multilayered flux and flow. Haslam (2000: 274) uses the metaphor of a 're-mix' to highlight both continuity and change in the city of Manchester, describing how musical tracks are reworked by producers, writers and DJs. Cycles, loops and patterns from the past are repeated and developed, hence Manchester 'is recognizably the same, but new elements have reappeared, disguising, reinforcing or extending the original version'. Yet the remix suggests a vision of city life that is rather too ordered and controlled, when the case material presented in this book has shown how events can unfold in ways that are messy and unco-ordinated, sometimes quite surprising and dramatic and often haphazard. Drawing upon Morton's study of traditional Irish music-making (2005), I am therefore tempted instead to think of Liverpool in terms of musical improvisation. The city is in this sense a performance based on recognizable musical elements and repetitions and infused with traces or echoes from the musical past. There may be variations on a familiar theme, but musical and social elements may also interact in such a way that events acquire a momentum of their own and develop in unpredictable ways. This might well result in the disruption of the performance and a breakdown in social and musical interaction. On the other hand, depending upon the particular circumstances involved and the particular social and musical mix, there is also the possibility that it might produce an experience through which something different, progressive and inspiring could unfold.

I would like to end, however, by returning to the metaphor with which this book began, and that highlights the peculiar ability of popular music to tell us about how cities are imagined, but also how they feel and how they are lived, For Coleman pop is a metaphor for the city and a continuation by other means of the urban mind, and has 'taught us to be intrigued by cities, to fear them, to face up to them' (*The Independent*, 11 April 1995). This book has focused on popular music in order to explore what it can tell us about cities within a 'post-industrial' context, and about experiences of loss and notions of decline but also a parallel struggle for renewal.

Appendix:
Methodology and Approach

This book has drawn upon a series of research projects that I directed during the 1980s and 1990s. Each project had its own distinct aims, objectives and research context and addressed its own specific themes and issues. I have nevertheless tried to relate the projects to the particular themes and aims of the book and knit together their research findings. The purpose of this appendix is to provide further information on the projects and the methodology involved, although there is only space for a brief description of each project.

The Research Projects

The Major Projects

The research involved three major projects, the first of which was a three-year project entitled 'Popular Music in Liverpool's Twentieth Century Cultural and Economic Development'. It ran from 1991 to 1994 and was funded by the Leverhulme Trust. It was based around a series of case studies on country music; Irish music, culture and identity; the musical life of the Jewish community; dance bands of the 1930s; and the music-making of local black musicians. The bulk of the research was conducted by Kevin McManus and myself, but the case study on dance bands was conducted by Tricia Jenkins with the assistance of sixth-form girls from St Hilda's Church of England High School in Sefton Park, Liverpool. All the case studies involved extensive face-to-face interviewing, and most also involved participant observation and archival research.

The second project was entitled 'Popular Music, Tourism and Urban Regeneration'. It was a two-year comparative study of popular music and tourism in Liverpool and New Orleans that ran from 1995 to 1997 and was funded by the Economic and Social Research Council of Great Britain (ESRC). The Liverpool-based fieldwork was conducted by Connie Atkinson and myself and involved a focus on Beatles tourism. The fieldwork in New Orleans was conducted by Connie and focused on jazz tourism. The Liverpool-based research involved face-to-face interviews with over 200 people – including tourist entrepreneurs and policy-makers, tourists and local musicians – and it also involved extensive participant observation.

The third project was entitled 'Music Policy, the Music Industry and Local Economic Development'. It was a two-year comparative study of music-industry policy-making in Liverpool, Manchester and Sheffield, and it ran from 1996 to 1998 and was also funded by the ESRC. It was a joint project directed by myself at the Institute of Popular Music (University of Liverpool) in association with

Justin O'Connor and Adam Brown at the Manchester Institute for Popular Culture (Manchester Metropolitan University). The project was based around a series of case studies: the In the City music industry convention and the Northern Quarter in Manchester; the National Centre for Popular Music and the Cultural Industries Quarter in Sheffield; and the Merseyside Music Development Agency and the RopeWalks in Liverpool. The project involved face-to-face interviews with music- and policy-makers. Adam conducted the interviews in Manchester and Sheffield, whilst many of the interviews in Liverpool were conducted by Abigail Gilmore, who was employed as a research assistant on the project for one year.

The Pilot Studies

These three major projects were supported by, and emerged out of, a series of six-month pilot studies funded or co-funded by the Research Development Fund of the University of Liverpool. The project on popular music in twentieth-century Liverpool emerged out of a 1990 study that focused on music and kinship on Merseyside, and was co-funded by the National Museums and Galleries on Merseyside. The research was conducted by Kevin McManus and myself, and it focused on the musical lives and histories of a number of local families and kinship networks. It was designed to test out ideas and approaches for a larger project and was deliberately not confined to one particular music genre, or to the musical life of a particular social group or neighbourhood. The research involved gathering oral histories from family members and participant observation at family gatherings and musical events (see Cohen, 1995 for further details on the study and its methodology).

The project on popular music, tourism and urban regeneration emerged out of a study of music and cultural twinning that focused on the twinning of Liverpool and New Orleans in 1989, and was entitled 'Sister Cities Liverpool and New Orleans: A Case Study in Cultural Exchange'. The research was conducted in 1993 by Connie Atkinson and myself, and involved desktop research and interviews with musicians, policy-makers and city marketing officials. The project on music policy, the music industry and local economic development emerged out of a study on the music industry and European funding, which was entitled 'Merseyside's Music Industries and Objective One'. The research was conducted in 1994 by Adam Brown and myself and it involved interviews with local policy- and music-makers.

Other Projects

In addition to these major projects and related pilot studies the book drew upon several other projects. The main projects were:

- A survey of the music industries on Merseyside that I conducted in 1989 on behalf of Liverpool City Council, which involved contact with 289 businesses and sole traders. Its key findings were printed in the Music City Report (Liverpool: Ark Consultants, 1991). The survey was based on questionnaires completed during face-to-face interviews, but it also involved a sampled telephone survey of pubs and social and working men's clubs.

- A three-month research project on rock musicians and local identity that I undertook in 1993. The project was funded by the Performing Right Society of Great Britain, and one of its aims was to encourage musicians to reflect upon their music and the various factors that had influenced it. The project was based on group forums that focused on particular topics and involved discussions amongst a number of invited musicians. The musicians were selected in partnership with the Picket, a local community music venue and advisory service, and the discussions took place at the Picket and at Liverpool University.

- A four-month consultancy project on popular music in Detroit, Liverpool, Manchester and Leipzig that I undertook in 2003–04 with Rob Strachan. The project was part of a three-year international comparative study entitled 'Shrinking Cities', which was funded by the German Federal Cultural Foundation. The study brought together artists, architects and academics in an exploration of urban 'shrinkage', involving the vacation of urban spaces by local industry and a decreasing population. It aimed to approach that process, and responses to it, from new perspectives, and the purpose of our project was to examine the response of musicians. The study largely involved desktop research, textual analysis and email correspondence with researchers in Detroit and Leipzig.

- A three-year research project on rock culture in Liverpool that I undertook between 1983 and 1986 as part of my doctoral studies in Social Anthropology at Oxford University. The research was funded by a studentship from the Economic and Social Research Council of Great Britain and the ethnographic approach and methodology that it adopted are discussed in more detail elsewhere (Cohen, 1991a).

During the 1980s and 1990s I was also involved with a number of other projects, and whilst the book does not draw upon them directly they have nevertheless helped to inform some of its observations. They include, for example, ICISS – an international comparative project directed by Justin O'Connor at the Manchester Institute for Popular Culture during the late 1990s and funded by the European Union's ADAPT programme. I contributed to the comparative dimension of the project and attended key meetings, but was also responsible for a case study on Dublin conducted by Marion Leonard and Rob Strachan at the Institute of Popular Music in Liverpool. In addition to such projects, the book has been informed by experiences and observations relating to my personal and professional life in Liverpool and I will reflect upon this below as part of a broader discussion on the approach and methodology of the projects I have described. Each of the projects required an approach and methodology that was specifically tailored to the particular themes and issues it addressed, its aims and objectives and its research context. It is nevertheless possible to make some general points about the kind of approach and methods involved.

Ethnographic Approach and Methods

Many people kindly agreed to participate in the projects that I have described. They were involved with music in a variety of different ways and were connected to a broad range of social and occupational groups. They included musicians, music critics, music and tourist entrepreneurs, music fans and audiences, consultants and policy-makers. All of the main projects and most of the pilot studies involved unstructured or loosely structured face-to-face interviews, conversations and oral histories. The vast majority of interviews and oral histories were tape-recorded, although sometimes this was not possible – in which case they were recorded through written notes (sometimes, for example, there was just too much background noise). To my knowledge nobody objected to the use of a tape recorder, although very occasionally, as requested by a few interviewees, the recorder was switched off at particular points in the discussion. Most of the taped interviews and oral histories were transcribed, and transcripts and any written notes were usually numbered, catalogued and listed in a project index. They have been accessible only to the researchers directly involved with each of the projects concerned.

The research also involved participation in, and first-hand observation of, a wide variety of music activities and events, including music performances and rehearsals, festivals, launch events for specific music initiatives, public and private lectures and meetings about music, music-related guided tours and music seminars, workshops, conferences and conventions. Throughout the research we were continually surprised by the access we were given to public and private events, as well as by how warmly people responded to us and by the depth of interest in our research. Information and data gathered through the various forms of direct contact that we had with people were supplemented by those gathered from a variety of other sources, including popular publications, consultancy reports and policy documents, leaflets and publicity materials, newspaper articles, websites, statistics, minutes from meetings, radio and TV documentaries and song texts.

Throughout this research, due to the constraints of the individual projects – particularly time constraints – it has not always been possible to engage in long-term, in-depth anthropological fieldwork. For many of the projects we nevertheless tried, as far as it was possible, to adopt the anthropological emphasis on ethnography not only as a method but also an approach. We thus tried to highlight a range of different and often conflicting perspectives on popular music, and to relate what people said about music to what they actually did with it, considering the interrelationship between music as a social practice and a meaningful or ideological one. Efforts were also made, again wherever possible, to relate detailed observations of specific social events and practices to other aspects of people's lives that might not have been directly observed but were inferred from a combination of observation and interview. In this book, which has focused on connections between music and the city, I have tried to draw on the encounter between my own understandings and those of the people who participated in our research in order to develop my own interpretations of such connections. I thus used those ethnographic encounters as a basis for the development of theoretical discussion, adopting a 'bottom-up' approach to social theory and analysis, and I tried to emphasize this in the way that I wrote the book. Hence the book's chapters prioritized ethnographic description, using it as a basis for the development of an argument, rather than simply slotting in ethnographic descriptions here and there as apt illustration to justify an argument that was preconceived. I also tried to avoid producing a simplistic, generalized or reductive account of city cultures and identities, and to highlight instead their complexities and the specific tensions and contradictions that informed them.

The book's ethnographic approach and its focus on Liverpool as a case study will inevitably raise questions about generalization and typicality. One common criticism of ethnography is that it is impossible to make useful generalizations and address the bigger picture on the basis of detailed micro-sociological research on specific social groups and locations. I have deliberately tried, however, to avoid making generalizations about music's connections with the city on the basis of this one case study; although I have nevertheless used the research findings to highlight common social and economic trends that affected not just popular music in Liverpool but also in other European and North American cities. I have also tried to study the general in the particular, examining global trends and key questions about music and its relationship with the city by focusing on one case-study city. Focusing on the particular need not necessarily mean that the bigger picture recedes from view. Similarly, discussion on global trends and mediascapes should not overlook the fact that people still live in and relate to particular cities, consume local media and so on.

Ethnographic approaches and methodologies also raise questions about objectivity and reflexivity, and debates on such questions have been addressed in literature on qualitative methodology across the social sciences. Within social anthropology such questions have been commonly raised in relation to the notion of 'anthropology at home', which is applied to ethnographic research conducted by researchers who are members of the groups and cultures that they study. This book is based on research conducted in Liverpool between 1985 and 2005, and I have lived and worked in the city since 1988. Inevitably, therefore, my involvement with the city's musical life has changed over the years and I can no longer be categorized as simply a visitor or observer, but now also as a long-term resident and participant. At the same time, however, the book has emphasized the fact that the musical life of the city is broad and diverse, and whilst a small sample of the case material drawn on for the book represents groups that I was familiar and closely involved with, and events in which I was an interested party, much of the material has been drawn from groups with which I and my co-researchers were much less familiar and were involved with for relatively short periods of time. Throughout the book I have therefore tried to make explicit my relationship and involvement with the people and situations I have discussed. This has hopefully helped to make the reader better informed so that they are in a more advantageous position to judge the book's key findings and arguments. Other music ethnographers have occupied a similar position in relation to their research on music (see, for example, Finnegan, 1989 and Shank, 1994).

My close and long-term involvement with the city's musical life has certainly assisted my research, although on rare occasions it has also made it more complicated and difficult. The Institute of Popular Music (IPM), for example, has provided an excellent base for the research, and benefited it in ways that are too numerous and substantial to give justice to here. Amongst other things we were able to produce outputs from the research that took different forms and were aimed at various audiences and not just at other scholars. Some of those outputs were produced through institutional collaborations, such as our collaboration with the National Museums and Galleries on Merseyside that resulted in exhibitions, publications and special events. On a couple of occasions, the position and status of the IPM nevertheless appeared to impinge upon the research process rather too closely (see, for example, Chapter 5), although this is a familiar situation and one that researchers based at other universities and institutions have also had to confront and contend with.

Bibliography

Abercrombie, N., Lash, S., Lury, C.E. and Shapiro, D.Z. 1992. 'Flexible Specialisation in the Culture Industries'. *Regional Development and Contemporary Industrial Response: Extending Flexible Specialisation*. Eds H. Ernst and V. Meier. London: Belhaven, pp179–94.

Appadurai, A. 1990. 'Disjuncture and Difference in the Global Cultural Economy'. *Theory, Culture and Society*. Vol 7, pp295–310.

Appadurai, A. 1996. *Modernity at Large: Cultural Dimensions of Globalisation*. Minneapolis: University of Minnesota Press.

Appiah, K.A. 2005. *The Ethics of Identity*. Princeton: Princeton University Press.

Atkinson, C.Z. 1997. 'Whose New Orleans? Music's Place in the Packaging of New Orleans for Tourism'. *Tourists and Tourism: Identifying People with Place*. Eds S. Abram, J.D. Waldren and D.V.L. MacLeod. Oxford: Berg, pp91–106.

Bailey, C., Miles, S. and Stark, P. 2004. 'Culture-led Urban Regeneration and the Revitalisation of Identities in Newcastle, Gateshead and the North East of England'. *The International Journal of Cultural Policy*. 10: 1, pp47–65.

Barrow, W.M. 1925. 'Studies in the History of Liverpool 1756–1783'. MA thesis. Liverpool: University of Liverpool.

Belchem, J. 2000. *Merseypride: Essays in Liverpool Exceptionalism*. Liverpool: Liverpool, University Press.

Bell, D. and Jayne, M. 2004. *City of Quarters: Urban Villages in the Contemporary City*. Aldershot: Ashgate.

Ben Tovim, G. 2003. 'Futures for Liverpool'. *Reinventing the City? Liverpool in Comparative Perspective*. Ed. R. Munck. Liverpool: Liverpool University Press, pp227–45.

Bennett, T., Frith, S., Grossberg, L., Shepherd, J. and Turner, G. (eds) 1993. 'Introduction [to Part One]'. *Rock and Popular Music: Politics, Policies and Institutions*. London: Routledge.

Bianchini, F. 1989. 'Urban Rennaissance? The Arts and the Urban Regeneration Process in 1980s Britain'. *Working Paper No. 7*. Centre for Urban Studies, University of Liverpool.

Bianchini, F. 1991. 'Urban Cultural Policy'. *National Arts and Media Strategy Unit Discussion Document*. London: Arts Council of Great Britain.

Bianchini, F. 1993. 'Remaking European Cities: The Role of Cultural Policies'. *Cultural Policy and Urban Regeneration*. Eds F. Bianchini and M. Parkinson. Manchester: Manchester University Press.

Bianchini, F. and Parkinson, M. 1993. *Cultural Policy and Urban Regeneration: the West European Experience*. Manchester: Manchester University Press.

Blacking, J. 1976. *How Musical is Man?* London: Faber.

Boniface, P and Fowler, P.J. 1993. *Heritage and Tourism: in 'The Global Village'*. London: Routledge.

Boyle, M. and Hughes, G. 1991. 'The Politics of the Representation of "The Real": Discourses from the Left on Glasgow's Role as European City of Culture, 1990', *Area*, Vol. 23, pp217–28.

Brocken, M. 1994. 'Introduction'. *"Let's Go Dancing": Dance Band Memories of 1930s Liverpool*. By T. Jenkins. Liverpool: Institute of Popular Music.

Brocken, M. 1996. *Some Other Guys*. Liverpool: Mayfield Publishing.

Brown, A., Cohen, S. and O'Connor, J. 1998. *Music Policy in Sheffield, Manchester and Liverpool: A Report for Comedia*. Manchester Institute of Popular Culture, Manchester Metropolitan University and Institute of Popular Music, University of Liverpool.

Brown, A., O'Connor, J. and Cohen, S. 2000. 'Local Music Policies Within a Global Music Industry: Cultural Quarters in Manchester and Sheffield'. *Geoforum*. Vol. 31. Exeter: Pergamon, pp437–51.

Burnett, R. 1996. *The Global Jukebox: The International Music Industry*. London: Routledge.

Cavicchi, D. 1998. *Tramps Like Us: Music and Meaning among Springsteen Fans*. New York: Oxford University Press.

Chambers, I. 1985. *Urban Rhythms: Pop Music and Popular Culture*. Basingstoke: Macmillan.

Chambers, I. 1994. *Migrancy, Culture, Identity*. London: Routledge.

Chappell, H. 1983. 'Mersey Dreams', *New Society*, 6 October, pp5–6.

Cixous, H. 1976. 'The Laugh of the Medusa'. *Signs*. 1: 1, pp875–93.

Clifford, J. 1992. 'Traveling Cultures'. *Cultural Studies*. Eds L. Grossberg, C. Nelson and P.Treichler. New York: Routledge, pp 96–116.

Cloonan, M., Williamson, J. and Frith, S. 2004. 'What is Music Worth? Some Reflections on the Scottish Experience'. *Popular Music*. 23: 2, pp205–12.

Cohen, S. 1991a. *Rock Culture in Liverpool: Popular Music in the Making*. Oxford: Oxford University Press.

Cohen, S. 1991b. 'Popular Music and Urban Regeneration: The Music Industries on Merseyside'. *Cultural Studies*. Vol. 5, No. 3. London: Routledge, pp332–46.

Cohen, S. 1994. 'Mapping the Sound: Identity, Place and the Liverpool Sound'. *Ethnicity, Identity and Music: the Musical Construction of Place*. Ed. M. Stokes. Oxford: Berg. pp117–34.

Cohen, S. 1995. 'Popular Music in 20th Century Liverpool: A Case Study in Popular Music'. *Perspectives III*. Ed. Peter Wicke. Berlin: Zyankrise, pp289–96.

Cohen, S. 1997. 'Men Making a Scene: Rock Music and the Production of Gender'. *Sexing the Groove: Popular Music and Gender*. Ed. S. Whiteley. London: Routledge, pp17–36.

Cohen, S. 1998. 'Sounding Out the City: Music and the Sensuous Production of Place'. *The Place of Music*. Eds Andrew Leyshon et al. New York: Guilford Press, pp. 269–90.

Cohen, S. 1999. 'Music Scenes'. *Popular Music and Culture: New Essays on Key Terms*. Eds B. Horner and T. Swiss. Malden, MA: Blackwell.

Cohen, S. 2003. 'Local Sounds'. *Continuum Encyclopedia of Popular Music of the World*. Vol. 1. Eds J. Shepherd et al. London: Continuum.

Cohen, S. 2005. 'Country at the Heart of the City: Music, Heritage and Regeneration in Liverpool'. *Ethnomusicology*. 49/1.pp25–48.

Cohen, S. and McManus, K. 1991. *Harmonious Relations*. Liverpool: National Museums and Galleries on Merseyside.

Cohen, S. and Strachan, R. 2005. 'Musical Representations of the Shrinking City'. *Shrinking Cities, Volume 1: International Investigation*. Ed. P. Oswalt. Catalogue for the'Shrinking Cities' exhibition. Berlin: Institute for Contemporary Art.

Connell, J. and Gibson, C. 2003. *Sound Tracks: Popular Music, Identity and Place*. London: Routledge.

Cooper, M. 1982. *Liverpool Explodes!* London: Sidgwick and Jackson.

Cope, J. 1994. *Head On*. London: HarperCollins.

Crafts, S.D, Cavicchi, D. and Keil, C. 1993. *My Music*. Hanover, NH: University Press of New England.

DeNora, T. 2000. *Music in Everyday Life*. Cambridge: Cambridge University Press.

Doss, E..L. 1999. *Elvis Culture: Fans, Faith and Image*. Lawrence: University Press of Kansas.

Du Noyer, P. 2002. *Liverpool: Wondrous Place*. London: Virgin.

Evans, G. and Foord, J. 2003. 'Shaping the Cultural Landscape: Local Regeneration Effects'. *Urban Futures:Critical Commentaries on Shaping the City*. Eds Malcolm Miles and Tim Hall. London: Routledge, pp167–81.

Everett, W. 2001. *The Beatles as Musicians: the Quarry Men Through Rubber Soul*. Oxford: Oxford University Press.

Fainstein, S.S. and Judd, D.R. 1999. 'Global Forces, Local Strategies, and Urban Tourism'. *The Tourist City*. Eds D.R. Judd and S.S. Fainstein. New Haven: Yale University Press.

Feld, S. 1984. 'Communication, Music and Speech about Music'. *Yearbook for Traditional Music*, 16, pp1–18.

Feld, S. 1990. *Sound and Sentiment: Birds, Weeping, Poetics and Song in Kaluli Expression*. Philadelphia: University of Pennsylvania Press.

Finnegan, R. 1989. *The Hidden Musicians: Music-Making in an English Town*. Cambridge: Cambridge University Press.

Finnegan, R. 1998. *Tales of the City: A Study of Narrative and Urban Life*. Cambridge: Cambridge University Press.

Forman, M. 2000. '"Represent": Race, Space and Place in Rap Music'. *Popular Music*. 19: 1, pp65–90.

Forman, M. 2002. *The 'Hood Comes First: Race, Space, and Place in Rap and Hip-Hop*. Middletown, CT: Wesleyan University Press

Frith, S. 1981. 'The Magic That Can Set You Free: the Ideology of Folk and the Myth of the Rock Community'. *Popular Music*. 1. Cambridge: Cambridge University Press.

Frith, S. 1983. *Sound Effects: Youth, Leisure, and the Politics of Rock'n'Roll*. London: Constable.

Frith, S. 1987. 'The Industrialisation of Popular Music'. *Popular Music and Communication*. Ed. James Lull. Newbury Park, CA: Sage Publications, pp53–77.

Frith, S. 1993. 'Popular Music and the Local State'. *Rock and Popular Music: Politics, Policies and Institutions*. Eds T. Bennett et al. London: Routledge, pp14–24.

Frith, S. 2002. 'Illegality and the Music Industry'. *The Business of Music*. Ed. M. Talbot. Liverpool: University of Liverpool Press, pp195–216.

Fryer, P. 1984. *Staying Power: the History of Black People in Britain*. London: Pluto.

Garcia, B. 2004. 'Urban Regeneration, Arts Programming and Major Events: Glasgow 1990, Sydney 2000 and Barcelona 2004'. *The International Journal of Cultural Policy*. 10: 1, pp103–18.

Gardner, H. 1993. *Creating Minds: An Anatomy of Creativity Seen Through the Lives of Freud, Einstein, Picasso, Stravinsky, Eliot, Graham and Gandhi*. New York: Basic Books.

Garnham, N. 1987. 'Concepts of Culture: Public Policy and the Cultural Industries'. *Cultural Studies*. 1: 1, pp23–37.

Gentleman, H. 1970. 'Merseyside and its Region'. *Merseyside Social and Economic Studies*. Eds R. Lawton and C.M. Cunningham. London: Longman.

Gibson, C. and Connell, J. 2005. *Music and Tourism: On the Road Again*. Clevedon: Channel View Publications.

Gibson, C. and Homan, S. 2004. 'Urban Redevelopment, Live Music and Public Space: Cultural Performance and the Re-Making of Marrickwille'. *The International Journal of Cultural Policy*. 10: 1, pp47–65.

Gifford, Lord B.W. and Bundy, R. 1989. *Loosen the Shackles: First Report of the Liverpool 8 Inquiry into Race Relations in Liverpool*. London: Karia Press.

Gillett, C. 1983. *The Sound of the City*. London: Souvenir.

Gilmore, A. 2004. 'Popular Music, Urban Regeneration and Cultural Quarters: The Case of the Rope Walks, Liverpool'. *City of Quarters: Urban Villages in the Contemporary City*. Eds D. Bell and M. Jayne. Aldershot: Ashgate, pp109–30.

Gilroy, P. 1993. *The Black Atlantic: Modernity and Double Consciousness*. London: Verso.

Glasgow, J. 1987. 'An Example of Spatial Diffusion: Jazz Music'. *The Sounds of People and Places*. Ed. G.O. Carney. Lanham, MD: University Press of America.

Gotham, K.F. 2002. 'Marketing Mardi Gras: Commodification, Spectacle and the Political Economy of Tourism in New Orleans'. *Urban Studies*. 39, 1735–56.

Hall, P. 1998. *Cities in Civilisation: Culture, Innovation and Urban Order*. London: Weidenfeld & Nicolson.

Hall, P. 2000. 'Creative Cities and Economic Development'. *Urban Studies*. 37: 4, pp639–49.

Hall, S. 1995. 'New Cultures for Old'. *A Place in the World? Places, Cultures and Globalization*. Eds D. Massey and P. Jess. Milton Keynes: Open University Press, pp175–213.

Hargreaves, D. 2005. '"Jumping on the Bandwagon": Scenes, Place, Media and Post-Millennium Liverpool'. MA dissertation. Institute of Popular Music, University of Liverpool.

Hargreaves, D. and North, A. 1997. *The Social Psychology of Music*. Oxford: Oxford University Press.

Harvey, D. 1989. "Down towns", *Marxism Today*, 33 (January), 21.

Harvey, D. 1990. *The Condition of Post-modernity*. Oxford: Blackwell.

Haslam, D. 2000. *Manchester, England: the Story of a Pop Cult City*. London: Fourth Estate.

Hesmondhalgh, D. 1998. 'The British Dance Music Industry: A Case Study of Independent Cultural Production'. *British Journal of Sociology*. 49: 2, pp234–51.

Hesmondhalgh, D. 2002. *The Cultural Industries*. London: Sage.

Hewison, R. 1987. *The Heritage Industry: Britain in a Climate of Decline*. London: Methuen.

Hobsbawm, E. and Ranger, T. 1983. 'Introduction: Inventing Traditions'. *The Invention of Tradition*. Eds E. Hobsbawm and T. Ranger. Cambridge: Cambridge University Press.

Holcomb, B. 1999. 'Marketing Cities for Tourism'. *The Tourist City*. Eds D.R. Judd and S.S. Fainstein. New Haven: Yale University Press.

Hugill, S. 1969. *Shanties and Sailors' Songs*. London: Jenkins.

Jenkins, T. 1994. *'Let's Go Dancing': Dance Band Memories of 1930s Liverpool*. Liverpool: Institute of Popular Music.

Jensen, J. 1993. 'Honky-Tonking:Mass Mediated Culture Made Personal'. *All That Glitters:Country Music in America*. Ed. G.H. Lewis. *Bowling Green, OH*: Bowling Green State University, pp118–30.

Johnson, B. and Homan, S. 2003. *Vanishing Acts: an Inquiry into the State of Live Popular Music Opportunities in New South Wales*. New South Wales: the Australia Council and the New South Wales Ministry for the Arts, pp1–71.

Johnson, P. 1996. *Straight Outta Bristol: Massive Attack, Portishead, Tricky and the Roots of Trip-Hop*. London: Hodder and Stoughton.

Jones, D.C. (ed.) 1934. *Social Survey of Merseyside*. Vol. 3. 1934. London: University Press of Liverpool.

Jones, M. 1998. *Organising Pop: Why So Few Pop Acts Make Pop Music*. PhD thesis. Institute of Popular Music, University of Liverpool.

Jones, P. and Wilks-Heeg, S. 2004. 'Capitalising Culture: Liverpool 2008'. *Local Economy*. 19: 4, pp341–60.

Kaijser, L. 2002. 'Beatles Tourism in Liverpool'. Paper presented at the Institute of Popular Music, University of Liverpool on 10 December.

Kettle, M. 1981. 'The Toxteth Troubles', *New Society*. 9 July, pp60–61.

Kilfoyle, P. 2000. *Left Behind: Lessons from Labour's Heartland*. London: Politico's.

Kneafsey, M. 2002. 'Sessions and Gigs: Tourism and Traditional Music in North Mayo, Ireland'.*Cultural Geographies*, 9, pp354–8.

Kneafsey, M. 2003. '"If It Wasn't for the Tourists We Wouldn't Have an Audience": The Case of Tourism and Traditional Music in North Mayo'. *Irish Tourism: Image, Culture and Identity*. Eds M. Cronin and B. O'Connor. Clevedon: Channel View Publications, pp21–41.

Kong, L. 1998. 'The Invention of Heritage: Popular Music in Singapore'. *Popular Music: Intercultural Interpretations*. Ed. Toru Mitsui. Kanazawa, Japan: Kanazawa University, pp 448–59.

Laing, D. 1997. 'Rock Anxieties and New Music Networks'. *Back to Reality? Social Experience and Cultural Studies*. Ed. A. McRobbie. Manchester: Manchester University Press.

Landry, C. 2000. *The Creative City: A Toolkit for Urban Innovators*. London: Earthscan.

Landry, C. and Bianchini, F. 1995. *The Creative City*. London: Demos

Lane, T. 1986. 'We are the Champions: Liverpool vs the 1980s'. *Marxism Today*, January: pp8–11.

Lane, T. 1987. *Liverpool: Gateway of Empire*. London: Lawrence and Wishart.

Lash, S. and Urry, J. 1994. *Economies of Signs and Space*. London: Sage.

Lau, S. 2003. 'The Chinese Community in Liverpool: A Study in Music, Ethnicity and Identity'. MA dissertation. Institute of Popular Music, University of Liverpool.

Law, I. 1981. *A History of Race and Racism in Liverpool, 1660–1950*. Ed. J. Henfrey. Liverpool: Merseyside Community Relations Council.

Lawson, A. 1998. *It Happened in Manchester!: the True Story of Manchester Music 1958–1965*. Suffolk: Multimedia.

Leeuwen, T. Van. 1999. *Speech, Music, Sound*. Basingstoke: Macmillan.

Lefebvre, H. 1991. *The Production of Space*. Oxford: Blackwell.

Leigh, S. 1984. *Let's Go Down the Cavern: The Story of Liverpool's Merseybeat*. London: Vermilion.

Leonard, M. 2001. 'Gender and the Music Industry: An Analysis of the Production and Mediation of Indie Rock'. PhD thesis. Institute of Popular Music, University of Liverpool.

Lipsitz, G. 1990. *Time Passages: Collective Memory and American Popular Culture*. Minneapolis: University of Minnesota Press.

Lipsitz, G. 1994. *Dangerous Crossroads: Popular Music, Postmodernism and the Poetics of Place*. London: Verso.

Loftman, P. and Nevin, B. 2003. 'Prestige Projects, City Centre Restructuring and Social Exclusion: Taking the Long-Term View'. *Urban Futures:Critical Commentaries on Shaping the City*. Eds Malcolm Miles and Tim Hall. London: Routledge, pp76–91.

Low, S.M. and Lawrence-Zuniga, D. 2003. *'Locating Culture'. The Anthropology of Space and Place*. Eds S.M. Low and D. Lawrence-Zuniga. Malden, MA: Blackwell.

Lynch, K. 1960. *The Image of the City*. Cambridge, MA: MIT Press.

Lynch, K. 1972. *What Time is this Place?* Cambridge, MA: MIT Press.

Lynn, I.L. 1982. *The Chinese Community in Liverpool: Their Unmet Needs with Respect to Education, Social Welfare and Housing*. Liverpool: Merseyside Area Profile Group.

MacCannell, D. 1976. *The Tourist. A New Theory of the Leisure Class*. New York: Schocken.

Maitland, S. 1986. *Vesta Tilley*. London: Virago.

Masser, F.I. 1970. 'The Analysis and Prediction of Physical Change in the Central Area of Liverpool'. *Merseyside Social and Economic Studies*. Eds R. Lawton and C.M. Cunningham. London: Longman.

Massey, D. 1994. *Space, Place and Gender*. Cambridge: Polity Press.

Massey, D. 1999. 'Cities in the World'. *City Worlds*. Eds D. Massey, J. Allen and S. Pile. London: Routledge, p99–156.

Maxwell, J. 2004. 'A Social Semiotic Approach to Communication Between Popular Songs and Listeners'. PhD thesis. Institute of Popular Music, University of Liverpool

McCartney, P. 2002. 'Foreword' to *Liverpool: Wondrous Place* by P. Du Noyer. London: Virgin.

McGuigan, J. 1996. *Culture and the Public Sphere*. London: Routledge.

McManus, K. 1994a. *'Nashville of the North': Country Music in Liverpool*. Liverpool: Institute of Popular Music.

McManus, K. 1994b. *Ceilies, Jigs and Ballads: Irish Music in Liverpool*. Liverpool: Institute of Popular Music.

McNulty, R. 1988. 'What Are the Arts Worth?' *Town and Country Planning*. 57: 10, pp266–70.

McRobbie, A. 1999. *The Culture Society: Art, Fashion and Popular Music*. London: Routledge.

Meegan, R. 1988. 'Life Without Work'. *New Society*. 20 May, pp12–14.

Meegan, R. 1995. 'Local Worlds'. *Geographical Worlds*. Eds J. Allen and D. Massey. Oxford: Oxford University Press, pp 53–104.

Meegan, R. 2003. 'Urban Regeneration, Politics and Social Cohesion: The Liverpool Case'. *Reinventing the City? Liverpool in Comparative Perspective*. Ed. R. Munck. Liverpool: Liverpool University Press, pp53–79.

Meyrowitz, J. 1995. *No Sense of Place: The Impact of Electronic Media on Social Behaviour*. New York: Oxford University Press.

Middleton, R. 1990. *Studying Popular Music*. Milton Keynes: Open University Press.

Miles, M. and Hall, T. (eds) 2003. *Urban Futures: Critical Commentaries on Shaping the City*. London: Routledge.

Mitchell, T. 1996. *Popular Music and Local Identity: Rock, Pop and Rap in Europe and Oceania*. London: Leicester University Press.

Mitchinson, A. 1988. 'Style on the Mersey'. *New Society*. 20 May, pp14–17.

Moore, K. 1997. *Museums and Popular Culture*. London: Cassell.

Morton, F.L.G. 2005. '"The Music of What Happens": Spaces of Performance of Irish Traditional Music in Galway City, Ireland'. PhD thesis. Department of Geography, University of Bristol.

Murphy, A. 1995. *From the Empire to the Rialto: Racism and Reaction in Liverpool, 1914–1948*. Birkenhead: Liver.

Myerscough, J. 1986. *The Economic Importance of the Arts on Merseyside*. London: Policy Studies Institute.

Myerscough, J. 1988. *The Economic Importance of the Arts in Britain*. London: Policy Studies Institute.

Neal, F. 1988. *Sectarian Violence: the Liverpool Experience 1819–1914*. Manchester: Manchester University Press.

Negus, K. 1992. *Producing Pop: Culture and Conflict in the Popular Music Industry*. London: Edward Arnold.

Negus, K. 1995. 'Legislators or Interpreters: Some Questions About the Politics of Popular Music Studies'. Paper presented at the biennial conference of the International Association for the Study of Popular Music. Strathclyde University, Glasgow, July.

Nightingale, M. 1980. *Merseyside in Crisis*, issued by the Merseyside Socialist Research Group. Birkenhead: The Group.

Palmer, R. and Rae Associates. 2004. *Study on the European Cities and Capitals of Culture and the European Cultural Months (1995–2004)*. European Commission.

Parkinson, M. 1985. *Liverpool on the Brink*. Hermitage: Policy Journals.

Parkinson, M. and Bianchini, F. 1993. 'Liverpool: A Tale of Missed Opportunities?' *Cultural Policy and Urban Regeneration: the West European Experience*. Eds F. Bianchini and M. Parkinson. Manchester: Manchester University Press, pp155–77.

Peck, B. 1993. 'Case Study on The Liverpool Institute for Performing Arts'. Unpublished paper presented at an international seminar entitled Arts and The Development of the Local Economy, held at St George's Hall, Liverpool, organised by Brouhaha International.

Peterson, R. 1997. *Creating Country Music: Fabricating Authenticity*. Chicago: University of Chicago Press.

Raban, J. 1974. *Soft City*. London: Hamilton.

Reynolds, S. and Press, J. 1995. *The Sex Revolts: Gender, Rebellion and Rock'n'Roll*. London: Serpents Tail.

Robins, K. 1991. 'Traditions and Translation: National Culture in its Global Context'. *Enterprise and Heritage: Crosscurrents of National Culture*. Eds J. Corner and S. Harvey. London: Routledge, pp21–44.

Robinson, D. Buck, E. and Cuthbert, M. 1991. *Music at the Margins*. London: Sage.

Rose, P. 2005. 'Post-Fordism and Regional Joint Venture Record Labels.' BA dissertation. Institute of Popular Music, University of Liverpool.

Rose, T. 1994. *Black Noise: Rap Music and Black Culture in Contemporary America*. Middletown, CT: Wesleyan University Press.

Russell, D. 1987. *Popular Music in England, 1840–1914: a Social History*. Manchester: Manchester University Press.

Sassen, S. 1991. *The Global City: New York, London, Tokyo*. Princeton: Princeton University Press.

Schafer, R.M. 1977. *The Tuning of the World: Toward a Theory of Soundscape Design*. New York: Knopf.

Scott, A.J. 2000. *The Cultural Economy of Cities: Essays on the Geography of Image-Producing Industries*. London: Sage Publications.

Shank, B. 1994. *Dissonant Identities: The Rock 'n' Roll Scene in Austin, Texas*. Hanover, NH: University Press of New England.

Shaw, F. 1971. *My Liverpool*. London: Wolfe.

Sheddon, I. 2001. 'Echoes of the Past'. *The Australian*, July 21, R16–17.

Shepherd, J. 1987. 'Music and Male Hegemony'. *Music and Society*. Eds R. Leppert and S. McLary. Cambridge: Cambridge University Press, pp151–72.

Shepherd, J. and Manuel, P. 2003. 'Urbanisation'. *Continuum Encyclopedia of Popular Music of the World, Volume 1*. Eds John Shepherd et al. London: Continuum.

Shimmin, H. 1856. *Liverpool Life: Its Pleasures, Practices and Pastimes*. Liverpool: Egerton Smith.

Short, J.R. 1996. *Imagined Country: Society, Culture and Environment*. London: Routledge.

Simmel, G. 1997. *Simmel on Culture: Selected Writings (Theory, Culture and Society)*. London: Sage.

Slobin, M. 1993. *Subcultural Sounds: Micromusics of the West*. Hanover, NH and London: Wesleyan University Press and University Press of New England.

Small, S. 1991. 'Racialised Relations in Liverpool: A Contemporary Anomaly'. *New Community*. 17: 4, pp511–37.

Spivak, G. (1990). *The Post-Colonial Critic: Interviews, Strategies, Dialogues*. New York: Routledge.

Stahl, G. 2001. 'Tracing out an Anglo-Bohemia:Music-making and Myth in Montreal'. *Public*. 22/23. Eds J. Marchessault and W. Straw. Toronto: York University, pp99–121.

Stevenson, D. 2004. '"Civic Gold" Rush: Cultural Planning and the Politics of the Third Way'. *The International Journal of Cultural Policy*. 10: 1, pp119–31.

Stokes, M. (ed.) 1994a. 'Introduction'. *Ethnicity, Identity and Music: the Musical Construction of Place*. Oxford: Berg, pp1–27.

Stokes, M. 1994b. 'Place, Exchange and Meaning: Black Sea Musicians in the West of Ireland'. *Ethnicity, Identity and Music: the Musical Construction of Place.* Oxford: Berg, pp97–115.

Stokes, M. 1999. 'Music, Travel and Tourism: An Afterword'. *The World of Music.* 41: 3, pp141–56.

Strachan, R. 2003. *Do-It-Yourself: Industry, Ideology, Aesthetics and Micro Independent Record Labels in the UK.* PhD thesis. Institute of Popular Music, University of Liverpool.

Strachan, R. and Cohen, S. 2005. 'Music Cultures and the Appropriation of Urban Space'. *Shrinking Cities: Volume 1.* Ed. P.Oswalt. Berlin: Hatje Cantz Verlag, pp398–431.

Stratton, J. 1983. 'Capitalism and the Romantic Ideology in the Record Business'. *Popular Music.* 3, pp143–56.

Straw, W. 1991. 'Systems of Articulation, Logics of Change: Communities and Scenes in Popular Music'. *Cultural Studies.* 5, pp368–88.

Straw, W. 2003. 'Scenes'. *Continuum Encyclopedia of Popular Music of the World, Volume 1.* Eds John Shepherd et al. London: Continuum.

Street, J. 1993. 'Global Culture, Local Politics'. *Leisure Studies.* 12/3, July, pp191–201.

Street, J. 1995. '(Dis)located? Rhetoric, Politics, Meaning and the Locality'. *Popular Music: Style and Identity*, proceedings of the Seventh International Conference of the International Association for the Study of Popular Music. Eds W. Straw et al. Montreal: Centre for Research on Canadian Cultural Industries and Institutions, pp255–63.

Street, J. 1997. *Politics and Popular Culture.* London: Polity.

Tagg, P. 1979. 'Kojak – 50 Seconds of Television Music: Towards an Analysis of Affect in Popular Music'. *Studies from Gothenburg University, Department of Musicology.* Vol.2. Gothenburg: Gothenburg University Press.

Tagg, P. 1982. 'Nature as a Musical Mood Category'. No. 8206. *IASPM Norden Working Paper Series.* Institute of Musicology, University of Gothenburg.

Tagg, P. 1990. 'Music in Mass Media Studies. Reading Sounds for Example'. *Popular Music Research.* Eds K. Roe and U. Carlsson. Nordicom-Sweden. 2, pp103–15.

Tagg, P. 1991. *Fernando the Flute.* Liverpool: Institute of Popular Music.

Taylor, I. 1998. 'Foreword'. *The Beatles: An Oral History.* Eds D. Pritchard and A. Lysaght. Toronto: Stoddart.

Taylor, I., Evans, K. and Fraser, P. 1996. *A Tale of Two Cities: Global Change, Local Feeling and Everyday Life in the North of England.* London: Routledge.

Theweleit, K. 1987. *Male Fantasies.1: Women, Floods, Bodies, History.* Cambridge: Polity Press.

Thornton, S. 1995. *Club Cultures: Music, Media and Subcultural Capital.* London: Routledge.

Toop, D. 1995. *Ocean of Sound: Aether Talk, Ambient Sound and Imaginary Worlds.* London: Serpent's Tail.

Toynbee, J. 1996. 'What's the "Alternative" in Music Projects?' Paper presented at a UK Popular Music Forum organized by Generator and held in Leeds on 11 April.

Toynbee, J. 2000. *Making Popular Music: Musician, Aesthetics and the Manufacture of Popular Music*. London: Arnold.

Turner, V. 1982. *From Ritual to Theatre: The Human Seriousness of Play*. Baltimore: PAJ Publications.

Unwin, F. 1983. *Reflections on the Mersey*. South Wirral: Gallery Press.

Urry, J. 1990. *The Tourist Gaze: Leisure and Travel in Contemporary Societies*. London and Newbury Park: Sage Publications.

Urry, J. 1999. 'Sensing the City'. *The Tourist City*. Eds D.R. Judd and S.S. Fainstein. New Haven: Yale University Press.

Wade, P. 2002. 'Musical Nationalism in Transnational Perspective: Colombian Popular Music'. *I Sing the Difference?: Identity and Commitment in Latin American Song*. Liverpool: Institute of Popular Music, pp106–16.

Wallis, R and Malm, K. 1984. *Big Sounds From Small Peoples*. New York: Pendragon Press.

Wenner, J. (ed).1987. *20 Years of Rolling Stone: What a Long Strange Trip It's Been*. London: Ebury Press.

Williams, R. 1977. *Marxism and Literature*. Oxford: Oxford University Press.

Williamson, J. and Cloonan, M. 2004. 'Rethinking "The Music Industry": Towards a New Paradigm'. Unpublished paper.

Willis-Pitts, P. 2000. *Liverpool: The 5th Beatle: An African-American Odyssey*. Colorado: Amozen.

Wong, M.L. 1989. *Chinese Liverpudlians: A History of the Chinese Community in Liverpool*. Birkenhead: Liver Press.

Zukin, S. 1989. *Loft Living: Culture and Capital in Urban Change*. New Brunswick: Rutgers University Press.

Zukin, S. 1995. *The Culture of Cities*. Oxford: Blackwell.

Index